Praise for Tilar J. Mazzeo

Eliza Hamilton

"In Tilar J. Mazzeo's vivid, compelling, and unputdownable new biography, Eliza Hamilton finally takes her place in the pantheon of remarkable American women who, no less than the men they loved, built this nation."

—#1 *New York Times* bestselling author
Christopher Andersen

"[The] first-ever comprehensive biography of a woman who is known solely for the man she married but whose courage and generosity are revealed here. Fast-paced and reads like a novel."

—Kate Andersen Brower, #1 *New York Times*
bestselling author of *First Women*

"Mazzeo has made me fall in love with the enchanting but refreshingly real Eliza Hamilton. An important portrait of a woman as intriguingly complicated and now as deservedly memorable as her husband."

—Stacy Horn, author of *Damnation Island*

"Drawing from an impressive breadth of sources . . . this is an expertly told story that's certain to captivate Hamilton fans and intrigue anyone interested in early US history."

—*Publishers Weekly*

"A luminous biography that brings Eliza to life as a relatable survivor, and will appeal to lovers of history and biography as well as fans of the musical."

—*Library Journal* (starred review)

"Mazzeo's Eliza appears stoic, loyal, and canny."

—*Kirkus Reviews*

"Tilar Mazzeo has given us the profound gift of getting to know more fully the extraordinary woman whose legacy we are honored to carry forward today. Eliza Hamilton inspires!"

—Jess Dannhauser, president and CEO of Graham Windham

Irena's Children

"[An] incredible account."

—*The New York Times Book Review*

"An important, often harrowing, and, until now, little-known story of the Holocaust: how thousands of children were rescued from the Warsaw ghetto by a Polish woman of extraordinary daring and moral courage."

—Joseph Kanon, bestselling author of *Leaving Berlin*

"Mazzeo chronicles a ray of hope in desperate times in this compelling biography of a brave woman who refused to give up."

—*Kirkus Reviews*

"A fascinating narrative of a devastated city, Nazi depravity, and the extraordinary moral and physical courage of those who chose to fight inhumanity with compassion. This is a book that stays with you long after you've turned the last page."

—Chaya Deitsch, author of *Here and There:*
Leaving Hasidism, Keeping My Family

"This account of tremendous bravery is recommended for teens and adults who are drawn to inspirational stories."

—Library Journal (starred review)

"Mazzeo has put together an almost granular record of the cruel madness of the Warsaw ghetto and the astonishing feats of deception it took to help a small portion of its doomed residents survive. Even if you have read volumes on the Holocaust, you will find this book harrowing, surprising, and riveting."

—Joseph Berger, longtime reporter for the New York Times
and author of Displaced Persons: Growing Up American
After the Holocaust

"A taut, dramatic account of the nearly inconceivable bravery of Irena Sendler and those who worked with her to protect and save children in wartime."

—Booklist

"Mazzeo's portrait of Sendler . . . is harrowing; some passages are admittedly difficult to get through, but it feels so important that we do."

—Goop

Also by Tilar J. Mazzeo

Irena's Children
The Hotel on Place Vendôme
The Secret of Chanel No. 5
The Widow Clicquot
Plagiarism and Literary Property in the Romantic Period
Back Lane Wineries of Sonoma
Back Lane Wineries of Napa

Eliza Hamilton

THE EXTRAORDINARY LIFE AND TIMES
OF THE WIFE OF ALEXANDER HAMILTON

Tilar J. Mazzeo

G
GALLERY BOOKS
New York   London   Toronto   Sydney   New Delhi

G

Gallery Books
An Imprint of Simon & Schuster, Inc.
1230 Avenue of the Americas
New York, NY 10020

First Gallery Books trade paperback edition July 2019

GALLERY BOOKS and colophon are registered trademarks of
Simon & Schuster, Inc.

For information about special discounts for bulk purchases,
please contact Simon & Schuster Special Sales at 1-866-506-1949 or
business@simonandschuster.com.

The Simon & Schuster Speakers Bureau can bring authors to your
live event. For more information or to book an event, contact the
Simon & Schuster Speakers Bureau at 1-866-248-3049 or visit our
website at www.simonspeakers.com.

Manufactured in the United States of America

10   9   8   7

The Library of Congress has cataloged the hardcover edition as follows:

Names: Mazzeo, Tilar J., author.
Title: Eliza Hamilton : the extraordinary life and times of the wife of
    Alexander Hamilton / Tilar J. Mazzeo.
Description: New York, NY : Gallery Books, an imprint of Simon & Schuster,
    Inc., [2018] | Includes bibliographical references.
Identifiers: LCCN 2018008245 (print) | LCCN 2018026003 (ebook) |
    ISBN 9781501166327 (ebook) | ISBN 9781501166303 (hardcover : alk. paper)
Subjects: LCSH: Hamilton, Elizabeth Schuyler, 1757-1854. | Hamilton, Alexander,
    1757-1804—Family. | Politicians' spouses—United States—Biography.
Classification: LCC E302.6.H22 (ebook) | LCC E302.6.H22 M29 2018 (print) |
    DDC 973.4092 [B]—dc23
LC record available at https://lccn.loc.gov/2018008245

ISBN 978-1-5011-6630-3
ISBN 978-1-5011-6634-1 (pbk)
ISBN 978-1-5011-6632-7 (ebook)

For Adelaide, Xavier, and Frankie

Love is the whole history of a woman's life;
it is an episode in a man's.

—GERMAINE DE STAËL,
The Influence of the Passions (1796)

Contents

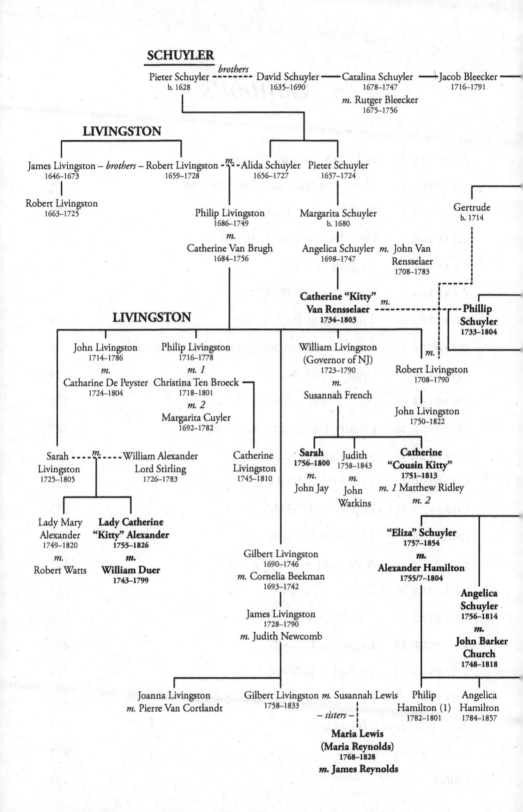

SCHUYLER

Pieter Schuyler
b. 1628
— *brothers* — David Schuyler
1635–1690
— Catalina Schuyler
1678–1747
m. Rutger Bleecker
1675–1756
— Jacob Bleecker
1716–1791

LIVINGSTON

James Livingston
1646–1673
— *brothers* — Robert Livingston
1659–1728
m. Alida Schuyler
1656–1727
Pieter Schuyler
1657–1724
Gertrude
b. 1714

Robert Livingston
1663–1725

Philip Livingston
1686–1749
m.
Catherine Van Brugh
1684–1756

Margarita Schuyler
b. 1680

Angelica Schuyler *m.* John Van
1698–1747 Rensselaer
1708–1783

Catherine "Kitty"
Van Rensselaer *m.* Phillip
1734–1803 Schuyler
1733–1804

LIVINGSTON

John Livingston
1714–1786
m.
Catharine De Peyster
1724–1804

Philip Livingston
1716–1778
m. 1
Christina Ten Broeck
1718–1801
m. 2
Margarita Cuyler
1692–1782

William Livingston
(Governor of NJ)
1723–1790
m.
Susannah French

m.
Robert Livingston
1708–1790

John Livingston
1750–1822

Sarah
Livingston
1725–1805
m. William Alexander
Lord Stirling
1726–1783

Catherine
Livingston
1745–1810

Sarah
1756–1800
m.
John Jay

Judith
1758–1843
m.
John
Watkins

Catherine
"Cousin Kitty"
1751–1813
m. 1 Matthew Ridley
m. 2

Lady Mary
Alexander
1749–1820
m.
Robert Watts

Lady Catherine
"Kitty" Alexander
1755–1826
m.
William Duer
1743–1799

Gilbert Livingston
1690–1746
m. Cornelia Beekman
1693–1742

"Eliza" Schuyler
1757–1854
m.
Alexander Hamilton
1755/7–1804

Angelica
Schuyler
1756–1814
m.
John Barker
Church
1748–1818

James Livingston
1728–1790
m. Judith Newcomb

Joanna Livingston
m. Pierre Van Cortlandt

Gilbert Livingston *m.* Susannah Lewis
1758–1833

Philip
Hamilton (1)
1782–1801

Angelica
Hamilton
1784–1857

— *sisters* —

Maria Lewis
(Maria Reynolds)
1768–1828
m. James Reynolds

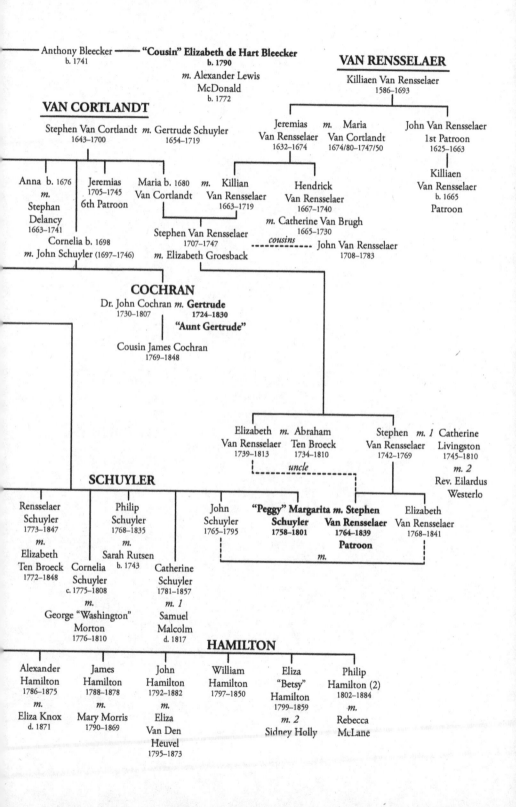

Prologue

Best of Wives, Best of Women

Eliza blushed. It was a beautiful letter.

Beyond the window of the front parlor of the Schuyler family home in Albany, the autumn leaves were crimson and gold, and now and then she could catch a glimpse of some small boat or another tacking back and forth, slowly beating its way against the river current. The lawns of the house ran down to the river, and in those days, the Hudson was a frontier highway.

It would be dark soon in the afternoons. Winter was coming. Never before had Eliza looked forward so eagerly to winter and its bitter chills. This year, December would bring Alexander.

Eliza and her mother were already busily planning the wedding. When the snows did come at last, Eliza knew already: they would exchange their vows in front of this window.

She touched the letter tenderly. Would it be too vain of her to read it again? At the Dutch church on Sunday mornings, where Eliza sat in the family pew with her parents, the minister warned against the sin of vanity. But no young woman in love could resist another look at such a letter:

I have told you and I told you truly that I love you too much. You engross my thoughts too intirely to allow me to think any thing else. You not only employ my mind all day, but you intrude on my sleep. I meet you in every dream—and when I wake I cannot close my eyes again for ruminating on your sweetness. 'Tis a pretty story indeed that I am to be thus monopolized, by a little nut-brown maid *like you and from a statesman and soldier metamorphosed into a puny lover. I believe in my soul you are an inchantress; but I have tried in vain, if not to break, at least, to weaken the charm—you maintain your empire in spite of all my efforts—and after every new one I make to draw myself from my allegiance my partial heart still returns and clings to you with increased attachment. . . .* I will not be delayed beyond November.

A nut-brown maid. It made Eliza smile to remember.

It was a reference to a popular folk song of that same title—"The Nut-Brown Maid"—revived in music books in the 1760s and 1770s. All last winter and into the spring at the camp in Morristown, she and Alexander had sung that old duet in Aunt Gertrude's front parlor. Eliza had plucked out the notes of the ballad on the pianoforte. Alexander had brushed close to her as he turned the well-worn pages, using any excuse to be romantic.

Alexander, his voice rich and deep with feeling, had sung the part of the lowly knight, in love with a baron's daughter. "Alone, a banished man" was the knight's mournful refrain at the end of every stanza. When Alexander sang the words, there was weight and feeling. Eliza knew that Alexander felt alone in America and an outsider.

Her family's embrace would change that. And so she had sung the part of the loyal nut-brown maid, whose refrain was "I love but you alone," looking into his eyes so he would know how much she meant it.

Weren't his long, poetic love letters another way of Alexander singing that same part in their ballad? The words were different but not the meaning. Over and over, Alexander, the outcast knight, wanted her reassurance. "I love but you alone" were the words he wanted.

Eliza always tried her best, but words were not her strength. Separated by war and not yet married, she and Alexander hadn't seen each other in months. Eliza fiddled with the pen in front of her now. Busy voices and an industrious clatter drifted in from other quarters of the house. She should be helping her mother and her sister make the last of the preserves and put up the winter canning. Early October was a busy season for an agricultural plantation on the edge of the New York wilderness.

Alexander had complained, however sweetly, at the end of the letter before her, reminding her, "I ought at least to hear from you by every post and your last letter is as old as the middle of September," and she couldn't deny that she had put off writing. Each time she composed in her mind the first sentence, self-doubt gnawed at her, and she blushed again, thinking of how poorly she spelled and how awkward her expression was. She showed her love better in the little gifts of affection that she carefully embroidered and in tender gestures.

If there was any distance between them in this love affair, it was this. They were different people. Her heart was full now. But she could not seem to get beyond the first words of her letters. *My dear Alexander . . .*

In the years that followed, when children's music lessons filled their home, when her spirited sister Peggy plucked Alexander away from his books and his writing and got him singing, they returned to that old ballad. It remained, too, in the spirit of their letters.

The nut-brown maid. It was their script, the love song at the heart of this complicated thing that was marriage. Sometimes, Eliza's knight errant would laugh as he sang the words. Sometimes, in the years to come, he would have reason to be penitent.

The words of the song endured. When Alexander's foes surrounded them and secrets pressed upon her, did Eliza sing softly to herself these words from the ballad: "If that ye were with enemies day and night, I would withstand, with bow in hand, to grieve them as I might, and you to save; as women have from death men many one: for, in my mind, of all mankind I love but you alone"?

The grateful knight's reply was, Eliza knew, "Mine own dear love, I see the proof that ye be kind and true; of maid, of wife, in all my life, the best that ever I knew."

Alexander in his letters made just a small revision to those words: "best of wives, best of women."

CHAPTER I

Home on the Hudson, 1751–65

Eliza Schuyler was born on August 9, 1757, into a world unraveling.

What history now remembers as the French and Indian War swept all the settlers of New York's Hudson River Valley up into it. Eliza and her family knew it only as hardship and chaos.

When Eliza was one day old, the French torched Sir William Johnson's British encampment at Fort William Henry, north of the Schuyler family land patent in Saratoga, and France's Huron allies scalped and murdered the unarmed retreating column and their families in a massacre that shook the Hudson Valley.

When Eliza was three months old, in November, French, Canadian, and Indian marauders attacked the outpost at German Flatts along the Mohawk River. Hatchets and arrows dispatched a dozen settlers. Those who could fled for the forests and did not stop running until the flames and the smoke of the burning settlement were far behind them. Those unlucky enough to be captured—more than half the village population—were frog-marched into the wilderness as slaves and war bounty. When wounded refugees made their way days later to Albany, telling terrible stories, the Schuylers turned a family barn into a makeshift hospital. Eliza's mother, Kitty, and her paternal aunt, Gertrude, worked late into the night as volunteer nurses.

When Eliza was six months old, her father Philip's childless uncle passed away, leaving Philip heir to a vast forest empire. Included in the legacy were two thousand hotly contested acres of Schuyler family lands in Saratoga, on the site of traditional Mohawk hunting grounds, where Eliza would pass much of her childhood.

A generation later, Eliza's distant cousin James Fenimore Cooper would romanticize the story of this moment in history in his best-selling novel *The Last of the Mohicans*. For Eliza and her family in the late 1750s and 1760s, confrontations between the natives, their European neighbors to the north, and the valley's settlers were the subjects of stories repeated anxiously from neighbor to neighbor at farmyard gates and in front of roaring winter fires, and there was nothing romantic about them.

The cultures had lived, sometimes more and sometimes less easily, cheek by jowl with each other for generations, but the fuse had already been lit that would lead to destruction and enmity. The explosive circumstances that followed would give shape to the largest contours of Eliza's frontier girlhood.

One of the great explosions came the summer that Eliza turned one. The British army and the settlers, guided by the charismatic Brigadier General Lord Howe, waged a pitched battle against the French and the Indians at a small outpost farther up the Hudson River at a strategic fort later known as Ticonderoga. Eliza's father, Philip Schuyler, a proud and stern military man, stood at the ready, one among the more than fifteen thousand valley soldiers preparing to fight to breach the enemy's defenses. When a French sniper picked off Lord Howe before the campaign started, things quickly went sideways for the settlers, and, even in the countryside in the 1750s, bad news traveled quickly.

When Eliza's mother, Kitty Schuyler, saw a young post rider hurtling toward her on horseback with a message, her heart sank, and a hand rested for a long moment on her swollen, pregnant belly. She was already the mother of two small children, little Eliza and her older sister, two-year-old Angelica.

The sweaty letter was thrust into Kitty's hands, and the sight of Philip's handwriting made her jubilant. *Dead men don't write letters.* It was the first thought that passed through the mind of any frontierswoman. But the rest of the news was heartbreaking. Even now, Philip was ferrying south by barge as quickly as he could some of the thousands who were dead and wounded. His wife, he knew, would organize the relief effort with as much intelligence as any general. Kitty Schuyler was not only a handsome and rich young woman, she had brains and courage. Swishing her satin skirts and ignoring her swollen ankles, she ordered a servant to look after the girls and directed the family slaves and farmhands down to the wharf on the river. When Philip's boats arrived, they would be waiting for him with biers and doctors.

For nearly a week, the lamp in the Schuyler barn burned late into the night, while Kitty and the local ladies tended the soldiers, and, before the girls knew it, their father was gone to the front again. War commanded everyone's attention. When Kitty's labor pains started one day in late September, Philip was still far from home, fighting. In her mother-in-law's best bedroom, Kitty held the hand of her sister-inlaw, Gertrude, and listened to the firm and quiet words of Dr. Stringer.

On September 24, 1758, Kitty gave birth to her third daughter. The little girl's name was Margarita, but she grew up being called Peggy. She was, from the beginning, the wildest, most high-spirited Schuyler daughter.

Kitty Schuyler was the wife of a soldier in the midst of a war, raising three small children in the home of her mother-in-law, and, at twenty-three years old, she might have preferred to be dancing at assemblies. But the most frustrating part for the young housewife was the fact that—despite having borne three children in as many years of marriage and, tongues clucked in the neighborhood still, a hasty wedding to legitimize Angelica's early arrival—she hardly saw her husband except in the bedroom.

Kitty Schuyler did not complain. She came from a long line of pragmatic and courageous women, each connected to one another in an intricate network of marriages, sisterhood, and cousinhood that gave them, over the generations, names like Schuyler, Livingston, Van Schaick, Van Cortlandt, Ten Broeck, De Lancey, and Van Rensselaer. These were the names of the most prominent Dutch entrepreneurial families in the New World, and they were bound by a culture and an ethos that did not permit retreat or grousing. Kitty's mother, Engeltje—Angelica in English—came from the great country estate at Livingston Manor, along the river leading to New York City. But her father, Colonel John Van Rensselaer, was one of the heirs to the greatest estate of all, the million-acre fiefdom of Rensselaerwyck, which spread for hundreds of miles in all directions around Albany. Many of the Schuyler family properties were large tracts that had, over time, in marriage after marriage, been carved out, along with the city of Albany, from inside the Rensselaerwyck boundaries.

And so Kitty did not complain, but it was not easy being the young bride of an officer, with war in the countryside, and with three small children—and a mother-in-law—at home. Kitty had been one of the famous belles of Albany, the "morning star" in a firmament of local beauties, according to the young gentlemen and clucking town matrons, and her marriage to Philip Schuyler was a marriage of passion. She longed sometimes to cut loose just a little. So when Philip was posted to a command in Albany in autumn of 1758, just after Eliza's first birthday, there was excitement and a celebration. At last Kitty could enjoy the company of her handsome husband for more than a short conjugal visit. At the Dutch Reformed Church in Albany on Sundays, where the family attended, the older matrons tutted over Philip and Kitty's shameless habit of arriving late at church just so they could make a splashy entrance in their finery. They were an undeniably fashionable couple. And even the matrons had to confess that Kitty was a striking woman, with a figure that, despite a quick succession of children, was much admired.

For a year, the family luxuriated in domestic happiness, and Angelica, Eliza, and Peggy bounced on the knee of their father. But in the spring of 1761, Philip Schuyler was given a new posting, as quartermaster charged with managing accounts and supply chains. The posting would take him now across the Atlantic. When Philip set sail from the harbor in New York City aboard the *General Wall* destined for Britain on March 3, 1761, Kitty Schuyler once again was pregnant.

Philip Schuyler nearly didn't make it home from this adventure across the Atlantic. A transatlantic journey meant a month at sea in the best of times, more if the weather and war were uncooperative, and well before the *General Wall* reached the halfway point in the voyage to London, somewhere in the vast emptiness south of Greenland, the captain of the ship grew feverish and perished.

Philip was long accustomed to boats and navigation. He'd run schooners up and down the Hudson River. He was a steady military officer of considerable experience by now, as well, and the officers onboard quickly nominated Major Schuyler as the new captain. His first test was a nightmarish encounter with a "ghost ship"—an abandoned and crippled slaver, whose fleeing crew had left behind their still-chained human cargo. Food supplies were short and options were few, and there is nothing heroic about Philip Schuyler's decision. He ordered the enslaved men and women set free from their bonds and then cast off the line. The *General Wall* sailed away, leaving the survivors to their own devices.

Troubles did not stop there. French bounty hunters attacked the ship, and the *General Wall* was captured. As Philip Schuyler sat shackled in biting irons, contemplating the grim prospect of the plank, and perhaps considering more fully the plight of that "human cargo," the privateers debated what to do with their prisoners. Luckily, Philip's time at a French boarding school as a youngster now served him well, and he set about haggling over a fine ransom. Another warship, however, appeared on the horizon and engaged the

General Wall in a second harrowing sea battle. When the ship was recaptured by the British, Philip now had to persuade his own side that he was one of their agents and not an enemy French commander. By the time a sea-weary Major Schuyler and his crew arrived in the metropolis of London, the story of the epic misfortunes of the *General Wall* was being recounted in public houses and newspapers on both sides of the Atlantic, and friends congratulated him "on your escape and arrival and extreme good fortune."

His wife, Kitty, however, was not cheered by this harrowing story when it made its way back across the Atlantic to Albany. It terrified her to think of how near they had come to losing Philip, and he was even still on the other side of the ocean. What would happen on his return journey if this was the state of seafaring? Kitty was exhausted and exasperated for other reasons too. She and the children were living on North Pearl Street, in the village house of Philip's widowed mother, Cornelia Schuyler, along with at least one of Philip's brothers; his widowed sister, Gertrude; and Gertrude's two saucy preteen children. The house was spacious by colonial standards, but colonial standards were not generous.

Her husband commiserated. And he did more than that. Before Philip departed, he'd given Kitty free rein to design and build a new family mansion. Kitty couldn't see it completed fast enough. She ordered local masons to raise up a house of pale brick and planned long green lawns running down to the family's private wharf on the Hudson River. She fussed over designs for a grand ballroom for the girls on the second floor and designed intricate marble chimneypieces.

Kitty also built the estate they called "the Pastures" to be a veritable fortress. She was no stranger to war. The walls were thickened to withstand attacks, and the doors fitted with brass locks and heavy brackets. In the years to come, Kitty's foresight and those fortifications would save the lives of Eliza and her family on at least one very dramatic occasion.

Kitty's construction budget was 1,400 pounds sterling—something on the order of $1.5 million in contemporary terms—and in the letters to Philip that drifted slowly across the Atlantic, she set him to the task of buying flocked wallpaper and expensive window curtains.

Privately, Kitty was also mourning. On July 29, 1761, as word of Philip's adventures at sea were making their way back to New York, she gave birth to twins. The little boy, named John after his maternal grandfather and after a family friend, John Bradstreet, died at birth. The baby girl she christened Cornelia, after Philip's mother. Philip would never meet his small daughter either. On August 29, a month after the infant's birth, Kitty awoke to a dead baby. Angelica and Eliza were just old enough to remember later the loss of their baby sister.

When their father returned home at last in 1762, it was to a freshly completed family home, with pretty gardens and a bright-blue front parlor. Angelica, Eliza, and Peggy would spend their childhoods shuttling between here and the family wild lands in Saratoga. Behind the house and the barns of the Pastures rolled eighty acres of farmland and woods. Beyond the front gardens, large windows and a portico faced east to the sunrise and the Hudson River. Despite the damage done to Philip Schuyler's health by the sea voyages, Kitty was again pregnant in no time.

One of Eliza's childhood friends, Anne MacVicar, later left an account of growing up with the Schuyler girls and their cousins in Albany, and it is the story of a carefree and happy childhood, despite the conflicts and unsettled countryside around them. Anne, the daughter of a Scottish officer in the British army who had fought with Philip Schuyler in the battle at Ticonderoga, was eleven the year she met Angelica, Eliza, and Peggy, and for the next three years the girls were constant playmates.

The world Anne MacVicar describes was full of laughter and freedom. Those who met the Schuyler family remarked, almost to a one, on the easy intimacy and emotional warmth they extended to each other and to strangers. Eliza's parents were not bohemians, not in the least. Philip and Kitty were disciplined people and moderately pious. The Schuyler family were members of the Dutch Reformed Church and certainly religious, although their Calvinism was of the sort that fostered entrepreneurship and independence rather than social restrictions, and Eliza's family was more English than Dutch when it came to playing cards or dancing. Eliza and her sisters also grew up on the frontier, surrounded by a wilderness that began less than a day's journey from Albany. The keenly class-conscious Sir William Johnson, a friend of their father and an outsize presence in the valley, kept his teenage daughters locked up in a wing of his house and ordered an eagle-eyed governess to watch them, as was common practice regarding young aristocratic women in fashionable London. Philip and Kitty Schuyler found the idea repugnant. The Schuyler girls were to be integrated into the complex and sometimes dangerous world of war and politics that went on around them.

It was a world that schooled a young Eliza in some hard realities. The death rate on the frontier was astonishingly high, and the Schuyler family was not spared those losses. Forty percent of children born in the 1760s died as infants or toddlers. A year after the death of the twins, Kitty gave birth again, to a long-awaited son and heir, whom they once again hopefully named John Bradstreet Schuyler. But the winter that year was particularly hard, with the first snows coming in early November, and the summer that followed was swampy, humid, and sickly. Between the biting cold and the summer putrid fevers, it was an unlucky year to be born, and this second John was no luckier than the first little John had been. He, too, died before his first birthday. By twenty-nine, Kitty Schuyler had given birth to six children and buried half of them.

Smallpox continued to plague the Mohawk and Hudson Valleys that year, as well. Sir William Johnson built a new, bespoke mansion, named Johnson Hall, and the family there was struck down with the disease, which left those fortunate enough to survive disfigured and disabled. By late summer, New York and Philadelphia were in the grip of the fearsome yellow fever. American cities were small during

Eliza's girlhood, and the horror of contagion at close quarters was a predominant factor. Then there were the unexceptional deaths, the ones that resulted from childhood diseases like mumps and measles, from carriage accidents and bucking horses, from pleasure boats tipped into swirling rivers, and from age. Eliza's grandmother, Cornelia, died in 1762, the year Eliza turned five, and the body was laid out in black crepe in the front blue parlor. Eliza missed the warm scent of her grandmother.

Despite the loss and mourning that inevitably came with colonial life in America, Eliza and Anne both later remembered their childhoods as idyllic, pastoral. The children played on the rivers and in the forests, accompanied by Prince, Kitty's most trusted African slave, to watch over them.

The constant presence of enslaved people must be noted as a historical fact, too, in Eliza's girlhood story. The Schuyler family owned as many as a dozen slaves during the lifetime of Eliza's parents, men and women born in the New World but whose bloodlines had their origins in Africa, the native peoples of North America, and, especially, Madagascar.

Cousins piled into canoes for summertime trips to harvest wild berries, and Angelica, Eliza, and Peggy learned from the local Indian girls who camped in the fields near their home, heading to and from summer council meetings each year, how to make willow baskets and string belts of brightly colored wampum from beads and shells to tell a story. Needlework was an essential part of a young girl's education, and the Schuyler girls, like their parents and their aunts and uncles, all spoke at least bits and pieces of the Iroquois languages. They took lessons from a dancing master in Albany, learning the intricate steps of the minuet and how to rise and fall on the balls of their feet while turning in circles. From their mother, they learned to cut out patterns for clothes and how to preserve strawberries for winter. The girls read Shakespeare and the Bible aloud to their greataunt, Margarita Schuyler, and learned to speak French, as well as English and their family's native Flemish; in the winter, when the river froze, the girls eagerly pulled on their warm fur muffs and the smart beaver caps that their father had ordered especially for all the children and went for skating parties and sleigh races.

Soon, that childhood would also include long, wild summers in what seemed to Eliza and her sisters a magical forest kingdom. The French and Indian War was behind them now, and, upon the death of Eliza's grandmother Cornelia Schuyler, another sizable inheritance passed to the girls' father, including more land in Saratoga and the money Philip would need to commercialize and develop it. Kitty gave birth at last to a healthy son, whom they again named John Bradstreet, the third infant to bear the name and the first survivor. Philip Schuyler already dreamed of the day he would leave his son and, in smaller shares, his daughters a great legacy in Saratoga.

CHAPTER 2

Fine Frontier Ladies, 1765–74

If Eliza swung high enough, she could nearly touch the branches. When Angelica scolded, she pulled back on the ropes and swung higher.

If she'd looked out from the treetops, she could have seen her mother directing the family slaves as they planted lilac bushes along the new foundation. Mother had promised them a strawberry garden, where they could eat their fill, and the girls had a great swing in a tree on the lawns, which Prince had made for them.

The Schuyler family spent the summer of 1765 not at the Pastures, but camping on Eliza's father's new lands in Saratoga. They lived, army style, in roomy canvas shelters that snapped in the breezes, while work was going on all around them. Father oversaw the laborers, who brought down great virgin pines that shuddered and fell, and the men next raised up a sawmill and planed the logs into timber with which Mother said they would build a home. It would have two stories and such pretty flowers.

For Angelica, Eliza, and Peggy, this frontier plantation was a second childhood home, just as much as the grand riverfront compound in Albany, and the family increasingly spent all but the harshest months of the winter at the edge of the wilderness in Saratoga.

Eliza was nine in 1766, the summer when the house at Saratoga was completed. By now her father was a rich businessman with contracts running the ferry trade from Albany to New York City and on his private fleet of schooners, and he would soon be promoted to the rank of colonel. After Stephen Van Rensselaer and James Duane, both relations of her mother, Philip Schuyler was the third-richest man in the Upper Hudson, and all around them at Saratoga that wealth was growing.

These were working estates, where much of the family's food and income was produced, running to large acreages, and dozens of tenants and slaves provided the grand landowning families like the Schuylers with the income that allowed them to live like the colonial aristocracy of which they considered themselves part.

The privilege did not go uncontested. Periodic uprisings, by tenants and, later, by slaves, preoccupied men like Philip Schuyler throughout New York and New Jersey. That spring, the plantation owners were especially edgy after an upstart Westchester County manorial tenant named William Prendergast incited a rent war that unsettled estates all along the Hudson River as far north as Albany. A thousand angry farmers or more stormed the countryside, demanding that the doors of the landlords' debt prisons be thrown open, and at the estate of Kitty's father, John Van Rensselaer, fisticuffs gave way to bullets. At Rensselaerwyck, the Albany County sheriff, Harmanus Schuyler, laid siege to a farmhouse, and large landowners scrambled to the frontier to assess the mood among their own distant tenants.

The Schuyler plantation at Saratoga was at the crossroads that summer of several especially important land patents, many of which were owned by the Schuyler family's relations. Eliza and her sisters listened quietly in front of the fireplace on cool summer nights that year, while the grown-ups talked passionately and sometimes angrily of danger from their tenants and, increasingly, about bitter politics. Eliza's Van Cortlandt, Van Rensselaer, and Livingston cousins all made the trip upriver to Saratoga to stay with the family in late June and to check on property. Eliza and her sisters, along with their constant playmate Anne MacVicar, raced to meet younger cousins on the docks as the sloops arrived from downriver. Twelve-year-old

Mary Watts, a china-doll beauty and a De Lancey cousin, was one of those arrivals, and she may have come alone for the summer because her family was already quarreling with the Livingston relations. Angelica and Eliza also became fast friends sometime this summer, or one soon after, with their cousin Kitty Livingston, from a New Jersey branch of the family, and Eliza and Kitty sent each other gossipy letters as teenagers.

There was a great deal to discuss urgently in the political realm, and it wasn't only the prospect of revolting tenants that had the grand landowners like Eliza's father so agitated. Resentment toward the British crown was also part of what the adults discussed in the evenings. Eliza heard terms now like the "Stamp Act" and understood that the new law made her father and her uncles angry. Eliza also heard now words like "tyranny" and "taxes." Soon, the tenants were not the only ones beginning to murmur of revolution. Some of her visiting kinsmen talked of something now called the Sons of Liberty, a secret movement whose motto was "No taxation without representation."

William Prendergast would have to pay for his treacherous rent war. All the visitors agreed with Philip Schuyler and Eliza's angry Van Rensselaer relations. Prendergast stood trial at the end of that summer, facing down a court whose judges were primarily landowners.

Unsurprisingly, the landlords found against a tenant revolution. The sentence, when it came down, was gruesome: Prendergast was ordered "hanged by the neck, and then shall be cut down alive, and his entrails and his privy members shall be cut from his body, and shall be burned in his sight, and his head shall be cut off, and his body shall be divided in four parts, and shall be disposed of at the king's pleasure." This was the price of rebellion against the British crown a decade before the American Revolution.

Angelica, who had been invited to New York City at the end of the summer for a stay with new British governor Sir Henry Moore,

his wife, and their teenage daughter, Henrietta, had a front-row seat
for some of the drama of the Prendergast trial. The wife of William
Prendergast, a woman so beautiful that jurors at her husband's trial
were sternly cautioned not to let that influence proceedings, roared
up to the front courtyard of the governor's mansion on a steed and
pleaded with Sir Henry to commute her husband's terrible death sentence. Angelica watched agog with excitement. Sir Henry, moved as
much by Mehitable Prendergast's beauty as by her speech, gallantly
overturned the verdict and immediately issued William Prendergast
a full pardon.

It was a disastrous misstep with the great landowners of New
York. The governor's pardon turned William Prendergast into a
tenant folk hero, fueled resentful talk of counter-revolt, and unleashed fresh complaints about years of British mismanagement
among the wealthy of the colony, including Philip Schuyler. The
governor had just unwittingly helped to light one of the fuses of the
coming revolution.

It was another minor revolt, though, that captured Angelica's imagination that fall, during her first grown-up visit to New York City.
The governor's wife doted on the ten-year-old social butterfly, and
for her part Angelica idolized the governor's haughty and impulsive
daughter. The stylish seventeen-year-old Henrietta promptly added
a dose of great excitement to Angelica's trip when, disobeying the
dictatorial commands of her father, she climbed over the garden wall
and ran off with a young captain in one of the society scandals of the
season. Her impulsive actions would forever define Angelica's idea
of the romantic.

When Angelica returned from her city sojourn, the other girls
jealously and sometimes suspiciously noted the change. When Eliza
ran across the lawns down to the river to meet the boats, Angelica
cringed with embarrassment and would no longer race her. Angelica practiced mincing daintily down the gravel path and lifting her

skirts above the dust like Henrietta instead. Angelica sat primly on
the edge of the seat when company came and fussed in the mornings
longer with her bonnet ribbons. This or that was all the New York
fashion, she solemnly informed her sisters. She shrugged off Eliza's
urgent whispers to hurry or Papa would be cross. Eliza and Anne
MacVicar still joked together decades later over "Angelica's early
air of Elegance & dignity when she first returned from New York."
When Kitty and Philip Schuyler noticed the change, they decided it
was time to send both the older girls off to boarding school. They
had on their hands budding young ladies. Those early airs and graces
would need to be honed and disciplined at school if in a few years'
time the girls were to become eligible young brides and, as Philip
Schuyler insisted should be the case, obedient daughters.

Eliza may have gone away to school earlier than the fall of 1768,
but she was definitely in New York City by the autumn of the year
she turned eleven. Mrs. Grant, a fussy, respectable widow living on
Hanover Square in Lower Manhattan, agreed to board "two of the
children for 50 a year, two pounds of tea, one of loaf sugar each,
their stockings & shoes mended, but new work must be paid for the
making." Their father, as a man on the rise in the world of New York
politics now, was in and out of the city, but Eliza's parents primarily
entrusted the girls to the care of her mother's cousins, Elizabeth and
John Livingston, who soon reported back to the girls' parents that
"the young ladies are in perfect health and improve in their education
in a manner beyond belief, and are grown to such a degree that all the
tucks in their gowns had to be let out some time ago."

The education of wealthy colonial girls like Eliza and her sisters
had a clear and definite focus: that of training young women in the
social graces and household skills that would make them desirable
wives and estate mistresses. Angelica and Eliza already knew how
to read. Aunt Gertrude had seen to that and had insisted that the
girls practice reading Shakespeare aloud while she did her needlework. Music was an essential element of a family's private entertainment, and all three of the Schuyler girls learned to play the English

"guittar," although Eliza had to admit that her sisters were more skillful, no matter how long she practiced. Peggy was the one with real musical talent.

Writing and penmanship, especially, set clever upper-class girls apart from the middle classes. It was expected that, like their mother, Angelica, Eliza, and Peggy would someday manage large household accounts, so clear, neat penmanship and basic arithmetic were important skills. Very young girls learned their first numbers and letters by embroidering samplers, and needlework was a universal skill among ladies. Mastery of the subtler points of grammar and spelling, though, was considered particularly "elegant," and only a young woman who was an unusually "fine scholar" would consistently spell correctly.

In the 1780s, Thomas Jefferson would write a letter to his eleven-year-old daughter, Polly, offering a glimpse of the education of girls in elite colonial circles. He advised:

> With respect to the distribution of your time, the following is what I should approve:
> From 8. to 10. o'clock practise music.
> From 10. to 1. dance one day and draw another.
> From 1. to 2. draw on the day you dance, and write a letter the next day.
> From 3. to 4. read French.
> From 4. to 5. exercise yourself in music.
> From 5. to till bedtime, read English, write [i.e., practice penmanship], &c.
> ... Write also one letter a week. ... Take care that you never spell a word wrong. Always before you write a word, consider how it is spelt, and, if you do not remember it, turn to a dictionary. It produces great praise to a lady to spell well.

The education the Schuyler girls received closely mirrored that which Thomas Jefferson wanted for his daughter a decade later, and

Angelica flourished as a young scholar and bloomed as a fine young lady.

Eliza struggled. She was never good at spelling, and she found writing awkward. She was self-conscious of her letters. Angelica danced more prettily. The French master despaired of Eliza's accent and how she stumbled on her verbs, while Angelica chattered like a native. Angelica found her introduction to New York society thrilling. Eliza, whose great talent was the careful, intricate embroidery that Angelica didn't have the patience for, longed to be home in the country.

Boarding school was only one half of the Schuyler girls' education, though. Eliza and her sisters were caught between two worlds, and each would have to decide which of those worlds they would make their lives in. The Schuyler girls belonged to a merchant family with deep roots in the Hudson, and their parents anticipated that all their daughters would marry someone from a similar background. Indeed, they might reasonably have expected that their daughters would marry into an extended network of family cousins and second cousins. So Eliza was also educated in the life of the frontier and equipped by her parents to succeed in building and managing an agricultural and entrepreneurial estate on the edge of the wilderness, and it was here that she shone. Eliza doled out her pin money carefully, on sensible, industrious girlhood purchases: a new set of strings for the guitar, a bit of fine muslin for her embroidery. Angelica was perfectly capable of blowing her entire allowance on a whim if a bit of finery in a window caught her eye. Eliza, a precocious little treasurer, shook her head at her sister's impulsiveness, but there was no shadow between the girls. Angelica kissed her sister fondly and turned to her ribbons.

During the girls' summers home in Saratoga, Kitty and Philip attended to the other half of their daughters' education. Eliza lived for those summers. She wanted nothing more than to be outdoors and especially on horseback. She loved riding fast in the open countryside and the feeling of flying. She never minded dusty boots and did not always remember to wear a bonnet. Had they been living in Jane Austen's *Pride and Prejudice*, Angelica would have been Jane Bennet and Eliza, Eliza.

Philip Schuyler was a forbidding man, but the sight of his outdoorsy younger daughter made him smile, and he knew that if there were one of his girls he wanted with him on a military campaign, it was not the fussy and fine Miss Angelica but her tough-minded tomboy sister. In the summer of 1770, when Eliza was approaching her thirteenth birthday, Philip Schuyler planned to attend the grand Indian council of the Six Nations, where fifty Iroquois sachems, from all the clans of all the nations, would gather at a site two days' travel farther west even than Schenectady. They would ride for days, through the great pine forests, and a young girl would need to be a steady horsewoman. When her father wanted to speak to her, Eliza's heart sank. What had she forgotten? Her father did not have patience for disobedience and insisted on military order. When instead he asked if she thought she were old enough for an adventure, she hugged Papa and promised to be as brave as any soldier. Even the stern Philip Schuyler laughed. She was plainest of his three daughters, but when her dark eyes lit up with excitement, she turned into a beauty.

The grand council meeting was in July, and Eliza packed her satchel with the discipline of any general. She rolled her needles and some sturdy thread into a bit of cloth, tied neatly with a ribbon. There would be no time or place for heavy books, and anyhow Eliza didn't care about reading. She cared about her riding gloves and extra bootlaces.

Eliza and her father, accompanied by at least one household slave, would travel by barge and then by horseback days through pine barrens and rough countryside. As they journeyed west along the Mohawk River, they almost certainly stopped overnight at Johnson Hall, the estate of Sir William Johnson, where Eliza met Sir William's elegant and cloistered teenage Anglo daughters and perhaps some of Sir William's half-native children. Sir William Johnson was also going to the grand council, and Eliza and her father probably made the final stages of the journey with Sir William and his entourage. Philip Schuyler went as both a major landowner and an elected member of the New York Assembly. He and Sir William joined more than two thousand representatives of the Iroquois and Cherokee nations and a delegation of British officers.

Eliza understood that Sir William was an important figure at these meetings. The natives trusted him, her father explained, to keep fair records of the council agreements with the settlers. Agreements were recorded on wampum belts among the Iroquois, and each design in colored shell- and beadwork told the story of a conversation. To accept the gift of wampum meant to accept an agreement as binding, and frontier girls learned to string wampum as readily as they could work samplers. Eliza, an especially accomplished needlewoman, made beautiful pieces of wampum that drew admiration.

Council meetings were exciting and deeply political, and it was not typical for a young woman like Eliza to attend them. If Philip Schuyler had had a son old enough, it is unlikely that Eliza would have accompanied her father. Her brother John, however, was only five, and her newest baby brother, Philip Jr., was still a toddler.

As she and her father arrived at council, all around Eliza were Indian families setting up camp along the banks of the river. All day, there were long speeches with debating. At family meals on the late summer nights, the Iroquois women pounded out summer corn, and boys pulled wriggling fish from the Hudson.

Her father was well known and well regarded among the Iroquois, and so Eliza tried to remember to act like a lady. She tried to be like the Iroquois girls, who listened carefully to everything that was said at council. The Schuyler family's political ties with the native clans went back already generations, and it was Eliza's first serious introduction into that world of politics. Philip Schuyler explained now to his daughter why some matters were easy and others were so difficult and contentious.

Philip Schuyler also explained that Eliza herself was part of an old network of ties and alliances. Her father and her grandfather had both been initiated into the Mohawk and Onondaga tribes as honorary members. Now, the sachems welcomed Eliza in a naming ceremony. With her brown hair tied in braids like that of the Indian girls, she stood tall and quiet when the tribal elder in his robes and feathers placed a string of beads around her neck. Eliza was now a member of the Iroquois family, and she was proud of her Indian name, which her father said meant "One of Us." Eliza liked the idea that she belonged to the frontier and to the Onondaga. Eliza was a girl of the woods, who could scramble over rocks as fast as any of the Mohawk girls, and who learned to speak some of their language. Philip Schuyler knew, but probably did not explain yet to Eliza, that these rituals of allegiance might someday preserve the safety of his daughter and her family on the frontier. He knew that relations with the Iroquois were dangerously fragile.

In New York City and at school again come autumn, Eliza felt the stark contrast between her two worlds, and was homesick. The Schuyler girls were too young to stroll across the Kissing Bridge or dance at the Governor's Ball in June, but there were "routs," where Eliza practiced dancing with the other young people from the colonial upper classes. She tried not to wriggle as a servant teased and pulled her hair into a dramatic updo for parties, and she learned how to wear high-heeled satin shoes on cobblestone streets without spraining an ankle. She wore, in the fashion of the day, satin and brocade dresses cut low enough to raise modern eyebrows and tucked bits of fine lace into her swelling teenage bosom in cold drawing rooms during the winter. On Sundays, she and Angelica sat primly in a family pew at Trinity Church, alongside their Van Cortlandt and Livingston cousins, attended by the slave their father had sent with them. The family owned at least five slaves during these years, including Eliza's mother's favorite, Prince, who stood behind Kitty's chair every night at dinner; additionally, there were Cutt, John, Peter, and Bett. The girls were not alone in having an African servant. Slaves made up roughly a quarter of the population of New York City in the fall of 1770.

Before long, their younger sister Peggy joined the two older girls at school in the city, and each girl had her own family role and personality. Angelica was the most sophisticated and socially ambitious of the three sisters, and she thrilled to the romances she discovered in novels and poetry. "A very Pretty Young Lady," as one visitor noted emphatically, she looked the most like their mother, who had been a beauty. Angelica was also a flirt and obsessed with the social graces and accomplishments that would make her a fine lady. Peggy, on the other hand, was dark-haired, plump, and, some said, the prettiest of all the three sisters, with a sarcastic sense of humor that intimidated those less clever and less witty. She possessed the lion's share of family musical talent, and played the guitar with real skill and sang moving ballads in a clear soprano. She also inherited her father's imperious demeanor, and she and Philip Schuyler clashed on more than one occasion. She was his willful child and, with her saucy tongue, his most exasperating daughter.

Eliza was the classic middle sister and the peacemaker. She took after her father, with a strong-boned face a bit too thin and angular to be called beautiful on a young woman. She had an enviable figure and a healthy, athletic build from hopping over fences and riding horses fast. But she also had a stubborn independence and a native modesty that made it easy to overlook her amid her flashier sisters. Eliza was, someone who knew her said, "a Brunette with the most good-natured, lively dark eyes . . . which threw a beam of good temper and Benevolence over her whole countenance." Angelica was the socialite, and Peggy could be a bit of a laddish rebel. Eliza was a quiet force who kept the three sisters together.

By 1773, the Schuyler girls' formal educations—such as they were—were over. New York City, however, was increasingly where Eliza's parents and her family spent time during the 1770s, thanks to Philip

Schuyler's burgeoning political and military career. When the family
was at home in Albany or Saratoga in the summers, handsome young
captains were also increasingly frequent visitors, as the word spread
that Philip Schuyler had a particularly fine wine cellar and three entertaining and lively daughters. Social conventions on the frontier
were famously relaxed, and Kitty and Philip Schuyler understood
from personal experience how one thing might lead to another and
how carts can come before horses. Philip Schuyler cast a discerning,
fatherly eye over the callers, and on more than one occasion showed
a young gentleman to the end of the wharf, pointing in the direction
of downriver. Visitors to the Pastures, after all, might fall as easily
in love with the family's wealth as with one of his daughters, and
Philip was wary of these bounty hunters. His concern was not un-
warranted. Officers remarked in their private journals that Philip
Schuyler lived like a prince in a veritable woodland palace, and his
property ran to the tens of thousands of acres. With three increasingly boy-crazy country girls and, by 1773, three young sons now to
contend with—John, Philip Jr., and baby Rensselaer—Kitty Schuyler
was feeling beleaguered and understandably tired.

Romance was on the mind of all three of the Schuyler sisters. In
the summer of 1766, their cousin Mary Watts had come to stay for
the Saratoga season. Then, Mary—known to everyone just as Polly—
had been a rare, "china doll" beauty. Now "Lovely Polly," as she was
known, was nineteen and more striking even than she had been as
a girl. She was also high-strung, snappy, and snobbish. "Rich and
nervously irritable" was how one person who knew Mary put it, and
now, it seemed, she had found a perfect partner: Colonel Sir John
Johnson, the careless and randy son and heir of Philip Schuyler's
friend Sir William. John quietly jettisoned his common-law wife, a
local working-class Dutch girl, packed off their two small children,
and proposed to Mary Watts. The Schuyler girls found the idea of
their glamorous cousin marrying a baronet very romantic.

The wedding took place at the end of June in New York City, and
in July the Schuyler girls watched the river eagerly each morning for

the newlyweds' arrival. What would Lady Mary wear? How long would the bride stay in Albany on her wedding visit to their common aunt, Judith Van Rensselaer? When would she and Sir John call on Father? In their bedroom at the Pastures, the girls debated these fine points, and when Lady Mary and Sir John arrived in Albany, Mary was pleased to be given a celebrity reception.

Already, however, family tensions were brewing. Talk of revolt and tyranny and taxes still occupied the gentlemen in the public houses and around the fireplace after dinner. Increasingly, cousin Mary's new husband was staking out a position that placed her on a collision course with kinsmen like Philip Schuyler and Aunt Judith.

When, in the year that followed, Sir William Johnson died and Sir John inherited, the newlyweds found themselves at the center of a powerful political network, just at the moment a new war was on the horizon. This time, the war would not be between the British and the French but between the British and the "American" settlers. Everyone in the Hudson and Mohawk Valleys would have to choose sides in the coming bloody conflict.

Philip Schuyler already knew that, when the time came, he would throw in his lot with the Sons of Liberty and the patriots, and he was already laying down the contacts that would make him an important Revolutionary War spymaster. Eliza and Angelica would act as his eyes and ears in the Hudson Valley and gather sensitive military intelligence to forward to General Schuyler. They weren't spies exactly. But they weren't not spies either.

Behind enemy lines, their recently married cousin Mary Watts would get drawn into espionage, as well. She, too, would have to choose sides and decide whom to spy for.

CHAPTER 3

First Romances, 1775–77

For the moment, though, boys were what mattered.

Eliza was afraid of the coming war. But the times were also thrilling for the young ladies. War meant the arrival of officers, who were dashing and sometimes handsome. Everyone knew, too, that officers threw balls for entertainment. While General Schuyler's thoughts in August were on the campaign and his fragile Mohawk alliances, the thoughts of Eliza, Angelica, Peggy, and another of their cousins, the fifteen-year-old Maria Van Rensselaer, turned to new romances.

All the girls had crushes that summer, including Eliza. The trouble was that Eliza had not one but two rivals for the affections of the gentleman whose eye she hoped to catch.

Eliza turned eighteen in the summer of 1775. The older girls had stayed on in New York City to gain a bit of polish while Peggy finished school, but now all three of the Schuyler sisters were coming to the end of their educations. Eliza returned home to Albany to be tutored by Kitty and her aunts in what everyone expected would be the real life's work, as practiced by other young women from her background: estate management.

She would have to learn to do this work, like her mother before her, in the midst of a war being fought in the countryside. By 1775, the American colonies were in open revolt against their British colonial rulers, and a great conflict was coming. Philip Schuyler, a seasoned officer from the days of the French and Indian War, joined the patriots at the First Continental Congress and was given command of the Americans' entire northern army. He served under a man who quickly became a friend, George Washington.

Eliza's father was in and out of Albany, sometimes away with the army patrolling the valley, sometimes home with a bevy of young captains and lieutenant colonels in tow, plotting defense strategy. Dispatches were constantly sent from and received at the Schuyler family's riverfront estate, which quickly became command central, especially after the patriots in Massachusetts sent a man on horseback to warn the Americans in April that shots had been fired at Lexington and Concord. As her father put it in the days before the revolution began, it was a matter of principle and passion for the colonists: "Much as I love peace," Philip Schuyler wrote to a friend,

> much as I love my own domestic happiness and repose, and desire to see my country-men enjoying the blessings flowing from undisturbed industry, I would rather see all these scattered to the winds for a time, and the sword of desolation go over the land, than to recede one line from the just and righteous position we have taken as freeborn subjects of Great Britain.

In June, Philip was promoted to major general of the Continental army. When he led the American troops into Albany, bonfires lit the streets; red, white, and blue ribbons streamed from ladies' bonnets; and Eliza joined her sisters and their neighbors in welcoming home the patriots and their local hero, General Schuyler.

Ahead of the boys was war. Philip and his troops marched north that summer, and Kitty and the girls traveled with the men as far north as Saratoga. They planned to say their goodbyes at dawn and to watch the army set off with the sun for outposts farther upriver.

Just after midnight, the urgent shouts of the sentinels and the heavy clatter of boots and her father's booming voice jolted Eliza from sleep. Heart pounding, Eliza rushed to pull her gown over her linen shift, and in the dark she and Angelica fumbled as they quickly tied each other's dress laces.

Eight hundred Iroquois were coming down the valley on the war-path. Many suspected that Sir John Johnson was behind this. Saratoga lay in their path. There would be no retreat to country estates that summer. Papa and the troops marched to stop the rogues, and Eliza's mother promptly packed the family back to the presciently fortified Pastures.

It was there at the Pastures that Eliza first set sight on a flirtatious, slightly paunchy southern officer in his early thirties named Tench Tilghman. His family owned a large plantation in Maryland, and Tench came as an envoy to the summer Indian council as part of the converging American political delegation.

Tench Tilghman met the Schuyler girls within days of his arrival on the scene in Albany. Angelica—"Ann"—he described as a "brunette with dark eyes, and a countenance as animated and sparkling as I am told she is." Eliza—"Betsy"—also charmed Tench. "I was prepossessed in favor of this Young Lady the moment I saw her," he noted in his diary. "Mr. [Walter] Livingston informed me that I was not mistaken in my Conjecture for that she was the finest tempered Girl in the World." This was high praise from her cousin. Tench also met, however, the very elegant Miss Lynch, a confection of feminine elegance and helplessness and the daughter of a visiting military commander from South Carolina. Miss Lynch was the first of Eliza's rivals. The second of Eliza's rivals was her richer and prettier younger cousin, Maria Van Rensselaer.

The morning of August 23, 1775, broke bright and clear, and Eliza was grateful. She hadn't wanted this day to be spoiled by drizzle.

And she didn't want to be late either. She hurried out of bed, dressed with extra care, and rushed through her prayers and breakfast. A party of young people and their chaperones was making an excursion up the Hudson River to Cohoes Falls, a popular beauty spot, and Eliza was invited. So was Tench Tilghman.

It was still early when Eliza set off along the river path toward the town house of another cousin, Abraham Cuyler, where they would depart in carriages. But, despite her good start, Eliza arrived just in time to see Tench handing Miss Lynch into his fast, two-seater phaeton. Miss Lynch smiled down at Eliza innocently. Cousin Abraham gave a hallo and patted the seat beside him in a solid, heavy coach. One look was all it took to tell Eliza that she would spend the next hours of their journey crushed between Cousin Abraham and a portly military matron. The sun seemed to shine a bit less brightly. Eliza was far too polite to let on how bitterly she was disappointed.

Cousin Abraham's coach lurched into motion, and the matron swayed heavily toward Eliza. Ahead, Eliza could see the cloud of dust kicked up by Tench's sleek horses, and sometimes there was a glimpse of Miss Lynch's bobbing bonnet disappearing around the bend in the roadway.

Miss Lynch's dramatic femininity piqued Eliza. At the picnic grounds, the rocky terrain was too uneven for Miss Lynch to walk alone. She fretted with her charming drawl that she feared to turn an ankle. Tench gallantly held her elbow every minute. With Captain Tilghman's help, she thought she just might be able to manage. The carriage was so high. Tench would have to help her mount it. Miss Lynch desired some berries. Captain Tilghman would fetch them. It was an art of flirtation incomprehensible to Eliza, who could only wonder how anyone could be so hopeless. Miss Lynch's innocent smiles weren't entirely innocent either, she thought irritably.

Eliza didn't know afterward what had come over her. By the time the party set out for a stroll to the falls after their picnic, she was out of patience. Miss Lynch brought out her contrary streak—Eliza was made of sterner stuff, and why not flaunt it? Her romance was not turning out as she and Angelica had planned. Tench had hardly given her a second glance, so absorbed was he with this southern belle.

Ahead were steep rocks leading off the path, heading directly up toward the waterfall. That was where the best views were, so Eliza lifted her skirts and set off on a scramble. The recklessness of Miss Schuyler! exclaimed the southern ladies. As the cries reached her, Eliza laughed at them and scrambled higher. Eliza "made herself merry at the distress of the other Ladies," as Tench told the story later. And he did admire Miss Schuyler's courage and spunk. But he wasn't looking to find a wife, and his pleasure was in flirting with the more coquettish ladies.

High bonfires were crackling and throwing sparks in the middle of the streets when the party rolled back into Albany that evening. Miss Lynch rode home beside Tench Tilghman. An Iroquois feast and dance was beginning. As the sun set, the Iroquois opened the council ceremonies, Tench wrote in his diary, by "beating their drum, striking sticks together in Exact time and yelling after Their Manner. They were almost intirely naked." Miss Lynch, who had never encountered something so savage and shocking, relied utterly upon Captain Tilghman. Eliza was exasperated. She had had enough of batting eyelashes. Surely there were Indians as well in South Carolina.

Eliza was not shocked at the sight of half-naked Iroquois men dancing at council. She had seen it all before, every summer council of her childhood. She was not shocked either the next day when the chief of the Onondaga initiated Tench into the native family by bestowing on him an Indian name. She still wore her string of initiation beads when the Iroquois came for council. Eliza understood, too, that Tench would be offered a native "wife" as part of the bargain, and no girl who had grown up on an agricultural estate could miss the basics of sexual relations. The sachem, who took the measure of Tench Tilghman quickly, promised that Tench's Iroquois wife would "be one of the handsomest they could find." As Tench recorded in his diary, "I accepted the proposal with thanks. Miss Lynch and Miss Betsy Schuyler have promised to stand bridesmaids."

Eliza made a joke of being bridesmaid, but among the young women marriage was a serious business. Miss Lynch, Eliza, and Angelica were all at the age where marriage was their primary object. Tench, a large landowner and a decade older, was a highly eligible bachelor. He enjoyed the young ladies competing for his affection, but he had no intention of proposing marriage that summer. That didn't stop the ladies, though, from trying.

Tench wasn't joking when he accepted the sachem's offer of an Indian "bride" either. Tench confided to his diary that, just as soon as the young American ladies were out of the way, he planned to bed some of the Indian girls. They "are pretty and extremely cleanly they speak tolerable English too," Tench wrote, "so that I believe I must make an Acquaintance among them when my fair Country women are all gone, for I think they are superior to any of the Albanians."

He hoped to bed some of the English and Dutch girls, too, given half a chance. He was keeping a little black book of conquests. Tench rated the Indian girls prettier than Miss Lynch, Eliza, or any of her sisters, but he did make one exception: "Miss Ransolaer." She "is the Belle of the Town and therefore a little of the Coquette," Tench confided. "I will have a Tete a Tete with her before I go. And give her a place in my Journal." "Miss Ransolaer" was Eliza's younger cousin, fifteen-year-old Maria Van Rensselaer, a girl of great beauty and vast wealth, who was, despite her youth, rumored to be of a free inclination.

Eliza had had her chance at catching a beau, and by the next week it was too late. Her father's plans were for the entire family to decamp to Saratoga, and that would be the last she would see of Tench Tilghman. The young captain would soon be leaving the Hudson Valley.

They would set off, her father reminded her, on the morning of August 29, and the family would need to be ready. On the morning of their departure, Tench joined them for breakfast, and his affection was genuine. "I sat among them like an old Acquaintance, tho' this is only the seventh day since my introduction," Tench wrote. "It would be seven years before I could be as intimate with half the World. But there is so much frankness & freeness in this Family that a man must be dead to every feeling of Familiarity who is not familiarized the first hour of his being among them." Tench liked Eliza especially, and there was enough of a spark between them that it wasn't unreasonable to hope that romance might blossom. But now it was too late for this summer. Tench waved goodbye as the coach set off and turned back toward his quarters. He had one week left in Albany before his return voyage south. His laddish thoughts were on Maria Van Rensselaer and fair Indian maidens.

Eliza's feelings were more complicated. No one ever recorded precisely what occurred next inside the Schuyler family carriage as it departed, but whatever it was must have been dramatic and impassioned. It is not hard to guess that there were tears and some heartbreak. The Schuyler sisters stuck together, and poor General Schuyler is likely to have found himself cast by Angelica and Peggy as the cruel father, whisking Eliza away from a romantic precipice. Eliza would never have said so, but her sisters would not have hesitated. By the end of a long day on the road with three boy-crazy daughters, Philip and Kitty were beaten down sufficiently for General Schuyler to let his daughter do something absolutely extraordinary.

Sometime on the second day of their journey, just as they were nearing Saratoga, Eliza was allowed to turn around. She would travel alone, in the midst of a war, through open country, with just one of the servants as a guard, back to Tench and Albany. Whether by design or by chance, Eliza asked for permission to stay in Albany at the home of her cousin Maria Van Rensselaer.

Back in Albany alone, Eliza wasted no time in letting Tench know she was in town. "Who should bless my eye sight this evening," Tench wondered, "but good natured agreeable Betsy Schuyler just returned from Saratogha." Miss Lynch and her party had departed for the south. The field should have been open.

But when Tench called on Eliza and her cousin the next day, all his attention was on Maria. "Miss Ransolaer," he recorded in his journal, "is pretty, quite young and fond of jokes about her humble servants. As I had made myself master of a good deal of her private history, I could touch upon such matters as I knew would be agreeable to her." It was all rather less agreeable for Eliza.

Had Eliza and Tench had more time together, perhaps something might have blossomed between them. Tench was fond of Eliza. As the evening came to an end, "I lamented that my short stay in Albany would so soon deprive me of so agreeable an Acquaintance and a deal more of such common place stuff," Tench wrote. "This was a mere Compliment to her [i.e., Miss Rensselaer], but I told Miss Schuyler so with truth." Whatever Tench's feelings, Eliza was smitten. But, then, being smitten was the primary occupation of the young women.

Tench departed, and whatever else was the case he set off without proposing marriage to Eliza. Any romance would have to bloom on another occasion, but, now that her parents knew of her feelings, it was not impossible that there would be other occasions to meet Tench Tilghman.

Soon there were other gallant distractions, too. Handsome visitors came and went from General Schuyler's home, and Eliza was in the mood to have a romance. A few weeks later, the captured British officer John André stayed briefly in the Schuyler family as a prisoner of war while being transferred farther from the front. He passed several days in polite captivity, doing sketches of her cousin Abraham Cuyler and his wife, Janet, and flirting with the general's second daughter. Eliza promptly fell in love with John André as well. Mooning about him, however, was something Eliza knew would not meet with a patient response from her father. A general's daughter could not expect to fall in love with a captured enemy officer and have her father permit it, not during the War of Independence. The Schuyler sisters knew many of the British officers from the days before the war, and their father liked many of them as gentlemen and soldiers. But any of his daughters marrying a Loyalist was out of the question. So Eliza and her sisters swooned over John André and Eliza's star-crossed romance in hushed late-night whispers.

Tench Tilghman and John André were not the only gentlemen visitors, that year or the next. One of the gentlemen to visit the family in April of 1776 was charming and a favorite of the Schuyler girls, especially Eliza, but he was neither young nor eligible nor a bachelor. This visitor was Benjamin Franklin, who came with a delegation to see Eliza's father and travel to Ticonderoga.

The long river journey from New York City up to Saratoga exhausted the elderly Franklin, who stopped for a week to rest and recover. There, in the sunny front parlor, he taught Eliza how to play backgammon. "The lively behavior of the young ladies makes Saratoga," noted one of the other guests, "a most pleasing sejour," and Benjamin Franklin could not have agreed more wholeheartedly.

The old gentleman set off with the other men for a hunting trip to Johnson Hall the following week, but it didn't take long on the trail to persuade Benjamin Franklin that he wasn't cut out for wilderness travel and carousing. He preferred the company of cheerful young ladies and backgammon. Pleading old age and failing health, he turned back and spent another week instead with Eliza, Peggy, and their mother.

One of the other visitors in 1776 was far less welcome by either the general or Kitty. That year, the Schuyler girls first encountered at their father's house a mysterious, flirtatious, and secretive young officer in the American army named John Carter. John Carter, a notably short and slight man, with bright, pale eyes and delicate features, arrived at the Pastures one day with a letter of introduction from Philip Schuyler's neighbor and sometime business partner, a fast-dealing British-born commercial agent named William Duer. In time, Eliza would come to despise Duer and his penchant for crooked dealing. Without a letter from Duer now, Carter would never have gained admission to the mansion or to the Schuyler daughters so readily, and

Philip Schuyler would later rue the day he let Mr. Carter cross the threshold.

What happened at that first meeting of John Carter and the Schuyler sisters? The girls never left an account of that drawing-room visit. But Mr. Carter would have bowed, the young ladies would have nodded, and it seems that John may have reminded Angelica that they'd danced together once at an assembly ball the previous winter in Philadelphia. Not that Angelica needed any reminder. Dancing with a gentleman with whom one was barely acquainted at a public ball was not proper, but the recollection certainly added a frisson of excitement to this introduction, and by November 1776, John Carter was a regular visitor, dashing off cordial notes of thanks to the Schuyler girls' mother and sending his "compliments" to "the young ladies"— especially to Miss Angelica.

Where John Carter came from or what his family connections were no one knew, except that he was British and had been appointed in July as a commissioner to the Continental Congress, charged with auditing the accounts of the northern army in Albany, an army that General Schuyler headed. The rest was murky. Eliza wondered, how had he come to America and why had he said so little about his family? The sisters had read in romance novels about young men forced to flee cruel parents and orphans stripped of their rightful fortunes by unscrupulous guardians. Poor Mr. Carter. There must be, Angelica assured her sisters, some wildly romantic story.

The more he saw of the young man, the more Philip Schuyler sensed something was amiss. Philip was deeply suspicious and doubted very much that this young man was what he represented. That he was a British agent sent to infiltrate the general's home was certainly not impossible.

General Schuyler was the patriot spymaster in the Hudson, and sensitive information came and went from the household constantly. The Schuyler sisters were already part of that network. There was a fine line between local gossip and military intelligence. When Eliza heard a bit of news about the movements here or there, when someone or another suspected of Loyalist sympathies departed town suddenly, she made a note to tell Angelica, who gathered up these bits of information and shared them with their father.

The sisters passed along especially any news about their cousin Lady Mary and her sister Margaret, who were being held captive by Aunt Judith on the orders of General Schuyler and General Washington. Cousin Mary's husband, Sir John Johnson, had fled through the wilderness to Canada, pursued by the rebels. Heavily pregnant, with two small children in tow, Lady Mary was forced to remain behind and was promptly incarcerated. Philip Schuyler already suspected that, despite her house arrest, she was somehow leaking intelligence back to the British. Lady Mary for her part now hated Philip Schuyler. The revolution divided families, and on the New York frontier, where communities were small and tightly knit, the pain was disproportionately heightened.

One had to ask the same question of John Carter and his allegiances. Was he a true patriot or a covert loyalist? His British birth and recent arrival in America tolled against him. But no one knew what was in the heart of another man, no matter what uniform he wore in battle. The war for independence was only beginning, and in 1776 there had already been unpleasant surprises. There were more to come. General Schuyler knew it. And something just didn't add up when it came to John Carter.

While General Schuyler cautioned his daughters that the history of Mr. Carter would bear some looking into, the girls knew that was only to be expected. In the novels of Mrs. Brooke and Mr. Goldsmith, which arrived from London, drowning heroines were always being plucked from rivers by gallant suitors only to find their love thwarted by a stern papa. When their father declared not long after that the gentleman was not welcome any longer and ordered that his daughters break off contact, Angelica felt just like a heroine in a story.

But Philip Schuyler was right to worry about this mysterious gentleman. John Carter was not his name, and he definitely had designs on the general's daughter.

Philip Schuyler was a man accustomed to having his orders followed and assumed that this would be the end of any thoughts of romance with Mr. Carter. For Eliza, it would have been. Eliza had good sense and a head on her shoulders. Anyhow, it wasn't her romance. She had thoughts of Tench Tilghman and John André to occupy her. Angelica, however, declared herself now madly in love with John Carter, and her father's command only fueled the flames of passion. Angelica thrilled to the forbidden allure. When a secret letter arrived, Angelica swore her sisters to secrecy, and Eliza's heart sank when she read it. John begged Angelica to meet him. She could not deny him a farewell, not when he so fervently admired Miss Angelica Schuyler. Eliza begged her not to go. But any warning was futile. Angelica was determined to carry on seeing John Carter.

From their mother's perspective, there should have been dangers enough to keep Angelica, Eliza, and Peggy busy, and she should have been able to count on the girls obeying their father. The Revolutionary War was unfolding around them, and their father was a general. The countryside was alive with danger. Philip Schuyler—and, by extension, his family and home—was a target on a number of fronts, and the Schuylers' home at the Pastures was an armed fortress for good reason.

Kitty and the girls were not at the front, but the front was all around them. They were in constant danger, not only from the troops of the British general John Burgoyne from the north but, more important, from the Indian attacks that were increasingly frequent and violent. The Mohawks were firmly aligned with the British and with the Johnson family Loyalists, who continued to fight against the Americans from Sir John's outpost in Canada, with the help of intelligence that, just as Philip Schuyler feared, was smuggled out by cousin Lady Mary.

Stationed outside the doors of the Schuyler family mansion in Albany now and at the estate in Saratoga were a half-dozen guards and soldiers. Philip Schuyler was taking no chances. Eliza and her sisters were friendly with a young woman named Jane McCrea who lived with her brother in Saratoga and was nearly the same age as Angelica. Miss McCrea's brother, Colonel John McCrea, fought in the Albany militia with their father. Word of Jane's murder and scalping in the spring ignited passions against the natives and General Burgoyne in the countryside. Eliza and her mother were in Saratoga when the word of the scalping spread through the Hudson, and Eliza remembered afterward that her "father was so alarmed by the killing of Miss McCrea" that he sent an armed escort to fetch his wife and daughter back to Albany. The accounts of the murder quickly took on fantastic and exaggerated elements in the retelling, but the risk of attacks from the natives was real. A plot to have the Schuyler family murdered in their home by an Indian brave was averted at the final moment only because the Iroquois man said that he could not finally kill a man at whose table he had eaten.

In the spring of 1777, John Carter was still in Albany, too, and from Kitty and Philip's perspective it was the worst timing. The girls had a new heartthrob, a young captain named Richard Varick, their father's military secretary. Kitty warmly supported him as a choice for one of her daughters. Richard and their cousin Henry Livingston were assigned the pleasant task, once the countryside grew safer, of escorting Angelica and Eliza back and forth between Albany and Saratoga, and the young people arrived in peals of laughter. Also charged by their father with rounding up deserters, Richard one day brought in a tailor turned soldier, and Eliza promptly joked that they should keep the deserter as a family captive and set him to work as her dressmaker. Before long, Richard Varick was practically a member of the family and given assignments such as finding new curtains for General Schuyler's field bed and ferrying plant cuttings up to Saratoga for Eliza's flower garden. Richard was, like the Schuyler and the Van Rensselaer families, from the New York Dutch community and spoke their language, both literally and figuratively. Here was the kind of man Kitty and Philip Schuyler would be glad to see one of the girls marry.

Angelica and John Carter, however, were already exchanging passionate vows behind the backs of her parents. By spring, John was ardently pressing a besotted Angelica to run away from her father's home with him. Angelica knew that her father took a dim view of Mr. Carter and his shady past. She remembered with a thrill, too, how exciting and romantic it had been when the governor's daughter, Henrietta Moore, climbed over the gate of her father's garrison to elope with her forbidden officer. Of course there were some blustery words. But the governor had forgiven Henrietta. Despite the risks, knowing that she would incur her father's fury, in June 1777 Angelica agreed. She gambled—without calculating just how hurt her mother and father would be—that it would be better to ask for forgiveness than for permission. She may have realized, as well, that there might not long be an option. Angelica was not pregnant yet. But that she might be was no longer an impossibility either.

John Carter arranged horses and a secret assignation. This time, Angelica told no one of her plans, not even Eliza. Eliza was glad for that later. She would have had to tell Papa.

When Angelica saw John waiting at the end of the lane, she was giddy. She was also frightened. Angelica and John were not married, though marrying seems to have been the intention. But if John Carter did not follow through now, Angelica would be ruined. The fleeing couple made for the Van Rensselaer estate, which was spread out around Albany. The new "patroon" of the manor was Angelica's thirteen-year-old cousin Stephen, who, despite his feudal title, was not old enough to help them. Angelica turned instead to her maternal grandfather, John Van Rensselaer, crying and proclaiming her father a heartless tyrant. Her grandfather had a different concern. Had the relationship already been consummated? Why was his granddaughter not already married? When the young Mr. Carter was quizzed about the state of the affair, it became clear that, whether General

Schuyler liked it or not, there would have to be a wedding. The only question now was how to control the damage.

Angelica's grandfather immediately saw the runaway couple married on June 21 at the manor house. Then John Van Rensselaer set about the grim business of informing his daughter Kitty and son-in-law General Schuyler that their reckless eldest child was married to a man they detested.

CHAPTER 4

Angelica, 1777

Eliza watched in awe as her father tossed into the fireplace Angelica's letters, unread and unopened.

Philip's hands shook. Eliza had never seen her father so angry. Angelica and that bounder would never get a penny, Philip Schuyler tartly informed his father-in-law. The doors of this house were closed forever to Angelica.

Poor Grandfather. He had come to broker peace, but Eliza could see the process was not going smoothly. Her mother wasn't helping. While her father paced furiously, Kitty slumped in the corner, weeping. Eliza had never heard such harsh words from her mother either. Mother had already yelled at Grandfather, and that made Grandfather angry. When Eliza passed Prince or the other servants in the corridors, no one wanted to make eye contact, least of all Eliza.

Would Papa forbid Angelica's letters to her sisters too? Mother raged that Angelica was a bad influence. Eliza already knew she would never do something so foolhardy as run away from the Pastures. She guessed from the pathetic tone of Angelica's letters that it was beginning to dawn on her that she had gambled unwisely. Eliza knew that her sister had spent most of the first days of her marriage crying.

For the newlyweds, being cut off from Angelica's parents' home and, especially, from the Schuyler family fortune posed a serious and deeply unpleasant dilemma.

John Carter did not have a fortune. He did not have the money to support a wife, let alone a wife from a wealthy background. John had a position in the army, but he was not financially independent. He had pursued Angelica, in part, because of her family's wealth and connections in America and had counted on the generosity of her father. Philip Schuyler, however, not only planned to cut Angelica out of a share of the family inheritance but was not inclined to support his disobedient and now-married daughter with a private income or marriage settlement.

No one had broken the worst news of all yet to Philip Schuyler either. John Carter was, as Eliza's father had feared, an imposter.

John Carter was not a British spy. That was some consolation, at least, to Philip Schuyler. Eliza's grandfather had extracted most of the sorry story from the young man already. John Carter confessed that his real name was John Church, and he hastened to reassure John Van Rensselaer that he did come from a wealthy mercantile background in London, from a family not unlike the Schuyler family. He was a gentleman in his tastes and education.

Just not a gentleman in his conduct then. Philip Schuyler was not moved so far by this story.

The rest of the story behind John Church's flight from Britain and his transformation into John Carter did nothing to endear Angelica's new husband further to Philip or Kitty, although it did have some stock romantic elements to thrill the young ladies. John Church was orphaned at a young age; his guardian was a wealthy uncle in London: John Barker, an important man in the insurance and sugar trade in the West Indies. John wanted desperately as a lad, so the story went, to join the British army and dreamed of adventure. His stern uncle took a dim view of such an unsteady occupation and insisted that John work in the trading house of a rich neighboring merchant, whose daughter and only child was a plain, dull young lady less than charitably described as having "nothing remarkable to distinguish her save her gilding." The work was boring, and so was the merchant's daughter.

At first, John obeyed his uncle's orders. The tedium, though, was unrelenting. He wasn't cut out for the countinghouse and insurance contracts. He was a wealthy young man with rich, fast friends, and he wanted some excitement. So he toiled days for the merchant and his uncle and at night threw himself into wild parties.

Partying in London in the 1760s and 1770s mostly meant running riot in bawdy houses and participating in high-stakes gambling. John soon managed to lose 10,000 pounds—the modern equivalent of more than $1.5 million—in the aristocratic gambling dens in the capital and in reckless stock-market speculation. Certain that he would win big and more than repay the stakes, John had "borrowed" the money from his uncle's business accounts, and now faced a very thorny problem.

Uncle Barker, furious, hit upon a solution to the problem of his wayward nephew and his mounting debts. He announced to John that it was high time for him to propose to the daughter of the rich business associate.

John balked. The girl was not pretty enough for his fine tastes. She was not witty or funny. He would not marry her, John announced. His uncle retorted that a young man 10,000 pounds in debt was not in a position to be picky. In the standoff that followed, Uncle Barker washed his hands of his charge. He cut off John's income and declined to bail out his feckless ward. By August 1774, bailiffs were on John's tail, and the London newspapers were reporting that he was bankrupt.

This was the story that John Carter had told Angelica and her grandfather. Unfortunately for Angelica, her father did not find his bold escape from a loveless marriage quite as romantic as she did. All Philip Schuyler saw was disobedience. Even more unfortunately for

Angelica, John Church had also not yet come clean with the entire story and had glossed over some other unfortunate bits.

Before fleeing Britain, the young John Church had also managed to get tangled up in a duel. Dueling was illegal, and it was never clear later which of the combatants ended up making a visit to the surgeon. Chances are it was John who was grazed by the bullet. His uncle wasn't the only person from whom John had "borrowed" his gambling stake. Tongues still wagged, even a decade after his marriage to Angelica, that John had "entered into a partnership with another man, but then took 5000 guineas of the pair's money and faked his own death before fleeing from England" under the assumed name of John Carter.

John booked a transatlantic passage and fled his troubles. On his arrival in America, John then did what he'd wanted to do all along: he joined the army. The only army that was likely to take him—because he and British major John André were old schoolmates and his identity would have been uncovered in the British camp immediately— was that of the Americans. Conveniently, John decided at that point that he was an ardent supporter of the cause of the patriots.

For a month, Eliza's grandfather worked behind the scenes to calm the waters, and Eliza watched as her mother cried every night in the front parlor and her father's jaw set tighter and tighter. There were fiery family conferences, and even from her refuge in the garden Eliza could hear angry voices. Grandfather John quietly pressed his daughter and his son-in-law to think of the fate that awaited Angelica, tied to a bitter, resentful, and cash-strapped imposter, if they refused to aid the young couple.

Meanwhile, Angelica's elopement was the talk of New York society all that first summer, causing Eliza and her family keen embarrassment. Letters with the news were flying. One of Eliza's cousins reported,

Dear Alice, Gr. Grandfather Trumbull writes his wife as follows, Albany, 30 June 1777, Monday last Miss Angelica Schuyler

*became Mrs. Carter. The Ceremony passed at the Manor without
the knowledge of Parents—the new married couple came to
Town Wednesday following—have not yet been to her Father's
House nor seen her Mother—they remain at Grand Papa's over
the River. This the News of Town.*

When Philip Schuyler finally permitted the couple to return to
the family home, it may have been as much to quash the gossip as
anything else. Angelica parading through Albany on the arm of her
new husband, just a few miles from the Pastures, was impossible to
ignore, and already the tittle-tattle had spread as far as relatives in
Manhattan.

By July, Philip and Kitty were worn down and relented. As Philip
Schuyler explained to William Duer, the man who had introduced
John to the family: "unacquainted with his Family, his Connections,
and Situation in Life the match was exceedingly disagreeable to me."
However, Philip Schuyler went on, "as there is no undoing this Gor-
dian Knot . . . I frowned, I made them humble themselves, forgave,
and called them home."

The chilly reception and the groveling apologies Angelica's father
demanded of the couple should have been a hint to John and Angelica not to inflame the situation. It was certainly enough to persuade
Eliza that she would never marry except with her papa's permission. Neither John nor Angelica, however, ever showed much sense
in matters of finances or diplomacy. John, who took a liberal view
of his right to the money of other people, considered that he was
entitled to a share of the family fortune as a marriage portion. He
was a man who took what he wanted from life without so much
as a by-your-leave and thought it enough afterward to smooth any
ruffled feathers with a gallant thank-you. That others saw this as
underhanded and manipulative he could never fathom. His young
wife, on the other hand, was simply spoiled. It had never occurred
to Angelica that she would need to think about money. Papa had always paid for everything.

Angelica and John, having no home of their own, now moved into the Schuyler family home in Albany, and the tension was soon unbearable. The newlyweds immediately began running up extravagant bills, expecting Angelica's increasingly irate father to pay them. A day after first being permitted to meet his new in-laws, in what went down in family lore as a famously cold welcome, John Carter picked up the pen and passed a pleasant morning placing orders for luxury items at his father-in-law's expense. "Mrs. Carter requests you to buy her 5 or 6 Pounds of Hyson Tea, be the Price what it will," he blithely instructed in one letter. Angelica wanted "a set of strings for her Guitar and two setts of upper G Strings." He placed the order for those too. Other requests quickly followed.

The impertinence of the order for a half-dozen pounds of tea was especially rich given the economic uncertainty at the start of the American Revolution and what tea represented. The "American" dollar was just six months old in the summer of 1777, and its value was plummeting. Wartime inflation was running in the double digits, and even rich men like Philip Schuyler were short of ready money and watching their wealth vanish on paper. When John placed his order for tea—"be the Price what it will"—a barrel of the precious leaves cost the modern equivalent of about $3,500. By the time that order arrived, two months later, the cost had risen to well over $5,000. By the summer of 1778, a year on, the cost would approach $30,000, as the American currency entered what some feared was a death spiral.

John Carter, though, didn't worry about such trifles. When the bill arrived in the autumn, John dashed off a quick note, assuring his creditors, "The General will pay you for them when you come here, and any other sum you have been so kind as to lay out for me." As one biographer of John Carter trenchantly observes, "Whether or not Schuyler had agreed to assume Carter's debts in addition to his married daughter's is not clear, but knowing the initial antagonism that existed between Schuyler and his son-in-law it seems safe to assume that Carter was being presumptuous."

There were constant quarrels all that summer at the Pastures. Eliza felt sorry for her mother, who still felt deeply wounded by Angelica's betrayal and showed it. Kitty snapped, and Angelica pouted. No one much appreciated Peggy's wry and witty running commentary. Angelica put on new airs as a married woman, and, as John downed one generous glass of her father's expensive Madeira after another, Eliza fled them all and retreated to the gardens or the stables. It was enough to give anyone a headache.

General Schuyler was away more often than not as the summer wore on and, thankfully, was spared witnessing the greatest incursions into his wine cellar. Had he been home, there surely would have been fireworks—but he had his own fireworks to contend with. The battle with the British general John Burgoyne and the climax of the Saratoga campaign at Ticonderoga were barreling toward the Americans in July.

Papa's safety was a constant worry. General Schuyler was a high-value target, with a price on his head already. A native assassin nearly succeeded in claiming the bounty that month when Eliza's father was at Saratoga. Only a household slave catching a glint of metal reflected in the light of the fireplace, and, with great presence of mind, calling out for help from imaginary sentinels prevented Philip Schuyler from being murdered in his bed by the intruder. Worry kept everyone edgy. The Schuyler girls at home all lived with the knowledge that another attack on the family in Albany might come at any moment. Eliza was alert to even the smallest sounds outside her window, and armed guards patrolled the manor house as a military compound.

The campaign in Ticonderoga was not going well for the Americans. Defeat was not impossible. What then would become of them? In the back of everyone's mind was the terrible sentence that had been handed down to William Prendergast for treason. The American rebels understood clearly that, if their cause failed, the price would be monstrous. The British were gaining ground, and when word came that they had taken the peak at Sandy Hill, Eliza knew enough to be frightened. From there, the route to the entire Hudson River lay open to them.

Philip Schuyler, from his campaign outpost in the north, already saw clearly that his estate at Saratoga lay in the path of the British. The general composed a hasty letter to his wife and sent a messenger racing across the countryside to Albany. The letter reached Kitty and the girls at the Pastures at the end of July, and Kitty's hand went to her throat as she read the words. The British could not be stopped from reaching Saratoga.

Eliza marveled at her mother's composure now. Kitty Schuyler was the wife of a soldier, and she had lived her life on the edge of the wilderness. Although her career was as a mother and mistress of a domestic estate, as her youngest daughter later remembered, "she possessed courage and prudence in a great degree." Well, if the British army could not be stopped from reaching the family summer estates, then Kitty Schuyler was determined to make sure that they would not find there anything of use or value. She, too, could thwart the British. Kitty scribbled a quick note to Philip and ordered a servant to prepare the fast coach and to harness four of the family's horses. An armed servant mounted the seat beside her, prepared to deal with anyone who tried to stop her. Leaving the older girls in charge of the estate and reminding them to check the locks on the doors carefully, Kitty Schuyler set off in a cloud of dust for Saratoga.

Albany to Saratoga was forty miles, through country lanes and a trail through the pine forest. When Kitty was less than a half-dozen miles from her destination, panicked refugees rushing in the other direction blocked the roadway. Families living farther north up the river were fleeing the advance of the British troops and their Iroquois allies. Farmers and their wives begged Kitty to turn back. Ahead, only a savage death awaited her. She would have to travel through two miles of dense forest on the last approach to the house, risking an easy ambush, and Kitty's heart was racing. She had lived with war her entire life on the frontier, though, and Kitty knew how small things could tip the outcome in a battle. She squared her shoulders and announced, "The wife of the General must not be afraid," before she swished the heavy reins and urged the carriage forward.

The Saratoga house in late July was in full midsummer beauty. Her orchards were heavy with green fruit, which would ripen in autumn, and the carefully tended gardens were blooming. In the distance, the mountains rose up from the valley floor, and Kitty knew that somewhere to the north the patriots were fighting. She turned and ordered the household staff to begin packing up the family silver. When an army rider raced into the courtyard, her heart stopped. She took into her hand another message from the general. The situation was worse than he had feared. He had received her message. There was one more thing he needed her to do before she returned to the children and the safety of Albany.

Burn everything in the fields. Those were the instructions. Kitty must destroy everything they had worked all summer to produce. They had to hope the local tenants would follow suit if she led by example. If they did, when General Burgoyne came down the Hudson River with his troops, he would find scorched earth all around him. Everyone in the valley knew precisely how hard it could be to survive a hungry New York winter. General Schuyler wanted that aching hunger for the British.

Horses were of immense value in the midst of battle. As a soldier's wife, Kitty saw that Philip and his officers would need the animals, now that the tide was against them. Kitty ordered the post rider to take back to the general at Fort Edwards all four of her mounts and a reply letter, promising that she would do instantly what he requested. The servants were to hitch oxen instead to her carriage for her return trip in the morning.

Then Kitty Schuyler walked out into the wheat fields in the fading sunshine. One of the family slaves carried a torch, but when she told the man to set the fields on fire, the frightened servant refused. To burn a crop was a serious thing, and a slave who did such a thing on purpose might easily swing from the gallows. "Very well," Kitty sighed. "If you will not do it, I must do it myself." Lighting one stick after another, lifting each high overhead before she flung it from her, taking care that the sparks did not fall into the fold of her skirts, Kitty set the fields alight corner by corner. When she finished, her hands were black with soot, and she watched as the flames swept across the dry earth and as smoke billowed up from the cornfields. As night fell, the ground shimmered red with embers.

As the sun rose the next morning, she was ready. Kitty set off past the blackened fields driving a heavy ox-drawn carriage. The household servants walked behind for the slow, long journey back to the girls and Albany, where the story of the general's courageous wife quickly became a legend. A century later, when people came to tell the story of small acts that helped to win the American Revolution, the tale of Catherine Schuyler burning her fields was still being repeated and depicted in illustrations.

When the battle finally came at Ticonderoga, the Americans suffered a stunning defeat. Philip commanded the northern army, and the blame fell on him as the general. He was stripped of command amid politicized charges of dereliction of duty; incensed by the humiliating allegations, Philip demanded a full court-martial to clear his name of the trumped-up charges. As political infighting threw the American campaign into further disarray, British troops were battling their way down the Hudson. General Burgoyne was determined to drive the king's army through New York, dividing the northern colonies from the southern colonies, with an eye to conquering both and destroying the American uprising. In the summer of 1777, that all looked increasingly possible. John Church's professional charge as an army commissioner, assigned to audit the account books of the Northern Department at the moment of his father-in-law's embarrassment, did nothing to ease tensions at home between a newly unemployed Philip Schuyler and his spendthrift son-in-law.

In the Schuyler home as the summer came to a close, everyone was angry. Kitty was still fuming silently, John bristled, and Angelica was caught in the middle. Eliza retreated to work in her gardens and lamented that the countryside was too dangerous now for fast horseback riding. By September, "wearied out with the Disputes and Bickerings," John had had enough. The young man decided once again to flee an uncomfortable position of his own creating. "I have determined to remain no longer in Commission," he informed friends, "and have this Day sent my Resignation." The next morning, John and Angelica set off for a new life in Boston. Both Angelica and Kitty were pregnant.

When General Burgoyne reached Saratoga with his troops, Kitty Schuyler's charred fields and an empty mansion awaited him. The British officers took possession of the family mansion, and, after a brief period of riotous revelry, during which Philip Schuyler's wine cellars were emptied and the house looted and vandalized, General Burgoyne ordered the mansion and all the farms and mills on the property torched too. Richard Varick, Philip's military secretary and the man Kitty was still hoping Eliza might marry, reported to General Schuyler, "No part of your buildings escaped their malice except a small outbuilding, and your upper sawmill, which is in the same situation we left it. Hardly a vestige of the fences is left except a few rails of the garden." Losing her childhood home was a blow that hit Eliza keenly.

The final battle at Saratoga came in early October, and the tide now turned in favor of the rebels. When the British surrendered, General Burgoyne was captured, and Philip Schuyler's moment for revenge arrived. Word of admiration for Eliza's father spread as far as Britain when he refused to take it.

Baroness Frederika Riedesel was there with her military husband at the capitulation, and, as she put it later, "I must candidly confess that I did not present myself . . . with much courage to the enemy." The baroness trembled as she stepped from her carriage at the American camp. She had never been a prisoner. Her eyes met those of a tall man who held out his hand to her. "Do not be alarmed," he assured her, and he lifted her three little girls carefully down from the carriage. The man, she learned soon after, was General Schuyler.

It was the turn of General Burgoyne, who had destroyed Philip and Kitty's summer mansion, to be astonished next, when General Schuyler offered him and his men accommodation in the family home at Albany along with the baroness. They would be his prisoners, it was true. But Philip assured General Burgoyne that he would be welcomed as a fellow officer.

"You are too kind to me—who have done you so much injury," he told Philip.

"Such is the fate of war," Philip replied gallantly. "Let us not dwell on this subject."

"This gentleman," General Burgoyne recounted later, "conducted me to a very elegant house and, to my great surprise, introduced me to Mrs. Schuyler and her family."

Baroness Riedesel recorded, "Our reception from General Schuyler, and his wife and daughters was not like the reception of enemies, but of the most intimate friends," and the generosity and civility of the Schuyler family in the midst of war would be remembered long after the war was over. Among those who made the most charming impression on the officers and their wives was General Schuyler's eldest unmarried daughter, Eliza. Later, there were toasts to the beauty and graces of Eliza and her sister Peggy at boozy dinners behind British lines by some of their new admirers. Those toasts to Eliza and Peggy would carry on throughout the conflict.

General Burgoyne and his entourage stayed three days with the Schuyler family in Albany. The baroness and her husband stayed longer, until the prisoners were transported to Boston and placed on parole—essentially under town arrest—in the sleepy river village of Cambridge. British men were barred from leaving Cambridge or entering Boston, but the wives of the captured officers could request passes for social visits and shopping. Few had the temerity. The reception among the patriots' wives and daughters was not friendly. Baroness Frederika Riedesel, though, felt sure that she would find a gracious reception in at least one American household. She had yet to meet Angelica, now a socialite in Boston. She would shortly.

In the midst of all the hustle and bustle of war, sometime in November 1777, something else important transpired.

One of the officers fighting in the campaign was a young man dispatched to deliver an urgent letter to General Schuyler at his residence in Albany. The officer rode a fine horse along the country lane that led in the direction of his duty and considered himself lucky when he spotted coming toward him a young lady with lively dark eyes and cheeks flushed from fast riding, accompanied by a family slave for protection. With a handsome bow, he introduced himself as General Washington's aide-de-camp, Lieutenant Colonel Alexander Hamilton, and dared to wonder whether the lady could direct him to the Schuyler mansion.

Eliza smiled at the gallant courtesy and twisted a bit in her saddle to get a look at this gentleman. She could never say what it was afterward, but something about him made her want to tease him gently. He took himself so seriously. She certainly hoped she could help, Eliza quipped lightly, seeing that the man he wanted was her father.

Come on then, her look said, as she set off toward the Pastures. Wisps of dark hair blew in the wind. She was not a beauty, the young man noticed, but when Miss Schuyler laughed something wonderful happened.

CHAPTER 5

Hamilton, 1778–80

It was not love at first sight.

Apart from this brief encounter in Albany, it would be more than two years before Eliza would see Alexander Hamilton again.

While the Revolutionary War continued to unfold on the northern front, Eliza was not there to witness the campaign or to meet with any of the young officers fighting it, although Alexander was a frequent presence. By the end of December 1777, Eliza had moved to Boston, where she was living with Angelica and John, helping her sister through her first pregnancy.

When Eliza had time to dream of romance during those next two years she would spend in New England, she thought still of Tench Tilghman. Tench had not proposed. Her father, though, she was certain, would not refuse the match if he did. Tench, with his connections to their shared Livingston kin and his comparable wealth and status in colonial America, was just the kind of man a girl like her could expect to marry. He was a far more eligible bachelor, say, than the impoverished immigrant Colonel Alexander Hamilton.

Mostly, though, Eliza was too busy in Boston to think much at all about the future. Angelica was struggling as a new bride. She had married at twenty-one. Her husband was thirty, and Angelica was learning that life as the young wife of a scoundrel was not always easy. John dressed in the latest styles, sparing no expense on his embroidered waistcoats and neck stocks, and he wanted to be surrounded by opulence at home also. Angelica's dinner menus, the sisters quickly learned, were not up to her husband's exacting standards. "I entreat you to purchase for Mrs. Carter," John requested of an agent, "one or two of the best cookery books, as she is a young Housekeeper and wants to gain Experience." Not that Angelica or Eliza did a great deal of the actual cooking. John and Angelica owned at least one slave, a young African man named Ben, and they almost certainly owned at least one or two female domestics. Angelica, however, was responsible for managing the housekeeping budget and directing the menu, and in wartime Boston procuring food and supplies was a constant struggle. Budgets were never Angelica's strong point. Eliza wrote down the figures for her sister in careful columns and tried to make sense of Angelica's impulsive orders to tradesmen.

John Carter, as he still styled himself, spent his days hustling for new business opportunities, with projects that included a bit of banking and shipping insurance and, more to his liking, some high-risk currency and land speculation. When cash was tight, he made up the difference by gambling.

John was not liked by many. When the Baroness Riedesel arrived in Cambridge, still on parole with her husband, she quickly obtained a city pass, and one of her first visits was to Angelica, "who, with her sister Betsy, was living in Boston." "Curiosity and desire urged me to pay a visit to Madame Carter, the daughter of General Schuyler," the baroness wrote later, "and I dined at her house several times." The baroness quickly came to the same conclusion as Philip Schuyler with respect to his son-in-law's character. "Madame Carter," the baroness decided, "was as gentle and good as her parents, but her husband was wicked and treacherous."

The British officers who invited him to their parties also grew wary. John Carter quickly gained a reputation in Boston as a skillful card shark. Baroness Riedesel's husband tried to warn General Burgoyne: gambling with John was a good way to lose a fortune. At first, the general laughed off the baron's advice. Later, chagrined, Burgoyne confessed, "I did not understand you . . . in what you mention'd in your note about Carter. But [General John] Anstruther, who is just now come in to dinner, tells me of Carter's gambling—I was not of the party nor out of my house all day yesterday which was lucky, for I hear the little man carried off money in all his pockets."

John and the baroness quickly squared off as bitter antagonists, and the dinners where they exchanged pointed barbs were exhausting. Eliza hated conflict. Her brother-in-law's humor was crass and combative, his demeanor entirely unlike that of her disciplined father. John took great pleasure in shocking the baroness. If she were discouraged from visiting his wife as a result, so much the better. It would save him instructing his wife to cut her. John Carter gleefully informed the baroness on one memorable occasion that he was advising the Americans to chop off the heads of the British generals and their allies, her husband's noble head included, "salt them down in small barrels, and send over to the English one of these barrels for every hamlet or little town [the British] burned down." The baroness, whose command of irony was limited, flushed red, then white, and stammered in fury. John thought it was hilarious.

While John flitted about Boston, carousing and gambling with the increasingly wary officers, Eliza tended to her sister, now ungainly and swelling heavy with pregnancy. In mid-April, when Angelica's labor pains started, Eliza pressed cool, wet cloths to her sister's forehead during the worst of the long hours when the sisters clung to each other. Childbirth did not always end happily, and the sisters had looked on as their mother buried one child after another. Women, too, died in labor. The thought of losing Ann—as her sisters called her—put knots of fear in Eliza's stomach. Eliza put on a brave face and murmured quiet words to Angelica when the pain carried her, but both sisters wished for their mother. When the baby gave a throaty cry and the ordeal was over, Eliza felt more relieved than celebratory and left John as the proud father to announce the news to her parents. John, tickled that the child was a son, informed the family in Albany that "the little Fellow of two Days old 'grows finely.'"

Angelica and John, hoping to consolidate the peace with her father, who was still footing bills for household luxuries, named the boy Philip. When his sister was born a year and a half later, they strategically named her Kitty. Their first missteps with Eliza's parents had come at a price. They were learning.

Eliza stayed on with Angelica and John in the year that followed, too, during her sister's second pregnancy. Only their father's court-martial in October 1778 interrupted those first years of the war in Boston. They were years that bound Eliza and Angelica to each other more tightly than ever.

Their father's trial was unmitigated misery and sorrow. General Schuyler's court-martial for dereliction of duty at Ticonderoga set off a fresh storm of gossip that wounded everyone in the family old enough to understand it. By now, the household included several younger siblings—Eliza's three brothers, John, Philip, and Rensselaer, and another sister, too, little Cornelia, named after her late grandmother—but the eldest of these siblings was barely thirteen and Cornelia just a toddler. Eliza's sister Peggy, however, was twenty that year and still living at home, and she bore an especially heavy share of the emotional burden with her parents. Eliza would have felt guiltier had she not been away, managing the domestic whims and caprices of John Carter.

The Schuyler family was tight-knit and clannish, and they drew together in moments of crisis. They had rallied before, when the British swept through the Hudson Valley and when they had witnessed the aftermath at Saratoga. They would all gather for the trial, and they would survive together, whatever happened, behind a wall of silence that, despite the family's friendly, easygoing demeanor, did not readily admit outsiders. Angelica and Eliza set off from Boston in late September to join their parents and Peggy in support of their father. The outcome—especially if General Schuyler were found guilty—would profoundly affect all their future prospects.

The verdict from Congress was slow in coming. The wait was excruciating. Her father was not sleeping and tried not to fuss, but Eliza worried. For weeks on end, the family lived in cramped, rented accommodations, beset with ugly rumors and gossip that not only damaged Philip Schuyler's reputation but threatened to blight the marriage chances of Eliza and Peggy if their father were found to have conducted himself dishonorably. If their father were guilty, who would want to marry a Schuyler? And for a time, even after the verdict came, it seemed that the answer was no one.

On December 3, 1778, the verdict was announced at last. It brought both satisfaction and fury. Eliza and her sisters waited in the parlor until the word was delivered. Needlework was cast aside, and the girls watched at the window. When the message came, it was the news they hoped for—the news justice demanded. The court unanimously acquitted General Schuyler, with highest honors. It was a tacit acknowledgment of what the family had fumed about for a year in private: that these had always been vindictive, trumped-up charges. But Philip Schuyler, freed from shame and stress, was now nothing but angry and indignant, and he could not be mollified. He resigned from the army and, only after some arm-twisting, agreed to serve as the Indian commissioner. In the year that followed, his work in this capacity would bring Philip Schuyler's relationship with the Mohawk agents in his spy network to a point of crisis.

When the trial ended, Eliza and Angelica returned to Boston. Days passed as the sisters managed a wartime household, rocking baby Philip to sleep and haggling with merchants. At night, when John was home, there were rounds of dinner parties and assembly balls all winter. The idea of the flirtatious Angelica acting as the chaperone to her younger, steadier sister raised more than one astonished eyebrow. Angelica was known, especially, for her risqué fashion choices, and people tutted that it was the young Mrs. Carter who needed a chaperone.

Despite the social whirl, despite the dances, no marriage propos-
als came for Eliza. Would she miss her chances? Some unlucky girls
did end up old maids and spinsters.

When John's work as a military supplier called for him to move
from Boston to Newport, Rhode Island, in the autumn of 1779,
Eliza might have moved again with her sister, but her mother and
father thought better of it. Perhaps having her live with Angelica and
John was not the best way to get Eliza established with the right kind
of partner. Philip Schuyler continued to hear stories about his son-
in-law's gambling and carousing.

General Schuyler wrote instead to his sister Gertrude and her jo-
vial husband, the army surgeon John Cochran, asking whether they
might have need of Eliza's help and companionship that winter in
Morristown, New Jersey. Eliza was twenty-two already, and Aunt
Gertrude grasped the situation immediately. It was high time Eliza
found a husband. Of course, Eliza must pass the winter of 1779–80
with her aunt and military uncle at winter camp.

Philip Schuyler knew that Tench Tilghman would be there. Soon,
so did a delighted Eliza.

Winter camp at Morristown, conveniently located between the
British troops at New York and Philadelphia, was a lively place
in the autumn of 1779 and into the winter and spring of 1780.
Eliza was not the only young lady arriving for a round of balls
and parties and to attend to the serious business of finding a husband. Senior officers brought their wives and children, including
their eligible daughters, and the great landowning families of the
area hosted thrilling winter balls and dance assemblies to bring the
young people together.

Tench Tilghman was an aide to General Washington and lived in
rooms at headquarters with a number of other young officers in the
general's "family." One of the men who bunked in his room—where
late-night conversations were frank and, as Tench noted, "where

all is under the secure lock and key of Friendship"—was Alexander
Hamilton.

Eliza Schuyler had come to Morristown to look for a husband.
Alexander was also of a mind that winter to get married. Their
finding each other, however, was far from certain. Some of the
stiffest romantic competition, once again, would come from Eliza's
cousins.

Eliza's favorite cousin, Kitty Livingston, lived at a grand estate
near Morristown, with her father, the governor of New Jersey.
Kitty was considered something of a beauty, with thick, dark hair,
fashionably high cheekbones, and wickedly expressive eyebrows.
Kitty was irreverent. It made Eliza laugh to see and hear her cousin.
Poking fun would never get Kitty a husband, but she didn't care.
She was young, and beaux were a dime a dozen. Marriage wasn't
everything anyway. There was one gentleman, though, who seemed
intrigued by Kitty Livingston's flirtatious mockery: Alexander
Hamilton.

There was just one problem. Caty Greene, the wife of General
Nathanael Greene, had other plans in mind for Colonel Hamilton.
Those plans did not include Kitty Livingston as the bride of her
favorite bachelor.

Trouble followed Caty Greene wherever she went, and that meant
trouble followed Alexander. Flirtation was Caty Greene's favorite
pastime, and matchmaking was flirtation as an art form. Caty Greene
loved arranging marriages for her favorites, which meant never mind
Miss Kitty Livingston. Caty's eye fell on Cornelia Lott, daughter of
the wealthy but rather shady merchant Abraham Lott, the local estate
manager of a rich Dutch West Indian planter. Cornelia, a young lady
"of delicate sentiments and polite education," was sixteen, and that
was admittedly young even in the eighteenth century to be thinking
about marriage. But the general's wife didn't trouble herself about
details.

Alexander Hamilton was looking for a bride. He turned to several
friends for assistance in matchmaking and did not mind in the least

Caty Greene's officious involvement. He did have, as he explained to his friend John Laurens, a couple of particular requirements:

> *Such a wife as I want will, I know, be difficult to be found, but if you succeed, it will be the stronger proof of your zeal and dexterity. Take her description—She must be young, handsome (I lay most stress upon a good shape), sensible (a little learning will do), well bred . . . chaste and tender (I am an enthusiast in my notions of fidelity and fondness). . . . But as to fortune, the larger stock of that the better. . . . Though I run no risk of going to Purgatory for my avarice; yet as money is an essential ingredient to happiness in this world—as I have not much of my own and as I am very little calculated to get more either by my address or industry; it must needs be, that my wife, if I get one, bring at least a sufficiency to administer to her own extravagances.*

His wife did not need to be a great beauty, but he didn't want a bride who was unattractive. Most important, she needed to be rich. That was crucial. While Alexander Hamilton played the lovestruck gallant for the crowd, he was also running a careful private calculus when it came to courtship and marriage.

Marriage was an expensive business, and the cold, hard fact was that young men were wise to be picky. The camps offered an important opportunity for a man like Alexander Hamilton, a rare chance at social mobility. The great families tended to marry within their own circles, just as the Schuyler family had been connected for generations to the Van Rensselaer and the Livingston clans. Alexander Hamilton knew that for young men not in possession of a fortune the eighteenth-century marriage market was no less a matter of urgent thought and reflection than for Jane Austen's heroines a generation later.

Alexander had been pursuing Kitty off and on for two years already when Caty Greene began to play matchmaker. As early as the

spring of 1777, Alexander penned to Kitty some decidedly amorous
letters, and at that time a gentleman and a young woman engaged
in private correspondence were considered already halfway to an
engagement. Alexander gushed to Kitty in one wordy missive:

> After knowing exactly your taste, and whether you are of a
> romantic, or discreet temper, as to love affairs, I will endeavour
> to regulate myself by it. . . . You and I, as well as our neighbours,
> are deeply interested to pray for victory, and its necessary
> attendant peace; as, among other good effects, they would
> remove those obstacles, which now lie in the way of that most
> delectable thing, called matrimony;—a state, which, with a kind
> of magnetic force, attracts every breast to it, in which sensibility
> has a place, in spite of the resistance it encounters in the dull
> admonitions of prudence, which is so prudish and perverse a
> dame, as to be at perpetual variance with it.

Eliza and her cousin Kitty were pen pals, and perhaps Eliza already
knew something of the flirtation between her cousin and Alexander
Hamilton when she first met him in Albany. When she gave him a
sideways glance on the ride back to the Pastures at that first meeting,
was she sizing up her cousin's love interest? Nothing is more likely.
The girls exchanged all sorts of intimate chitchat in their notes to each
other, from family gossip to dress patterns, and before Morristown
Eliza likely thought of Alexander—if she thought of him at all—only
as her cousin's admirer.

The love affair between Kitty and Alexander might have led to
a proposal. Alexander certainly wanted to talk in his love letters of
marriage. Her replies, however, frustrated the young colonel—she
did not respond to him with the requisite counterdisplay of ardor.
Kitty was a bit too cool and ironic. Her passion for Alexander Hamilton was tepid.

Caty Greene knew just the girl instead: Cornelia. In her, Alexander found a more encouraging and fevered reception. By late autumn

of 1779, Alexander was courting Cornelia Lott in particularly flamboyant and public fashion. No young lady likes being snubbed for
a rival, but Kitty was not heartbroken. Alexander's fellow officer
and another aide-de-camp, Colonel Samuel Webb, to the delight of
General Washington's inner circle, penned some comic verses on
Alexander's passion for the young lady in January of 1780, verses
that slyly noted other "shrines" at which Colonel Hamilton had pre-
viously worshipped. Samuel Webb joked, "What bend the Stubborn
knee at last, / Confess the days of wisdom past, / He that could bow
to every shrine, / And swear the last the most divine / . . . / Now feels
the inexorable dart / And yields Cornelia all his heart!" It had not
been the first time Alexander Hamilton had declared himself in love.
It would not be the last time either.

In Alexander's defense, it was hard not to get caught up in the
wartime enthusiasm for romance. Camp weddings were frequent
and fashionable. Tench Tilghman's cousin, Margaret "Peggy" Shippen, threw over the handsome Major John André—the same John
André who had caught Eliza's fancy a few years earlier—and married Major Benedict Arnold in a wedding that had everyone talking.
Soon, Benedict Arnold would go down—and not in a good way—as
a legend of the American Revolution. What no one at Morristown
knew yet was that Peggy Arnold was already an enemy informant
and an agent for the British spymaster John André. Within months,
she would bring her disgruntled husband into the network, culmi-
nating in a stunning betrayal.

At the end of January, despite the public courtship, Alexander suddenly jilted Cornelia Lott, just before Eliza's arrival at Morristown. Maybe the passion fizzled—Alexander was famously fickle.
There was probably more to the story, however. Colonel Abraham
Lott was a wheeler-dealer with a taste for high living and financial
gambles, and he had already been hauled up in front of Congress
to account for more than 20,000 pounds—several million dollars

in modern values—that had mysteriously vanished. If Alexander inquired further into the finances of Cornelia's father, as he surely would have done before proposing marriage, he would have learned that Abraham Lott was hopelessly indebted, embroiled in a situation that would soon see him imprisoned as a bankrupt. A dowry for his daughter was out of the question. Cornelia and her sisters remained, unsurprisingly, unmarried for decades.

Alexander Hamilton now turned his eye instead to Tench Tilghman's eighteen-year-old cousin Mary, known as "Polly," the daughter of Colonel Edward Tilghman. The abrupt shift in his affections set tongues at camp freshly wagging, and a smitten Polly seemed certain that a marriage proposal was imminent. At just this juncture—as Alexander Hamilton was assiduously courting Polly—Eliza arrived at Morristown.

Eliza traveled to Morristown under military escort and carrying letters from her father to General Washington and General Friedrich von Steuben sometime in late January or early February of 1780, with plans to spend the winter season with her aunt and her Livingston cousins. Home would be the small cottage that her aunt and uncle shared with General Washington's personal physician, Dr. Jabez Campfields, on the road between the headquarters and the village.

Eliza's journey down to Morristown was cold and blustery. A blizzard in January left snowdrifts up to six feet high across the roads, and, as she rattled toward New Jersey, the wind swept into the cracks in the carriage door and the coachman sometimes slowed for icy sections. Travel conditions were difficult throughout January and February, and the winter of 1779–80 was not only the worst winter of the war, it was among the worst winters in an entire century. The ice on the Hudson River froze a dozen feet deep, worsening inflation made the cost of basic supplies beyond the reach of many, and the snow simply kept coming.

Eliza arrived at Morristown with little fanfare, and within days had seen Tench Tilghman. Tench, however, was not interested in romance with Miss Schuyler. The situation was hopeless.

Tench Tilghman was madly in love with another young lady. The object of his desire was his twenty-five-year-old cousin, Anna. Anna Tilghman was a young lady who knew precisely how to manage her skittish bachelor relation. When Tench proposed, she turned him down smartly. There were delighted letters among the Tilghman cousins, applauding Anna for not "surrendering at the first Summons." Nothing could have more inflamed Tench's passion. Tench was determined to marry only Anna. And Anna was determined to keep him wondering and waiting.

For Eliza, it was a painful start to life at Morristown. Then, unexpectedly, Alexander Hamilton appeared on her uncle's doorstep.

Alexander had not come looking for Eliza. Or, at least, that was not his ostensible errand. He had been sent from headquarters to deliver some papers to her uncle Cochran, he explained, excusing his sudden appearance in Aunt Gertrude's parlor. Eliza gave him a friendly welcome. There was her smile again, he noticed.

Eliza had an appraising eye as well. Alexander, as one nineteenth-century biographer observed, "was evidently very attractive and must have possessed a great charm of manners, address, and conversation." He had beautiful deep-blue eyes, and, as someone who knew him reported, "his complexion was exceedingly fair and varying from this only by the almost feminine rosiness of his cheeks. His might be considered, as to figure and colour, an uncommonly handsome face."

This time, the spark between them was instantaneous.

Alexander went back to headquarters late and in the days that followed promptly threw over Polly Tilghman. He dashed off a letter instead, inviting Eliza and her cousin Kitty Livingston to go sleighing—though when work at headquarters forced him to cancel, he cajoled Tench into taking out the ladies.

Embarrassed and miffed at her lover's sudden desertion, the unlucky Polly fled home. Cousin Tench felt badly for her, writing to his brother:

"Alas poor Polly! Hamilton is a gone man. . . . She had better look out for herself and not put her trust in Man. She need not be jealous of the little Saint—She is gone to Pennsylvania and has no other impressions than those of regard for a very pretty good tempered Girl, the daughter of one of my most valuable acquaintances."

The "little Saint" was Tench's teasing nickname for Eliza, and everyone understood that the change of heart was entirely in character for Alexander.

Word of Hamilton's newest infatuation traveled quickly in Morristown circles—not least because Alexander talked of nothing now but Eliza. John Cochran noticed that Colonel Hamilton was drinking gallons of tea and spending a great many hours in his front parlor. When, returning to headquarters one night from a late evening spent there with Eliza, the giddy Alexander forgot the password at the checkpoint and was accosted by an overzealous young sentinel alert to the dangers of political assassination, there was great merriment in General Washington's household at the newest love interest. But few were prepared to lay bets on whether it would all end at the altar. It was not the first time the young colonel had abandoned himself to his passion for a young lady, after all. It was the third time in the space of a month, actually. This might not be the last time this winter, either, some of his fellow officers wagered.

Would Miss Elizabeth Schuyler meet the same fate as Cornelia and Polly when Alexander Hamilton's attention wavered? And would Eliza have him?

Some of the wiser heads at camp asked another question too. Alexander came from nothing and nowhere. Eliza was the daughter of a colony aristocrat. He was a lowly knight. She was a baron's daughter. Why would General Schuyler ever agree to such a marriage?

CHAPTER 6

The Winter Ball, 1780

Angelica arrived on the scene in New Jersey at a crucial moment. The first winter ball of the season was just a week away, on Wednesday, February 23, timed to celebrate the birthday of George Washington a day earlier, and no one at camp was laying great odds on the chances that the fickle Alexander Hamilton would still be courting Miss Schuyler so many days in the future.

True, Alexander talked of nothing now but Eliza. His fellow officers groaned when he waxed poetic after a few tankards in the Morristown tavern and teased him for his "cavalry-like advances on the latest feminine arrival." This week, the colonel was in love with Miss Schuyler and her eyes. But only a few weeks ago it had been Miss Lott's dark tresses. The other fellows felt for the girls and especially for poor Polly Tilghman. Still, the lads supposed, it was up to the ladies in the end to catch a husband. But it would take a rare lady, indeed, to catch and to keep a playboy like Alexander, and the good-natured Eliza Schuyler did not yet strike any of them as a ruthless tactician.

It turns out they were underestimating the Schuyler sisters.

Angelica swept into camp with her usual dramatic flair on her way to Philadelphia in the second part of February, bringing her little boy Philip, her three-month-old baby Kitty, and more trunks of extravagant French fashion than was strictly decent in wartime. The sisters quickly closeted themselves for a long talk—Angelica wanted to hear at once all the gossip—and Eliza poured out her heart. Angelica quickly assessed the situation. Her sister was in love. So was the colonel. Tench Tilghman was no more. Well, then, they would have to see to it that there was a marriage, *n'est-ce pas*? Angelica couldn't get through a sentence these days without dropping in some French expression or another, Eliza noticed. There was a ball to plan for and the small matter of arranging a marriage proposal. Angelica laid out gauzy silk ball gowns and their strategy, and they quickly drew their sharp-witted cousin Kitty Livingston—Alexander's old friend and love interest, a strategic advantage—into their lively war council. Then, behind closed doors, the girls put their heads together, laughing.

The snow fell thick and heavy all the next week, and when the night of the ball at last arrived the girls traveled by horse-drawn sleigh with their aunt and uncle to the Continental Store above the village green. The military storehouse had been commandeered for the festivities. Wrapped in thick cloaks, their hands protected in beaver muffs, the girls tucked the fabric of gowns neatly underneath them and wiggled just a bit to stop their stays from pinching. As they were handed down from the sleigh in a cloud of powdery snow, the sisters were in high spirits, and Angelica recognized among the gentlemen General Henry Knox, General Washington, General Greene, and Eliza's old beau Tench Tilghman. Their cousin Kitty Livingston was there with her sisters. Eliza's eyes searched for and quickly found Alexander. When their eyes met, her heart pounded.

The wide-pine-board floors gleamed with polish, and Eliza saw that the doors along the length of the second-story veranda were thrown open to let in cold, fresh air when the dancing started. Would Alexander ask her to dance? Or had his interest already faded? Angelica had advised her all week in the coquettish arts of keeping a man's attention. There were three times as many officers as ladies, and some of the girls would end up sad wallflowers.

The ball opened with a dainty minuet, danced by a series of couples, one after the other, and Lucy Knox, the wife of General Knox, led off the dancing that night—a mark of her social superiority—with the famously handsome eligible bachelor General Walter Stewart, a heartthrob among the ladies. General Greene's wife, Caty, fumed quietly, tired of being perennially ranked one notch below her archrival. The incongruity of the leading couple did not go unnoticed on the dance floor, and Caty Greene didn't let pass the opportunity for snide, whispered commentary to members of her party, who included Cornelia Lott and her sisters. Lucy Knox's waistline was bigger than ever, she snickered.

Lucy was keenly interested in fashion, especially faddish and outrageous headdresses. The exaggerated styles of the day, Eliza had to admit, did not favor Lucy's especially ample figure. As one particularly unsympathetic observer described Lucy Knox in the 1780s, "Her hair in front is craped at least a foot high . . . and topped off with a wire skeleton . . . covered with black gauze, which hangs in streamers hangs down her back." Eliza liked Lucy. Still, the effect was ridiculous.

Eliza touched her neck gently. The room was warm, and a lady's fan could hide blushes. Had she and Angelica misjudged her artfully chosen fashion choices this evening? An extravagant beehive updo was the height of style in London and Paris, and American patriots added whimsical touches to the elaborate designs to include frigates of war that billowed under full sail on the dance floor and miniature cannons camouflaged by hair powder. Coiffures dressed à la Americaine featured thirteen fat curls at the back of the neck, in homage to the thirteen rebellious colonies, and a fluttering wake of red, white, and blue ribbons. Even Benedict Arnold's wife, Peggy, had sat for a wedding portrait the previous year with her hair teased two feet tall and festooned with trailing ribbons, Angelica assured her.

Eliza hadn't gone quite that far—few went as far as Lucy Knox—but, in fairness to Lucy, she was not the only lady that winter to indulge in this whimsy. Eliza and Angelica, after all, had called in the hairdresser, and all afternoon he had teased their hair into high rolls, molded around pads of itchy cow hair. Eliza's headdress that season was a dramatic and patriotic confection of ribbons and feathers, made up in the style *à la Bostonne* and sent to her as a gift from one of her father's commercial agents in Paris. Eliza called it later her "Marie Antoinette coiffure."

Now, there was a moment's hesitation. But when Eliza looked up to see Alexander making a little bow of greeting before her, any trace of worry was forgotten.

She must have said yes, because the next thing she knew she was dancing.

As the night went on, the band played faster, and the formal minuet soon gave way to reels and quadrilles, and there at camp, in the midst of an uncertain war and a hungry winter, everyone sang along to the refrain of tunes like "The Liberty Song," with lyrics that went "Come join hand in hand, brave Americans all." In front of fifteen ladies and nearly sixty officers, the romance between Eliza and Alexander blossomed. When he asked her to dance a second time, the other officers exchanged glances. Just a hint of a smile passed between Angelica and their cousin Kitty. Colonel Hamilton would find himself engaged if he weren't careful. When he found his way to Eliza and Angelica's side for supper, it was clear that Alexander was indeed a "gone man," as Tench Tilghman had predicted. So, the field belonged after all to Miss Schuyler, the gentleman chuckled.

If Alexander didn't propose that night, he proposed the next morning. Dancing twice with the same unmarried lady was tantamount to a declaration. By the time Angelica left camp the following week, to join her husband, John, at his new post in Newport, Rhode Island, Alexander and Angelica were fast friends, and John Cochran thought it wise to send off a hasty note to the general, advising him of Colonel Hamilton's respectful attentions to his daughter. Within days of the ball, Alexander sent off a gallant letter introducing himself to their younger sister Peggy, declaring his love for Eliza and affection for all this charming family. He wrote that Eliza was all "good natured affability and vivacity unembellished with that charming frivolousness which is justly deemed one of the principal accomplishments of a *belle*." Time after time, those who knew Eliza best would say the same things. Those who loved her did so for these reasons.

The young people were making their plans, talking, their hands brushing, for hours in Aunt Gertrude's front parlor. Aunt Gertrude was a hopeless romantic and found all sorts of reasons to leave Alexander and Eliza whispering alone in front of the fire. But, her aunt reminded her, Alexander would need to speak to her father before these castles in the air had any real foundation.

Alexander was more than a little anxious. Alexander knew he was nothing but an upstart. His background was distinctly checkered, and he had too much good sense to be anything other than completely honest with General Schuyler. Alexander was the illegitimate son of a woman who had abandoned her husband for a lover, and he had grown up an orphan in impoverished circumstances on the West Indian island of Nevis. Precious few in America were privy to the story of his origins, but Alexander was determined to come clean with the general. His background was not the kind of thing you let a man discover after you married his daughter—especially when that man already had one duplicitous son-in-law. Alexander might have been born out of wedlock, but he was a gentleman and meant to act like one.

That Alexander had completed university with a law degree and risen to the rank of colonel in America spoke to his immense intelligence, but he did not possess even a small fortune either. There was hardly any point in trying to hide that from the general. They would need to depend on some of Eliza's family inheritance in the beginning to make it. Not all parents from Eliza's elite background were likely to accept talent and promise as sufficient. As Alexander candidly put it to his friend John Laurens, "I am a stranger in this country. I have no property here, no connexions."

Whatever else they talked about, head bowed together by the fire, the couple never considered eloping. Eliza had witnessed firsthand the hurt and anger that Angelica's elopement had caused, and Eliza was not the family rebel. So when General Schuyler passed through camp briefly in early March, not entirely by chance, Alexander jumped at the chance to speak to him in person. What would Alexander say that could persuade her father? Eliza was on tenterhooks. She hoped Alexander would find the right words, because she already knew that she would not disobey her father. If her father said no and told her to break off the connection, it would be the last time she would see Alexander.

The clock in Aunt Gertrude's parlor ticked relentlessly. At last, Alexander emerged stunned and bewildered, sooner than Eliza had dared to imagine. To Alexander's great surprise, General Schuyler had taken his hand as though Alexander were his son and had welcomed him wholeheartedly into the family without hesitation.

Alexander Hamilton was a rising star, and for Philip Schuyler his acumen and ambition far outweighed the young colonel's small purse and modest background. He could see clearly that his daughter was in love with a young man whom he liked and respected. Why throw up obstacles when the young people had gone through the proper and dutiful motions? Besides, even the general was not so old a relic that he couldn't see that Alexander was any young lady's idea of extremely handsome. He could only shake his head in wonder and wish for the best for the young people. "You cannot, my dear sir," Philip Schuyler wrote to Alexander in the days that followed,

be more happy at the connexion you have made with my family than I am. Until the child of a parent has made a judicious choice, his heart is in continual anxiety; but this anxiety was

*removed on the moment I discovered it was you on whom she
had placed her affections.*

But Eliza's mother would also have to be asked, the general
warned Alexander. If "she consents to Comply with your and her
daughters wishes," then Philip Schuyler would bless the marriage. *If.*
Men may have ruled over women as a matter of law in the eighteenth
century, but Philip and Kitty Schuyler enjoyed a long and happy
marriage, in part because he did not undercut her household authority as either mistress or mother. Philip knew how wounded Kitty
had been by Angelica's elopement and deception. He also knew that
the main issue was that she wanted the confidence of her daughters
and the pleasure of a family wedding. "You will see the Impropriety
of taking the dernier pas [final step] where you are," Philip warned
Alexander and Eliza sternly. Don't spoil it all now by jumping the
gun and upsetting your mother. That was the gist of the message.
Getting married in a hasty "do" at Morristown was simply not an
option. "Mrs. Schuyler did not see her Eldest daughter married. That
also gave me pain, and we wish not to Experience It a Second time."
When her next daughter married, Kitty Schuyler wanted a proper
hometown wedding. A big one. With white paper chains on the tables and the Schuyler-family wedding cake, made according to a recipe passed down for generations. A wedding where all the neighbors
could see how finely the Schuylers did things.

Kitty Schuyler had never met Alexander Hamilton, and she was
less immediately certain about the wisdom of this match. She took a
full month to give her answer. But if Eliza's mother had seen the ardent love letters passing between the couple, she would have known
that it was already far too late to ask her daughter to end things with
Alexander. The romance was passionate, and they were already laying out together the foundations of what would be an extraordinary
marriage.

They had to write letters, because General Washington sent Alexander away on assignment for several weeks in mid-March, tasking the young colonel with arranging an exchange of war prisoners with the British. Perhaps the thought occurred to General Washington that his old friend General Schuyler might appreciate a bit of distance between the ardent young lovers. General Washington knew from firsthand experience that Alexander was not a young man who easily took no for an answer.

The Schuyler sisters had long been favorites among the British officers, as Alexander soon discovered at the British camp. The redcoats and the Americans might be on opposite sides now, but Eliza and her sisters had grown up with many of these officers in and out of their father's house before the Revolution. "If I were not afraid of making you vain," Alexander wrote to Eliza, "I would tell you that Mrs. Carter, Peggy, and yourself are the dayly toasts of our table; and for this honor you are chiefly indebted to the British Gentlemen." Sometimes Alexander couldn't help feeling a bit jealous. He depended on Eliza's letters to assure him of her love and devotion.

When Eliza's letters arrived, all was well, and Alexander was happy. "I cannot tell you what extacy I felt in casting my eye over the sweet effusions of tenderness [your letter] contains," Alexander enthused in one missive. "My Betseys soul speaks in every line and bids me be the happiest of mortals. I am so and will be so. You give me too many proofs of your love to allow me to doubt it and in the conviction that I possess that, I possess every thing the world can give."

His letters to his male friends were boastful and far more laddish. Eliza might have been less swept off her feet had she seen them. "Have you not heard that I am on the point of becoming a [newlywed]," Alexander asked his friend John Laurens,

I confess my sins. I am guilty. Next fall completes my doom. I give up my liberty to Miss Schuyler. She is a good hearted girl who I am sure will never play the termagant; though not a genius

she has good sense enough to be agreeable, and though not a beauty, she has fine black eyes—is rather handsome and has every other requisite of the exterior to make a lover happy.

Not a beauty. Not a genius. Alexander's friends thought he was underrating Miss Schuyler.

By April, the engagement was official, and Kitty Schuyler quickly arranged a house for the Schuyler family in Morristown. The wedding would be a gala affair in Albany come December. Kitty was determined to see to it that no early infant arrival or swelling belly would force a rushed marriage before then. She wanted that wedding.

For one glorious season, Eliza was given free rein to shine as one of the belles of the ball, even if she was "not a beauty," and throughout the spring and summer Eliza and Alexander danced at a round of assemblies, laughed late into the night at parties. Eliza bounded out of bed each morning happy, knowing that before the morning was out, Alexander would come to call or would send a note. She spent her afternoons making social calls and busily planning her trousseau and wedding with her mother.

For everyone at camp, it was a brief season of celebration, at least among the officers and their wives. Eliza's mood matched the mood of those around her. For the enlisted men, life was harsher. But the officers were jubilant that spring. The war was hard going, but the French were joining the fight. That would turn the tide. Everywhere, everyone said so. When the French troops arrived, amid splendid fanfare, the sky above Morristown was lit with fireworks, and, as one of their fellow camp officers, Captain John Beatty, remembered of that season, we "kicked up a hell of a dust" until June, when the party ended.

As the spring drew to a close, Eliza's mood shifted. The war began again in earnest with the summer, bringing with it a dawning new reality: Eliza was in love with a colonel caught up in a war that the Americans would not win for several years still, at a moment when, despite the French intervention, an American victory was not guaranteed. As the winter camp broke up and Eliza and her mother bent over leather trunks, folding away the ball gowns and satin slippers, Eliza's heart was heavy. Who knew how long it would be before she saw Alexander again? It might not be until December.

At the end of June, the women set off in the coach that would take them along the bumpy roads to the boats that would bear them north to Albany. Eliza craned her neck for as long as she could to keep Alexander and her father in sight, and held close to her heart, carefully folded into a locket, a love poem Alexander had written.

If that poem is any evidence, not only was Alexander Hamilton not a great poetic talent, but Eliza had heeded her mother's warning and not consummated their relationship before the wedding:

> *A love like mine so tender, true*
> *Completely wretched—you away,*
> *And but half blessed e'en while you stay*
> *. . .*
> *Deny to you my fond embrace*
> *No joy unmixed my bosom warms.*

Alexander professed a love "tender, true," but he did want to point out that she was refusing his "embrace" and denying him a lover's pleasure.

In coarse, private letters to John Laurens, Alexander bemoaned his sexual frustration more bluntly. "I intend to restore the empire of Hymen [i.e., marriage] and that Cupid [i.e., erotic love] is to be his prime Minister," Alexander wrote. "I wish you were at liberty to transgress the bounds of Pennsylvania. I would invite you after the fall to Albany to be witness to the final consummation." A ménage à trois or a mere witness to the marriage? Alexander was not blind to the double entendre.

Alexander loved Eliza, but she did have two other flaws as a bride he felt he needed to point out to her: her conversation skills and her letter writing. Alexander couldn't help but try to mold Eliza and press her to be a bit more sophisticated in her book learning. A bit more, say, like her sister Angelica. "I love you more and more every hour," Alexander told her,

> The sweet softness and delicacy of your mind and manners, the elevation of your sentiments, the real goodness of your heart, its tenderness to me, the beauties of your face and person, your unpretending good sense and that innocent simplicity and frankness which pervade your actions; all these appear to me with increasing amiableness and place you in my estimation above all the rest of your sex.

But then he added:

> I entreat you my Charmer, not to neglect the charges I gave you particularly that of taking care of your self, and that of employing all your leisure in reading. Nature has been very kind to you; do not neglect to cultivate her gifts and to enable yourself to make the distinguished figure in all respects to which you are intitled to aspire. You excel most of your sex in all the amiable qualities; endeavour to excel them equally in the splendid ones. You can do it if you please and I shall take pride in it. It will be a fund too, to diversify our enjoyments and amusements and fill all our moments to advantage.

He wished Eliza had a bit more book learning. Her response to the rather tactless suggestion that she might think about some intellectual self-improvements has not survived. But when Alexander's letter arrived, she knew instantly the sight of his elegant and easy hand and eagerly looked forward to the pleasure of reading words of longing and devotion in private.

When she folded up the thin sheet of paper, her heart must have raced. Alexander's words cut her to the quick. They struck at the heart of Eliza's greatest insecurity—that she was tongue-tied in speech and clunky and halting in her letters. That she was dull and stupid. Eliza knew she had in her heart a world of feelings. But she could never find the words to express them. Alexander pushed. He wanted to know everything. But her love didn't work like that. She felt like a failure. When Eliza was hurt or angry or even just worried, she retreated. In time, Alexander would come to understand that he should worry most when Eliza's voice grew quiet.

More embarrassed than angry, she retreated now. Alexander's letter sat unanswered in Eliza's wooden writing box, and she searched for the words to apologize for how she stumbled in the arts of courtship and conversation. She tried to turn her mind to one of the thick history books Alexander had recommended. The words swam, and she felt like crying.

Alexander waited days for Eliza's reply. None arrived. Soon, Alexander was in a panic. "It is an age my dearest," he wrote, "since I have received a letter from you; the post is arrived and not a line." Alexander spoke too fast, wrote too fast, sometimes without fully considering. He knew it. It was slowly dawning on him that he had upset Eliza.

"I know not to what to impute your silence; so it is I am alarmed with an apprehension of your being ill," Alexander wrote,

Pardon me my lovely girl for any thing I may have said that has the remotest semblance of complaining. If you knew my heart thoroughly you would see it so full of tenderness for you that you would not only pardon, but you would even love my weaknesses. For god's sake My Dear Betsey try to write me oftener and give me the picture of your heart in all its varieties of light and shade. Tell me whether it feels the same for me or did when we were together, or whether what seemed to be love was nothing more than a generous sympathy. The possibility of this frequently torments me.

Eliza melted. In the next week, she cheerfully wrote Alexander three letters. And she had been thinking of him: she enclosed as a gift a bit of embroidered neckwear that she had passed her afternoons patiently making for him. Eliza showed her love through small acts of work and patience. The subject of letters, though, would remain a touchy point between Eliza and Alexander as they started their life together. Letters, lost and found, written and unwritten, would define, too, how their marriage unfolded.

Letters—and money. Despite the wealth of Eliza's family, or perhaps because of it, Alexander was also at pains during their months apart before the wedding to explain to Eliza that he did not have a fortune and could not promise her the lifestyle of her parents or, indeed, even the lifestyle of the free-spending John and Angelica Carter. A happy marriage did not include the bitter complaints of a wife who would later regret that she hadn't married someone richer. "Do you soberly relish the pleasure of being a poor mans wife?" he quizzed her:

> *Have you learned to think a home spun preferable to a brocade and the rumbling of a waggon wheel to the musical rattling of a coach and six? Will you be able to see with perfect composure your old acquaintances flaunting it in gay life, tripping it along in elegance and splendor, while you hold an humble station and have no other enjoyments than the sober comforts of a good wife? . . . If you cannot my Dear we are playing a comedy of all in the wrong, and you should correct the mistake before we begin to act the tragedy of the unhappy couple.*

Alexander dreamed, too, of a career building a republic, if they were to win their independence, and he warned Eliza that this would also come at a price in their life together. Was Eliza prepared to sacrifice to the republic in ways that were not only financial? "I know too you have so much of the Portia in you," he wrote, "that you will not be out done in this line by any of your sex, and that if you saw me inclined to quit the service of your country you would dissuade me from it. I have promised you, you recollect, to conform to your wishes, and I persist in this intention. It remains with you to show whether you are a Roman or an American wife."

Eliza understood the reference to Portia. The classical history of Valerius Maximus was a staple of a young man's education and one of the sober, improving books in her father's library that Eliza was especially determined to finish. Her preference inclined toward romance novels. Portia was the Roman wife of Caesar's assassin, Brutus, and showed herself strong enough to bear any pain to keep the secrets of her husband. Alexander and Eliza spoke often of the sacrifice and loyalty of the Roman wife in service to the republic. Was Eliza courageous enough to be a Roman wife? She promised herself she would rise to the challenge.

By "an American wife," Alexander meant someone like Angelica—always dressed in the latest fashion, her carriage lined with satin and velvet, her lifestyle extravagant. Eliza didn't long for that. She had found the social whirl of Morristown exhausting, and it was her growing friendship with the older Martha Washington that most inspired her. Martha Washington—with her homespun dresses and quiet modesty—was Eliza's ideal. Eliza had loved the afternoons when she and Martha sat together at camp, chatting quietly over tea and patiently working on their embroidery, a shared passion. Theirs was a friendship that would sustain Eliza more and more in the times ahead of them, though Eliza yet had only a dim inkling of the sacrifices that would be required of her. At the hardest moments, Martha would be there for her. If a life of modest domestic tranquility was all Alexander feared he could offer her, she teased him in her letters, she could manage. Could Alexander? That was the real question.

That Eliza didn't constantly write him letters, even after they had made up their lovers' tiff, unnerved Alexander, though he had the grace to laugh at his insecurities. Eliza was home in Albany throughout the summer, and in August, having written three letters to her one—and having obstinately counted—Alexander warned her playfully, "When I come to Albany, I shall find means to take satisfaction for your neglect. You recollect the mode I threatened to punish you in for all your delinquen[c]ies." Eliza responded teasingly by sending Alexander a cockade she had sewn for his hat and a now-lost satirical poem, set to music by Peggy, on the subject of what ridiculous things they would do together in their happy poverty. But Eliza's promise that money would never come between them was one of the other bedrock foundations of their marriage.

In September, after three months apart, the scandal of Benedict Arnold's treason broke, rocking the army. At General Washington's headquarters, Tench Tilghman raged at the dawning realization that his cousin's husband had played him a fool, at Peggy Shippen's urging. Benedict Arnold slipped behind British lines and quickly fled for London. Eliza's youthful crush, the British major John André, the spymaster, was not so fleet-footed and was captured behind American lines.

Benedict Arnold had conspired to deliver the American troops into the hands of their enemies for a bounty of a mere 20,000 pounds—a couple of million dollars today—and luckily had failed, but his betrayal brought home to everyone how fragile a thing was their revolution. "If America were lost," Alexander assured Eliza, "we should be happy in some other clime more favourable to human rights. What think you of Geneva as a retreat?"

Alexander also acknowledged what all the Schuyler women understood: more likely than not, if the campaign failed, General Washington's officers would fall in battle. Death was a constant presence, always possible. "I was once determined to let my existence and American liberty end together," Alexander told Eliza. "My Betsey has given me a motive to outlive my pride, I had almost said my honor; but America must not be witness to my disgrace." Eliza and her family had made him feel that he had a true home in America. That was everything to Alexander, an orphan and an immigrant. More than anything now, he wanted to live and to start a life with Eliza. The Schuyler family, for their part, drew him into their circle.

There was one other deeply personal betrayal awaiting the Americans that autumn and Philip Schuyler especially, and it was part of the wall of silence that encircled the Schuyler family. It would place the life of Eliza and her family in even greater personal danger as the war unfolded.

John André wasn't the only spy risking his life. The patriots also maintained spy rings buried deep in the rural communities up and down the Eastern Seaboard, and their operations were crucial to the Americans' progress. Eliza's father led the espionage network embedded in upstate New York, with the help of his native mistress, a high-ranking Mohawk woman named Mary Hill. What Philip Schuyler did not yet know was that Mary had betrayed him and his network to the enemy that autumn. All he knew was that the Indian raids were growing closer and closer. The Schuyler house was already a fortress. The general had to warn Alexander of the chances. "I have no body between me and the Enemy except two poor famalies and about one hundred militia with me," Philip wrote now to Alexander. "We are surrounded from every quarter and the Inhabitants flying down the Country. I believe my turn will be in a few days unless troops are sent."

The idea of Eliza in danger gnawed at Alexander. Everyone knew the story of the scalping of poor Jane McCrea, Eliza's neighbor. All autumn, Alexander searched for any chance to travel north, even for a few days, to hold her and to know she was safe and still loved him. But the war made it impossible. General Washington could not spare officers. Alexander urged her to be careful, urged her father to take greater precautions. He promised Eliza in long letters that he would arrive in Albany by the first of December for their marriage.

Could he keep that promise? Eliza, the daughter of a general, knew as well as anyone that in the midst of a war that had not gone well that year for the Americans, anything could happen. They kept loaded guns by the thick oak door, and all night shadowy sentinels stood watch in the garden.

At night, as she drifted off to sleep, Eliza listened to the creak of the wood beams, moaning and settling in the cold autumn air, and wondered if the falling snow beyond her window had been loosened by the breeze or if it heralded the start of the attack they dreaded. With any luck, December would come and bring Alexander.

In the meantime, as her pragmatic mother briskly reminded the girls each morning, there was nothing to do but hope for the best. They needed to get to work planning a Schuyler family wedding.

CHAPTER 7

All the Girls Together— and Peggy, 1780–81

O n Wednesday, December 13, 1780, the Schuyler, Livingston, Cuyler, and Van Rensselaer clans gathered, and in the large back kitchens of the Pastures the family slaves were unwrapping a wedding cake for the next day, spiced with molasses and brown sugar, stuffed with raisins, and aged for weeks in generous lashings of rum and brandy, in accordance with an ancient Schuyler family recipe. Eliza and her mother had been tending the cake since early autumn. Pickled oysters by the barrelful sat in their salty brine, and cured hams and great shanks of venison waited in the larder, well out of the reach of the exasperatingly disobedient seven-year-old Rensselaer Schuyler, Eliza's little brother. As evening fell, the house rang with laughter and the clink of glassware, but in the waiting darkness beyond armed sentinels stood careful watch against the war parties. General Schuyler remained a high-value target for kidnapping or assassination, and he was not the only high-ranking officer at his daughter's wedding.

Upstairs, a pregnant Kitty Schuyler looked in on a feverish four-year-old Cornelia, while servants put the final touches on Eliza's bouffant hairdo, dusting it white with powder, a gift from Martha Washington. Eliza had time alone with her thoughts to consider.

In the morning, she and Alexander would be married quietly before lunchtime, afforded all the dignity of a Dutch religious service, in the cheerful front parlor where Eliza had stood so many times in the preceding months, reading Alexander's love letters.

Now, Alexander was here at last, and her sober pearl-gray silk gown was already waiting in the bedroom. Tomorrow, they would be married. They would share a bed. It was hard to think of every-one in the family knowing that about them. Eliza fingered gently a piece of fine linen embellished with her painstaking embroidery; she had made Alexander a matching kerchief as a wedding present. She would tuck hers along the low-cut neckline of her gown as a modest shawl in the morning.

Tonight, her sister Peggy was having none of that. Peggy tended toward the rambunctious and irreverent. This evening, their mother was going to have the party that Angelica's elopement had denied her, and Peggy was determined that they were all going to kick up their heels a little. Little surprise that Eliza's younger sister quickly became a favorite with Alexander.

The tables were heavily laden with rich foods and treasures from Philip Schuyler's wine cellars. Everything was ready. They waited only for Eliza. At the bottom of the staircase, as Eliza descended, Alexander was waiting on the landing to take her elbow. It was a perfect beginning.

On the morning of December 14, the day of the wedding, the sun didn't rise over the horizon until after seven o'clock, but the girls had already been awake for hours. Some of the gentlemen, perhaps, found that last night's Madeira had left them a little bit less chip-per. They would be up, the ladies supposed, before too much longer. Eliza, Peggy, and Angelica—home only briefly and without John or the children—dressed in darkness, happily chattering in low voices, helping each other with their gowns as they had always done. Down-stairs, household servants were shifting logs in the fireplaces to stoke the fires and Eliza's father, the general, was already waiting. The Schuyler family and Alexander began the morning with prayers and a quiet wedding breakfast. Alexander had no relations with him, but his friend and fellow aide-de-camp, the Irish-born surgeon James "Mac" McHenry, had traveled up with Alexander as a representative of the young men who called themselves General Washington's "family."

At noon, Eliza's father gave the signal, and the din of the guests grew quiet. The small group of friends and family—nearly all of them Schuyler connections—gathered silently in the reception room; Eliza once again made her way down the staircase, for her bridal entrance. Eliza saw that Aunt Gertrude and John Cochran were beaming. It was in their home that their love affair had first started, and kindly Aunt Gertrude deserved some of the thanks and credit. On a pale, flowered carpet in front of the large window overlooking the garden, Eliza took her place, just as she had practiced. Alexander stood beside her. From the window, she could see the icy river and the pines and the landscape of her childhood. Alexander's childhood tropical island, Nevis, would have been so different. It was her world he was entering. Eliza turned and faced Alexander.

The minister read the vows and the service, and then Alexander slipped onto her finger a small gold ring, engraved simply ELIZA-BETH, which bore a secret notch where her ring could join his own in an interlocking, infinite puzzle. Onto his finger, she slipped its twin, marked ALEXANDER &. Alexander leaned to kiss her, and just like that, Eliza realized she was Mrs. Hamilton.

George and Martha Washington had sent a courier with a note of good wishes. The luncheon passed with toasts and laughing, and Mac read a poem he'd composed as a wedding present for Alexander. Mac had come quickly to the conclusion that his friend Hamilton was a luckier man than the lads back at camp imagined. The roguish Tench had called Eliza a "little saint," affectionately mocking her pleasure in attending church and her naïve, housewifely good nature. Mac took the measure of Eliza more deeply and more accurately. "Hers," he said, "was a strong character with its depth and warmth, whether of feeling or temper controlled, but glowing underneath, bursting through at times in some emphatic expression." Eliza said little of what she felt, but she felt life deeply.

The first week of married life was a whirlwind. Couples didn't get away for honeymoons in the eighteenth century. Eliza's extended family was large and spread out around the Albany region, and social custom required wedding visits. By the end of the week, Alexander might have wished the Schuyler family were slightly less extensive. Eliza and Alexander passed what remained of December bundling themselves into heavy cloaks, tucking their feet up against hot bricks wrapped in flannels, and setting off through the bitter cold in a horse-drawn sleigh to do their duty by her relations.

But it was still romantic, and Eliza didn't wish for anything different. She was with Alexander. In between the cups of tea and polite chitchat, there were long hours when she and Alexander leaned close against each other in the bright winter weather while the horse kicked up snowy powder. Alexander warmed her fingers. In the evenings, the Schuyler family gathered together in the parlor, where Alexander accompanied Peggy in singing Scottish ballads. At night, when the bed curtains were drawn closely against the drafts, he held her under the thick down coverlet. Eliza drifted off to sleep, happy.

Eliza and Alexander would stay in Albany until the New Year. Angelica, probably escorted by Mac, returned south before Christmas, to Newport, Rhode Island, where the French navy was blockaded and where John Carter, as he still styled himself, was raking in a fortune as a broker. John and his partner, Jeremiah Wadsworth, managed the supply chains for the French military in America, and John took a generous cut out of each transaction. Angelica couldn't stay for the holiday with the Schuyler family, but she did send them a present to enliven their quiet domestic circle in Albany—although her mother was less than delighted with the present's timing. Just before Christmas, several French officers, including François de Beauvoir, the Marquis de Chastellux, arrived by schooner at the wharf of the Pastures, friends of Angelica's. Eliza's father sent a sleigh to meet the houseguests.

The Schuyler home, the marquis remembered, was "a handsome house, halfway up the bank opposite the ferry, [that] seems to attract the eye and to invite strangers to stop." These strangers were made very welcome by Eliza and her father. The marquis remembered Eliza's mother, in her late forties, stout, gout-ridden, again heavily pregnant—for a twelfth time—and weary of houseguests, as short-tempered. It was better, the guests quickly concluded, not to cross Mrs. Schuyler.

But there were plenty of compensations for a cranky hostess. We "found ourselves in an instant in a handsome drawing room near a good fire," the marquis recalled, and there was a merry dinner the first night and for the next several nights with the family, before Philip Schuyler wisely set off with his guests a few days after Christmas to tour the battlefield at Saratoga. Alexander might otherwise have gone with the officers. He chose, instead, to stay with Eliza and Peggy. These were the last days in Albany and the end of any wedding holiday. Soon, they would return to camp, this time as a married couple.

The thought of managing a new household on her own filled Eliza with both excitement and trepidation. Her mother didn't need to warn her. Eliza could see for herself that marriage was not the same as courtship.

Alexander set off for camp immediately after the New Year and, after more than a week of traveling through frigid weather by schooner and then on horseback through the mountains, reached General Washington's headquarters at New Windsor on January 10 or 11, 1781. Eliza set off from Albany two days later, bringing with her trunks filled with wedding linens, gowns, and a few good pieces of silver, traveling more slowly and more comfortably, by boat and then carriage, expecting to arrive on January 17 to begin her new life as a young wife and housekeeper.

As Peggy saw her sister off, she was filled with despair, frustration, and perhaps, if she were honest, even a bit of jealousy at Eliza's good fortune. Peggy was twenty-two and eager to find a husband. She was tired of being stuck at home with her mother, looking after younger siblings and managing the canning. She had her beaux, and she knew that some people said she was the prettiest of the Schuyler sisters. She had turned down one or two dull gentlemen. She couldn't help but wonder, though, why none of the admirers she fancied had ever made a marriage proposal.

Peggy was not the only one to wonder if she would ever find a husband, though many had a better sense than she did of the root of the problem. Their old family friend Benjamin Franklin asked a mutual acquaintance in 1778 if she were married yet, and the answer came back, "I have not heard that the wild Miss Peggy has found a match to her liking." Peggy was still unmarried more than two years after that letter, and her sisters advised her now to be less choosy when it came to marriage offers. Alexander, seeing she was desperate, advised her not to marry just anyone, no matter what her sisters urged her. Eliza might "persuade all her friends to embark with her in the matrimonial voyage," Alexander told Peggy, but he sounded a note of caution:

> *I pray you do not let her advice have so much influence as to make you matrimony-mad. 'Tis a very good thing when their stars unite two people who are fit for each other. . . . But its a dog of life when two dissonant tempers meet, and 'tis ten to one but this is the case. When therefore I join her in advising you to marry, I add be cautious in the choice.*

Caution, however, was not in Peggy Schuyler's nature. She was suffering from a string of disappointments brought on by her indiscretion. As recently as October of 1780, rumors had swirled at camp that François Louis Teissèdre, the Marquis de Fleury, planned to propose to her. The marquis himself confided that he was in love with Peggy. "Mrs. Carter told me you was soon to be married to her sister, Miss Betsy Schuyler," the French nobleman wrote to Alexander:

> *I congratulate you heartyly on that conquest; for many Reasons:*
> *the first that you will get all that familly's interest, & that a*
> *man of your abilities wants a Little influence to do good to his*
> *country. The second that you will be in a very easy situation,*
> *& happin's is not to be found without a Large estate. The third*
> *(this one is not very Certain) that we shall be connect'd or*
> *neighbors. For you must know, that I am an admirer of Miss*
> *Pegguy, your sister in Law; & that if she will not have me;*
> *Mr. Duane may be cox'd into the measure of giving me his*
> *daughter.*

The marquis, however, either changed his mind or was a singularly unlucky gentleman, because he married neither Peggy nor her Livingston cousin, Mary Duane. Alexander threatened teasingly to write a play for his new sister-in-law on the topic of her marriage quest. "I am composing a piece," Alexander wrote, "of which, from the opinion I have of her qualifications, I shall endeavour to prevail upon [Peggy] to act the principal character. The title is 'The way to get him, for the benefit of all single ladies who desire to be married.'"

What changed his noble friend's mind about marriage to Peggy, Alexander never said. Perhaps the marquis learned that Miss Peggy had been so bold as to kiss one of her other beaux on a visit to Hartford, Connecticut. Perhaps word reached him that she declared next, as Alexander put it, that she was in love "with an old man of fifty." Whatever the case, Peggy remained worryingly single.

Alexander's friend Mac thought he understood why Peggy was having trouble catching a husband. Comparing Angelica and Peggy, Mac observed,

Mrs. Carter is a fine woman. She charms in all companies. No one has seen her, of either sex, who has not been pleased with her, and she has pleased every one, chiefly by means of those qualities which make you the husband of her Sister. Peggy, though perhaps a finer woman, is not generally thought so. Her own sex are apprehensive that she considers them, poor things, as Swifts Vanessa did [i.e., with scorn]; and they in return do not scruple to be displeased. In short, Peggy, to be admired as she ought, has only to please the men less and the ladies more. Tell her so. I am sure her good sense will soon place her in her proper station.

Peggy, however, was not in a mood to listen. She looked down her nose at the other young ladies and didn't care a fig that they looked for ways to ostracize her. She enjoyed talk with the men and flirting. She couldn't see how that should affect her marriage chances. But that it did was certain.

Army headquarters in the winter of 1781 was dull for a married woman. Peggy had no reason, Eliza quickly discovered, to feel jealous. It was, by any start, a rocky first year with a surprisingly volatile and moody Alexander. This wasn't what Eliza had expected.

At Morristown, Eliza had been courting. In New Windsor, she was a young military wife. Between the two was a world of difference. The transition was one from pleasure to duty. Martha Washington and Aunt Gertrude welcomed her warmly to their circle of camp matrons, but Angelica and John were passing the winter gaily in New York City, and Eliza secretly longed to join them. Alexander was so busy, she hardly saw him in the evenings, and she was lonely.

Letters from her cousin Kitty Livingston were a consolation—and a source of lively gossip. "Pray do you talk of a Jaunt to New York?" Kitty asked Eliza. "I have heard such a rumor, if you do say everything from me to Ann that you Know I would myself repeat—How

is Col. Tilghman? Miss Brown says very ill. I hope he is recovering—
Farewell once more, I wish I could tell you so in person."

When Alexander came into the room, Eliza quickly tucked Kitty's
letters into her sewing basket. It wasn't because Eliza feared talk of
Tench would make Alexander jealous—though it might have. And it
wasn't that Eliza fretted that Alexander still carried a torch for her
cousin either. It was a bit of solidarity among the girls, who were embarrassed by the poverty of their education and the silliness of their
confidences.

Kitty and Eliza knew that the polished and clever Angelica out-
shone them. Angelica wouldn't need to be embarrassed by Alexander seeing her letters. Angelica spoke fluent French and wrote long,
witty letters to important, clever men—men like Thomas Jefferson
and Benjamin Franklin—that charmed even the most discerning
among them. It was the same with Kitty's sophisticated sister, Sarah
Livingston Jay, a diplomat's wife and cut from the same cloth as
Angelica.

Eliza and Kitty stumbled over their words and their spelling. "If
I did not know any apology made a bad thing worse," Kitty confided to Eliza, "I would endeavor to say something in behalf of this
poor letter, pray do not let Colonel Hamilton see it. His forte is writing I too well know, to submit anything I can say tonight to his
inspection—from your Friendship I know I have nothing to dread."
Ashamed of how dull they might seem to a brilliant man like Alexander, Eliza quietly rallied behind her cousin, and they often destroyed each other's letters in solidarity.

In New Windsor, Eliza saw far less of Alexander, and it was hard not
to be a little homesick. She was particularly glad, therefore, to make a
new friend among the younger officers' wives. Marie-Charlotte Antill was a young Anglo-Quebecois woman with a thin, pretty face,
and, although she was just a bit older than Eliza, Marie-Charlotte
had a horde of children already.

Her new friend, Eliza knew, had a tragic story. Marie-Charlotte's husband, Colonel Edward Antill, had been a guest at the Schuyler family home in Albany as recently as 1777, when he arrived bearing an urgent message from Montreal for the general.

Not long after Colonel Antill's flying visit to the Pastures, though, Edward had been captured by the British. He and Marie-Charlotte had wasted away together for years in the prisoner-of-war camps on Long Island in deadly conditions, alongside their small children. Alexander, as aide-de-camp, had had the job of opening and reading General Washington's correspondence, including Edward's increasingly desperate letters.

Someone—perhaps Alexander—persuaded George Washington to make sure the prisoner exchange to free Edward took place in December of 1780, just as Eliza and Alexander were getting married. Eliza arrived now at camp to learn that Edward faced the scandalous indignity of a January court-martial. He would have to prove that he hadn't let himself be captured on purpose.

The trial consumed headquarters in the first weeks after Eliza's arrival in the latter part of January. Everyone from the officers' wives to the laundrywomen talked of it. Marie-Charlotte appeared, and conversations faltered. Marie-Charlotte kept her head high and threw back her thin, tired shoulders. She and the children had starved on Long Island as British prisoners, and she couldn't shake the cough that plagued her. Marie-Charlotte never complained. Like Eliza, Marie-Charlotte was a woman who held close her emotions. In her eyes, though, Eliza thought she read anger and sadness.

The other ladies avoided making awkward social calls to see Marie-Charlotte. Not Eliza. Eliza remembered all too well her father's court-martial and all her family had suffered. Eliza was profoundly loyal to those she chose to protect, and she chose now to stand with Marie-Charlotte and Edward. Besides, Eliza loved spending time with Marie-Charlotte and Edward's babies. Everyone hoped that it would not be long before Eliza was pregnant. No one hoped for it more than Eliza.

On February 18, the Antill verdict finally came down, and the ladies sat vigil in tense anticipation. Edward was completely vindicated. "Lieutenant Colonel Antill appears to have been captured while in the execution of his duty," the court-martial announced, and "he is not Censurable in any part of his conduct but is deserving the Approbation of every good officer." It was just what Eliza knew was warranted. A pact had been sealed between the two couples now. As long as she had the friendship of Marie-Charlotte and the reassuring presence of Aunt Gertrude and Martha Washington, Eliza knew she could manage.

Until Alexander's impetuous temper turned everything topsy-turvy in the midst of the Antill verdict and threw Eliza's plans into bitter chaos. It happened just as Eliza was getting settled.

Headquarters was tense, and everyone worked too hard and in crowded conditions. Tempers were short. The war was uncertain. Eliza did not need anyone to explain that. Alexander was miffed at not being promoted to a field command position, where he could lead the charge, and, as their patience with each other frayed, George Washington and Alexander Hamilton quarreled on the staircase at headquarters. Alexander had been looking for a fight. He came home indignant. Eliza couldn't believe what he had done. Alexander knew her father would be disappointed and worried. But he was defiant.

General Washington tried to heal the rift, but Alexander remained hotheaded and stubborn. He would not retract his resignation as aide-de-camp and shunned headquarters. Suddenly Eliza had at home an unhappy and unemployed husband. Then Alexander let her know that he was sending her back to Albany.

His impulsive decision threw into turmoil their camp housing arrangements. Alexander could not have her there while things were so uncertain. Money was tight, and, although Alexander might not have said as much, Eliza understood. A wife would only be a burden. A little over a month into their marriage, already Eliza was making the long, cold journey over snow back to the Pastures. She dreaded explaining Alexander's rift with General Washington to her father.

Eliza stayed in Albany until springtime, and, although there were visits from Alexander, it wasn't the start to a new life that she had imagined in December. She would have to be patient until April, when Alexander rented accommodations at De Peyster's Point, a rural hamlet just across the Hudson River from the New Windsor, and Eliza traveled south again to join him. Alexander kept busy writing and lobbying for a command position. Eliza, at last, set up housekeeping.

Orders flew to John Carter's business partner, Jeremiah Wadsworth, requesting household goods. They ordered a pound of green tea and a dozen new knives and forks. They purchased a "table 4½ feet long 3½ wide for a dining table" and a slave woman from the wife of General George Clinton. Any claims that Alexander Hamilton was an ardent abolitionist are complicated by several such transactions in the 1780s and 1790s. Alexander also bought a small boat, which he put into immediate use, rowing across the river to spend rowdy evenings in the pub with the officers. Eliza sat home alone. When Alexander returned, he was inevitably tipsy and amorous.

Most of Alexander's letters to his brother-in-law John, though, were about getting money rather than spending it. He and Eliza were woefully short of funds, and Alexander did not want to rely on the generosity of General Schuyler. In 1781, James McHenry sardonically observed that Angelica's husband had "riches enough, with common management, to make the longest life very comfortable." Alexander wanted to know how he had made it happen. The truthful answer was through speculation and some shady practices, although people were mostly too polite to say so. But John was on the make, and growing richer and richer. He never stopped being a bounder.

Above all, though, what Alexander wanted was to lead a regiment in battle. He wanted to be a hero and to prove himself as a soldier and a patriot. For Alexander, an immigrant, it was especially important to do so. Otherwise, the war would end, and he would be one of those men who would have to confess to never having seen action. He was determined to loiter about camp until General Washington relented. He might not be an aide-de-camp, but he was still a colonel. The climax of the revolution was surely coming. Alexander was desperate to be part of it.

It meant yet another separation. Eliza struggled to accept it. Winter camp broke up in June, as the campaign season again started, and Eliza would need to go again for the summer to the Pastures, without Alexander. There was only one consolation. With her would go her sister Angelica, uncomfortably pregnant with a third child, and Marie-Charlotte. Edward Antill had been ordered to "proceed immediately with Colonel [Moses] Hazen's Regiment to Albany," and Marie-Charlotte and the children followed.

Eliza tried to be happy that summer when General Washington, in a peace offering, gave Alexander his long-wished-for command position. But she knew enough about war to worry. "Though I know my Betsy would be happy to hear I had rejected this proposal," Alexander chided gently, ". . . I hope my beloved Betsy will dismiss all apprehensions for my safety." Alexander was also pressing her already for letters. She couldn't write him too often. "I impatiently long to hear from you the state of your mind since our painful separation," he wrote. "Be as happy as you can, I entreat you, my amiable, my beloved." But Eliza was not happy. She missed Alexander.

Eliza had particular reason to worry about the safety of her husband. She had suspected something wonderful for weeks, as her stomach churned and she felt sometimes light-headed. She and Angelica had nursed her secret. At last, she confided her suspicions to her mother, who didn't think there could be any doubt but called for the local doctor. The kindly old gentleman confirmed her guess. Mrs. Hamilton was four months pregnant by August. Eliza looked forward to writing to Alexander to let him know. When the letter reached him, his response was speedy and excited. "I am inexpressably happy . . . to find that you seem at present to be confirmed in your hopes." Now if only Alexander would stay safe to meet the baby.

What none of them understood fully until that summer was that the gravest danger faced not Alexander Hamilton but General Schuyler and his family at the Pastures. Eliza would also have to explain this in her letter.

Sunset came late in the summer so far north, and the sentries still stood guard. But this time, it didn't matter. The attack was planned and ferocious.

August 7 was a hot day, and Eliza was over the worst of the morning sickness. She noticed now the swelling beneath her stays and wondered that Angelica—unwieldy and awkward in her eighth month of pregnancy—could bear the heat and the clammy weight of rich dress fabric. Somewhere in the house came the cry of an infant. Their mother had recently given birth to their last sister, baby Catherine.

By nine o'clock in the evening, the family gathered in the front hall for dinner, where the breeze was coolest, and the sisters talked in quiet voices as the sky darkened. Three armed guards, all named John to the amusement of the girls, lazed on the front steps of the house, their guns leaning against the woodwork in the entrance. Three more guards, who would keep watch come dark, snoozed in the cellars, and Peggy noticed that baby Catherine had finally fallen asleep in a cradle.

Somewhere in the back kitchen, Prince, their mother's favorite servant, heard the tinkle of a latch and creak of wood and looked out to see a man at the gate to the garden. In any other time and place, the sight might have seemed pastoral, a stranger at the gate on a summer night in August in the hour after twilight. But in Albany in the summer of 1781, with a bounty on the head of General Schuyler, with the British making incursions up and down the countryside "carry[ing] off some of the most inveterate and active Leaders in the Rebellion"

and executing them in retaliation for the hanging of Major John
André, this was danger. Prince's heart beat fast. He started running.

Prince burst through the parlor door, crying the alarm. Philip
Schuyler jumped from his chair as papers scattered. He raced to the
foyer and swung shut in a heavy arc the great wooden door and drew
down the iron bars to lock it. The slam shook the plaster. The sentinels at the front of the house were on their feet now, reaching for
their guns—but their guns were missing. By now General Schuyler's would-be assassins were at the portico. Somewhere, someone
screamed in terror. Just beyond the parlor windows, the groggy sentinels, still searching for the weapons that Angelica had moved out
of the reach of the children, landed a few blows but were quickly
overpowered and dragged away, still struggling, beyond the garden.
Trussed and tied, they would be hauled away as captives. Inside,
Kitty and the girls ran upstairs frantically with the toddlers, urging the other children on, and rushed into a second-floor bedroom.
There, General Schuyler barricaded the door, dragging and pushing
furniture, and took up a position at the window, pistol cocked, determined to fight to the end and to ward off his attackers.

Eliza never forgot the awful sound of the front door cracking as
it broke open. "The attack and defense of the house was bloody and
obstinate, on both sides," British officer Barry St. Leger reported
of the mission to capture General Schuyler later. The children were
hysterical by now, and in that moment a terrible realization swept
over Kitty Schuyler. She had forgotten baby Catherine downstairs in
the cradle. Eliza watched as her courageous mother crumbled.

Kitty was on her knees. Angelica was crying. Eliza looked on in
horror. Peggy took in the scene and, ever impetuous, acted. *Someone
needs to get the baby.* Eliza read the thought on the face of her sister,
but the wheels in her brain turned too slowly. Peggy swept her skirts
up into a fist and, with a defiant flounce, turned on her heel and
bolted down the staircase. Before Eliza could think to move, Peggy
was already in the hallway.

With the assailants in the next room and the sound of crashing and the clank of silver, Peggy flew down the stairs and caught up her infant sister. Then she gripped the banister and prepared to lurch toward the landing. Before she could move, a burst of air blew past her. Only as she heard a dull thud and felt something tugging at her skirts did Peggy realize that a tomahawk had pinned her dress to the stair's wooden railing. Jerking the fabric free and clutching her infant sister tightly, she turned to run and came instead face-to-face with Captain John Meyers—formerly a tenant farmer from the neighborhood and now a Loyalist assassin—coming out of the dining room where the raiders were stealing the family silver.

Peggy's heart sank. She would be taken captive.

"Wench, wench, where is your master?" demanded John Meyers.

Wench, indeed, thought Peggy. But the fool had mistaken her for a servant and not the general's daughter. Peggy, thinking fast, played along. "Gone to alarm the town," Peggy quipped defiantly.

Listening at the top of the stairs, gun cocked and anxious for his daughter, General Schuyler took up the ruse and bellowed for the imaginary reinforcements.

"Come on, my brave fellows, surround the house and secure the villains, who are plundering."

John Meyers stopped and stammered. Then he decided to hightail it. The attackers fled, taking the family silver and the three sentinels in the yard with them as bounty and captives. But they left Peggy and the baby.

When Alexander learned of the assault a week later, he wrote urging his father-in-law to beef up the protections. "Upon the whole I am glad this unsuccessful attempt has been made," he wrote to Eliza. "It will prevent his hazarding himself hereafter as he has been accustomed to do." It was suddenly occurring to Alexander as well that Albany might not be the safest place for his pregnant wife and unborn baby.

As their separation stretched into the end of August, Eliza and Alexander hadn't seen each other for two months. Again. It felt like those long months of their courtship all over. The army was heading south for the coming battle at Yorktown, and Alexander would, at last, lead a fighting regiment, but being so far from Eliza when danger lurked on the frontier was distressing and triggered all of Alexander's old insecurities and obsessions. "I am unhappy my Betsey," he wrote. "I am unhappy beyond expression, I am unhappy because I am to be so remote from you, because I am to hear from you less frequently than I have been accustomed to do." No matter what she did, Eliza could never write enough, and it was worse when war and distance delayed their letters further. Alexander seemed not to understand that there was a house full of clamoring children and that the summer linen needed airing. He did not see that the garden was heavy with crops at the end of the summer or that it all needed curing and preserving. He knew she was pregnant, but what he could not see was how often she was tired. There were relatives who came for morning calls, and new arrivals in Albany.

One of those new arrivals was a law student who quickly made friends with the Van Rensselaer family and found his way into the sitting room at the Pastures at teatime with Eliza and her sisters. A slight young man with black eyes and thinning hair, he announced himself as Aaron Burr, but to Eliza he needed no introduction. Everyone knew the scandal about Lieutenant Colonel Burr. Her Livingston cousins said that he was carrying on an adulterous love affair with the wife of a British officer. Eliza looked at him curiously. What was so special about him that Theodosia Prevost was willing to gamble her reputation?

With distractions like this, it was easy to miss making the post when her father called, especially when the right words to say to Alexander in a letter came to her slowly and never carried the fullness of their meaning. And what were the words with which to say to Alexander that she was frightened? She wanted to be supportive. But she hated the idea of him fighting.

Alexander was excited about heading into battle. September was an anxious month on the front lines. Things looked dicey. But in October, the tide turned at Yorktown at last decisively in favor of the Americans. Alexander was jubilant.

Even in the midst of war, though, he could not help chiding Eliza yet again for not writing letters to him often enough. If she gave birth to a son, he joked, he might forgive her. A daughter, he wrote, would surely inherit all the charms of her mother and "the caprices of her father and then she will enslave, tantalize and plague one half the sex."

And it wasn't only war and the thought of losing Alexander that panicked Eliza. As her belly swelled, so did Eliza's apprehensions. Marie-Charlotte had lost her two-year-old son John. Eliza wept at the thought of such a little casket. Every woman privately feared the agonizing and all-too-common death from childbed fever. Eliza had been with Angelica during the birth of her first two children in Boston. She now sat with her older sister in September as she delivered her third baby—named John, after his father—in their old bedroom in Albany, with nothing more to ease the racking pain than a generous slug of their father's brandy.

As Alexander and Edward marched toward Yorktown, Eliza and Marie-Charlotte had another worry to consider. When camp fever took Martha Washington's son at Yorktown, his twenty-five-year-old widow lost not only her husband but the custody of her two children. The law was not a friend to young widows, even to widows who were the daughters of wealthy families. Even for those lucky few, children and estates passed to the care of fathers and uncles, sons and brothers. For impoverished widows with children, Eliza shuddered to think about the desperate realities of penury and the poorhouse.

If something happened to Alexander, Eliza would not get to make the decisions about how to raise the baby even now growing inside her. The injustice left Eliza anxious—and indignant. Someday, someone would need to do something about it. No one yet had any inkling—herself included—that this someone would one day be Eliza.

CHAPTER 8

Peggy, 1781–84

In early November, Alexander made his way home at last to Albany and Eliza.

She had been watching for him. Her father read the military news. It would not be long, General Schuyler said each night at dinner. Alexander was ebullient now in his letters. His fondest wish had been granted: he had seen active service as a commanding officer. "Two nights ago, my Eliza, my duty and my honor obliged me to take a step in which your happiness was too much risked," Alexander had written in one letter that autumn, assuring her the danger was past—but not wanting either to diminish too much the adventure. All the men said that the tide was turning in Yorktown.

At the wharf in the mornings on their way back from church, Peggy and Eliza would stop to ask for news of the schooner masters. When Alexander came at last up the broad avenues of trees from the river and swept her up in his embrace, Eliza could hardly believe the wait was finally over.

The Americans won their independence with the surrender at Yorktown in October, but in the autumn of 1781 the decisive nature of the victory was not yet apparent. It would take two years to hammer out the withdrawal of thirty thousand troops and a peace treaty, amid ongoing skirmishes and frontier raids. But the British were fighting too many wars, in too many foreign theaters, and Yorktown had the welcome effect of clarifying priorities. The campaign, at any rate, was over for the winter, and Alexander was back in Albany.

His arrival came not a moment too soon. Eliza was exasperated with spending so much time apart. She was weary, too, of living with her parents. Alexander reassured her that from here forward, her wish for the future would be what mattered. She had, he had written tenderly during his last weeks at Yorktown, "the assurance of never more being separated. Every day confirms me in the intention of renouncing public life, and devoting myself wholly to you. Let others waste their time and their tranquillity in a vain pursuit of power and glory; be it my object to be happy in a quiet retreat with my better angel." That was all Eliza wanted. And for a little while, it seemed possible.

The news of that new winter season in Albany together was the death of Eliza's great-uncle.

Kiliaen Van Rensselaer, the father of Eliza's wayward younger cousin, Maria, was buried in December at a family funeral in nearby Rensselaerwyck, where the new heir and feudal patroon was the seventeen-year-old Stephen, a heavy-drinking and headstrong young lord of the manor fresh from his first term at Harvard. Alexander, who arrived home and promptly got sick with a cough that lasted for weeks, was not well enough to attend the service, but Eliza and Peggy went with the family. Aaron Burr, living by now with the Van Rensselaer family while studying to pass the bar examination in Albany and in and out of General Schuyler's law library at the Pastures, was also almost certainly in attendance.

Marriage was still very much on the minds of the Schuyler sisters. Alexander called them simply "the Girls," and the girls were furious with Alexander's friend Major Nicholas Fish for jilting one young woman of their acquaintance. "I am told Miss is in great distress," Alexander warned Fish, and "you must be cautious in this matter, or your character will run some risk, and you are sensible how injurious it might be to have the reputation of levity in a delicate point. The Girls have got it among them that this is not your first infidelity." Peggy was also still man hunting.

The young teenage patroon Stephen Van Rensselaer, home at the estate in Albany for the funeral and holiday season, too, took one look at his sexy and sarcastic older cousin, the now twenty-four-year-old Peggy Schuyler, and became infatuated. Wiser heads quickly packed him back off to college. That would not, however, be the end of the story.

For Eliza, the beginning of 1782 was the last month of her pregnancy and was exhausting and uncomfortable. Alexander fussed solicitously, and she worried that his cough lingered. On January 22 she finally gave birth safely to a little boy, whom they promptly named Philip after her father.

After several weeks of rest, Eliza and Alexander then moved into a small farm owned by her parents, not far from the Pastures, where the new young family happily threw themselves into housekeeping. Alexander confessed to a friend, "You cannot imagine how entirely domestic I am growing. I lose all taste for the pursuits of ambition, I sigh for nothing but the company of my wife and my baby." He cast aside his law books and his papers, sat by the fire rocking the cradle, and turned his mind to sorting out their glassware and china. He was putting together a little wine cellar and planned some elegant entertaining. Could an acquaintance help him find four pint-size wine decanters? A dozen wineglasses? Beer tumblers? Eliza sorted little jars of seeds and planned for springtime and their vegetable garden. There on their little farm, they spent the winter nesting.

Alexander retired from the military and found employment as a state tax collector. They were short of cash, and Eliza sometimes wondered how to make the household accounts come right, but she was happy. She loved being a mother, and Alexander was a devoted, doting father. Alexander had wondered in his letters before his marriage if she could live simply. He need not have worried about the good-natured Eliza. What more could she need except this?

All spring and into the summer, they lived quietly in Albany. Alexander was engrossed in studying for the bar examination, with an eye toward becoming qualified as a lawyer. General Schuyler had the second-finest law library anywhere in New York, and in the afternoons Alexander read in his father-in-law's study. Also granted permission to use the law library and to live, for a time, at the Pastures, was the twenty-six-year-old Aaron Burr, who had been introduced to the Schuyler family by the good offices of General Alexander McDougall. Large estate homes frequently opened their doors to other members of the well-networked gentry, and the Pastures was no exception. But when Aaron Burr soon became fast friends with Stephen Van Rensselaer, Aaron confided in his amorous letters to Mrs. Prevost that the teenage patroon gallantly arranged for him to live instead with Schuyler and Van Rensselaer aunts in Albany. Aaron and Alexander, whose futures would someday be bound together so disastrously, studied side by side in companionable silence in the early 1780s.

In the evenings, Eliza and Alexander rode together along the lanes that Eliza had known as a girl, and Alexander shared her enthusiasm for fine horses and galloping. He listened with interest as Eliza and her mother talked about the deer in the garden and the plant specimens they were always hunting. Aaron Burr came for tea in the front parlor. Kitty sent her daughter gifts of fresh fruits to preserve for the winter, and new potatoes. Alexander wrote and studied, and they sat in church on Sundays in the family pew with her parents. "I have been employed for the last ten months in rocking the cradle and studying the art of fleecing my neighbors," Alexander reported cheerfully to his friend the Marquis de Lafayette.

Changes came with the autumn. Alexander passed his bar examination and was honored with an appointment to the Continental

Congress in Philadelphia as a New York representative. Now started the hard work of building a country. In November, Alexander went south ahead of Eliza and baby Philip to find a new home for the family. So much for Alexander's promise to abandon ambition and a public life for domestic quiet.

Eliza understood. And she tried to be patient. She had promised to be a Roman wife, and she believed in the republic. But it meant time apart again, and Eliza hated it. Once again, Alexander could not help pressing Eliza for letters, however affectionately. "Remember your promise," he wrote. "Don't fail to write me by every post. I shall be miserable if I do not hear once a week from you and my precious infant. You both grow dearer to me every day. I would give the world for a kiss from either of you."

The separation would grow longer than either expected, as one delay after another cropped up. Angelica and John were already living in Philadelphia, and Peggy was spending the winter with them, still husband hunting. When a letter arrived at the Pastures warning that Peggy and Angelica were both gravely ill, their parents rushed south in a panic to join Alexander and John, leaving Eliza behind to look after her younger siblings, nine-year-old Rensselaer and six-year-old Cornelia. By the time her parents returned north, relieved at the survival of both the girls, the roads were too sloppy for a carriage to pass. Eliza was forced to wait several weeks more for the winter snow, so a sleigh could carry her and baby Philip as far as New Jersey, where she could visit with her cousin Kitty Livingston and wait for Alexander to fetch her. "When you are in the Jerseys write me of your arrival and I will come for you," Alexander urged, reminding her tenderly to pack rum for the cold journey.

As Eliza traveled south to Philadelphia at last in January, weeks later than planned, Peggy returned north to Albany to help their mother with the children, and there was one other addition to the Schuyler household in the winter of 1783. Their nineteen-year-old cousin, another Kiliaen Van Rensselaer, took a position as Philip Schuyler's estate secretary. Cousin Kiliaen was especially close with their impetuous cousin Stephen Van Rensselaer, who was away until June at school in Harvard.

When Eliza returned home for a summer visit in June, not long after Stephen Van Rensselaer's return to Albany, she walked into a household rocked by chaos.

Peggy was determined to marry, and she would turn twenty-five in the autumn. Finding a husband, even for a rich and pretty young woman, was far from certain. Seven years of war had translated into the death of a generation of young men, and in America in 1783 there were 120 would-be brides for every hundred-odd eligible gentlemen. Eliza's favorite cousin, Kitty Livingston, was both older and richer, and she still hadn't managed to catch a husband. Twenty-five was practically an old maid, and Peggy saw her window quickly closing.

Stephen Van Rensselaer was a scrawny young man. He had high, dark eyebrows; a long, thin nose; friendly eyes; an easy laugh; and extremely deep pockets. His fortune still ranks today, centuries later, as one of the largest ever in American history. He liked to drink fine wine and, like Peggy, enjoyed boisterous dinner parties.

Stephen arrived home from Harvard in June and, still enchanted by his feisty older cousin, promptly proposed marriage. Peggy, in no mood to turn down any suitor, accepted with great alacrity.

General Abraham Ten Broeck, the teenage patroon's uncle and guardian, exploded with fury. Abraham was Philip Schuyler's oldest and dearest friend, since their earliest days at school together, but Stephen was too young to be thinking of marriage, and it all looked very opportunistic on the part of the lady. Philip Schuyler agreed entirely and promptly took matters in hand by calling off the engagement, forbidding his daughter from accepting the proposal, and packing the entire family off to remote Saratoga for the summer, where, the burned-out summer house still in ruins, there were only tents for accommodation. That, Abraham and Philip agreed, should cool the young man's ardor.

The problem with the young patroon's marriage, everyone agreed, was not Peggy Schuyler. The trouble was the youth of a teenage Stephen Van Rensselaer. In a few years, when Stephen had come of age and was no longer a minor, when his fortune was his to manage, and he had found his sense of himself as a man and estate master, then, of course, no one could object to one of General Schuyler's daughters, even "wild Miss Peggy." If Stephen felt the same way at twenty-two or twenty-three, the path was open. If. After all, crushes came and went, and young men were often fickle.

But in three or four years, Peggy would be approaching thirty. If the rest of them had missed that fact, Peggy certainly hadn't.

Peggy Schuyler was not about to wait years to see if the young man changed his mind and risk losing her certain chance to get a husband. Their unfortunate cousin Kiliaen Van Rensselaer was pressed into duty as a secret messenger, despite his protests, and Stephen set off in a boat for Saratoga. Peggy carefully folded a mauve silk gown, worked with an overskirt of damask flowers, and some of her nicest bits of lace into a satchel and, when the signal came, slipped away from their summer encampment and down to the river with her suitor. The next morning, Peggy got her wish. They eloped and were immediately married. No minister in Rensselaerwyck was going to refuse the patroon.

When Peggy was missing in the morning, there was little doubt as to what had happened. Philip and Kitty Schuyler heard the confirmation of the marriage that afternoon, and this time they were more disappointed in their daughter than enraged or worried. But Abraham Ten Broeck was furious, and Philip Schuyler sympathized with his old friend in his anger. He knew what it was like when a disobedient child ran off on the sly to marry. Philip still thought that Angelica's husband was a cad and a fraud. John was even now masquerading as late as 1783 under his assumed identity as "Mr. Carter" to shirk responsibility.

Stephen Van Rensselaer was kin, part of that interconnected web of Dutch landowners, and the lord of a vast feudal manor that reached for miles around their hometown of Albany. Scandalized letters flew in the weeks that followed, and Cousin Kiliaen was in an especially uncomfortable situation. "Stephen's precipitate marriage has been to me a source of surprise and indeed of regret," one friend wrote him. "He certainly is too young to enter into a connection of this kind; the period of his life is an important crisis; it is the time to acquire Fame, or at least to prepare for its acquisition. . . . Our friend has indulged the momentary impulse of youthful Passions, and has yielded to the dictates of Remorseful Fancy."

Stephen would regret it, the locals tutted. Some went further and said that Peggy Schuyler, facing down spinsterhood, had taken advantage of the impulsivity of a young man to catch a husband.

Peggy didn't care. Let the gossips moan and flutter, she thought. She was tickled when Alexander nicknamed her "Mrs. Patroon." Stephen had no regrets either. He was young, hopelessly rich, and reasonably handsome. He drank far too much fine wine, he sometimes gambled, and he reveled in flirtatious women and raucous parties. Peggy—always the impulsive Schuyler girl—was smart, funny, haughty, beautiful, and she never tired of dancing. And he was in love with her. The couple promptly moved into a mansion in the center of Albany.

Did Eliza, in Saratoga with the family for the holiday, know of her sister's plans? It is unlikely that Peggy would have confided in Eliza. Eliza was closer to Angelica than to Peggy. Peggy talked fast and loud, and she had a fiery, explosive temper. Eliza was famously easygoing and thoughtful. Peggy boiled. Eliza simmered slowly. If she had known, Eliza might not have tattled. But she would have tried to talk Peggy out of disobeying Father.

Instead, Eliza stayed on to console her parents. The situation was an embarrassing one for General Schuyler. What would the world think of a military man who could not control even his daughters? June was wet and cold that summer, and they camped near the hot springs in Saratoga. In the mornings, Eliza walked the land with her father, who was determined now to build a small, two-room summer cottage near the medicinal waters. But tenting in the rain was sure to make everyone ill and bad-tempered, and the damage was done with Peggy. The family returned to Albany, traveling back and forth between the house and camp all summer. Soon Alexander would come to join the family, and then they would travel back south together as a family to Philadelphia.

But in July, Eliza was still waiting for Alexander to turn up. One letter after another from him announced some delay, gave some reason. Eliza did not like the pattern she saw emerging. She had been waiting what seemed like forever to live in their own house together.

Other old friends from Morristown were already arriving in upstate New York while Eliza waited for her husband. Saratoga was increasingly famous as a summer retreat, and the tourist population was growing. George Washington, who dreamed of a horseback tour through the Hudson River and Mohawk country, arrived that month to tour the military sites at Saratoga and to look for land in the area to purchase. The end of the war set off a frenzy of land speculation. Real estate—holding, developing, subdividing, flipping—seemed like a certain path to riches, and everyone wanted to get in on the action as prices skyrocketed.

General Washington brought with him many of Eliza's old friends—General Henry Knox, General Nathanael Greene, her old flame Richard Varick, and even a recently married Tench Tilghman. His cousin Anna had finally agreed to have him. The house in Albany was full of laughter and celebration. Philip Schuyler, Abraham Ten Broeck, and Peggy's new husband, Stephen Van Rensselaer, joined the touring party, which as it set off numbered nearly forty.

On August 3, the military men arrived back in Albany, and Abraham Ten Broeck threw a raucous dinner at a local tavern, followed by a more sedate reception with the ladies of Albany at the Schuyler mansion. Eliza, in her mother's absence, played hostess. Alexander, still trying to make his way north and acutely conscious of his wife's growing impatience—and of the fact that he was missing the party—

was becoming increasingly exasperated with his mother-in-law, who was traveling up with him and who insisted on visiting New York City.

Part of what delayed Alexander and his mother-in-law, Kitty, at the end of July was news that brought Eliza sorrow. Angelica and John were leaving America, and it might be years before the sisters met again. They had seen each other through thick and thin, held each other's hands during childbirth, and shared their most private thoughts with each other as new wives and householders.

On July 27, John, Angelica, and their children set sail for Paris. Alexander and Eliza's mother watched them depart from Philadelphia. John was now a vastly wealthy man. The account books for 1783 showed that he and his partner, Jeremiah Wadsworth, had raked in profits of nearly 35,000 pounds—earnings upwards of a modern equivalent of $46 million. The partners were owed more payments from the French government for unpaid wartime bills, and they were traveling to France to collect. But John Church—still living under the assumed name of John Carter—also wanted to go home to London. He had fled as a bankrupt in disgrace, with the bailiffs hard on his heels, a decade earlier. The scandal of his dueling was long forgotten, and he was now in a position to clear his debts and cancel the warrants. He also wanted to show Uncle Barker that he had made something of himself after all in America.

When they sailed, Angelica had in tow three toddlers—Philip, Kitty, and John—and she was five months pregnant with a fourth child, who was destined to be born in Europe. A smooth transatlantic voyage meant a month at sea, but the late summer of 1783 was a risky time to travel. Banks of fog and a persistent haze blanketed harbors across Europe and America—the effects of a volcano in Iceland—and Angelica and John were fortunate to arrive safely at the start of September.

John set off almost immediately to settle affairs in London, leaving Angelica and the children in Paris, and, by the end of October, Jeremiah Wadsworth reported, "Mr Carter has found all his friends

and relatives well a most cordial reconciliation has taken place between them and his Uncle is perfectly amended. He therefore as-
sumes his real name John Barker Church."

The prodigal son was welcomed home, and, on December 7,
Angelica gave birth in Paris to a daughter. "I intended to have called
my little girl Eliza after Mr. Church's mother," Angelica wrote to
Eliza, "but she thinks Angelica is a much prettier name. Mr. Church
is also of that opinion, but I promise that the next girl I make shall
be called Betsey."

By the time Eliza received the news, she and Alexander were settling—at last—into a new life of their own in New York City, in a
rented house at 57 Wall Street, near the corner of Wall and Broad
Streets, in what was then the urban center of the city, where Alexander now opened a law practice. This would be his postwar career. He
had had enough of politics. He would be an attorney. They would
raise a big family. He promised.

Old friends were congregating in New York City in the months
after the British evacuation, and Alexander and Eliza's social circle in the city now was dominated by Alexander's fellow attorneys,
Eliza's extended network of more or less remote cousins, and other
families associated with a controversial fraternity, the Society of the
Cincinnati, an elite group of patriot senior officers that some bitterly charged with establishing a new American aristocracy. Among
those friends and neighbors in the Cincinnati fraternity, Eliza could
count her old flame and attorney Richard Varick; chief judiciary and
kinsman Richard Livingston; and Peggy's patroon husband, Stephen
Van Rensselaer, who'd turned twenty-one at last in the autumn and
had celebrated coming into his vast inheritance with a riotous house
party. Perhaps most ominous, though, was Alexander's growing
friendship with the inveterate gambler and wheeler-dealer William
Duer, the man who had introduced John Church to the Schuyler
family and who was now married to another of Eliza's Morristown
cousins, Catherine Alexander.

Alexander was consumed with legal work, political writing,

a banking project in the city, and the Cincinnati. He worked long into the night in his office and repaired inevitably after to the nearby Fraunces Tavern. His and Eliza's lives were increasingly separate.

Eliza lived largely among other women, children, and servants. Her nearest friends were her cousins, Catherine Alexander Duer and Sarah Livingston Jay, and Marie-Charlotte Antill. All four of the women attended the same Anglican church services at the nearby Trinity Church, and in 1784 they were also all mothers or, like Eliza again that summer, pregnant. Marie-Charlotte's chubby toddler, Harriet, was Eliza's special favorite.

They were all part of the cast of characters in a drama that, before the decade was out, would change life for Eliza and Alexander forever and cause Eliza more grief than she ever could have imagined.

CHAPTER 9

New York, 1785–88

The spring brought unexpected good news. Eliza was jubilant. Angelica and John Church were to return from Paris in 1785, after more than a year's absence. They arrived in New York City just as a worn-down Marie-Charlotte was giving birth to her twelfth baby, a little girl named Fanny, and Eliza busied herself visiting Marie-Charlotte and trying to help her ailing friend with the houseful of Antill children.

Eliza's joy at Angelica's return was to be short-lived.

Angelica had arrived knowing that her and John's return to America was not permanent. John had purchased a large estate on Sackville Street, in London's Mayfair, near his elderly mother. She was still shocked and surprised, though, to learn that her husband was wrapping up his business interests at a breakneck speed and was planning to leave America for good. Angelica had imagined she would at least have the summer with Eliza and that they might return to Europe in the autumn. John had other plans. He intended, he informed Angelica, to sail back to Britain not after a leisurely family visit but on the next passenger ship. They had just spent an exhausting month at sea. He told Angelica to be prepared to do it all over again after just a few weeks in America. After assigning Alexander, his lawyer, power of attorney, and charging his brother-in-law with the management of his income and property, he booked a hasty return voyage. Like that, they were gone again.

Eliza was crushed. Her fondest wish was to watch her children and Angelica's grow up together as friends and cousins, and she missed her sister desperately. She was lonely in New York as a wife and new mother. Worse, the sisters and Alexander understood this probably was goodbye forever this time.

Eliza was too disconsolate to write, but Alexander put into words both their sadness in August, when Angelica was being tossed and buffeted in a ship somewhere in the middle of the Atlantic. "You have I fear taken a final leave of America and of those that love you here," Alexander wrote to his sister-in-law.

> Unless I see you in Europe I expect not to see you again. This is the impression we all have; judge the bitterness it gives to those who love you with the love of nature and to me who feel an attachment for you not less lively.... Your Good and affectionate sister Betsey feels more than I can say on this subject. She sends you all a sisters love.

Eliza just cried, and when she tried to focus on her needlework her eyes were swimming.

She turned to Marie-Charlotte for friendship and consolation, but Marie-Charlotte was dying. Complications from the delivery of Fanny had drained her last reserves of strength, and while the infant grew stronger, her mother lay feverish and lethargic until sepsis took her. Edward Antill buried his wife in St. Paul's churchyard at Trinity parish in the first week of September. Eliza mourned with her friend. A week later Eliza was in the parish again, standing as godmother to both baby Fanny and five-year-old Harriet Antill in a double baptism.

Alexander and Eliza worried now about the widowed Edward. Eliza's heart ached for his sorrow and for the darkness that engulfed him. Six of his twelve children were dead. He had buried their thirty-five-year-old mother. Left to him were a half-dozen daughters, for whom he had no dowries, and the ruins of his fortunes. Alexander rallied round the troops, enlisting the men of Society of the Cincinnati to donate funds to support their fraternity brother, but Edward couldn't lift himself from his depression.

Eliza took charge in the only way she could. She welcomed into their home her friend's motherless youngest children. Two of his teenage girls, Mary and Isabella, went to stay with their father's family in Albany, where the Schuyler family would be among their support network. But Eliza coaxed Edward into letting Harriet and Fanny stay in the nursery with her two children, toddler Philip and one-year-old Angelica. They needed a mother, these little ones. She promised Edward she would care for them. In the spring, a fifth child would join the Hamilton household. Eliza's third was born a little boy, named Alexander Jr. after his father.

It was becoming hard to keep track of the number of children coming and, sadly, departing in the households of the Schuyler sisters by the time of little Alexander's arrival. Death was a constant presence and held terrors for Eliza. Peggy was the mother of two small children in the spring of 1786, three-year-old Catherine and baby Stephen. Within a year, both were buried. Angelica was the mother of four that spring. She now buried her youngest, a happy ten-month-old boy named Richard. Eliza said a less tragic goodbye, too, to her favorite, little Harriet Antill, who traveled north to Canada with her father. Baby Fanny, though, stayed behind with Eliza and Alexander, and when word came that Edward had died on the northern frontier, Eliza steadfastly refused to abandon the Antill orphan. Alexander did not even try to persuade her.

When Angelica heard the news of the informal adoption in London, her response was that it was classic Eliza. Any of her own virtues, Angelica wrote to Alexander, "fade before the generous and benevolent action of My Sister in taking the orphan Antle under her protection." The thought of her children left alone in the world was Eliza's deepest fear, and orphans tugged at her heartstrings. Orphans and widows.

By the autumn of 1786, another specter haunted Eliza's imagination: bankruptcy. Bankruptcy was a crime in the eighteenth century, as John Church had discovered. For families who fell into its grasp, the ruin was complete. Only the luckiest families worked their way out of debtors' prison in time to salvage a future. Most families were not so fortunate.

Abraham Lott, the wheeler-dealer father of Alexander's early Morristown crush, Cornelia, did not fade from Alexander's life when the courtship of Abraham's daughter abruptly ended, and Abraham Lott's plight in the 1780s gained him both Alexander's and Eliza's sympathy. Eliza felt, especially, for poor Cornelia and her sisters. Abraham Lott was locked away as a debtor in the New Gaol, just to the north of St. Paul's Chapel, where Marie-Charlotte was buried. Eliza walked there often and looked with horror on the brick-and-stone building, three stories tall, surrounded by stockade fencing.

The brutality of impoverishment at the prison was crushing. Criminal inmates were fed and clothed by their jailers, however abjectly. Not so debtors. They survived—or not—on whatever food and, in winter, firewood, family or friends delivered. Between Abraham Lott and starvation stood only the unlucky Cornelia and her still-unmarried sisters, none of whom had prospects or incomes.

When Eliza first stepped foot in the debtors' prison that year, she pulled her thick cloak close around her and shuddered. As the lock clicked shut behind her, Eliza could only wonder what she and Alexander had been thinking. She decided there and then that she would move heaven and earth to prevent anyone in her family ending up in debtors' prison. It was bad enough to be a visitor.

Eliza squared her shoulders. She was there on a charity mission.

Alexander heard from a friend and fellow brother of the Cincinnati fraternity of the plight of a portrait artist locked away that winter for debts that were shockingly modest. Such a fate was not uncommon. Of the 1,162 debtors in New York City prisons that year, more than seven hundred were languishing for debts of less than a pound—not quite a hundred dollars in modern figures.

Alexander thought he saw a better solution. The incarcerated artist, Ralph Earl, could paint his way to freedom. Would Eliza help him? As one of the Hamilton sons remembered later, their father asked their mother to go "to the debtors' jail to sit for her portrait and she induced other ladies to do the same." She was there that day for her first of several sittings.

In the most famous painting of her, Eliza sits before velvet curtains, her dark hair powdered white and veiled in a gauze of lace, her throat encircled by a black ribbon. Her lively brown eyes, which Alexander so admired, sparkle as they look out of the portrait. The background is a polite illusion. The reality was something starker. Eliza sat motionless in a dank cell and for weeks listened to the moans and cries of the desperate. Within the year, Ralph Earl was free, but Eliza never forgot what she had witnessed. Fear of financial ruin stayed with her after.

Life in New York City had a daily pattern by 1788.

Mornings began early for Eliza. The family was up before 5 a.m., and Eliza bustled the children off to school at the astonishing hour of six o'clock in the morning. A servant brought them home again at eight, and Eliza gathered the children around her while they ate warm milk and bread for breakfast. She didn't mind that little fists left crumbs on her dresses. This was what she liked best about being a mother.

Philip, their eldest boy, was six in 1788, old enough for tutors and, soon, boarding school during the week on Staten Island. Alexander was already teaching him Greek and Latin. The little girls in the house, Angelica Hamilton and Fanny Antill, were learning their letters, and in the nursery Eliza's toddler, Alexander Jr., was joined by another Hamilton brother, infant James. Eliza patiently watched the girls trace out their first, crooked letters.

When the weather was poor, Eliza read to the children from the Bible by the fireplace and contented herself with the endless sewing a growing family required. But if the weather were fine, Eliza put on a pretty gown and joined Aunt Gertrude and one of Eliza's older cousins, the twice-widowed Judith Van Rensselaer Bruce, for morning weekday church services and, after, social visits. The ladies mostly attended the Episcopalian services at Trinity and St. Paul's Chapel, but sometimes they attended the Dutch church of Eliza's girlhood or went to hear a sermon at the Presbyterian church, where Eliza soon became friends with another newcomer to New York City, a Scottish woman in her forties named Isabella Graham, and her nineteen-year-old daughter, Joanna. Only Methodism, with its holy-roller enthusiasm, and Catholicism were seen as equally shocking.

The social visits were regimented affairs. New York high society at the end of the 1780s comprised a group of fewer than three hundred people and only a few dozen prominent families, most of them somehow related to each other and, more often than not, to Eliza. Society's leading ladies each had an "at home" day to save the confusion of everyone being out visiting at once, and Eliza, whether she liked it or not, was one of those leading ladies.

She mostly didn't like it.

Eliza's at-home day was Wednesday. On that day, each week, from eleven to three, she prepared to welcome sometimes as many as two dozen callers in the front parlor on Wall Street. The servants in the kitchen prepared refreshments to be passed around on silver trays, arranged the chairs around the edges of the room, and stoked a cozy fire. Eliza dreaded those hours. The conversation was studiously trivial.

Over cups of fine Chinese tea, ladies and the occasional gentleman critiqued sermons and traded news of family sickness, ominous reports of the spread of yellow fever, and the safe arrival of babies and boats from Europe, and rated their chances in the New York lottery—the prizes for which sometimes ran as high as $10,000, a veritable fortune in the eighteenth century.

Eliza shook her head along with the other ladies at the frequent reports of duels between young men across the river in Hoboken, though the ladies discussed this more discreetly in low voices. Even the son of the bishop was guilty of dueling, to the great embarrassment of his pious father. As another of Eliza's numerous kinswomen, Elizabeth De Hart Bleecker, put it sarcastically in her journal from those years in New York City, "Unfortunately neither of the children had the pleasure of receiving an honorable wound." Eliza Hamilton shared in the general view among the ladies that dueling was immature and foolish. Among the men, though, it was the fashion.

In between the social calls, Eliza walked along the seawall at the Battery or scoured the shopwindows for frippery and dress trimmings with her aunt and cousins. And in the afternoons, even a rich housewife oversaw the servants cleaning and baking. Bed curtains came up and down constantly with the season, and there was always mending. After supper, when Alexander came home, evenings often saw more callers, who stayed for games of whist and glasses of Madeira. Women like Eliza and her cousins confided to their journals the pain of toothaches they tried to ignore, worries about sick children, and their private annoyance at guests who stayed too long, kept them up past midnight, and bored them with what Eliza's cousin and friend Eliza De Hart Bleecker confided to her journal could be "rather a stupid visit."

On weekends, the entire family went to church services, at least once and sometimes twice on Sunday, although few of the men and women whose daring philosophical beliefs had fomented the American Revolution embraced rigid church hierarchies. Eliza and Alexander, like their friends in the Cincinnati fraternity, did not take communion at the altar. After morning church, a solicitous husband or father might hire a coach for a country drive, and balls and concerts made up part of the whirl of the social season. A married woman with children like Eliza attended gala events a few times a year, however, and not weekly, like the girls who were courting.

Eliza knew that this was the role of a wife and mother. She did not wish for a place in Alexander's busy world of law, finance, and increasingly New York–centered politics, where ratification of the Constitution was bitterly debated. By 1788, Alexander had already served in Congress, in the New York State legislature, and as a delegate to the Constitutional Convention. Eliza did resent the unflattering gossip about Alexander that sometimes made its way back to her, intimations about his easy gallantry, unfounded rumors of his mixed-race "Creole" blood and more accurate rumors about his bastard origins, which she tried to accept stoically as part of the rough-and-tumble of politics. Alexander sometimes came home exercised about backroom deals or thickheaded policies that imperiled the new republic. Eliza listened patiently and tried to steer Alexander toward moderation, but in the end politics was a man's business.

Still, Eliza longed for some role larger than morning social calls and fashion. She and her family had dedicated themselves to the building of the American republic and had sacrificed for the revolution. She wanted to do something useful. Her cousin Sarah Livingston Jay, with whom Eliza traded regular morning visits in the 1780s, privately expressed the same wish to her sisters and Eliza's cousins, Kitty and Susan Livingston, when she found herself writing of liberty and America: "But whither, my pen, are you hurrying me?" she chided herself. "What have I to do with politicks? Am I not myself a woman & writing to Ladies? Come then, ye fashions to my assistance."

Above all, Eliza longed for the return of Angelica. In 1788, a bitter rift in the Schuyler family spread to both sides of the Atlantic and suddenly made that wish possible.

The second wave of Schuyler children was now coming of age—the younger siblings of Angelica, Eliza, and Peggy—and, thanks to her sisters, runaway weddings were already a touchy subject for Eliza's parents.

Their eldest little brother and heir to the largest share of the family's fortune, John Schuyler, dutifully married the patroon's nineteen-year-old sister, Elizabeth Van Rensselaer, in a grand society wedding.

The next two boys, Eliza's brothers Philip and Rensselaer, however, exasperated their father. Rensselaer was ungovernable and had been since he was seven. Eliza's brother Philip Jr. was either too busy partying or too dull to pass his college courses at Columbia—nobody quite knew which was the problem. He was the only one of the Schuyler boys to go to college, and his father was determined to see through the investment. But it had not turned out with the boys as General Schuyler expected. Eliza's father candidly confessed to Angelica that her brother Philip Jr. was a disappointment, and Angelica sympathized with her father's concerns about gambling especially. In London, she confided to Alexander, John Church was making staggering bets at the horse races. He was also hobnobbing with a passion, while Angelica retreated to their country estate in Windsor with the children. John wanted a seat in Parliament. His "head is full of politics, he is so desirous of making one in the British House of Commons," that Angelica hardly saw him.

Just when General Schuyler's patience was completely exhausted, young Philip Schuyler made another rash decision and ran off to marry a local eighteen-year-old beauty and heiress. Philip Jr. didn't know which way to turn for family support, but he knew that Rensselaerwyck was not far enough away for him to escape the wrath of his father. So the newlyweds ran all the way to London and Angelica. Surely, Philip Jr. must have reasoned, his sister Angelica would know how to manage their parents' anger. But it looked as if Angelica had been party to the plot, and that brought up all the old hurt. Angelica was in the hot seat along with her wayward brother.

The transatlantic family quarrel that followed had just one silver lining, Eliza thought afterward. Philip Jr. needed to go home and face his father. Angelica had been pressing John to let her travel to America to see her family, but he had not been inclined so far, she wrote to Eliza, to "indulge me in returning to my family and my country, when he is intimately persuaded that no woman in London leads an happier or easier life." He knew, however, that her father would be furious. John—whose own insight into rifts and family peacemaking had matured since his youthful flight from London and impetuous elopement—now agreed that Angelica should travel home to America alone for a few months in the spring and fall of 1789, returning with her brother and his anxious bride to Albany. She would need to remember: it was to be a short visit. Make the peace with General Schuyler and return home to London and the children. That was as far as John was willing to go.

Eliza didn't care if it were only for a week. She wanted to see her sister.

In New York, Alexander's law career was at its postwar zenith. His political star, too, was on the rise, and he was celebrated as a prominent attorney and war hero. He had long since forgotten those early promises to Eliza that he was done with taking risks and chasing ambitions.

With fame, increasingly, came enemies. That was one of the prices Alexander and Eliza paid now. An ugly power struggle was unfolding in elite political circles, and Alexander's reputation flew so high in some camps that in other camps people wished for his complete destruction. In the newspapers, in private letters and gossip, wild assertions about his illegitimacy, dubious parentage, immigrant status, aristocratic tendencies, secret allegiance to the crown, and, increasingly, infidelities and sexual perversions swirled around him. John Adams was decidedly partisan, but even he would later repeat the crude tittle-tattle that said that Alexander Hamilton possessed "a superabundance of secretions which he could not find whores enough to draw off." What upset his political enemies were Alexander's words, which were elegant, powerful, and persuasive. They hated his mind. So what they talked about was the corruption of his body.

Alexander, who surely knew the gossip, shrugged it off while it remained bawdy talk among the gentlemen. Sometimes he had been too flippant. He had once during the war recommended an elderly minister for a camp post with a letter that read, "He is just what I should like for a military parson except that he does not whore or drink," though he meant it to be funny. But words had a life of their own after you wrote them, and, besides, like most elite men of the 1780s, Alexander Hamilton was probably not a stranger to so-called ladies of pleasure. Taverns doubled as brothels, and New York was a teeming seaport.

Eliza, as yet, knew nothing of any of this.

But Alexander Hamilton had always been known as something of a rogue, and his current situation had explosive potential. Into that situation arrived the fuel to the fire that was Angelica.

CHAPTER 10

Family Indiscretions, 1789

When Angelica's ship crept into the New York City harbor in early March, Eliza was waiting.

Philip Jr.'s new bride, Sarah Rutsen, was eight months pregnant and wanted to go home to have her baby. The young couple set off immediately up the Hudson as far as Rhinebeck. It would take Philip Jr. nearly two months to screw up his courage and travel to Albany to make his peace with his mother and father.

Angelica, meanwhile, came home to Alexander and Eliza.

She arrived in New York City dressed to the nines in Paris fashion, giddy and full of gossip. She had come alone, without John or the children, and Angelica wanted to cut loose. Stephen and Peggy had a pied-à-terre in Manhattan, not far from Alexander and Eliza's residence on Wall Street, and Angelica entertained them all with rumors and funny stories of human folly. Alexander laughed the hardest. One of the stories that Angelica shared with Alexander privately was the scandalous account of the private life of her new continental friend, Thomas Jefferson, whose dalliance in Paris with Sally Hemings, a fair-skinned African slave from his plantation, had resulted already in mixed-race children. Alexander tucked that story away in his memory.

The three older Schuyler girls maintained a tight sisterly friendship, and Eliza and Peggy had grown closer in New York City. Alexander found Peggy's irreverent sense of humor refreshing. The sisters closed the domestic circle around themselves ever tighter. There was a deep and abiding sense of family loyalty that made them appear clannish. The jocular easiness of their manners with each other was discussed and noted. Alexander and Stephen, welcomed into the family as brothers, were part of the merriment, and a fair bit of horseplay was common. Peggy knew the words to some bawdy drinking songs, and Alexander sang along. There were juvenile pranks, offcolor jokes, and amateur theatrics.

Angelica, Alexander, and Peggy were all flirts who sometimes overstepped the bounds of decorum. Angelica took pleasure in raising eyebrows with her embrace of outlandish fashion. A decade earlier, the French Marquis de Chastellux had noted wryly in Newport that "Mrs Carter, a handsome woman," paraded about town in "rather elegant undress" that earned from those passing by shock and censure. Her time in Paris and London had not exercised a moderating influence.

It was well known, too, that John Church was a rake and a gambler, whose interests ran from the hazard table to speculative stock trading. Gambling had bankrupted him once in the 1770s, and there were fresh ugly rumors now circulating. Each ship that arrived, it seemed, brought more news about John's debauched existence in London. John ran with a fast set there that included members of the government and the Prince of Wales, and their private entertainments included brothels, hellfire clubs with salacious mock masses, and high-stakes betting.

Angelica had the reputation of the wife of just such a husband. One of Alexander's colleagues and friends, Robert Morris, reported that in London Angelica turned away her morning callers one day "because she [was] engaged at cards with her children" and teaching them to gamble, shocking even the most jaded society figures. Morris told tales, as well, of their provocatively pretty French governess—"young enough and handsome enough" to arouse commentary—whom he suspected John was openly bedding.

Within weeks of Angelica's arrival, the rumors about her and

Alexander had started. Angelica, Alexander, and Peggy were all responsible for setting tongues wagging.

It happened at a society event sometime in late March or early April. The Schuyler clan were in high spirits. As the girls crowded into the carriage, there were cries to Alexander and Stephen not to crush the flounces of their gowns or their towering headdresses of ostrich feathers. Sleeves cascaded in lace at the elbows, and stockings in the style of 1789 were embroidered silk, worked in fanciful patterns, and, in an age before the invention of elastic, tied just above the knee with frilly garters, topping shoes festooned with bows. Either garters or shoe bows proved to be the fashion accessory that started the scandal. No one knew afterward quite which object started tongues wagging.

As a married woman, Angelica needed no escort, but she was sorely lacking for a dance and dinner partner without John to attend to her. Her brothers-in-law would look out for her, they promised. Some people said that it happened on the dance floor, when Alexander led Angelica there and stood up alongside Peggy and Stephen. As the dancers spun in their graceful motions, there was a small eighteenth-century calamity. One of Angelica's frilly garters fluttered to the dance floor, and down with it came her silk stocking.

Harrison Gray Otis, who was there, claimed that it wasn't a garter but a shoe bow and that Angelica lost it not on the dance floor but in the salon after dinner, though his account bears all the hallmarks of a polite whitewashing.

Whatever the case, in the 1780s, a lady losing a garter or a bow passed as a chivalric occasion. Peggy—still thought of as "a young wild flirt from Albany, full of glee & apparently desirous of matrimony" in the view of Mr. Otis, despite her marriage to Stephen—plucked her sister's frippery from the floor and put it suggestively in Alexander's buttonhole. To cover their blushes, Alexander hammed up the part of the knight and returned it to Angelica with a flourish, as legend said the gallant King Edward III had once done for his fair mistress. Angelica quipped her thanks and picked up the allusion.

She did not know, she retorted gaily, that he had been made royal Knight of the Garter.

Such merriment drew unfortunate attention. Peggy, a wit with a raunchy sense of humor, now chimed in acerbically that Alexander would be a Knight of the Bedchamber if he could, and the three rogues all thought it terribly funny. Eliza, long since inured to their tomfoolery, smiled and knew better than to take any of her sisters or her husband seriously. Those outside their circle, though, saw it differently, especially the wives of Alexander's political enemies. Behind their fans, the sober society ladies pursed their lips and tut-tutted. They lived in full view of the public. "I had little of private life in those days," Eliza remembered later. And not everyone who was watching was friendly.

Life was about to get even less private. George Washington was elected the first president of the United States in the spring of 1789, and New York City was abuzz with plans for fireworks, parades, and balls to celebrate the inauguration. Alexander was already being mentioned as a likely candidate for the first secretary of finance, and his political star shone increasingly brighter, along with the stars of Eliza's father and brothers. Eliza would learn to live with every action being scrutinized. Her sisters and Alexander took fewer precautions.

At the inaugural ball in early May, all eyes were on Eliza as one of the few ladies asked to dance by President Washington. He was an old friend of her father, and George Washington liked the level-headed Eliza. Martha Washington considered her a friend and kindred spirit. "I mingled . . . in the gaieties of the day," Eliza recalled. "I was at the inauguration ball—the most brilliant of them all," where the assembled guests included all of elite political society and more than a dozen of the Livingston cousins, some of whom Alexander was increasingly at political odds with that summer.

Despite her position as one of New York's leading socialites,

Eliza did her best to keep out of the limelight. Angelica was the opposite, and that also set tongues wagging. Eliza wanted a purpose—and tribal devotion to family was one she could embrace willingly, even if she yearned for something larger. Angelica longed to join the world of men and politics and their liberty. She once wrote to her mother, on hearing of her brother John's marriage and his inheritance of Saratoga, "I am glad to hear that my Brother is likely to be so well established. I wish to God I had been a boy, or an old maid." In her marriage, Angelica had few choices, and perhaps, as her father had predicted, she now questioned the wisdom of running off with a scoundrel. In New York City, she was determined to enjoy whatever freedom she could grasp, for however long John let her stay in America. The clock was ticking. She was starting the fourth month of what John had expected would be a flying visit to make amends with her father.

While Eliza danced with George Washington—the stately minuet, she later said, was a dance well suited to his dignity and office—some eyes flew elsewhere. Already rumors were spreading. No one was surprised now at who Alexander had chosen as his dance partner. What was going on between Mrs. Church and Mr. Hamilton? People were whispering the question. In March and April, Angelica lived with Eliza and Alexander. In early May, increasingly wary of the gossips and under the weather, she moved to a boardinghouse farther down Wall Street, which Alexander leased for her until October as John's attorney, and where the girls' mother promptly arrived for several weeks to visit.

While tongues wagged, in truth, Angelica and Alexander barely saw enough of each other alone to carry on a secret liaison, at least not in the Hamilton home on Wall Street. Alexander passed his days in his law office, and Angelica and Eliza were constant companions.

When Angelica and Alexander did see each other, they were crammed into a small house with Eliza, filled with children, servants, and usually one or the other of their parents.

Angelica once joked to Eliza that she should share her husband.

"I love him very much and if you were as generous as the Old Romans," she teased, "you would lend him to me for a little while." It was part of the inside joke at the heart of Eliza and Alexander's marriage. Eliza prided herself on being the Roman wife and told herself that all the annoyances of life in the public eye and Alexander's political enemies were her sacrifices to family and the republic. Angelica was jestingly asking the Roman wife to make the ultimate sacrifice.

But Angelica did wish that she had a husband like Alexander. John was far more imperious, far less tender. He spent weeks in London at his club, carousing with the lads. She had retreated to their country estate near Windsor. Angelica and Alexander's friendship was deep and abiding. There was love and heartfelt care for each other. There was some teasing mixed with flirtation. That was true also. All of it was mixed with a shared sense of the ribald Schuyler family humor.

Context is everything. The letters that passed among the three of them—because Eliza was always party to the reading, even if she hated writing—strike the modern eye as clandestine and amorous. To those raised in a culture of sensibility and sentiment, however, they were not proof of anything except deep and intimate affection.

By early June, their runaway younger brother and his bride had made peace with Eliza's parents, and General Schuyler was pressing all his children to come home together for the summer. Eliza and Alexander planned to stay in the city, barring perhaps a short holiday, but Angelica could not refuse her mother, who needed a travel companion back to Albany. Angelica and Kitty traveled together up to Albany early in the month, stopping to fetch Philip and Sarah at Rhinebeck, and Angelica stayed there until July, helping her brother mend fences with their parents.

Angelica discovered that month a terrible family secret. The wealth of the Schuyler family, her father confided, was vastly overrated. What there was of it was precarious. The war and the economic aftermath had been the ruin of their fortunes, and just paying the bills was a challenge. General Schuyler put his head in his hands. He was determined to find a solution. Angelica was certain John could advise her father. If John knew one thing, it was money.

The immediate problem was a house in New York City. General Schuyler, newly elected as state senator, needed a townhome for the legislative season, but he was short on funds, and space was cramped with Alexander and Eliza. Angelica insisted on making arrangements and drew Alexander and Eliza into the secret. "If papa requires money I hope that he will draw on Col. Hamilton who will supply him if he has any monies belonging to Mr Church, at my particular desire," Angelica pressed her parents. "Let not then my dear parents be under the least embarrassment whilst their Angelica has so much."

In mid-July, Angelica swept back into New York City to begin house hunting. She seems to have decided that she and John would set up a second residence there and throw open the doors to her parents. Perhaps she wrote to John, too, urging their return to America, citing his business acumen and the financial need of her father. Whatever the case, Angelica quickly scouted out a house on Broadway that would be, she believed, "an eligible situation, and if my Brother [Hamilton] should be appointed to the finance Eliza will be your neighbor." When that house fell through, her father traveled down on the sloop with Peggy to keep looking, and they soon arranged to take a different house on Broadway from the first of November, where Angelica planned to stay through the winter at least with her parents. "On the first floor there are two rooms," Philip Schuyler reported to his wife, "a parlor in front and dining room back with a good pantry. . . . On the Second floor, a drawing room in the near the whole breadth of the house, a large bedroom in front and a small one besides a closet between the two rooms sufficiently large for a bedroom for the Children."

As soon as that was settled, Angelica and Peggy took the sloop back upriver, for an August visit to spend some more time with Philip and Sarah. Alexander and Eliza remained in New York City,

Alexander now caught up in all the excitement of the presidential administration and working late hours. Eliza, under the weather for most of the month, was left alone at home with the children for long periods in July and August. She and Martha Washington, both of whom understood public pressures and how they grew wearing and who shared a love of sober, simple pleasures, passed quiet summer evenings together stitching needlework in the sunset. Martha Washington missed her rural home. Eliza understood her longing. They talked of the Pastures and of Mount Vernon and gardens.

By September, the city was returning to life after the summer recess, and Eliza looked ahead happily to a winter with Angelica and her parents no more than a few minutes' distance. Angelica dared to hope that John would arrive with the children in the spring, for a permanent return to America. In fact, she seemed to be counting on it. There would be dinner parties and family celebrations, and Angelica was proud to know that Alexander and her father would be among the men shaping the country's direction.

When the courier arrived, John's letter was already a month old. One of the children was sick in London. Angelica's presence was required. Any plan that Angelica had of her family returning to America was canceled. John was exasperated at his wife's long absence and demanded she take an immediate return passage. She had not seen her children in seven months, and John was not happy.

Whatever John wrote in his letter—and it was likely blunt and angry—sent Angelica into a panic. Servants in a mad rush threw dresses into trunks and banged them down the hallways, leaving the landlady to fume at the damages. Angelica abandoned the two fine horses that pulled her sleek carriage; Alexander ultimately auctioned them off at John's instructions. Worst of all, her departure would throw her parents' living plans into chaos, but she did not have time to travel upriver to tell them in person. She wrote a hasty, heartbroken letter, apologizing for everything. She made certain, too, that she was aboard the next ship with passage, as John expected.

On November 6, Alexander went alone to the wharf to see Angelica on board, while Eliza cried at home, comforted by her aunt Gertrude and cousin Judith Van Rensselaer Bruce. Angelica's greatest fear was that her parents would think of her in anger, and Alexander promised he would make peace for her as a brother. Then, disconsolate, Alexander walked home through the streets of New York, back to a sleepless Eliza.

In her cabin that night, anchored just beyond New York City, Angelica wrote a last letter, which the pilot crew leading the ship out to sea promised to deliver back in the harbor. "I am completely at sea and my poor heart unravels at quitting you all," she wrote to Alexander,

> *Do my dear Brother endeavor to sooth my poor Betsey, comfort her with the assurances that I will certainly return to take care of her soon. Remember this also yourself my dearest Brother and let neither politics or ambition drive your Angelica from your affections. . . . Adieu my dear Hamilton, you said I was as dear to you as a sister keep your word, and let me have the consolation to beleive that you will never forget the promise of friendship you have vowed. A thousand embraces to my dear Betsy, she will not have so bad a night as the last, but poor angelica adieu.*

So that Angelica would have a letter from them quickly after her arrival, and because they could think of nothing else to soothe their great sorrow, Alexander and Eliza wrote a letter to Angelica and sent it off on a ship leaving immediately after. "After taking leave of you on board of the Packet," Alexander wrote,

> *I hastened home to sooth and console your sister. I found her in bitter distress. . . . After composing her by a flattering picture of your prospects for the voyage, and a strong infusion of hope, that she had not taken a last farewell of you . . . little Phillip and myself, with her consent, walked down to the Battery; where with aching hearts and anxious eyes we saw your vessel, in full*

sail, swiftly bearing our loved friend from our embraces. . . .
I shall commit this letter to Betsey to add whatever her little
affectionate heart may dictate. Kiss your children for me. Teach
them to consider me as your and their father's friend. . . . Adieu
Dear Angelica! Remember us always as you ought to do—
Remember us as we shall you.

Eliza added only a postscript:

My Very Dear beloved Angelica—I have seated my self to write
to you, but my heart is so sadned by your Absence that it can
scarsly dictate, my Eyes so filled with tears that I shall not be
able to write you much but Remember Remember, my Dear
sister of the Assurances of your returning to us, and do all you
can to make your Absence short. Tell Mr. Church for me of the
happiness he will give me, in bringing you to me, not to me alone
but to fond parents sisters friends and to my Hamilton who has
for you all the Affection of a fond own Brother. I can no more
Adieu Adieu. heaven protect you.

It would be at least two months—a month there and a month
back for a letter—before they would hear anything from Angelica
in London.

Historians have long speculated as to whether there was any truth
in the rumors that were bandied about that year that Alexander had
taken his wife's sister as his lover and mistress.

Eliza dismissed the gossip.

Politics in 1789 were bitter and divisive, and Alexander was already a lightning rod in the new government. Eliza saw that clearly.
His ideas about finances and the role of the federal government set
him at odds with some of the republic's other Founding Fathers, especially one of the powerful factions led by Eliza's kinsman Robert

Livingston. They talked about it late into the night by the fire, after Alexander would come home exhausted and frustrated. Eliza hated the conflict with the Livingston clan, but she left such matters to Alexander and her father. All of them saw it as a fight for the heart and soul of America, she knew, and Alexander wielded a fierce power. He was appointed by President Washington in the autumn of 1789 as secretary of Treasury, which placed him in charge of the national economy. His political enemies were keen to destroy his reputation and to stop his agenda. Alexander didn't treat them with kid gloves, either, and in the next few years an ugly situation was about to get a whole lot uglier. If Eliza had known how much uglier, she might have worried more about the gossip.

But Eliza understood the stakes and the contours of this battlefield. She shrugged off whatever she heard of the tall tales that Alexander was having affairs both with Angelica and with Peggy. Benjamin Latrobe, who knew Alexander in the 1790s, snidely remarked that Alexander "went to church from the bed of the wife of his friend" and told his correspondent, "If you ever get to the East Indies . . . you will see little Hamilton . . . standing in the temple of Lingam (the Hindus Priapus) . . . in eternal and basaltic erection."

Alexander's lack of discretion did nothing to quash the rumors. In his swaggering way, Alexander liked to make jokes among the men about prostitutes, conquest, and the impressive size of his member. A youthful Alexander once advised his friend John Laurens in a crude joke to pass along to any interested ladies considering his hand in marriage the "size, make, quality of mind and body . . . do justice to the length of my nose." *The length of the nose* was a euphemism for "the size of the penis." He also wrote to John Laurens letters ardent and suggestive enough to make generations of historians wonder whether the two young men were lovers. It's unlikely, but it's not hard to see why joking talk about "intercourse . . . with my friend" led scandalized Victorian editors of his writing to scratch out whole passages. It was not much different from his jest about the camp minister whoring. Jokes like this were common enough and

were never meant to be shared outside the eighteenth-century political boys' locker room, but those who despised Alexander seized
upon the jokes as a confession.

Eliza half heard, half intuited some part of this gossip about her
sisters and developed the firm and indignant conviction that rumors
of her husband's infidelity were crass political attacks. The gossip
also had the effect of pulling the Schuyler family even closer. They
were a tight-knit bunch, no more so than when attacked, and Eliza,
more than any of them, was staunchly, stubbornly, some said blindly
loyal. That loyalty would be tested.

Speculation, 1790–91

In the spring of 1790, Alexander was consumed with work, and the bruising politics and manic pace were taking a toll on both him and Eliza. Eliza almost certainly heard in late March of the public attack on Alexander's character and of the accusations of financial misconduct made in the House of Representatives by Congressman Aedanus Burke of South Carolina. The insults would have to end in a duel, the pundits whispered, and Eliza's kinswoman and friend Elizabeth De Hart Bleecker confided to her journal that all the society ladies knew that it might end with pistols in Weehawken, New Jersey. The matter was so widely discussed in the city that Senator William Maclay of Pennsylvania noted in his diary on April 4, "So many people concerned in the business may really make the fools fight."

It had been, Eliza thought, a long winter. They had been thrust into the limelight, and Alexander's opponents were stirring up all sorts of trouble. She could trace it all back to Alexander's stunning political success over the creation of a United States federal bank in February.

At the end of 1789, President Washington had appointed Alexander secretary of Treasury. With the appointment to the administration, Alexander became a national figure. The financial system of the United States had to be built from the ground up, and Alexander was in the position of chief architect. He had played an outsize role in founding the Bank of New York in 1784, and he was determined to expand the banking system. All winter he had advocated the establishment of a federal bank, funded through a public stock offering. Whispers flew in the city that it would be the greatest investment opportunity of the century.

Alexander pushed hard for his federalist ideals and the creation of central banking. For Alexander, nothing less was at stake than the shape of the country. The opposition, though, was bitter and partisan. President Washington wavered. By the beginning of 1790, the moment of crisis and decision had arrived, and Eliza sat up until dawn with Alexander one night in February, reading drafts and making neat copies in her careful handwriting, as he hammered out a rationale for the bank. In the morning, the president read it. He signed the executive order. As Eliza described Alexander's role and vision later, "He made your government. . . . He made your bank. I sat up all night with him to help him do it. Jefferson thought we ought not to have a bank and President Washington thought so. But my husband said, 'We must have a Bank.' I sat up all night, copied out his writing, and the next morning, he carried it to President Washington and we had a bank."

Some people stood to make a fortune from the changes. The stock market was booming, and speculation swept the new republic in the years after independence. The nation was gripped with what in another century might be called irrational exuberance. The trouble was that some of those most visibly benefiting included members of Eliza's extended and powerful family.

Eliza's father, Philip Schuyler, was "one of the largest dealers in public papers" and was grasping at the chance to restore his failing fortune. In Britain, their old friend Gouverneur Morris was acting as an unofficial securities agent and raking in profits. John Church, ever the gambler, was caught up in American stock speculation with the French ambassador. Alexander was John's agent and attorney in America, and to some the pair's actions smacked of conflict and collusion. Political paranoia was rife, and not entirely without reason.

The extended family of Schuyler men were as careless about financial appearances at the start as Alexander and Angelica had been about flirting and joking.

Worst of all, Alexander had appointed William Duer, the wheeling-and-dealing husband of Eliza's high-flying Livingston cousin, Catherine Alexander, as his financial deputy in the Treasury. Alexander had an easy tolerance of bounders and schemers, and the appointment of William as his number-two man gave Eliza pause. She knew the spendthrift Duer from long experience. The appointment would cause unimaginable heartache and doom Alexander's ambitions for the presidency.

Congressman Burke had only said aloud what others were thinking. More than one representative opposed to Alexander's economic plans for the United States complained in his private journal or in the hallways to colleagues in a low voice that the secretary of Treasury was trying to ram through a financial program structured to benefit Eliza's powerful relations and other members of the colonial aristocracy.

William Maclay, the senator from Pennsylvania, fulminated in his congressional diary that Alexander Hamilton was engaged in "the most abandoned system of speculation ever broached in our country," and many of Alexander's enemies agreed with the senator's judgment. There were those looking for an occasion to catch out the secretary of Treasury and to launch a congressional investigation. Few periods in American history had been as viciously partisan as the 1790s, and Alexander was a divisive figure and, for some, a high-value target.

Alexander also made some rookie errors. Early on, he was not quick enough off the mark in understanding how the financial benefits flowing to Eliza's family network during these boom times would shape appearances and hamstring his policy decisions. He made at least one misstep that winter. On February 24, 1790, Alexander at an opportune moment placed an order for the sale of some of John Church's stocks—stocks the prices of which the secretary of

Treasury had the power to influence. It wasn't the particular details of the trade that rankled. It was the fact that Alexander acted at all for John in a financial transaction that was the central conflict. In time, such a misstep would be called insider trading. The 1790s were the crucible in which such financial restraints were fired and tested.

When John Church handily "won" election later that spring as the member of Parliament of a rotten borough, purchasing the votes for the astonishing sum of 6,000 pounds—the modern equivalent of $750,000—Alexander's role as his financial agent took on in retrospect an even darker aspect. John Church was now the agent of a foreign government. What, precisely, was his relationship to his brother-in-law? And was the secretary of Treasury loyal to the Americans or to the British? Alexander had made his legal career defending the property rights of ousted Loyalists. He was an immigrant from the British West Indies. The Hamilton family was Scottish. What if his own allegiances were in question?

By late spring, a new controversy gripped Congress—one that also had at its heart questions of money and power. Alexander once again was in the thick of it and drew political fire. Would Congress move to Baltimore or Philadelphia or remain in New York for the next session? More important, where would the nation's capital and the presidency be located? The decision was tied up with questions of public debt, and that led straight to the Treasury.

On Sunday, June 20, Alexander joined the politically influential James Madison and Thomas Jefferson for a small dinner at the latter's cramped bachelor pad at 57 Maiden Lane, in Manhattan, and over brandy, the three men hammered out a bargain. The horse-trading was less than entirely transparent. Alexander would support the capital moving south to what would become Washington, DC, if Madison would support public credit reform that Alexander believed was critical for the nation. Later, Alexander and the financier Robert Morris met, "as if by chance," on the Battery seawall, where there was a further agreement to propose Philadelphia as the capital for ten years and then a move southward. By the end of the summer, the location of the temporary capital and the permanent establishment in Washington were approved in Congress, along with the public credit measures, and Alexander once again celebrated a political victory.

A fresh wave of land speculation engulfed rural Maryland, the site of the future capital.

Eliza and Alexander were caught up in that postwar real estate craze as much as anyone. They were not rich, but Eliza's share of her mother's Van Rensselaer legacy especially included considerable property. Alexander—whose concerns for their personal finances were acute—noted in his account books that Eliza's property included more than a dozen farms in Saratoga, variously ranging from forty to 140 acres. Alexander was also swept up in the land-buying frenzy. He was one of a dozen or so speculators in the purchase of a large tract of land along the Saint Lawrence River, and his partners in the venture included Philip Schuyler, their old friends Henry Knox and Gouverneur Morris, and Peggy's husband, Stephen Van Rensselaer.

Owning and capitalizing on Eliza's farms would also get a bit trickier following one other important piece of legislation from the 1780s—the Pennsylvania Act for the Gradual Abolition of Slavery. Eliza understood immediately what the establishment of the new capital would mean: they would have to leave the house in New York and relocate to Philadelphia in the autumn. With them would go their property. But slaves arriving in Pennsylvania could be freed.

Alexander and many of the other men in his political milieu were members of "manumission" societies that advocated for the end of slavery in America. Most of those men, however, were also slaveholders. Eliza's father in 1790 owned thirteen enslaved people, and in early June two of them, Jacob and Cutt, were stirring up enough trouble on the estate that Philip Schuyler advised his wife, Kitty, "I believe it would be best to part with them, and if you approve of it I wish you to advertise them for sale and to get what you can for them." Eliza's brother John owned fourteen people, and Peggy and Stephen owned another dozen. Alexander and Eliza were not an exception. They owned both enslaved people and indentures.

Eliza listened to politics and followed the ins and outs as Alexander explained them in the evening before the late-spring fire. But her day-to-day life was consumed with caring for children and nursing sick family members. Everyone seemed to be ill in the spring and into summer of 1790. While the Senate was in session in New York, General Schuyler—a state representative—lived in town with Eliza's younger sister Cornelia, now fifteen and old enough to manage some housekeeping. When their father was struck with a high fever, Eliza and Cornelia spent several sleepless nights at his bedside.

Then one of the Hamilton household servants caught the yellow fever that was spreading up and down the seaboard that summer. In the small, hot attic bedroom of the Wall Street town house, the delirious servant vomited forth black bile in agony and died while Eliza watched, helpless and frightened. The toll it took on her was greater than she let on. Eliza was rattled. When Eliza succumbed herself at the end of July to chills and fevers of malaria, the household was in turmoil for weeks. Just as she was beginning to recover, her father succumbed to another infection, and she went back to late-night nursing.

It seemed to Eliza like an evil visitation by late summer. She tried to remember that resignation was her Christian duty. Philip Schuyler was still weak and bedridden when fresh disaster struck. The infant son of her brother John was also dying. Her father Philip composed a shaky letter to his wife explaining why he could not come to Albany to the deathbed of his small grandson. "Little as the prospect is that I should find My Dear Child Alive," he wrote, "I would set out immediately, but I am so weak that it is with difficulty I can write." By the time he was regaining strength and back in Albany, the baby had been buried. Even Alexander was suffering from kidney troubles, the result of his own untreated malaria. The infection would turn out to be chronic, and would trouble Alexander every autumn.

Manhattan itself was clearly part of the problem. The city was sticky and humid in the summer, and open sewers and rainwater sitting stagnant in barrels bred pestilence. The fearsome yellow fever was a modern plague in early America, and it hit New York City hard in the summer of 1790. Eliza's father said that everyone knew the island was a miasma, and he pressed her to bring the children to Albany for the summer to escape the fevers. "The accounts we have of the prevalence of the Yellow fever at N York and of its progress tho every part of the city," he wrote to her,

> have excited the most painful sensations, Citizens are quitting the city, to fly from the effects of this fatal disorder, and as yet I cannot learn that any preparations are making on your part to leave. . . . I have written to my Dear Hamilton, I have urged him not to remain, but with you, the Children & Family to come up, use all your influence my dear Children to prevail on his to accompany you.

But Alexander would not go. Government business consumed him. The work in the Treasury was too compelling, too important. And if Alexander would not go, neither would Eliza. She was determined for them not to be apart as a family. Too many times an absence of weeks turned into months, and Eliza hated the idea of being stuck alone again without Alexander in Albany. It brought back memories of the earliest years of their marriage. Memories came to her of waiting at the wharf and quarreling about letters.

While they stalled, the health of both suffered. Finally, during the first week of September, Alexander gave in to General Schuyler's demands and the dictates of reason and accepted that the city was simply too unsafe for the children. Eliza, he explained to her gently, would have to go up to Albany at least until the cold weather came in the end of October. He was her husband, and those were his wishes. He asked her obedience in this matter, and, by law and by custom, Eliza had no choice as a wife but to give it.

She did not, however, have to like it. When Eliza was angry, her voice grew quiet. She did not want the family separated. Alexander pressed, Eliza resisted, and they ultimately negotiated a marital bargain. Eliza would go as he asked, for the sake of the children, but Alexander promised he would immediately follow them. Eliza also stood firm on the backup plan. She placed a time limit on the end of their separation. If Alexander did not come to her in September, she was coming back to the city by the end of October.

And, as she had known would happen, Alexander did not arrive in Albany. Alexander hoped to travel up the following week for a monthlong vacation together. Politics kept interfering. Britain and Spain were on the brink of war, threatening to involve the United States in a new conflict, and the administration was shorthanded. What else could he do? he asked in his frequent letters. Eliza didn't argue, but she wasn't surprised either. Work sometimes seemed to be Alexander's greatest passion. Forced to choose, would he choose the Treasury or Eliza and the children? It hung a painful and unspoken question.

In Albany, there was one bright spot. Eliza took pleasure in reuniting Edward's orphan daughter, little Fanny Antill, with one of her older sisters. Eliza and Peggy sat in the parlor after dinner working on embroidery, just like old times, and laughed at the antics of the children. But three weeks at home was the limit of Eliza's patience, and she would draw that line brightly in summers afterward. Eliza fretted about Alexander alone in the city, not only about his health and safety from fevers but also about the rabid tone of politics and the cumbersome logistics of house moving. Her elderly parents, with their gout pains and her father's fussy military-style habits, also drove her a little bit crazy.

When October came, Alexander knew better than to protest. He encouraged her to stay in Albany longer, where the air was fresher, but he knew Eliza well enough to know she hated being hemmed in and for their family to be apart. "I leave the matter to yourself," he wrote. "If you feel anxious or uneasy you had better come down."

Coming down now meant to the new house that Alexander had rented for them all in the capital of Philadelphia. Eliza and the children arrived there in the first days of November, only a few days later than she had sworn to Alexander. She was a woman who prided herself on keeping a promise.

Home now was a three-story redbrick row house on 79 South Third Street in the nation's temporary capital, just around the corner from the grand mansions that ran along Walnut Street. Looking at the house with a domestic eye, Eliza despaired. It was light and airy, and that was the critical thing she appreciated in this swampy city. But it was also in urgent need of some redecorating. Angelica—how she missed her sister!—would have laughed at something so hopelessly unfashionable. Alexander's colleague and their friend in New York City, the merchant banker William Seton, went searching at Eliza's request for yards of imported French upholstery. There would need to be fresh drapes, fresh paint, and a careful scrub and polish.

It was an elite neighborhood, but Eliza was still as ambivalent as ever about her role as a leading society lady. She found hosting so many visitors during her at-home morning each week tedious and a bit exhausting. But she didn't want to embarrass Alexander. As a political power couple in the new capital, Alexander and Eliza quickly struck up friendships with other political couples who lived nearby, and they were caught up in the whirl of balls and dinners. Alexander was often the vivacious life of the party. They were soon socializing especially with Anne Bingham, whose husband, William, was, like Alexander, involved in government finances. Like Angelica, Anne was sophisticated, worldly, and passionate about politics, and her evening salons soon became the favorite meeting place of Alexander and his political compatriots.

Down the road from them on Third Street, south of the intersection with Walnut, was the large home of Benjamin Chew and his daughters. Alexander, enthusiastic as always in his attention to beautiful ladies, set tongues wagging again that autumn with his indiscretions. He pressed his flattery on one of the Chew daughters so passionately that people later said he had "designs" on the young woman's chastity. No one would quite say afterward exactly what happened, and the young lady and her father brushed it off as idle gallantry. But Alexander had unwisely given his political opponents more ammunition. They squirreled away this rumor, alongside the ones about his "incest" with Angelica and Peggy.

If Alexander's favorite retreat was the salon of Anne Bingham, Eliza felt most at home in the salon of Martha Washington. The company was glittering and the power brokers still came and went, but the first lady always gave Eliza a secret smile that said, one old friend to another, she would rather be sitting quietly with some embroidery and her husband. Eliza shared the sentiment wholeheartedly. "Do you live as pleasantly at Philadelphia as you did at New York?" Angelica asked Eliza in her letters. "Or are you obliged to bear the formalities of female circles, and their trifling chit chat? To you who have at home the most agreeable Society in the World, how you must smile at their manner of losing time."

Beyond the salons and political dinner parties, the gala balls and the morning visits that Eliza endured with all the good grace she could muster, there was the hustle and bustle of Philadelphia all around her. Philadelphia was the second-largest city in the nation, although its population was under thirty thousand. By modern standards, everything in America in the 1790s had a small-town feeling. Visitors to American cities remarked with astonishment on the feral pigs that ran wild in the streets, forcing parks to be fenced off to keep out the animals, and only a short walk from Eliza and Alexander's new town house the streets opened up to pasture. Merchant ships swept in and out of the city along the Delaware River, and a market arcade ran for nearly a mile up High Street. Prostitutes frequented the market in the area running west from Second Street and blithely approached gentlemen with offers. The penalty for the prostitute, if caught, was thirty days' hard labor. Not for the putative gentleman.

In January, the election results for Congress came in. Her father had run for reelection but had lost his seat to their old acquaintance

Aaron Burr, who was now part of a firm coalition, led by Eliza's distant cousin Chancellor Robert Livingston, ranged against Alexander and her family. The chancellor, passed over for lucrative appointments and his pride wounded regarding the posts that Alexander had helped to secure for his father-in-law and for John Jay, William Duer, James Duane, and Gouverneur Morris—all of whom were also Livingston, Van Rensselaer, or Schuyler relations by either blood or marriage—was fuming. Chancellor Livingston might have been forgiven for thinking that Alexander was lining the pockets of the chosen few but cutting out one branch of the family.

The politics were bruising and ugly, and the Livingston family was caught up in a minor civil war of its own by 1791. The feud undoubtedly fueled Chancellor Livingston's suspicions and enmity. Eliza's father was furious with the Livingston family at the upper manor house but was for the moment still speaking to the chancellor's branch at the lower manor, in a quarrel that tangled up property and local politics and encompassed not only the Livingston and Schuyler families but the neighboring DuBois, Van Rensselaer, and Van Cortlandt clans. Soon, this arcane web of family connections and grievances would be at the heart of a scandal that would test Eliza and her marriage and would shape the rest of her life with Alexander.

At the center of this web was William Duer, a consummate financial gamesman and market gambler. William was a slight, baby-faced man with a perennially boyish look, despite being nearly fifty, and, along with his socialite wife and Eliza's cousin Catherine, had a taste for the high life and for expensive fashion. Like Alexander, William had roots that sank deep into the plantations of the West Indies, and the two men bonded over that common connection. William was also an old family friend. He had been doing deals with Philip Schuyler, moving lumber up and down the Hudson, since the 1770s. Unfortunately, he had his fingers in all sorts of other deals, the riskier and more speculative the better.

William Duer belonged not only to the Federalist party—the

highly contentious party of which Alexander was the de facto intellectual leader—but he was the assistant secretary of Treasury, and those working to engineer all their fall from political grace were determined and far from subtle. "There is so much Rottenness," William Duer wrote to Alexander in mid-January of 1791, "that I know not who to trust."

Alexander's mistake was that he trusted William. Friends tried to warn Alexander. "The Chancellor [Robert Livingston] hates, & would destroy you," one friend wrote, adding that William Duer "is unfit as a Leader, & unpopular as a man, besides with all his address, he is duped by some Characters without ever suspecting it. . . . Mischief is intended, & may be effected." Alexander, supremely confident and loyal to a fault in his friendships, did not heed the warning.

At home, Eliza knew the storm was brewing, but she was helpless. All she could advise Alexander when he unburdened his worries was that he keep his wits about him. Otherwise, she had her hands full with the required rounds of social calls and morning visits and the health of their four children—Philip, Angelica, Alexander Jr., and James—and, the fifth, Eliza's special charge, Fanny Antill.

In January, a heat wave unexpectedly hit the city, and the temperature went up as high as the mid-seventies. Boys went swimming in the Delaware River, and for a month the unusual weather continued. It set off a particularly vicious outbreak of influenza that threatened to stall the government, and then in April the weather turned to rain, and there were new fears of miasma and malaria.

Eliza and their littlest boy, three-year-old James, got sick just as the worst of the fever season was starting. By mid-May, Eliza's father was pressing her and Alexander to come north again with the children to Albany for the season, before the worst summer fevers set in, and he offered to send a boat down to fetch them. "I fear," Philip Schuyler wrote of Eliza to Alexander, "that if she remains where she is until the hot weather commences that her health may be much injured."

Eliza again resisted, and until the end of June she remained at home in Philadelphia. In July, she relented. She and Alexander set off together with the children for a trip to New York City in July, planning to see their friends Rufus and Mary King. They stayed in the city for a few weeks, sorting out some logistics about houses and schools for the children, and were looking ahead to moving to a new rented house in Philadelphia in the autumn close to the president and Martha Washington. By the end of July, nine-year-old Philip Hamilton was safely settled into boarding school, and Alexander traveled alone back to the capital, where he wrote to Eliza on July 27 to say he was returned to "the hot City of Philadelphia; but in good health." "I have been to see your new house," he reported cheerfully, "& like it better than I expected to do. Twill soon be ready and I shall obey your orders about papering &c. Adieu My Precious Wife Blessings without number on you & my little ones."

Later, when the political and personal storm broke around them, all these details of where Eliza was and when would be cruelly dissected.

From Manhattan, Eliza traveled with the children the rest of the way upriver to Albany, and the family were immediately thrown into crisis when little James Hamilton fell dangerously ill, striking fear into the heart of both his parents. Alexander dashed off long letters advising cures of rhubarb wine and "barley water with a dash of brandy." After an anxious week, the toddler began to mend, and Eliza wanted to return home immediately. Alexander encouraged her to stay in Albany, but he also knew from long experience that living cheek by jowl with her parents made Eliza restless and irritable. Philip Schuyler, a general and a man used to having his orders followed, could be imperious and insisted on a household regulated according to his preferences. "I am myself in good health but I cannot be happy without you," Alexander wrote to Eliza on August 9. "Yet I must not advise you to urge your return."

Eliza, quiet but strong-willed, insisted that twenty days in Albany was sufficient. It wasn't just Albany and her father—Eliza was frantic and had a terrible sense of foreboding. She wanted to come home. "Dear Betsey—beloved Betsey—Take care of yourself," Alexander pleaded. "Be attentive to yourself . . . But I charge you (unless you are so anxious as to injure you, or unless you find your health declining more) not to precipitate your return." Undeterred, Eliza made plans to avoid traveling through New York City and to come down instead at the end of the month with the children and Peggy through New Jersey, stopping for a few days at the house of some friends from their days at the winter camp in Morristown, where they would see their Livingston cousins.

On August 21, as Eliza was preparing to set off back to Philadelphia, where a yellow fever epidemic was raging, Alexander tried once more, writing, "my extreme anxiety for the restoration of your health will reconcile me to your staying longer where you are upon condition that you really receive benefit from it, and that your own mind is at ease." Eliza's mind, however, was not at ease. What was this source of Eliza's fear and foreboding in the summer of 1791? She was a tough-minded, practical, and loyal woman, in every respect like her mother, Kitty Schuyler, in courage and independence. But something had her in a panic.

Did Eliza already know that Alexander had that spring met another of her distant Livingston cousins, Maria Reynolds? If so, Eliza was right to sense danger. What happened next would change everything in her life and in her marriage and would force Eliza into making an agonizing decision.

Eliza would learn the truth sooner than she could imagine.

CHAPTER 12

The Affair, 1791–92

The idyll lasted only until just before Christmas.

Peggy traveled down to Philadelphia with Eliza and the children at the end of the summer and promptly threw herself into socializing and shopping. Peggy was delighted to take charge of re-decorating Eliza and Alexander's new rented house, and Eliza was delighted to have the company. Peggy had brought with her, as a playmate for the Hamilton cousins and Fanny Antill, her sturdy two-year-old little boy, named Stephen after his lost infant brother and his father, and Martha and George Washington, now immediate neighbors, were raising two of their young grandchildren, Nelly and Wash, who were the same ages as some of Eliza's brood.

Back home, Eliza relaxed. She remembered that autumn afterward as one of her happiest times as a mother. There were daily playdates with the Washington family, and the children were in and out of both homes constantly. Twice a week, the president's elegant carriage stopped in the lane and four of the youngsters—Angelica, Fanny, Nelly, and Wash—rolled off to dancing lessons under the kindly eye of Martha Washington. In the afternoons, when he wanted some peace and quiet, George Washington came to sit in Eliza's parlor and read the newspaper or watch the children play. The president appreciated that Eliza was a woman who did not need always to chatter. The first lady gave Fanny, who was learning to sew, the scraps of a silk petticoat to make into a pincushion, and Fanny remembered later how "once, on a reception evening, when the drawing-room in [the president's] house was filled with ladies and gentlemen, talking and laughing, and the children were amusing themselves in a corner, there was a sudden great stillness." The children had found a nook behind a folding screen, and George Washington with a sly smile and a finger to his lips ducked out of the social melee to join the children behind it.

Peggy stayed in Philadelphia for several weeks, until her husband, the patroon, traveled down to fetch her, and for the better part of the week of Stephen's visit there were lively dinner parties and long nights when Stephen and Alexander talked business over Madeira. Eliza and Peggy knew, if not all the details, the broad outlines of the two men's investment projects and the headaches they occasioned, and Eliza was already pressing Alexander to step back from politics. She dreamed of a move abroad, where they could be near John and Angelica, though she knew it was an idle fantasy. After Peggy and Stephen left, Eliza wrote to Angelica in a chatty, wry note, reporting,

> We have just taken house in Markett Street nearly opposet the President who you know lives in Robert Morris house. I delivered your compliments as you wished to Mrs Washington who received them affectionately and made many enquirys after you. Peggy has just left this city with Mr. Rensselear having spent three weeks with us she is in good health and spirits but bears no marks of usefulness to the Commonwealth. I also continue Idle. but pray my Lady what are you a bout all this time with your grave enquierys about the success of your Sisters Labours? My Hamilton and I often talk a bout you with great pleasure and earnestly wish that you could again be aded to our little circle but we dare scarcely hope for so great a happiness. We will not however despair of meeting again on one or the other side of the Atlantic.

As Eliza confided to her sister, she was working hard behind the scenes to persuade Alexander to move on from his role in the cabi-

net. Enough of politics and all the nasty business of it. She and Angelica shared the idea that diplomatic work would be the best fit for
both Alexander and their father. Being useful to the republic mattered to Eliza, and she wanted that for Alexander. She grew up in a
family committed to the American project and its independence. At
army camps and in the raids on her family's home and the efforts to
murder and kidnap her father, she had witnessed the sacrifices it had
taken. She was no fan of the capital, however.

If Eliza had a blind spot, it was also that, as a member of a powerful and deeply intertwined and interrelated patrician class, she had
trouble imagining a world in which her family, understood broadly,
did not operate the levers of power or turn the markets to their
wealth and advantage, despite the fact that in 1791 and into 1792 finances were chronically tighter than Alexander wished. Alexander
and Philip Schuyler and the men in the extended network of families Eliza called kin and cousins were waging a pitched battle for the
future of the nation, and Eliza didn't doubt for a moment that they
were meant to lead it.

When the Reynolds scandal broke a little more than a year later,
Eliza would view what came next through that prism.

What happened was a slow-breaking scandal that washed over a bitterly partisan city and swept all the major players up in it. Maria
Reynolds was at the heart of it.

The story as everyone knows it goes something like this: in the
summer of 1791, with Eliza in Albany with the children, Alexander carried on an illicit affair with a young woman named Maria
Reynolds, whom he had been bedding since springtime. When her
husband, James Reynolds, learned of the infidelity, he turned to
blackmail, threatened to tell Eliza, and extracted more than a thousand dollars in hush money from a panicked Alexander. Perhaps
blackmail had always been the couple's plan. Alexander claimed as
much later. Perhaps some of his political opponents were behind

Maria Reynolds's bold propositioning of the secretary of Treasury on his own doorstep. At any rate, Alexander soon discovered that his mistress was a bit unhinged, writing hysterical letters, and that her husband was an extortionist.

From there, so the accepted history goes, things came to a head in the late autumn of 1792, a year later, when some members of Congress got wind of the financial payments and accused Alexander of insider trading with James Reynolds. Forced to come clean, Alexander confessed his affair in a private meeting with other politicians, broke off his torturous liaison with Maria Reynolds, and for several years more, that was the end of the matter—until the story was leaked to a muckraking journalist. When the tale ultimately appeared in the newspapers, Alexander unwisely published a confession, in which he offered blow-by-blow details of the affair, including the fact that he'd brought Maria into Eliza's bedroom, humiliating his wife in the national press and striking a mortal blow to his reputation.

But what if that familiar story is a fiction? What if it was nothing more than a desperate public spin on a far more complicated and troublesome private and political backstory? What if sex was a cover-up for power and money? That is what Alexander's political enemies believed, and it is what Maria Reynolds always insisted.

What if it was all a story, and Eliza also knew it?

The other story goes like this, and it is a story that starts not with sex but with money.

By the spring of 1791, allegations—some public, most whispered—that Alexander Hamilton was not playing fair in the Treasury were reaching a crisis point in the capital.

They were not new accusations. Eliza was not deaf to political chatter. She knew as well as anyone who could read the newspaper that the attacks on Alexander increasingly focused on charges of financial impropriety. Congressman William Maclay was not the only person who looked askance at a number of investments by Eliza's family and members of their inner circle and at Alexander's role in the Treasury.

Money was being made, hand over fist, by many of the men in their social circle—and by some of the men in Eliza's family—who were gambling with debt in a wild, exuberant bubble.

The unseemly financial speculation in 1790 had put Alexander at risk. The speculation in 1791 was even worse and the appearances far more damaging. Philip Schuyler; John Church; John's business partner, Jeremiah Wadsworth; William Duer; Gouverneur Morris; Robert Morris; Eliza and Alexander's friend William Bingham; and both Peggy's patroon, Stephen, and his brother, Philip Van Rensselaer, were all playing the markets aggressively and trading in government securities and speculating on real estate development.

Eliza's father liquidated $67,000 worth of securities, pocketing something over $1.5 million by today's values and significantly easing the financial worries that had rattled Angelica. These were securities, however, that Alexander in his capacity as secretary of Treasury was privy to information and action regarding. The appearances were damning.

Philip Schuyler's windfall was small change compared to what John Church and Angelica made during the frenzy. Foolishly, Alexander, as John's attorney and agent, had still not fully stepped back from executing for his brother-in-law a number of those transactions. This would be no less scandalous today than in the 1790s. The secretary of Treasury was making trades for a family member in a market he regulated.

Then there were all the shady land deals. Wild speculation, driven by decisions being made in the administration and in the Treasury office, was driving up the price of real estate and set off an investor frenzy. John Church, Philip Schuyler, and Alexander were among a group of investors purchasing tens of thousands of acres at below-market prices artificially reduced by New York State land commissioners.

But the nail in the coffin was William Duer. Alexander's assistant secretary was handing out favors and manipulating army supply contracts with such flagrant abandon that he earned the dubious honor of sparking the first congressional inquiry into government corruption in American history. He was guilty. There was insider trading. Only Duer's resignation in disgrace from the Treasury that spring prevented his prosecution. The political damage to Alexander was devastating. It all smacked of family ties and conflicting interests.

Alexander then compounded his already bad judgment; feeling sorry for William and Catherine Duer, he threw his disgraced assistant secretary a bone. William Duer landed the appointment as governor of an influential manufacturing investment group, of which Alexander was a founder. Things went from worse to disastrous. William, an inveterate crook, promptly returned the favor by destroying Alexander's reputation further. He started a scheme to run up the value of stock options in the Bank of the United States—the federal bank that was Alexander's signature accomplishment. The stock option went crazy. Alexander, as the secretary of Treasury, had a bubble on his hands, one that was capable of bringing down the central bank and the national economy should it burst. By August—when Eliza was in Albany and in a panic—$25 worth of script was selling on the derivatives market for nearly $300, and, to Alexander's horror, people just kept buying. Not just rich people. Shopkeepers and small holders. He intervened aggressively, working with his and Eliza's friend William Seton in New York City, to use the banks to deflate the bubble, and for the moment economic disaster was averted.

But the blow to Alexander's reputation fell hard. What Alexander did not know yet but would discover soon enough was that, to persuade wary buyers that this was a guaranteed safe investment and to keep driving up the resale prices, William Duer bragged that he had the inside track directly from the man who managed the country's finances.

The chorus of voices—in Congress, in the city, in the papers—saying Alexander Hamilton was trading insider information to benefit his wife's family was growing stronger and louder.

Eliza was beside herself. She pressed Alexander to resign.

By November 1791, even Alexander was persuaded that his position in the Treasury came at too high a cost to his family. Eliza was a nervous wreck and foresaw terrible things coming. She exercised a powerful influence over the situation. Alexander's first obligation was to his family, whose own finances were far from stable, and, if Alexander would walk away from the Treasury, Eliza was prepared to be very flexible about the new situation. She now threw her weight behind a plan for all of them to move to Britain, preferably in a diplomatic position. "Betsey has lately given me stronger proof than she ever did before of her attachment to you," Alexander wrote to Angelica on the first of the month. "Things are tending fast to a point, which will enable me honorably to retreat from a situation in which I make the greatest possible sacrifices to a little empty praise, or if you like the turn better, to a disposition to make others happy. But this disposition must have its limits. Will you be glad to see us in Europe? For you will never come to America."

Their nine-year-old son Philip returned home from boarding school in New Jersey in late December, and Eliza busied herself with hunting down Latin textbooks and some fancy embroidery. As far away as London, Angelica heard reports that "our dear Hamilton writes too much and takes no exercise and grows too fat," she teased her sister.

A solution seemed so near now. Eliza felt confident that the hard part was almost over.

The last few weeks of 1791 were far too brief a reprieve before the *annus horribilis* of 1792. And Eliza's hopes were a delusion.

In January 1792, the next financial scandal broke. People were just realizing that a small group of investors, led by two real estate developers named Alexander Macomb and William Constable, along with William Duer, had pulled off a massive land grab at discounted prices. The primary beneficiaries were members of Eliza's extended family and Alexander's political party. Congressmen in the opposition fumed. The secretary of Treasury had his hand on the scale and was enriching his relatives, they protested furiously. Alexander would have done well to have taken his own advice, offered to a friend in 1789, that "suspicion is ever eagle-eyed. And the most innocent things may be misinterpreted."

William Duer "will speculate on you," William Constable realized by spring, "and after leading you into all the risque He will reap the profit." But it was too late for the ringleaders. They were overextended. To save their skins, they came up with a plan to run up the shares in the manufacturing group to make ends meet on their other obligations. William Constable strategically shorted the stock, but the stock went wild with the pumping, setting off a second mania of credulous investors eager to jump in on the bubble. For Alexander, who had thrown his weight behind the society, the political appearances were devastating.

There was a vicious game afoot, and Alexander's enemies among the Livingston clan saw blood in the water. Seeing the run-up as profiteering and relishing the idea of punishing the investors, they exercised their considerable financial clout; started pulling cash out of the banks, setting off a credit crunch; and did their level best to tank the stock. Down it tumbled.

The Panic of 1792 exploded on Alexander in March and ended with riots in the streets. William Duer was short nearly $300,000—something upwards of $7 million today—to meet demands and begged Alexander to intervene to save him.

This time Alexander refused.

When Duer failed, he took down with him not only Alexander Macomb, who was upside down to the tune of a half a million, but also Walter Livingston, the husband of Eliza's cousin Cornelia Schuyler, the daughter of Aunt Gertrude. Within weeks, all three men were locked away in debtors' prison. Eliza remembered the conditions there with horror. This time was worse for the prisoners. Mobs of furious investors stormed the jail and threatened to burn it down, with William Duer and Alexander Macomb in it. They were spared immolation, but Duer would die in debtors' prison seven years later. Gone were Catherine Duer's days of flaunting an aristocratic lifestyle. Eliza's heart went out to her.

But mostly, she worried about Alexander and money. Eliza was the family bookkeeper. Their old friend Mac wrote to Alexander affectionately in 1791, "I have learned from a friend of yours that [Eliza] has as far as the comparison will hold as much merit as your treasurer as you have as treasurer of the wealth of the United States." She knew what happened to every penny. And the budget at home was tighter than usual. Where were hundreds of dollars disappearing to? If she suspected, Eliza said nothing. But she already knew that she would do anything to prevent someone she loved from ending up bankrupt and in prison.

What kind of losses Philip Schuyler, John Church, the patroon's brother Philip Van Rensselaer, and perhaps even Alexander suffered in the rout is unclear. But land values plummeted by two-thirds, and the four cannot have fared well on those investments. Many of the letters among these men from this period did not survive. That was probably not an accident.

The fallout and recrimination went on for months. Alexander's archrival, Thomas Jefferson, did little to hide his disdain. Colonel Hamilton, Jefferson fumed to the president in the late summer of 1792, was "a man whose history, from the moment at which history can stoop to notice him, is a tissue of machinations against the liberty of the country," a man who had been "dealing out of Treasury-secrets among his friends in what time and measure he pleases."

That was the first act. The second act in this tawdry drama didn't unfold until late autumn, and Eliza had every reason to curse William Duer all over again. And perhaps, also, Alexander.

Alexander was working in the Treasury on a plan to cash out at face value some long-delayed notes offered to veterans of the Revolutionary War, as part of the process of tidying up loose ends in the new republic. Many veterans and their families continued to dump the notes on a secondary investment market for deep discounts, and if the deal went ahead, anyone who bought notes at less than face value before the news broke stood to make a tidy fortune. It was a classic setup for insider trading.

Before his stock market bubble had gone bust and he'd ended up in debtors' prison, William Duer, using insider knowledge, had leaked word to a small group of investors. Among those who raked in the profits were John Church's business partner, Jeremiah Wadsworth; a number of the men in Eliza's extended family; and some shady characters named Jacob Clingman and James Reynolds. Alexander looked the other direction.

All the evidence suggests that sometime in the spring of 1791—when the familiar story says the affair started—Alexander also asked James Reynolds to buy some of the notes, a couple of hundred dollars at a time and off the record, for his personal portfolio. Around him, the men in the extended Schuyler family were getting rich and could sleep easy at night knowing they had financial security for their families. Alexander alone was barred from taking advantage of the greatest wealth-building opportunity of the century. It was a mighty temptation.

The scandal broke a year after the fact, in the autumn of 1792, just as Alexander and Eliza were celebrating the arrival at the end of August of a fifth child, a boy named John Church Hamilton, after Angelica's husband.

The pieces started tumbling down when James Reynolds was arrested on charges of defrauding war veterans with this pension-buyback scheme. His business partner, Jacob Clingman, got hauled in next, and from his prison cell offered a deal: his freedom in exchange for proof that Alexander Hamilton was engaged in illegal financial speculation.

Word of this extraordinary claim—so long bandied about in the press and in Congress but never proven—made its way up the ranks in Congress until it reached the Speaker of the House of Representatives, Frederick Muhlenberg, who owned the firm where Jacob Clingman worked. Speaker Muhlenberg, on the other side of the aisle from Alexander and the Federalists, found this very interesting. He quickly pulled in three colleagues—Congressman James Monroe, Congressman Abraham Venable, and Senator Aaron Burr—and suddenly Alexander Hamilton was under de facto investigation by some of his fiercest opponents, who planned to turn evidence over to President Washington.

The trail that they hoped would at last indict Alexander Hamilton led them straight to James Reynolds.

Jacob Clingman's claims, if true, were stunning. Sometime in early 1791, he claimed that he had been surprised to encounter Alexander Hamilton at the home of his business associate, James Reynolds. He was even more surprised when this event was repeated in coming weeks. On one occasion, he said in a sworn statement, he witnessed packets being exchanged and delivered.

Curious, Jacob Clingman suspected game was afoot. He asked James Reynolds and his pretty young wife, Maria, what was the nature of the business. Maria confided that Alexander Hamilton and her husband had been doing business for several months already and that so far Alexander had recently given James more than a thousand dollars. She believed they were speculating.

James Reynolds was more confiding yet. He told Jacob Clingman, "in confidence, that if [William] Duer had held up three days longer [in the financial panic], he should have made fifteen hundred pounds, by the assistance of Col. Hamilton: that Col. Hamilton had informed him that he was connected with Duer. Mr. Reynolds also said, that Col. Hamilton had made thirty thousand dollars by speculation; that Col. Hamilton had supplied him with money to speculate." Most damaging of all for Alexander, "Mr. Reynolds has once or twice mentioned," Jacob Clingman reported to the assembled congressmen, "that he had it in his power to hang Col. Hamilton."

That got the congressmen moving.

They set off to interview James Reynolds at once. Finding the twenty-two-year-old Maria Reynolds alone in her parlor and her husband out, they pumped the young woman for information. Maria revealed that Alexander Hamilton and Jeremiah Wadsworth—James Reynolds's wartime employer, John Church's wartime business partner—had come to visit earlier that day. Alexander, Maria fretfully reported, had urged James to leave the house quickly. At Alexander's request, she also confessed that she had "burned a considerable number of letters from him to her husband . . . touching business between them, to prevent their being made public." But she had not burned quite everything. Maria, frightened and pressured, offered the investigators now several letters, in a disguised handwriting, which she claimed were from Alexander to her husband and proved that Alexander was giving James money.

It did not escape anyone's notice, either, that Alexander Hamilton didn't just have a family "connection" to William Duer, as James Reynolds had boasted. Alexander also had a family connection to Mrs. Reynolds. Maria Reynolds, the sister-in-law of Gilbert Livingston, was Eliza's third cousin. The proximate relations of all involved lent a certain credibility to the story.

Armed with this testimony—and more—the congressmen laid out the charges and demanded a meeting with Alexander Hamilton in hopes of obtaining an explanation.

On the morning of December 15, 1792, at dawn, Alexander was at home and frantic. Eliza could hear the incessant creak of the floorboards as he paced up and down the parlor. When James Reynolds arrived on a stealth morning visit near the seven o'clock hour, Alexander was striking his head with his fists in anguish. The visit was short, and what happened in the course of it was something the congressmen later very much thought needed a better explanation, because by afternoon, James Reynolds had completely vanished. Eliza also spent the day anxiously wondering.

When Alexander strode out of the house that Saturday morning less than an hour later, he was calm and confident again. When his inquisitors arrived at Alexander's professional office at 8 a.m., he was relaxed and jocular. Accusations were leveled. Alexander's indignant denial followed. There was no financial speculation, he informed his inquisitors. He was simply having an affair with Mrs. Reynolds and her husband was a vile blackmailer. The story seemed remarkably convenient, but Alexander insisted he had proof in the form of love letters and demands for payment. He invited the skeptical congressmen and senator to meet again at the Hamilton home that evening, if they wanted, and Alexander would show them the evidence.

What happened in the next twelve hours that followed is the mystery at the heart of Eliza Hamilton's extraordinary story.

By the time dusk fell, Alexander was ready to meet his opponents. Eliza did not stay for the conversation. Whether he took her into his confidence now or whether that happened later, Eliza never said, and she went to lengths later to disappear from this story. But, all things considered, the probability is that Alexander told Eliza some substantial part of his troubles. A man who intends to keep a secret from his wife doesn't invite his accusers to meet in his family living room on a Saturday evening.

What is certain is that Alexander went alone into the parlor with his interrogators and political enemies and laid out in front of them some handwritten letters and receipts said to be from Maria and James Reynolds. The letters were probably forged. The troublesome receipts were undoubtedly authentic. It would have made no sense to fabricate them, since their existence was the largest part of Alexander's dilemma. The legislators blushed and rose, professed themselves content as gentlemen, and departed.

And that, Alexander thought, was surely the end of that problem. He went away cheerful.

James Monroe, however, was convinced that Alexander was lying. The next day, James Monroe recorded a memorandum of the conversation, writing:

> *Last night we waited on Colo. H. when he informed us
> of a particular connection with Mrs. R.—the period of its
> commencement and circumstances attending it . . . the
> frequent supplies of money to her and her husband and on
> that account. . . . To support this, he shewed a great number
> of letters from Reynolds and herself, commencing early in
> 1791.—He acknowledged all the letters . . . in our possession,
> to be his. We left him under an impression our suspicions were
> removed.*

But they were not removed. Quite the contrary. The worst was still ahead for Alexander and, especially, Eliza.

Within days, the gossip was all over the capital. Thomas Jefferson's journal entry that Monday makes clear that he and another half-dozen congressmen had heard the story of Alexander Hamilton's confessed infidelity.

Jacob Clingman broke the news to Maria. The horrified young lady steadfastly denied having any affair with Alexander Hamilton and burst into tears at hearing the story. Jacob reported this new conversation to James Monroe, also, who added a new note to the bottom of his minutes. "Mrs. Reynolds," the note recorded,

> *appeared much shocked at it and wept immoderately—That
> she denied the imputation and declared that it had been a
> fabrication of colonel Hamilton and that her husband had
> joined in it, who had told her so, and that he had given
> him receipts for money and written letters, so as to give the
> countenance to the pretence.*

Maria Reynolds claimed she was the victim of a tawdry cover story—one set up by the two men to save their hides but that would ruin forever her reputation.

Who was telling the truth, Alexander Hamilton or Maria Reynolds? At least three congressmen in 1792—and James Monroe especially—did not believe Alexander.

It is not difficult to see why they were suspicious. On the face of it, the tale seemed ripped from an eighteenth-century epistolary novel, with an even flimsier premise.

The story that Alexander told that Saturday night at home was tawdry and salacious. He claimed that Maria Reynolds had turned up on his family doorstep in the spring of 1791, a "Beauty in Distress," and announced her family connection to Eliza. Alexander expected them to believe that, with his wife and children at home at the time, he came to the instant conclusion that this young lady was offering herself as a prostitute and rushed her off the property, money in his pocket, to see if he could turn her distress to sexual advantage.

And Alexander did all of this knowing that the young woman had a Livingston connection, despite being in a political struggle to the death with Chancellor Robert Livingston, and having been warned of what everyone in Congress took as a given: "The Chancellor hates, & would destroy you."

If the story were true, there was no conclusion except that Alexander Hamilton was the most debased of men, a creature of his sexual appetites, unthinking, unstrategic, and hopelessly foolish. James Monroe was perfectly prepared to accept the first two conclusions. But Alexander Hamilton was not unthinking, unstrategic, or foolish.

James Monroe also thought there was something that did not add up about the letters Alexander had shown them. Was it not possible that someone else—Alexander himself—had written them? Something didn't strike the right note. They were sentimental, lovestruck, hysterical, melodramatic. They bore more than a passing resemblance to the kind of letters one read in something like Samuel Richardson's best-selling epistolary novel from the 1740s, *Pamela*.

Richardson's celebrated heroine proclaimed, in hundreds of letters after a pattern, sentiments along the lines of "Never was poor Creature so unhappy, and so barbarously used, as poor Pamela! . . . To whom but you can I vent my Griefs, and keep my poor Heart from bursting! Wicked, wicked Man!—I have no Patience left me!—But yet, don't be frighted—for—I hope—I hope, I am honest!?"

In the spirit of Pamela, Maria Reynolds's letters were full of the same sentiments. "Alas my friend," went one epistle,

> want want what [I] can ask for but peace wich you alone can restore to my tortured bosom and do My dear Col hamilton on my kneese Let me Intreatee you to reade my Letter. . . . oh I am disstressed more than I can tell My heart Is ready to burst and my tears wich once could flow with Ease are now denied me Could I only weep I would thank heaven.

Mrs. Reynolds could have simply been a fan of novels. But in that case, why was her spelling so unusual? Did James Monroe note the curious fact that Maria could spell difficult words correctly but sometimes misspelled the easiest of words in ways that did not seem phonetic, and that she did even that erratically?

But perhaps what moved him most was the simple fact that Maria Reynolds steadfastly and tearfully denied having any affair with Alexander. Those were not the words of a woman wildly in love. And a woman wildly in love was what the letters suggested. James Monroe mulled and considered. Then he took out his notes and added another sentence. Maria Reynolds, in his view, "was innocent and . . . the defense was an imposition."

The only question now was whether Alexander Hamilton had forged the letters of Maria Reynolds and fabricated the story of his infidelity in order to divert attention from a financial scandal. Monroe thought he also already knew the answer.

He took the notes and folded them carefully away. His thoughts were his own, for the moment. It was wisest to see how things transpired.

But the congressmen talked. The story of Hamilton's raunchy affair and blackmail was just too interesting to keep entirely secret. All of Congress knew the rumors that Alexander had confessed to infidelity before Christmas. That included the men in Eliza's family. On Tuesday, as the fallout spread, Alexander wrote to John Jay, the husband of Eliza's cousin Sarah, "Tis the malicious intrigues to stab me in the dark, against which I am too often obliged to guard myself, that distract and harrass me to a point, which rendering my situation scarcely tolerable." Eliza's father and her brother-in-law Stephen Van Rensselaer inevitably heard the rumors, and so, possibly, did her mother and Peggy. Along with William Duer and John Church, they were all in the thick of the financial speculation markets and at risk from the financial scandal that threatened to consume Alexander. If Alexander went down, the finances of a number of men in Eliza's extended family would be affected.

None of these men would have shared the information with Eliza directly, however. To do so would have been a breach of gentlemanly conduct. And if Peggy or her mother learned of it, they would never have spoken of the scandal. But the story quickly reached the fashionable ladies' circles in New York and Philadelphia. It unleashed a torrent of gossip, in which Alexander was now charged with other sexual improprieties. It was Eliza, though, who bore the brunt of the snide, sideways comments.

Alexander was accused of "designs . . . on the chastity of Mrs. [Tobias] Lear," the wife of President Washington's personal secretary, and of a fit of passion for "a Daughter of Judge [Benjamin] Chew." The rumor spread—still repeated years later by no less than John Adams—that Eliza's cousin Sarah Livingston Jay told a story of how Alexander

contrived to get into Mrs. Jay's bedchamber. On meeting her, he
seized and caressed her, and entreated her compliance with his
desires—That she indignantly broke away from him, and fled,
with a complaint . . . to her husband—That Mr. Jay considered
Hamilton as of importance in a political view, and suppressed
his resentment, but exhorted his wife to beware of an exposure to
him for the future.

Sarah Jay reportedly repeated the story in a letter to one of her sisters—and the choices there were either Eliza's cousin Susan or her oldest friend and confidante, cousin Kitty. Eliza sat politely in Sarah's front parlor on social calls, suffering in silence.

What did Eliza know about the truth and when did she know it? How much did she know in 1792 and how much did she learn later, when the story broke in the papers? There is no way to answer that question for certain, in large part because Eliza and her family destroyed the letters that held the answers.

What do survive of the record, however, are letters that point to the tone and tenor of Eliza and Alexander's marriage. In the summer of 1791 and into 1792, Eliza was deeply and uncharacteristically anxious. She knew a storm was brewing. She knew there were charges that Alexander was abusing his position in the Treasury, and she knew that the men in her family were gamblers in the financial market. She was the household treasurer, and letters from her father and her brothers all point to Alexander trusting Eliza throughout their marriage not only with the secret of his anonymous political writings but with complex financial information. He praised above all her "unpretending good sense," and good sense was sorely needed.

At some point, Eliza became aware of charges that the letters and the affair with Maria Reynolds were fabrications. At the very latest, she learned it in the press in 1799, when the story became public.

But all the unspoken signs in Alexander and Eliza's letters and in the shape of their marriage point to Eliza learning of the storm breaking over them from Alexander and probably as early as December of 1792, on the afternoon he was at home forging the letters.

It is all too easy to imagine the scenario. Alexander was distressed. Eliza wanted to know what was happening. After James Reynolds slipped away early that December morning, having agreed to Alexander's cover story and disappearing, did Alexander make his bitter confession? Since the first days of the courtship, he had worried: would Eliza love him as a poor man? He did not doubt Eliza, but it was a matter of pride for a man. He wanted success; he wanted an easy life for Eliza and the children. He had wanted to help, too, the husbands of Angelica and Peggy, Eliza's father, her family. He had foolishly gambled. Eliza's greatest fear was not the loss of face; it was debtors' prison.

So Alexander had manufactured a solution.

Alexander said to Eliza in that early love letter, "It remains with you to show whether you are a Roman or an American wife," and it was the Roman wife whom Alexander was praising. He had asked Eliza whether she was prepared for the self-sacrifice and loyalty that building a republic would require. He asked that loyalty of her now. But Alexander never believed that story would become public. He had, as yet, no idea what he was asking, and neither did Eliza. He was confident that the story would remain private talk among the congressmen. That was the code of conduct for gentlemen. There would be a bit of gossip for a season, but people already said he was a scoundrel. It was hard to see the damage. Would Eliza be able to endure it?

Eliza never hesitated. Here was a role for her of national importance. If a scandal engulfed Alexander and the Treasury, it would not only bring disgrace and private sorrow, it would jeopardize the Federalists and the Washington administration. And here was the moment for the Roman wife to prove herself. Here was the moment for the nut-brown maid to live the refrain that said, if "you were with enemies day and night, I would withstand . . . and you to save . . . for, in my mind, of all mankind I love but you alone."

Yes, she would show him. Eliza's trust in Alexander and in their marriage was unshakable. He asked. She promised. She would take the secret to the grave with her.

Eliza Hamilton was not a woman who broke her promises.

CHAPTER 13

Reprieve, 1793–95

Alexander's ruse worked.

By the spring of 1793, the storm had passed. The congressmen had come and seen what Alexander said were Maria Reynolds's love letters, and, while the legislators had their doubts, the ongoing investigation shifted into a lower register. The gossip dwindled. Alexander's reputation had been tainted by the whispers among the men of Congress and such of the political wives who heard it, but theirs was a small, closed circle. Eliza bore the hints and sympathy stoically. Alexander was tender and solicitous of how much the sacrifice wore on her, and their marriage was stronger and closer than ever.

Maria Reynolds, stung by her husband's betrayal, hired, of all people, Aaron Burr as an attorney and filed for divorce from James Reynolds. Alexander's political enemies quietly tracked those proceedings and tucked away damaging bits of information. As one watching the divorce appeal to the courts noted, "Clingman [reports] that Mrs. Reynolds has obtained a divorce from her husband, in consequence of his intrigue with Hamilton to her prejudice, and that Colonel Burr obtained it for her: he adds too, that she is thoroughly disposed to attest all she knows of the connection between Hamilton and Reynolds." Aaron Burr's role in keeping the scandal and danger alive would not endear him to Alexander.

Eliza didn't go out as much anymore, disdaining high society more than ever. Martha Washington, observing this in her usual eagle-eyed way, invited Eliza out on her social rounds under her considerable protection. Martha certainly knew the gossip that was circulating and had no reason to doubt that Alexander was cheating on his wife. Martha felt protective of Eliza. "Mrs Washington sends her Love to Mrs Hamilton," Martha wrote in one early morning note. "She intends visiting Mrs Peters this fore noon, if it is agreeable to Mrs H to go with her she will be happy to have company." When Alexander fell ill, Martha Washington sent over some special bottles of Madeira as a get-well present, and wrote to Eliza, "I am truly glad my Dear Madam to hear Colo. Hamilton is better to day. You have my prayers and warmest wishes for his recovery. I hope you take care of yourself as you know it is necessary for your family," signing off, "your Very affectionate Friend M. Washington."

Eliza also relied, as always, on Angelica. In chatty letters, the sisters swapped news of family weddings, fashion, and politics. Their youngest brother, Rensselaer, married Elizabeth Ten Broeck, the daughter of her father's oldest friend, and Angelica teasingly wrote of their new sister, "I pray she may be handsome, for the sake of my nephews and niece who are to be Schuylers." Angelica was less lighthearted about the political news from Europe. The French Revolution, under way since 1789, was giving way to the violence of the radical "Jacobins" and to the executions known as "the Terror." The violence threatened to draw the Americans into the conflict: ten thousand people marched in the streets of Philadelphia, insisting that President Washington "declare war in favor of the French Revolution."

Eliza would never have trusted any secret to a letter. Letters passed between too many hands, over too many miles, to ever be considered private. But Angelica heard news of the attacks on Alexander in London all the same, and wrote to Eliza, "I hear the Jacobins have made a attack at home, but that [Alexander] defended himself. . . . Do pray tell me all these affairs." John Church knew from Jeremiah Wadsworth and Gouverneur Morris the gossip and at least part of the backstory. It is not impossible, given the odd involvement of Jeremiah Wadsworth in the efforts to hush up James Reynolds, that John Church was one of the people Alexander was protecting. John may not have said as much to Angelica, but he certainly would have shared with her the rumors of a liaison. Eliza confessed weariness to her sister, but all she would say further was that she blamed Alexander's political enemies for everything.

In public, Eliza stood fast. In private, she was out of patience with the entire political situation and with the risks to Alexander's reputation and to their family. Behind the scenes, Eliza pressed Alexander. It was time to end this. It was too dangerous, too burdensome, Eliza insisted. Although the gossip was beginning to abate by springtime, the investigation in Congress simmered and widened to include complex financial investigations into Alexander's dealings. The matter of James Reynolds, which until now had remained within Congress, threatened to reignite at any moment, and Eliza could see only one path to safety. Alexander needed to walk away. That was their bargain.

And Alexander did that springtime. In June, he offered George Washington his resignation from the Treasury, effective from the end of the term in Congress, so that it did not appear he was trying to sidestep the ongoing investigation. "Considerations, relative both to the public Interest and to my own delicacy, have brought me," he wrote, "after mature reflection, to a resolution to resign the office. . . . I am desirous of giving an opportunity, while I shall be still in office, to the revival and more deliberate prosecution of the Inquiry into my conduct." The president would be sorry to see Alexander go, but he and the first lady understood the pressures on the family.

As Angelica correctly intuited when the news reached London,

It has been whispered to me that my friend Alexander means to quit his employment of Secretary. The country will lose one of her best friends, and you, my Dear Eliza, will be the only person to whom this change can be either necessary or agreeable.

I am inclined to believe that it is your influence induces him
to withdraw from public life. That so good a wife, so tender a
mother, should be so bad a patriot! is wonderful!

Eliza smiled when she read the letter. But she was not sorry.

The summer of 1793 was unbearably hot and humid even by Philadelphia standards, and low-lying areas outside the city turned
muddy as the water tables fell in a long dry period. The mosquitoes
were fierce, and bred in rainwater barrels and pools, and the stench
of food rotting on the wharves in the holds of ships that could not be
unloaded fast enough mingled with the effluvia from the open sewer
along Dock Creek and the carcasses of animals in shallow gullies.

Refugees were pouring into the city, fleeing the revolution in
France and the slave uprising in the French colony at Haiti. The émi-
grés had Eliza's keen sympathy. Many of them were aristocrats and
wealthy planters, and some of them were known to her family from
as early as the 1760s. Soon, the city of Philadelphia would be filled
with refugees of another sort as well: orphans.

On August 19, the death of a man in the city named Peter Aston
set off panic. He had been struck down with a raging fever, and,
when his eyes and skin went jaundiced, there could be no question
that the city would have to brace for the dreaded yellow fever. In the
next few days, there were four or five more dead or dying. Then the
number climbed to a dozen. The church bells tolled each passing,
until the racket became universal and so distressing that the practice
was suspended. "I have not seen a fever of so much malignity, so
general," wrote Dr. Benjamin Rush to a fellow physician. Within a
week, "universal terror" was prevalent. Thousands of residents fled
the city, causing traffic jams, lame horses, and more panic. When
streets fell empty, those who remained locked their doors and hoped
to ride out the infection. Of those who stayed, four thousand—ten
percent of the city's total population—perished. Unlike with the in-

fluenza or the malarial fevers that crept up from the docks, those who were struck down most fatally were not the elderly or the children. Those whom the fever hit the hardest were in their twenties, thirties, or forties, like Alexander and Eliza.

Eliza and Alexander, to escape the summer heat in Philadelphia, rented a small summer home two and a half miles outside the city, and hoped to avoid the pestilence there with the children. At first, the strategy appeared successful. Alexander carried on commuting into his office in the city for cabinet business, where he was still combating charges of financial corruption and speculation that now appeared to be popping up in all directions. He hesitated to tell Eliza that the inquiry was gaining steam again. She would worry.

His reticence meant that when the blow struck, Eliza did not see it coming.

Others were worrying now for Alexander. The investigation into his suspected speculation and insider trading was pulling in all sorts of testimony. At the end of August, a former aide-de-camp of Catherine Duer's father wrote to Alexander, warning him, "Your enemies are at work upon Mr. Francis, who has been a clerk in the Treasury department. They give out that he is to make affidavits, criminating you in the highest degree, as to some money matters &ca. . . . I concluded to give you this intimation."

Quickly following on the heels of this note came more charges, that Alexander had acted improperly in another financial transaction for their old friend from Morristown, Caty Greene, who had been reduced to penury after the death of Nathanael Greene thanks largely to the greedy machinations and predatory sexual pursuit of John Church's former business partner, the undeniably sleazy Jeremiah Wadsworth. Once again, William Duer was smack in the middle of the problem. "As it is an affair of delicacy," Alexander confessed in a letter to Caty in early September, "I will thank you to request some gentleman of the law to give form and precision to your narrative. You perceive that it is not in one way only that I am the object of unprincipled persecution." He was reduced to asking old friends for sworn testimony to forestall new charges of corruption, as the determination of Alexander's enemies to have him pilloried for misconduct became increasingly scattershot and openly partisan.

Toward the end of the first week of September, all that ceased to matter for the moment. Alexander felt a flush sweep over him and then the telltale chills of fever. George Washington wrote on September 6, saying, "With extreme concern I receive the expression of your apprehensions, that you are in the first stages of the prevailing fever."

Eliza hustled all the children into a carriage and sent them to her parents' home in Albany, keeping behind only one-year-old baby John, their newest arrival, who was still nursing. Then she turned her attention to Alexander and called in a friend and doctor—a man who was also very likely Alexander's half brother—Dr. Edward Stevens, who had arrived that year in Philadelphia from the West Indies.

Alexander owed a great deal to her judicious choice of physician. The leading physician in the city, Dr. Benjamin Rush, advocated a treatment of blistering, bleeding, mercury, and bowel purges that often left patients weaker than when he started. The West Indies, long plagued by the disease, favored a gentler approach of cold baths to reduce fever. Almost immediately, Eliza was struck down too. In her delirium, she wondered, *Where is Alexander?* Who is with the baby? Her muscles ached all over, and her head pounded. The feverish thoughts came and went in a haze, and then the nausea took her.

Eliza and Alexander were battling death, and the worst symptoms of the disease were gruesome. The disease began with the fever and jaundice and progressed until the victim retched up black vomit and bled from every orifice. When there was nothing left to vomit forth, the dry heaves and convulsions started. On the third day, the fever broke briefly, only to return with a vengeance, and, before the end of a week, the patient either died or began the slow road to recovery.

By the second week of September, Alexander and Eliza were being counted among the lucky survivors. Eliza's brother-in-law

Philip Ten Eyck sent off a letter to her brother, John Schuyler, reporting somewhat over-optimistically, "I must give you some information concerning the dreadful distress which prevails in Philadelphia, which is a species of the Plague . . . hundreds have fallen victim to this disorder. . . . Col. Hamilton & his lady, has both had it but by the great attention of Dr Stevens from the West Indies, they are perfectly restored. . . . I believe they will proceed to Albany to your fathers his children left this last week for Albany and were all well."

When Edward Stevens did declare Eliza and Alexander out of immediate danger, he warned of a long, slow road to recovery. Dr. Stevens prescribed fresh air, carriage rides, and an immediate removal to the country. On September 15, a cool Sunday morning, Eliza, Alexander, John, his nurse, and their servants set off for Albany.

The journey was difficult. No town or city wanted to receive the contagion that was devastating Philadelphia. New York City was blockaded, and Alexander and Eliza fought to find a ferry that would take them across the Hudson. They traveled late into the night, trying to get as far from the city as possible, only to have the landlord of a roadside inn tell them that the other guests were terrified by their arrival. On September 23, after eight days on the road, they arrived at last across the river from Albany, where the city physician issued them a certificate, confirming, "We have visited Col. Hamilton and his lady at Greenbush, this evening, and that they are apparently in perfect health; and from every circumstance we do not conceive there can be the least danger of their conveying the infection of the pestilential fever, at present prevalent in Philadelphia, to any of their fellow citizens."

The order required that Eliza and Alexander leave their servants behind, lodge at an inn, and abandon all their clothing and luggage. With the baby in her arms, they tried to enter the city at last on Tuesday morning. They were not warmly greeted. The citizens of Albany, outraged at the thought of contagion, demanded that General Schuyler's entire estate be quarantined, and there followed several tense days, in which Eliza's father and Alexander negotiated with the town leaders.

By the time they returned to their little country house outside Philadelphia, a month later, the restorative air had done its work and the fever had abated. Still, the children stayed behind with their grandparents, as a precaution. "Exercise & Northern air have restored us beyond expectation," Alexander reported to George Washington the next morning. "We are very happy that Mrs. Washington & yourself escaped."

Then, a week later, Alexander was sick again with fever.

Although this new sickness was not the yellow fever, Philip Schuyler, learning the news, put his foot down and refused to return the children to their parents. "It is very natural," her father explained firmly, "that you and my Dear Eliza Should be anxious to have your children with you, but in this instance I apprehend your prudence has given way to your feelings. . . . I have concluded that It would be improper to Acceed to your wish." General Schuyler was exasperated with his ambitious son-in-law and his headstrong daughter. In another month or so, if the fever had not returned and the city was properly recovered, either he or Eliza's brother, Rensselaer, would bring down the baby and his nurse for Eliza. The "others we all agree must remain until Spring," he informed their shocked parents. Eliza and Alexander knew better than to quarrel with the general, however.

Eliza was bereft without the children. But she would not leave Alexander. As a result, all the Hamilton children were in Albany in mid-November, during the slave uprising there.

Late on the night of Sunday, November 17, the town watchmen roused the citizens of Albany with the alarm of fire. Flames caught hold on the wooden rooftops, and the wind lifted the fire from building to building and then along the long back stables. Only a heavy rain at six o'clock the next morning saved the city from complete ruin, but twenty-six houses had been destroyed, including some of the most prominent homes in the city.

On the Monday, as the downtown core smoldered, residents tracked down the source of the fire. A tipped lantern was found in the stables of the Albany merchant Leonard Gansevoort, and the hunt for the arsonist quickly led to four African slaves, including a young female slave named Bet, owned by Stephen Van Rensselaer's brother, Philip.

For decades, the rich city merchants had feared an uprising, and now the city committee issued an immediate emergency ordinance placing a curfew on anyone who was black or mulatto. It didn't matter, in the end, that a vengeful young lover, refused permission to court Gansevoort's teenage daughter, had bribed the Africans, who were not mounting a political insurrection. All four of the slaves confessed, and when they were hanged the next spring, Eliza heard the story of the whole affair firsthand from Peggy and Stephen.

In December, with no more reports of the fever, her father relented. Their oldest daughter, nine-year-old Angelica, who was studying French in Albany, wished to stay with her grandparents and numerous local cousins, but her father sent the other children home to their parents.

Despite the fortunate escape, Eliza and Alexander were sick off and on for much of the next year, and both their health had been permanently damaged. In January, Philip Schuyler was "alarmed at the state of my Dear Elizas health, nor are we without apprehension on your Account," he informed Alexander. Angelica inquired of her sister, "When am I to hear that you are in perfect health, and that you are no longer in fear for the life of your dear Hamilton?"

Eliza was also frustrated when Alexander again put off his departure from the Treasury, citing the volatile situation in France. It now looked like he was not going to resign after all, and Eliza was frustrated. Alexander found it hard to let go of prestige and the reins of power. As one French aristocrat whom Angelica and John helped to flee to America reported back to Eliza's sister, Alexander spoke too much of "grandes personnages." The same aristocrat also observed— in a sign of the tensions brewing in their marriage and in a sign, too, that the gossip about Maria Reynolds was still circulating—that Alexander noted too little the beauty of his wife. Martha Washington was not the only person whose heart went out to Eliza.

The summer of 1794 meant the return of sweltering weather and fever, and Dr. Stevens again ordered Eliza and baby James to the country for fresh air and exercise. Alexander, committed to his work in the Treasury, planned to stay behind. All plans of resigning were brushed aside for the moment, to Eliza's exasperation. Toward the end of July, Eliza and the two youngest children, James and John, set off for Albany, although Eliza was deeply unhappy about going. For the first time, at odds over Alexander's broken promise about resignation and putting family first, their marriage was faltering. When the baby fell dangerously ill in her first weeks in Albany, Eliza sat up with the infant for long, sleepless nights, frightened and exhausted. She longed to come home to her house, to her husband, and especially to her older boys, who had stayed behind in Philadelphia with their father.

Alexander would not support it and reminded her of his authority as her husband. By August, Eliza was considering her own uprising, and Alexander's response to her letters showed her to be feeling increasingly caged and desperate. Albany felt like punishment and exile. Finally, in mid-August, annoyed with Eliza but tired of her upsetting letters, Alexander relented. "You press to return to me," he wrote. "I will not continue to dissuade you. Do as you think best. . . . But let me know before hand your determination that I may meet you at New York with an arrangement for bringing you or rather write to Mr. Seton who I will request to have things ready." Alexander wasn't even sure he would be able to meet her in person for the last stage home. Eliza's eyes watered.

Hardly had Eliza settled back in at home that autumn when Alexander set off with the military to fight in the Whiskey Rebellion. An excise tax on distilled spirits had enraged farmers on the western frontier and sparked an armed uprising. The home of a tax collector was torched, and the federal government felt compelled to assert its authority. Nearly thirteen thousand federal troops marched toward western Pennsylvania, Alexander among them, at the end of October.

Eliza stayed in Philadelphia, dealing with sick children. She was overwhelmed and, within weeks of Alexander's departure, began suffering as well from what she knew by now was morning sickness. Her mother traveled down from Albany to care for the children and called for the doctor when on November 24, a Monday afternoon, Eliza bent over double with cramps and bleeding, sure signs of a miscarriage. Losing a baby, at a moment of such coolness and distance in their marriage, felt especially lonely, and all her pent-up sorrow washed over Eliza now. She couldn't stop crying.

Kitty Schuyler was worried. This was not like her tough-minded and resilient daughter. Someone needed to fetch Alexander. Whatever was going on needed to get worked out between Eliza and her husband. Kitty reached out to old wartime friends of General Schuyler. Henry Knox dashed off a letter to the president's army headquarters. George Washington—who, like Martha, had vast reserves of affection and sympathy for Eliza—sent a rider for Alexander. "My dear Hamilton," the president wrote, "[Mrs. Hamilton] has had, or has been in danger of a miscarriage, which has much alarmed her. . . . She is extremely desirous of your presence in order to tranquilize her."

Alexander set off instantly for Philadelphia, arriving in the last days of the month. Whatever conversation passed between them remains private.

But on Monday morning, December 1, 1794, Alexander Hamilton sent President Washington his resignation.

All told, Philadelphia had been a disaster from Eliza's perspective. Sickness, scandal, and slander had dominated their lives for three years, and Eliza had borne them patiently for as long as she could stand to. But now she needed it to end, and she would not regret leaving. She was a New Yorker at heart, and she did not want to spend one minute longer in this swampy capital than absolutely necessary. Angelica, still believing that every spring would bring her return to America, shared her sister's dislike of the city. "I confess I should not like to settle at Philadelphia," Angelica wrote, "and if my Brother resigns there will then be no reason for my not going immediately to New York and be under his and your care till Mr. Church can leave this country."

Alexander's business in Philadelphia was finished by the end of January, and this time there was no backtracking on the resignation from the Treasury. Eliza put down her foot now on another front as well. Enough with all the working. They all needed rest, and she wanted some quiet time with Alexander and the children. Alexander, committed to finding his way back to Eliza in their marriage, did not argue. They would arrange for accommodations in Manhattan for June. But her parents' house in Albany was empty while her father was serving in the New York legislature, and the Hamilton family was going to spend the spring on the Hudson. Together. Relaxing.

Her father threw his weight in behind Eliza. Kitty Schuyler had seen enough in Philadelphia to know that something needed correcting, and General Schuyler almost certainly knew the gossip that Alexander had confessed to an affair with Mrs. Reynolds. Everyone knew that Alexander had been under investigation for financial corruption.

Alexander could hardly resist the combined forces of his wife and her strong-willed father. As soon as the snow lay thick enough on the ground, Philip Schuyler sent a sleigh down to carry them back north. The family left behind the capital in the first weeks of February, and Eliza got her wish. For three months, from mid-February until mid-May, the entire family—Eliza insisted they pull even the older boys from boarding school for the term—recuperated from years of sickness and political turmoil in the home where Eliza had been born and married. She wanted to step back in time, to that moment in the beginning of their marriage, at their small farmhouse in Albany, when Alexander had vowed to eschew ambition and fame and had been happy to rock his infant son's cradle. She counted on the Hudson Valley to work its magic on them all. Slowly, she felt her tension unwinding.

James McHenry, Alexander's best man, also threw his weight now behind Eliza's arguments and vision of the future. Mac had a special investment in Alexander and Eliza's marriage, and he had long thought that people underestimated the treasure Alexander had stumbled upon in Eliza. Mac sent Alexander a friendly letter of advice when he heard news of the resignation. "I have built houses," he counseled his friend,

> I have cultivated fields, I have planned gardens, I have planted trees, I have written little essays, I have made poetry once a year to please my wife, at times got children and at all times thought myself happy. Why cannot you do the same, for after all if a man is only to acquire fame or distinctions by continued privations and abuse I would incline to prefer a life of privacy and little pleasures.

It was just what Eliza wished for her family. Alexander himself would be the only obstacle.

When they returned to New York City in June, much of the damage had been repaired, and they all were happier. Alexander reopened a private legal practice, and Eliza celebrated the new beginning. Finances were not robust by the standards of their peers and especially not compared to the wealth of her sisters, but the family was not impoverished either. Eliza's father assisted them in the purchase of a "Negro boy & woman," for which Alexander reimbursed his father $250, and by summer they were settling happily into their new home in the city—all of them, that is, except Eliza's orphan charge, Fanny Antill.

Fanny was now ten, a bright-haired and cheerful girl. Her older sister was the wife of a prominent Albany gentleman. During their long spring sojourn in the Hudson, Fanny had been reunited with her sister, and when Eliza and Alexander moved south, Fanny stayed. It was a bittersweet moment for Eliza. For more than a decade, the orphaned Fanny had been a second daughter.

Sometime later that autumn or perhaps that following winter, Eliza sat again for another portrait, with the British artist James Sharples. She looks out of her portrait now, a more subdued, self-contained, and informal Eliza. Gone are the powdered wigs and high fashion. Her rich, dark hair is left natural, and curls around her shoulders. In profile, she is still youthful, slender, and a slight smile on her lips says she was, at last, happy.

It was such a short reprieve for Eliza.

She did not know that the charges of financial corruption and self-interested dealing still dogged Alexander. She assumed—wrongly, as it turned out—that his leaving his post as secretary of Treasury would be the end of the bitter turmoil. But there was trouble on the horizon, and, as always, Alexander's pride would play a part.

Alexander's overreaction to the slights and gossip that still buzzed among the gentlemen in late 1794 and early 1795, especially, didn't help matters. Engaged in the delicate work of repairing their marriage, Alexander didn't tell Eliza what was happening. He didn't want to upset her or the peace she was after.

The trouble had started in March, when Alexander traveled alone down to New York City from Albany to make some business arrangements, in advance of their return to Manhattan in June. James Nicholson, the chief commodore of the Continental army during the American Revolution, made the bold claim among some gentlemen that he had evidence to prove "that Hamilton had vested £100,000 sterling in the British funds, whilst he was Secretary of the Treasury, which sum was still held by a Banking house in London, to his use and Interest."

Alexander's supporters called it slander and called on Nicholson to prove it. Nicholson retorted that he was prepared at any time to lay the papers before a committee and threatened that "if Hamilton's name is at any time brought up as a candidate for any public office, he will instantly publish the circumstance."

Word of the accusations made their way to Alexander, and, determined to make the fresh start his family needed, he wisely did nothing. But on a Saturday afternoon toward the end of July in New York City, Alexander got caught up in a squabble. One of the parties was Nicholson, who insulted him as an "Abettor of Tories" and mocked him for refusing to prove he was innocent of fraud and corruption. Alexander had turned the other cheek. Now he was being told that he had done so because he was a guilty coward. Alexander, furious, demanded satisfaction. Letters flew between the two men, their friends, and their seconds for days in anticipation of a duel between the gentlemen.

It was not the first time that Alexander had reacted to the charges of financial speculation by calling for weapons. He and Aedanus Burke, the congressman from South Carolina, came near to dueling in 1790. Nor was dueling unfamiliar to Alexander. He had been involved, either as a principal or as a second, in at least two threatened duels before he and Eliza were married.

Now, unbeknownst to Eliza, Alexander prepared his will and set aside for delivery to his friend Oliver Wolcott, in the event of his death, a packet of letters. Those letters were marked with the initials "J.R.," and Alexander asked his friend to look after the papers carefully.

"J.R." presumably stood for "James Reynolds."

Friends worked behind the scenes, and this time a duel was averted, but news of it spread throughout New York City, reaching at least as far as Eliza's Livingston cousins and some of the ladies who attended church with Eliza at Trinity. It was only a matter of time before Eliza learned of it.

Alexander was trying. But just practicing law wasn't enough. He was too long accustomed to the battle royal that was politics in the early republic and couldn't bear to step away from the action,

no matter what James McHenry counseled, no matter what seren-
ity Eliza hoped for. And the greatest risk to their tranquility, Eliza
knew, was Alexander's pride and temper. Alexander was too easily
provoked by the personal.

By the next year, Alexander was back in the midst of politics and
controversy. The presidential campaign of 1796 pitted Thomas Jefferson against John Adams, and, although Alexander disliked John
Adams personally, he despised Thomas Jefferson's policies. Alexander had for years been on the receiving end of scandalmongering and innuendo, but, thanks to Angelica's tittle-tattle, he had his
own arsenal of gossip. Alexander came out swinging against Jefferson and unwisely dropped hints that the candidate's public veneer
of "simplicity and humility afford but a flimsy veil to the internal
evidences of aristocratic splendor, sensuality, and epicureanism,"
this last insult a veiled reference to Jefferson's sexual relationship in
Paris with Sally Hemings. Alexander never forgot the stories Angelica had told him.

What Alexander failed to appreciate was that James Monroe, who
had been abroad for several years, had lodged his cache of documents
regarding the James Reynolds affair, gathered in the course of the
initial 1792 investigation, with a "friend in Virginia"—almost certainly Jefferson—for safekeeping on departure.

John Adams won the race. Thomas Jefferson had every reason to
blame Alexander. Before too long—no one ever could track how precisely it happened—a certain muckraking anti-Federalist journalist
named James Callender ended up with copies of the Monroe papers.
And James Reynolds was back on the agenda.

CHAPTER 14

The Scandal, 1796–97

Eliza didn't see it coming.

She was too busy in the winter of 1796–97 and into the spring of 1797 with sick family members and, as always, children. Her sister Peggy buried another child, a seven-year-old little girl named Catherine, throwing, Alexander wrote, "a gloom upon the family." Peggy had been extraordinarily unlucky as a mother. This was the second little Catherine she had buried. Only her son Stephen Jr., eight years old in 1797 and the third to bear that name, would survive childhood. Eliza's father had an infection that threatened to turn gangrenous. Alexander came down with the flu, and by spring Eliza was once again pregnant. She would turn forty that summer, and this pregnancy was her seventh.

On top of it all, Eliza had her hands full with a headstrong twenty-year-old, her younger sister Cornelia, who came to spend the winter, and whom Eliza tried without great success to chaperone. Cornelia had a reputation for being a terrible flirt and for having a sarcastic wit that rivaled that of her sister Peggy, and their cousin Robert Livingston bitterly complained that Cornelia was haughty with men she considered boring. He seems to have fallen into that unfortunate category. Cornelia's best girlfriend was Catherine Westerlo, the half sister of the patroon Stephen Van Rensselaer, and the two girls were boy crazy. "I shall be so free to tell you I hate you for not acquainting me how the beaus in N York are and what handsom

things they say of me," Cornelia saucily wrote to her brother-in-law
Stephen. "Should you chance to see my sweet heart Jones pray tell
him I am well, and think myself twenty times handsomer than ever
the men tell me."

Eliza and Alexander were regulars on the high-society ball and
dinner-party circuit, and Eliza offered to give her unmarried sister
a winter "season" like the one Aunt Gertrude had made possible for
Eliza at Morristown. She soon regretted having made the offer. Eliza
didn't worry when Cornelia became friends with another young
lady in the neighborhood, Eliza Morton, the sister of Alexander's
old school friend and war comrade, Jacob Morton, who lived just
down the street from them on Broadway. But, in hindsight, perhaps
she should have.

Eliza Hamilton was seven months pregnant, uncomfortable, and
weary by June, when Cornelia traveled down to Princeton, New Jersey, as a guest at the wedding of Miss Morton. Eliza Morton was
marrying one of the catches of the season, a young man named Josiah
Quincy, the scion of a wealthy Boston family. Cornelia, a "charming girl," who wore her dark brown hair in waves and had blue eyes
framed by impossibly long, dark lashes, immediately spotted Jacob
Morton's chubby, bad-boy younger brother, Washington, whose
reputation as a hothead and a roué with a mean streak Cornelia dismissed far too quickly. She was smitten.

Eliza might have paid more attention to what Cornelia was up to
if she hadn't had that month two other more important distractions.

At the end of May—after years of hoping and pressure—Angelica
and John Church returned at last, for good, to America. Eliza was
jubilant. In June, she helped her sister settle into a freshly white-
washed rental house until a mansion could be built on a plot of land
on Broadway, and they were full of plans for the future as neighbors.

It should have been a happy summer of homecoming for the
two sisters. Instead, a journalist named James Callender dropped a
bombshell.

New York City roiled with talk of the incendiary claims published that month in James Callender's *History of the United States for 1796*. The work included an exposé that ran to pages and laid out, in devastating detail, charges that Alexander had engaged in financial speculation in office. It also broke the news that Alexander had confessed to an affair with Maria Reynolds—and included information from James Monroe's secret dossier.

The most damaging and persuasive charge that James Callender made was that the affair with Maria Reynolds was nothing more than a cover story for financial misconduct.

"We now come to a part of the work, more delicate, perhaps, than any other," the article teased readers. "This great master of morality [Alexander Hamilton], though himself the father of a family, confessing that he had an illicit correspondence with another man's wife." This was bad enough. But James Callender went on, "If anything can be yet less reputable, it is, that the gentlemen to whom he made that acknowledgement held it as an imposition, and found various reasons for believing that Mrs. Reynolds was, in reality, guiltless."

It tended to lend credence to Maria Reynolds's claims that in 1793, long before the press got a hold of the story, she had quietly retained Aaron Burr to sue for a divorce from James Reynolds "in consequence of his intrigue with Hamilton to her prejudice." Maria Reynolds had maintained from the start that her husband and Alexander had concocted the story of the affair to save their own skins, with little regard for the fact that it was her reputation that was ruined.

Alexander spent the day of July 5, 1797, writing furious letters to Congressmen Muhlenberg, Monroe, and Venable—the gentlemen involved in the initial inquiry—demanding their public disavowal of the statement. Alexander understood clearly that if there was one thing that would make him look more base and more ridiculous than financial missteps or infidelity, it was having forged love letters and ruined the reputation of an innocent young woman—his wife's relation, no less—in order to concoct a cover-up.

Alexander would have been wise to have stopped to think. But instead he reacted and engaged the journalist. All it did was ratchet up the scandal.

Alexander immediately published a letter of denial, reprinted in newspapers up and down the seaboard, promising to publish a pamphlet discrediting the story. James Callender published a counterrebuttal days later, again floating the theory that Alexander had forged the love letters. He challenged Alexander to let the world see these purported letters and to submit them for forensic examination of the handwriting. "I have perused your observations," James Callender expounded, and "the facts which you there bring forward, and the conclusions which you attempt to draw from them, do not appear Satisfactory."

By now, all of America was watching the breaking scandal. What would Colonel Hamilton do now? people wondered. He was being pressed to open shameful correspondence to public view, in order to defend himself against worse allegations. Anything Alexander said could only humiliate both him and Eliza further.

The journalist had the bit in his teeth, though, and published another long public letter, quickly reprinted in newspapers, that further mocked Alexander for the logical holes in his story about Maria Reynolds. "According to my information," Callender informed the world, "these written documents consisted of a series of letters pretended to be written relative to your alledged connection with Mrs. Reynolds. You told the members a confused and absurd story about her, of which they did not believe a single word, and which, if they had been true, did not give a proper explanation as to your correspondence with her husband."

Then Callender egged Alexander on about his promise to "place the matter more precisely before the public" in a pamphlet. "You are in the right" to promise such an explanation to the world, Callender sarcastically announced, "for they have at present some unlucky doubts. They have long known you as an eminent and able statesman. They will be highly gratified by seeing you exhibited in the novel character of a lover."

On July 11, Alexander demanded a meeting with James Monroe, accompanied by John Church, and the meeting at James Monroe's Wall Street home devolved predictably enough into a heated confrontation that left both men and their friends swapping letters threatening a duel for several weeks after.

Unfortunately, on July 12, Alexander read Callender's second installment in his exposé, which included a document that escalated the forgery issue and included "the very derogatory suspicion, that [Alexander] had concerted with Reynolds not only the fabrication of all the letters and documents under his hand, but also the forgery of the letters produced as those of Mrs. Reynolds—since these last unequivocally contradict the pretence communicated by Clingman."

A duel had been averted. It was now back on. The more Alexander thought about it, the more convinced he was that Monroe was behind it all and that getting the retraction of the congressmen was an affair of honor. Monroe, though, was convinced that Alexander was lying and said so. He would not back down and steadfastly refused to state that he accepted the truth of the affair or the letters. Friends again worked behind the scenes to cool tempers so the two men didn't kill each other.

Leaving friends to pressure Monroe in New York City, Alexander set off in a huff the next morning for Philadelphia, planning to meet in person with his other accusers in Congress. His arrival in Philadelphia was greeted with snide commentary in the anti-Federalist *Aurora* newspaper that "Alexander Hamilton has favoured this city with a visit. He has certainly not come for the benefit of the fresh air. . . . Perhaps, however, he may have been called to town for the purpose of clearing up the mysterious business." The nation was riveted by this extraordinary drama.

On the morning of July 13, Eliza sat quietly in her front parlor and read in the newspaper the second of Callender's letters. She read the sentences about the affair with Mrs. Reynolds. She read the sentences that claimed that the love letters were a forgery. She rested her hands on her swollen belly. What did all this mean for the children, her family? How long she sat there we can only imagine, but there is no doubt that she knew the thing she feared the most was finally happening.

Her response to the news of Alexander's "affair" with Maria Reynolds suggests more than anything else that she was in on the secret of the cover story from the beginning.

"How is my Dear Eliza? We are anxious to know," her father wrote from Albany. How does Eliza take it? Alexander also wanted to know from Philadelphia.

John Church went around to see Eliza that afternoon. He expected tears, maybe a tantrum. For a lady to learn of her husband's peccadilloes in the papers was a hard thing, and it was difficult for John to see what he could do. He shuddered to think how Angelica would take such a newspaper article.

When John stepped into the parlor, Eliza was restless, but there was no crying. The summer air was hot and sticky, and Eliza moved awkwardly and slowly at eight months pregnant. She was calm and defiant. When Eliza saw John, she didn't say a word, but turned to pick up the newspaper and handed it to him. Then she waved her hand dismissively. The whole knot of those opposed to Alexander are scoundrels, her gesture seemed to say.

"Eliza is well," an astonished John Church assured Alexander. "It makes not the least Impression on her." Her reaction was extraordinary. Unless, of course, Eliza already knew that Alexander's affair with her cousin was a fabrication. The other choice is that Eliza was Alexander's dupe, and nothing that came afterward supports that picture of Eliza and their marriage. Alexander, hemmed in on all sides by political enemies, betrayed by Duer and having overstepped the mark financially, had told a fib, confidentially and among gentlemen, five years earlier. Now he would have to defend the cover story. Already, the cover-up was proving the worst part of the scandal. Eliza knew, too, that the worst was not yet over. But she was determined to defend their secret and Alexander.

That was all Alexander needed to know. "Alone, a banished man."

Did the errant-knight's refrain in their old ballad come to him now? Eliza's abiding loyalty filled his heart with gratitude, and he poured out his love in letters. A week later, Alexander was still in Philadelphia, and Angelica and Eliza were riding out the gossip storm in New York City together. "The affair, My Dearest Eliza, upon which I came here has come to a close," Alexander wrote,

> *But unavoidable delays in bringing it to this point & the necessity of communicating the result much very much against my will keep me here till the departure of the mail stage tomorrow, which will restore me to my Betsey on the day following. I need not tell her how very happy I shall be to return to her embrace and to the company of our beloved Angelica. I am very anxious about you both, you for an obvious reason, and her because Mr. Church mentioned in a letter to me, that she complained of a sore throat. Let me charge you and her to be well and happy, for you comprize all my felicity. Adieu Angel.*

Alexander would be gone at least another week more, and sympathetic letters arrived regularly from her father, who was unaware that Eliza might have known already the full story. "I apprehended the vile calumny of my Dear Hamilton's villainous enemies might disturb your peace of mind," Philip Schuyler wrote in one letter, "but your husband's reputation is too well established to suffer in the public opinion from anything his wretched enemies can do." Eliza had more sympathy than she knew, even among strangers. Even Alexander's political opponents felt on "poor Mrs. H. Account whose feelings on the Occasion must be severely injured, if not expressed."

On August 4, Eliza gave birth in New York City to a son named William, just a week shy of her fortieth birthday. She might have in front of her another half decade of childbearing. Her mother had delivered their last sibling, Catherine, at forty-seven, and the Schuyler women were famous for their reproductive stamina.

The acrimony in the city was intense. John, Alexander, and Angelica agreed that Eliza should escape for a few weeks to Albany to take care of herself and the baby. But the climate everywhere was ugly. One man, recognizing Eliza, unleashed on her a storm of contempt and accusations, upsetting Eliza and depressing Alexander, who left it to John Church to manage. Eliza also fumed about James Callender.

Walking home from the wharf after seeing her off, melancholy and embarrassed, Alexander stopped to see Angelica, and the next morning Angelica wrote her sister a consoling letter:

> *When my Brother returned from the sloop, he was very much out of spirits and you were the subject of his conversation the rest of the evening. Catherine played at the harpsichord for him and at 10 o'clock he went home. Tranquillize your kind and good heart, my dear Eliza, for I have the most positive assurance from Mr. Church that the dirty fellow who has caused us all some uneasiness and wounded your feelings, my dear love, is effectually silenced. Merit, virtue, and talents must have enemies and is always exposed to envy so that, my Eliza, you see the penalties attending the position of so amiable a man. All this you would not have suffered if you had married into a family less near the sun. But then the pride, the pleasure, the nameless satisfactions, etc. . . . Adieu with all my heart and redoubled tenderness.*

The press storm, however, was far from over.

Alexander himself would initiate the next volley. At the end of August, Alexander published his long-promised pamphlet, composed during Eliza's absence and without her moderating influence. Perversely, he turned his entire and formidable intellect toward proving that his affair with Maria Reynolds was not invented. "I have been [charged]," he insisted, "with being a speculator, whereas I am only an adulterer."

Downplaying Maria Reynolds's connections to the Livingston

family, Alexander cast her as a strumpet and a prostitute and offered salacious details of bedroom romps. He cast himself as a rogue and a villain and, by emphasizing that his wife was out of town and that those romps took place in their bedroom, unwittingly turned the spotlight on Eliza. The press speculated as to how any woman could stay with this man. "Art thou a wife?" the newspapers mocked Eliza. "See him, whom thou hast chosen for a partner of this life, lolling in the lap of a harlot." Eliza knew that her absence from Philadelphia that summer was exaggerated, and even she couldn't understand why Alexander was telling this story. She did not doubt Alexander's loyalty. But even those who loved him most questioned now his judgment.

The pamphlet was a disaster. Alexander had done himself more damage than his political enemies ever could have managed, and he soon confessed to a family clergyman in despair that he regretted the publication. Watching Alexander twist in the wind as his pamphlet backfired was entertainment enough for his enemies. They patiently waited.

For the moment, his opponents were busy adding to their storehouse of ammunition. Maria Reynolds continued to insist that there had been no affair, and, according to hints in the press, drew up the draft of her defense and turned it over to William Duane, the publisher of the Jeffersonian *Aurora*; the newspaper held the draft in reserve "in the event of certain political movements." The implication was that if Alexander Hamilton ever considered a run for office, it would be used to reignite the scandal.

And Alexander never did run for office. It was not a coincidence.

Just as the worst of the scandal was crashing around Eliza, the family was thrown into a series of other crises.

By the beginning of September, Eliza was back home in New York City, nursing baby William, when her eldest child, Philip, was struck down by one of the deadly summer fevers. When the rash spread across the teenager's body, Eliza knew it was typhus. William

Seton's father-in-law was Dr. Richard Bayley, the city's foremost expert in infectious fevers, and he advised the family to call in his former student, Dr. David Hosack.

It was Dr. Hosack's first introduction to the Hamilton family, and he remembered later how rattled Eliza was by the scandal. "Great distress then existing in [the] family," Dr. Hosack recollected, "added to the anxiety pervading their numerous friends." It was too much for Eliza, who broke down in hysterics. His "Mother, overwhelmed with distress," Dr. Hosack recorded, Philip, "by my advice, was removed to another room that she might not witness the last struggles of her son." Eliza was overwhelmed by the entire nightmare of the summer.

Philip Hamilton narrowly survived the fever, and then, fresh on the heels of this family drama, came two others.

Eliza's brother Rensselaer, an indiscriminate risk taker since childhood, was among the men in the family caught up in gambling and speculation. Alexander had urged his father-in-law when he was in the Treasury not to let the Schuyler brothers, especially Rensselaer, "speculate in the public securities lest it should be inferred that their speculations were made upon information furnished by Hamilton; or were made in part on Hamilton's account."

Rensselaer had been hiding immense gambling debts—and he gambled as much in stocks as in card games—for which he had taken out loans at up to five percent interest a month and had no hope of paying. His creditors now were dunning Eliza's father, and even the reinvigorated Schuyler family fortune was not enough to cover the debts for Rensselaer. The debts "are too numerous," Philip Schuyler wrote grimly. "No alternative is now left other than an attempt to procure the benefit of the Act for the relief of Insolvents." The only thing that saved the twenty-four-year-old man now from languishing in a cell was a relatively new bankruptcy law, hastily enacted after the crash of 1792 put some of the city's leading citizens in debtors' prison. Rensselaer's troubles did nothing to tamp down the controversy surrounding Alexander's time in the Treasury.

Then there was Eliza's younger sister, Cornelia. She had met Washington Morton in June, and the two were still mutually enamored. He was not a steady young man, though he was undeniably a rich one. Washington Morton was one of the "young bloods" of his day and already had something of a reputation for making foolish bets and taking ludicrous wagers that saw him walking on a dare from New York to Philadelphia. He was not yet qualified to practice law and did not appear to have the temperament of a man ready to marry and support a wife and a family. But in September he was in love with Cornelia, she was in love with him, and he accordingly traveled up to Albany, where Cornelia had returned, to ask her father for permission to marry.

The interview did not go well. Washington Morton managed to pick a fight with Kitty Schuyler almost immediately on arrival, and, as he put it, "Her mother and myself had a difference which extended to the father."

Philip Schuyler advised the young man that any talk of marriage to his daughter would need to wait until Washington had "slackened his pace to the sober rate befitting a steady-going married man." The young gentleman, rather than biding his time, argued with General Schuyler as well, who did not take kindly to an impertinent suitor challenging him in his library. His impression of Washington Morton as a hothead hopelessly confirmed, Philip Schuyler marched his guest personally down to the dock and made sure he was on a boat heading southward. Striding back up the lawn, he encountered an anxious Cornelia:

"Come into the library," he directed, and he explained to his daughter in no uncertain terms that, based on the conduct of her suitor, he was not only denying consent for the marriage but was ordering that she break off all contact with Washington.

"My wishes will, of course, be respected. Promise me to have nothing hereafter to do with him, either by word or letter."

"I cannot, sir," Cornelia retorted.

"What! Do you mean to disobey me?"

"I mean that I cannot bind myself by any such pledge as you name, and—I will not."

The quarrel between the father and his equally stubborn daughter upset the entire household, and Cornelia, having already braved her father's rage, was now determined to be with Washington. The young suitor persuaded a servant to smuggle a note to Cornelia, proposing the time and the method for an elopement, and the following week Washington Morton and a school friend arrived at midnight outside the Schuyler mansion with a rope ladder. Down climbed Cornelia, and they made their escape first by rowboat across the river and then by horseback rode thirty miles to Stockbridge, Massachusetts. As Washington bragged later to his family, "I got my wife in opposition to them both. She leapt from a Two Story Window into my arms and abandoning every thing for me gave the most convincing proof of what a husband most Desire to Know that his wife Loves him."

Kitty and Philip Schuyler were worried for their daughter, and by late November they came to the conclusion that Cornelia needed sympathy more than anger. Philip Schuyler now confided to Eliza that he wished Cornelia happy, "if she can possibly enjoy it, with a man of such an untoward disposition as her husband—I apprehend very much that he will render her miserable, and increase my affection."

When her parents invited Cornelia and Washington to Albany to make the peace, however, they abandoned hope. "His conduct, whilst here has been as usual, most preposterous," Philip Schuyler reported, in despair for his daughter. "Seldom an evening at home, and seldom even at dinner—I have not thought it prudent to say the least word to him . . . as advice on such an irregular character is thrown away." Sadly, her father's predictions were not unjust. Cornelia had years to regret her youthful impulse, and the marriage was rocky from the beginning.

Alexander published his ill-advised pamphlet in August, and, while the press gnawed on the scandal all autumn, Eliza let herself hope that the worst of it was behind them.

James Callender, however, was not finished muckraking. Not long after the new year in 1798, he published another long, forensic exposé, and he made in excruciating detail the case for the Maria Reynolds letters—which Alexander had unwisely published in his pamphlet—being forgery. Callender's piece was a two-pronged attack on the credibility of Alexander, and the journalist was eager to urge Alexander on to more reckless action.

First was the question of why Alexander would not release the handwritten documents he claimed were in his possession. "If the letters published by Mr. Hamilton in the name of Maria are genuine," James Callender opined, "it would be very easy to obtain her attestation of the fact." And if—as Callender knew she would—Maria Reynolds claimed they were fabrications, why would Alexander not produce the letters and agree to allowing a judge to make a handwriting comparison? Maria Reynolds was quite willing.

Second, Callender drew the public attention to the many internal consistencies in the transcriptions Alexander had published in the pamphlet. "These letters from Mrs. Reynolds," Callender noted,

> are badly spelt and pointed. Capitals, also, occur even in the midst of words. But waving such excrescences, the stile is pathetic [i.e., moving] and even elegant. It does not bear the marks of an illiterate writer. The construction of the periods disagrees with this apparent incapacity of spelling. . . . A few gross blunders are interspersed, and these could readily be devised; but, when stript of such a veil, the body of the composition is pure and correct. . . . The whole collection would not have required above an evening to write. . . . You speak as if it was impossible to invent a few letters.

Alexander knew the pamphlet had been a mistake and confessed now that he wished to recall it, aware of how badly it had damaged his reputation. The Schuyler family rallied around him and tried to buy up all the copies of the pamphlet to destroy them. Alexander's critics responded with a rogue reprinting, adding a sarcastic title page with the note, "Copy Right not secured according to the Act of Congress."

Thomas Jefferson's view was that the pamphlet and the debate about the forgeries "strengthened [rather] than weakened the suspicions that he was in truth guilty of the speculations." Senator Maclay summed up neatly what everyone was saying about the letters and the financial gossip: "No Body can prove these things, but every body knows them." The pamphlet smacked of "the gentleman doth protest too much."

This time, Alexander exercised better judgment and kept quiet—in part at Eliza's urging.

By spring, Eliza wasn't living in daily fear of what the newspapers might say, and with Alexander out of public office the intensity of the gossip and the animosity abated.

But it never disappeared. Eliza lived with the knowledge that there was always the possibility of it returning to haunt them. The editors of the *Aurora* never let Alexander forget that they had something on him. Every so often, for years to come, the press wondered aloud about the scandal surrounding "a certain head of a department" and asked, "Why has the subject been so long and carefully smothered up?" Hanging overhead also, too, was always the possibility of Maria Reynolds or James Reynolds talking. Both had gone to ground and stayed out of sight and quiet. That could change at any moment.

Eliza knew whom she blamed for all the heartache, and it was not Alexander. She laid the responsibility for igniting the controversy about Maria Reynolds and the letters squarely at the door of James Monroe and Thomas Jefferson.

She would not forget. There were few things that made the even-tempered Eliza shake with fury and long for revenge. This was one of them.

CHAPTER 15

A Roman Wife, 1797–1802

Eliza had borne it silently, but the humiliation of it all was unbearable.

She did not regret the cover-up. Because no matter what happened or did not happen in the bedroom, financial indiscretions had been urgently swept under the carpet. She would have thrown her weight behind anything that prevented Alexander and the other men in her family from ending up like William Duer, who was still languishing in prison. The story had not been her invention, and she had been given few options in the matter anyhow.

If this story is the true one, Alexander and James Reynolds concocted the tale of the affair to explain the transfer of money, as Maria Reynolds claimed, and they had all believed that the fallout would be confined to snide gossip in government circles. Part of the deal in their marriage was that Alexander would leave politics. He had done that. But now, the story had hit the national papers, and Alexander had been forced to defend a years-old hasty invention.

Retreat from the glare of the spotlight seemed impossible, too. The return of Angelica from Britain had brought joy and consolation. But it also dashed any hopes that Eliza had of withdrawing from public attention. Angelica was the city's leading socialite and threw herself into the limelight. As the wife of one of the city's wealthiest citizens, Angelica flaunted European manners and the latest Parisian fashions. Even Harrison Gray Otis, a sympathetic Federalist politician, found Angelica "the mirror of affectation," and the former Loyalist turned Federalist Walter Rutherford complained of "a late abominable fashion from London, of Ladies like Washwomen with their sleeves above their elbows, Mrs. Church among them." Even Josephine DuPont, a French émigré and one of Angelica's friends, noted that Angelica "makes it a habit of receiving while lying down in her bedroom, which I cite to show how she flaunts this country's customs." Cornelia and Washington Morton continued to party conspicuously, too, and Peggy was as wild and sarcastic as ever.

Eliza's sisters kept the Schuyler girls firmly in the center of New York society, and Eliza felt the embarrassment keenly. "I rely on your promise to compose your dear heart," Alexander wrote her, and then he left town for extended legal business in Albany, leaving Eliza to manage a small baby and the gossip created by his pamphlet. On the weekends, when her house was filled with a passel of young boys, home from school on the island, Eliza was too busy to think about what the world said. Those were the days she felt most contented. But Alexander being away at such a difficult moment filled her with sadness and hopelessness. Eliza was struggling. Her heart ached.

It worried Alexander. But finances were tight, he was hustling to build his legal practice, and the work was in Albany. Alexander was away most of the spring of 1796, living upstate with Eliza's parents while traveling the legal circuit. Eliza stayed in New York City during the school year with the children, so they had somewhere to come home to on the weekends. They hardly saw each other all spring, and Eliza was under the weather. By the time he returned home, Eliza felt obliged to travel up the Hudson with the younger boys on the summer holiday to see their elderly grandparents. The older children would stay in the city during the break with Alexander.

Three weeks in Albany was a summer tradition, and it mattered a great deal to Philip and Kitty Schuyler, but when Eliza set off in early June she didn't want to leave Alexander or the older children and was close to a breakdown. Perhaps in the back of her mind were thoughts of what had happened the last time she'd left Alexander alone for a few weeks in the summer. The pamphlet had caused no end of heartache, and surely if she had been with Alexander she could have convinced him not to publish it.

When the time came to go, Eliza wept at the wharf. "I have been extremely uneasy, My beloved Eliza, at the state of health and state of mind in which you left me," Alexander wrote to her after her sloop departed upriver. "Let me entreat you as you value my happiness to tranquillize yourself and to take care of yourself. You are infinitely dear to me. You are of the utmost consequence to our precious Children."

A few days later, Alexander wrote Eliza again, assuring her that the "dear boys & myself continue in good health & that they thus far behave well. I hope they will continue to do so—for in our mutual love & in them consist all our happiness." The scandal regarding the Reynolds affair had drawn Alexander and Eliza into a tighter bond of family loyalty than ever, but circumstances had forced them to be apart for too long, and it was more than Eliza could handle. She did her duty. Then, exactly three weeks later, Eliza made her way home, where Alexander was anxiously waiting. There had been no new disaster.

In the summer of 1797, the United States was once again facing the possibility of war, as the French Revolution yielded to the imperial ambitions of Napoléon Bonaparte, and, at the end of July, Alexander's name was once again in the papers. This time, the coverage was less uniformly antagonistic and noted that Alexander Hamilton had been promoted to the rank of major general and inspector, making him second in rank in the military only to General George Washington. Angelica and John's eldest son, Philip Church, now nineteen, was eager to join the infantry as the American military mobilized, and Alexander wrote to President John Adams directly, requesting a commission for the young man, despite his inexperience.

Eliza refused to go to Albany for the summer this time. Over and over again, the letters Alexander wrote to Eliza during this period reveal in detail the unhappiness and anxiety these trips caused her. Now, more than ever, her commitment to staying together and protecting her family was tribal. When Eliza and Angelica proposed the two families rent a summer house together in the increasingly fashionable Harlem Heights during the fever season, instead of living apart in Albany, Alexander agreed readily. He was desperate to make Eliza happy and to return some measure of her devotion.

By the late 1790s, the Harlem Heights area was a popular summer retreat for the city's wealthy, and the socialite Josephine DuPont was one of their neighbors. Josephine found Harlem crashingly dull and dryly noted that the men mostly stayed in the city and left the women, bored, stuck on rural country estates with children. Angelica came to the same conclusion. Eliza, however, flourished. Far from the gossip, unburdened by tedious social calls and the dictates of city customs, she laughed with their children and spent long, delightful hours riding through the fields again and growing flowers.

Unlike the other city husbands, Alexander joined his wife there. In those days, the Bloomingdale Road extended as far as modern-day West 147th Street, and large summer homes straddled knolls of farmland, where the cool breezes came in from the river. Work took him a great deal to Philadelphia that summer, but when he was in the city, Alexander rode the dozen-odd miles out from Wall Street to Harlem to have dinner with Eliza. For the first time in years, Alexander saw her relaxing.

And so he struck upon a surprise for her in November. In a buoyant and flirtatious letter, Alexander wrote to Eliza:

> *You are my good genius; of that kind which the ancient*
> *Philosophers called a familiar; and you know very well that I am*
> *glad to be in every way as familiar as possible with you. I have*
> *formed a sweet project, of which I will make you my confidant*
> *when I come to New York, and in which I rely that you will*

cooperate with me chearfully. "You may guess and guess and
guess again Your guessing will be still in vain." But you will not
be the less pleased when you come to understand and realize the
scheme. Adieu best of wives & best of mothers. Heaven ever bless
you & me in you.

The letter is a rare peek at the heart of their marriage, and it is not
a glimpse into a marriage struggling with betrayal. It is a letter that
speaks of Alexander's love, of their continued intimacy, and offers
his thanks, in the private language of their relationship, for Eliza's
sacrifice and loyalty.

Alexander's secret plan was to make their renewed happiness that
summer and into the autumn permanent and to find a way to capture forever this emotional place and the depth of their commitment.
Their moments of greatest happiness together had come, over the
years, when they retreated to life together in the country as a family: the early days in Albany after Yorktown, the months in Albany
following his resignation from the Treasury, this pastoral idyll in
Upper Manhattan.

Alexander had found thirty-two acres of land for sale in Harlem
Heights. He was buying it. They would build together their dream
home in the country. Eliza's father promised to send down by river
from the Schuyler mills in Saratoga the wood to build their home,
and Alexander imagined a beautiful garden for Eliza. They did not
have the money for such an indulgence. It would take Alexander
years of work to pay off the loans to finance it. But he dared to look
ahead to the future.

When Alexander signed his note calling her the "best of wives,"
he was striking the theme that, privately, was at the heart of their
marriage and of how both Alexander and Eliza understood her public sacrifice in the scandal. When, long ago, Alexander had talked
of the Roman wife in his letters to Eliza, he had been thinking of
the famous Latin funeral oration on the tombstone of a Roman wife
named Turia, recounted in a law school text called *Factorum et Dic-*

torum Memorabilium by Valerius Maximus, a text that he knew well
as an orator and statesman and that sat in General Schuyler's law library at the Pastures.

At the beginning of their marriage, it was the virtues of the Roman
wife recounted by Valerius Maximus that Alexander was asking of
Eliza—loyalty, obedience, affability, reasonableness, industry, religion without superstition, sobriety of attire, modesty of appearance,
love for one's relatives, devotion to one's family. Alexander's earliest
letters to Eliza and to friends like John Laurens detailed his search
for a wife with just those qualities.

In the moment of their greatest crisis, Alexander knew that Eliza
had not wavered in her promise. And now he could not help thinking of the second part of that familiar oration on the best of Roman
wives. "Why," that fortunate Roman husband asked,

> *should I now hold up to view our intimate and secret plans and*
> *private conversations: how I was saved by your good advice when*
> *I was roused by startling reports to meet sudden and imminent*
> *dangers; how you did not allow me imprudently to tempt*
> *providence by an overbold step but prepared a safe hiding-place*
> *for me, when I had given up my ambitious designs, choosing as*
> *partners in your plans to save me your sister and her husband. . . .*
> *There would be no end, if I tried to go into all this. It is enough*
> *for me and for you that I was hidden and my life was saved.*

It was a sentiment remarkably near to the refrain of the "nut
brown maid" in Eliza and Alexander's old ballad, and it was the secret at the heart of the couple's marriage. "Best of wives" was, increasingly, a private code in Alexander's love letters.

Having made the sacrifice of the Roman wife, Eliza doubled
down on the role and its virtues, finding in them meaning and a mission. She embraced the identity. A new commitment to piety and
to public works of charity was part of that change for the Hamilton family after 1799. Eliza and the older children—Philip, Angelica,

and Alexander Jr.—attended church services on Sundays at Trinity, where Eliza soon began taking communion.

Eliza longed for a quiet life out of the public eye and her faith deepened. Alexander, however, remained Alexander. He and the rest of the Schuyler girls and their husbands continued to test the bounds of decorum with their pranks and sense of humor. Eliza grew exasperated.

One of those family pranks set off a new scandal in February 1799. Alexander, Angelica, and Angelica's eldest son, Philip Church, now in his early twenties, came up with a joke to play on John. Along with the help of a Polish gentleman, Count Julian Ursyn Niemcewicz, they went along with a gag to pretend that ghostly spirits of the dead were speaking to Alexander.

News of the haunting spread throughout the city, terrifying the credulous, and, as Peter Jay, the son of Eliza's cousin Sarah Livingston Jay, told the story,

> *Aided by our natural credulity and the respect paid to the names of the persons concerned, it obtained very general belief, gave rise to many very curious descriptions, and caused an interest and agitation of mind not easy to be conceived.*

The story grew and grew and with each telling became more ghoulish and outlandish, and eventually Alexander was forced to stop the panic by admitting that it had all been a contrivance "to frighten the family for amusement, and that it was never intended to be made public."

The society ladies were not amused, and when the truth came out the reputations of the pranksters suffered, especially Angelica's for being party to a trick on her husband. Another of Eliza's cousins in the city, Elizabeth De Hart Bleecker, noted in her private journal, "It seems it was a plot laid by General Hamilton, Mrs. Church, young Church, & [Count Niemcewicz], to deceive Mr. Church, which they did most completely—It was soon blazoned abroad & given credit

to by many. Ann [i.e., Angelica] Church is mortified exceedingly."
Alexander and Angelica continued to set tongues wagging with their
tomfoolery, fueling the old rumors. Following on the heels of the
Maria Reynolds scandal, their behavior added gasoline to a fire.

This same cousin also noted in her journal that in September,
John Church and Aaron Burr had fought a duel at Hoboken after a
quarrel over business.

The duel was a turning point in Alexander Hamilton's relationship
with Aaron Burr. More than anything else, it set in motion the succession of tragedies ahead of Eliza. The duel brought to a head two
events that had convinced Alexander that Burr was definitively a villainous scoundrel. The first had to do with a low trick that Burr had
played on Alexander in securing his support for a proposed water
company in Manhattan. In the summer of 1798, the yellow fever had
swept New York City again, and this time doctors thought they understood the reason for the pestilence: dirty city water. Alexander
threw his weight behind a plan to found a company to install safe city
infrastructure. When he learned that it was a bait-and-switch deal
and that the real plan was to fund a competing bank to his New York
project, Alexander was furious. Worse, the company put in wells
"dug in the filthiest corners of the town," which made the city's citizens sicker. The second involved a real-estate deal, a company called
the Holland Land Company, and some shameless stock market speculation. Alexander, who had made some genuine but relatively modest missteps during his time in the Treasury and paid an excruciating
price for them, understandably objected to what he saw as Burr's
flagrant abuse of his elected office in the New York legislature for
profit. John Church, repeating what he had heard from his brother-
in-law Alexander, "in some company intimated that Burr had been
bribed for his influence whilst in the legislature," prompting Burr's
challenge to a duel.

John Church, who took a dim view of Burr and was more than

a bit brash in his actions, accepted the challenge, and four gentlemen—the combatants and their seconds—were rowed across the
river to New Jersey one September afternoon before sunset. One
shot missed. Another shot tinged off a coat button. John Church,
thinking better of the affair after a first round of shots, promptly
offered an apology, which Aaron Burr accepted. Alexander, though,
was not satisfied. The subtext of the duel—in which he and his old
enemy Congressman Aedanus Burke were the seconds—nodded to
Alexander's time in the Treasury and to the debacle of the Reynolds scandal. Once, Alexander and Aaron had studied law side by
side in the library of General Schuyler and attended Van Rensselaer family events together in Albany. They had worked in the same
field as attorneys for years, sometimes on the same side, sometimes
as opposing counsel, but had maintained cordial relations. Since the
1790s, Alexander had had his doubts. He had doubts no longer. Burr,
Alexander was convinced, was a weasel of the first order. He would
move heaven and earth from this day forward to thwart Burr's ascent
in public office. Alexander would not always succeed. In fact, in the
election of 1800 his failure would be spectacular. But the die was cast
now, and the stage was set for what in a few short years would be a
disaster for the Hamilton family and a tragedy for Eliza.

The duel between John Church and Aaron Burr ended with a jolly
shaking of hands and laughter, even if Alexander stewed in private.
All four of the combatants, in fact, were lucky. These showdowns
ended badly as often as not, and dueling was against the law in Manhattan. Should death result, the man who fired the deadly shot faced
charges of willful murder, and all the seconds charged as accessories.

Dueling had long been a problem in the United States, and in 1799
duels disturbed the peace of the wives and mothers of New York
with upsetting regularity. Eliza was probably unaware that Alexander and John Church were caught up in a number of challenges over
insults and allegations.

Some of those challenges were absurd and seemed designed to
provoke Alexander. General John Skey Eustace, a political adven-

turer, informed Alexander early in 1799 that "a gentleman called this instant to tell me a duel was to take place between General Hamilton and myself—in the first place—and two successive combats with the Mssrs. Church, if I survived the first affair. As this report has arisen from some reflections I have sent to a printer . . . you may give the most prompt and efficient check to this more than ridiculous story."

Alexander, who had no interest in giving Eustace a platform for or satisfaction regarding this invention, replied coldly, "You are perfectly right, Sir, in calling the story you mention a more than ridiculous one. To confirm this conclusion, it is not necessary for me to tell you that I had not the most distant idea of your having written any thing which could give me displeasure." Alexander refused to be drawn back into combat with the press and judged that Eustace was an attention seeker. Renewing the controversy would distress Eliza.

There were still implications. Seventeen-year-old Philip Hamilton, raised in this milieu, was unfortunately inclined to view dueling as part of the ritual of manhood. His older cousin, Philip Church, told a riveting story, and Philip Hamilton admired his rich and rakish uncle John, as well. This was what it meant, then, to the teenager to be a gentleman. What came next had been set already in motion.

For most of the spring of 1800, Eliza was alone again with the children. Construction had begun on a large family home on the property in Harlem that they would call "the Grange," and Eliza and the younger children spent the summer living in a small farmhouse on the property, while Alexander traveled to court sessions across New York on business; when he could make it home, he camped with the older boys in tents, as Eliza and her sisters had done as children in Saratoga. Alexander "measured the distances [for the building] as though marking the frontage of a [military] camp," one of the boys remembered later. "When he walked along, his step seemed to fall naturally into the cadenced pace of practiced drill." They thought of their father, as Eliza had of hers, simply as the general.

Roughing it, though, wore on Eliza. Rheumatic gout, the effect of a kidney damaged by repeated fever and infections, had left Eliza's knees swollen and aching. It didn't help that she was heavily pregnant with their seventh child already that sticky summer, a daughter, another Elizabeth, born toward the end of November.

Eliza was lonely, and letters with her cousins sustained her. She was especially close with her cousin Gertrude Livingston, and their correspondence was frank and affectionate. One of Gertrude's letters added a postscript that hinted at some of the challenges Eliza faced with her eldest son, who people already said was as talented and as reckless as his father. Philip Hamilton had completed his studies at the recently renamed Columbia College and was being groomed by Alexander for a brilliant career as a lawyer. He was his father's golden boy, and Alexander adored him no less than Eliza did. But Alexander was too inclined to be soft on his son, even as the world praised the boy. "Tell the Renowned Philip," Cousin Gertrude wrote, "I have been told that he has out stript all his Competitors in the face of Knowledge and that he dayly gains new Victorys by Surpassing himself."

The world had high expectations for Philip Hamilton. And Philip was cocky.

Everyone seemed to struggle with bad health in the winter of 1800–1801. The new baby, Betsey, was sickly, and Eliza's sister Catherine couldn't shake a chest infection. Philip Schuyler's gout was painful enough in February 1801 that Alexander sent General Schuyler's sleigh down from Albany to fetch Eliza's sister Catherine home. "Don't be alarmed that Kitty is sent for," Alexander wrote. "Your father is much better and I am persuaded in no manner of danger. But he shews an evident anxiety to have your Sister Kitty with him. She is the pet."

The real health worry in the family, though, was Peggy.

Alexander was in Albany at the state court, and Eliza hoped to travel upriver in February to see him. But the roads were too sloppy for the carriage, and heavy clay in the soil was causing flooding at the Grange that she had to stay to manage. Alexander planned to be home before the end of the month, but when the time came it was clear to everyone that Peggy was dying. She had been failing for years due to complications of gout, a disease that plagued the Schuyler family.

Peggy asked if Alexander would stay a few days longer with her. He could not refuse the request of his beloved sister-in-law. Peggy's husband the patroon, Stephen Van Rensselaer, asked someone to fetch their young son from boarding school in New York City so he could see his mother. Eliza wished that she could have gone with the boy, but she couldn't leave her small children. She would have liked, though, to have said goodbye to her sister. She would have to trust Alexander to tell Peggy that she loved her. When the letter arrived, edged black with mourning, Eliza held it for a long moment, already knowing what it meant. "On Saturday, My Dear Eliza, your sister took leave of her sufferings and friends, I trust, to find repose and happiness in a better country," Alexander wrote. "Viewing all that she had endured for so long a time, I could not but feel a relief in the termination of the scene. She was sensible to the last and resigned. . . . Tomorrow the funeral takes place. The day after I hope to set sail for N York. I long to come to console and comfort you my darling."

But Alexander was seldom at home any longer.

Eliza's frustration was growing. Even when Alexander was in the city now, there were increasingly occasions when the three-hour journey back and forth from Wall Street to the Grange was too much, and he sent home by courier instead guilty notes to Eliza and presents of marbles for the boys and dolls for little Betsey. But what Eliza needed most was Alexander's help with the two oldest. Philip was drinking and partying. Their daughter Angelica was moody and erratic.

Alexander and Eliza had weathered together the crisis of public scandal. The numbing daily routine of middle age, chronic aches and pains, and marriage was a bigger challenge. They were apart again, and they had never done well long-distance as a couple. Alexander wrote defensive and irritable letters, and Eliza hated reading them and knowing he was unhappy with her. She was never a scribbler and found it harder than ever to write the letters he wanted when they were at odds with each other. It was an old pattern in their relationship and Alexander often repeated the refrain he had been iterating since the first days of courtship, but now his tone was less cajoling and wounded than scolding and paternal. "I was extremely disappointed, My Dear Eliza," Alexander wrote in early October, "that the Mondays post did not bring me a letter from you. You used to keep your promises better. And you know that I should be anxious to hear of your health. If the succeeding post does not rectify the omission of the former I shall be dissatisfied."

Eliza complied, but she was cross and unhappy.

Alexander was home briefly at the farmhouse in Harlem in October. Eliza finally lost her temper, and there was a bitter quarrel. Eliza didn't feel well, Alexander was never home, yellow fever was again terrifying New Yorkers, and there was always the looming humiliation of the Maria Reynolds gossip. She had two children under five, including a sickly one-year-old whom she was still nursing. On their weekends home from school, she looked after their three younger boys, her late brother John's fatherless son Philip, and now her late sister Peggy's motherless son Stephen.

And Philip was exasperating his mother. "Naughty young man," Alexander sympathized, adding uselessly to Eliza, "But you must permit nothing to trouble you and regain your precious health." She did worry about her eldest son's carousing, though. Word made its way back to Eliza that the boy was acting the part of the young buck in the city with friends, frequenting the theaters, drinking too much in the public houses, and debating politics with a venom that soon made even Alexander uneasy. And Eliza knew that if this was what was making its way back to his mother, things were probably worse than she imagined.

Eliza was not wrong in her supposition.

Philip Hamilton, with all the swagger of the handsome son of a famous father, was acting up. He was, in the words of one of his father's friends, a "sad rake" and something of a hooligan. Things were sure to end in disaster.

And then they did.

The tragedy started stupidly. Philip and a fellow Columbia classmate named Price—possibly Stephen Price, although the young man's identity is uncertain—went out drinking on the night of November 20, 1801, before heading off for a raucous night at the Park Theater in Lower Manhattan. A Friday night at the Park in the early 1800s was not a staid affair and largely did not involve watching a great deal of onstage drama. Prostitutes strutted in the cheap seats in the third-floor balconies, seats where young college lads, not coincidentally, also tended to congregate, and rowdy partiers threw peanuts at the actors. The real action was always offstage, though, and Philip and Mr. Price were carousing.

The previous summer a local attorney named George Eacker, twenty-seven years old and a supporter of Aaron Burr and his Republican party, had made a Fourth of July speech at Columbia that attacked Alexander and suggested that, during Alexander's time in the Treasury, he and John Church had colluded stealthily to bring back the monarchy. The relationship between Alexander and Burr had deteriorated further when Alexander, skirting the edge of his promise to Eliza to stay out of politics, had intervened in the presidential election. Such was Alexander's contempt for Burr that, faced with a choice between Burr and his ancient enemy, Thomas Jefferson, Alexander had supported Jefferson as president. But what stung Philip Hamilton most was the attack on the character of his father and his uncle.

The wine had been flowing, and the lads were foolish and rowdy. When Philip Hamilton spotted George Eacker in one of the next boxes on the balcony, in the company of one of the Hamilton cousins, a Miss Livingston, it seemed like a good idea to the impetuous young man to mock Eacker for the benefit of his fair relation. Young Philip Hamilton's loud commentary was, one witness recalled, "replete with the most sarcastic remarks." George Eacker was, unsurprisingly, irritated. Soon, all eyes were on the quarrel, and the show was forgotten. The three men took the argument outside, and on the pavement the situation degenerated. Eacker complained, "It is too abominable to be publicly insulted by a set of rascals," and made to throttle Philip Hamilton. Philip had it coming.

"Rascal" was a fighting word, and George Eacker knew it. That was an escalation. Circa 1801, "rascal" retained its original sense: the insult implied that a gentleman conspicuously lacked a certain virile organ. A contemporary vulgar translation would be something along the lines of calling a man a eunuch or a castrato. Philip Hamilton, with all the blustering machismo of youthful testosterone and certainly not prepared to give ground on the subject of his amours with the theatrical "ladies," responded with a furious, "Who do you call damn'd rascals?"

"We insist on a direct answer," pressed Price.

George looked from one to the other and shrugged. What a choice. "Well, then, you are both rascals," came the exasperated answer.

Friends urged the three to have a drink and try to resolve matters calmly. Further aspersions on each other's manhood and on the character of Alexander Hamilton continued in a nearby tavern. Whatever else was said in that tavern, no one ever recorded precisely, but there can be little doubt that some of what was said touched on the delicate subject of financial speculation, Maria Reynolds, and Philip's famous father. Then Eacker announced that he was going back to the theater with his friends and that he expected a challenge to duel, unless they were too much the cowards.

Rascals. Cowards. The young men were having none of that. Price immediately dashed off a letter challenging Eacker to a duel, and had it delivered to him dramatically mid-show in his box at the theater. Philip Hamilton named a second and then, as it was his first duel, rushed off first to speak to his cousin, Philip Church, and his uncle, John Church, about protocol and what to write in his letter. His challenge followed, just before midnight.

George Eacker, reasonably enough, indicated he could only fight one duel at a time and agreed first to meet Price, since he had sent the earliest letter. On Sunday afternoon, with pistols drawn, they fought a bloodless duel, shook hands, and returned to the city together. Now, he informed Philip, he was prepared to deal with his challenge. The young man turned again to John Church, who now advised his impetuous nephew that he had in fact been the aggressor. As such, finding a solution was his responsibility. John Church, having seen enough action to know, was wary of fighting when it wasn't necessary. Philip did offer to apologize and end the matter. But only if Eacker would retract the insult about his father.

Eacker declined to take back his criticisms of Alexander. He was of the view, in general, that Philip Hamilton deserved a sound thrashing. A duel was, he concluded, the only polite alternative to beating the young whippersnapper senseless. The showdown was set for the afternoon of Monday, November 23. Philip borrowed his uncle's dueling pistols for the occasion, and sometime around midday the news of what was happening reached a startled Alexander.

"On Monday before the time appointed for the meeting between E, & H," wrote one of Philip Hamilton's friends, Thomas Rathbone, "General Hamilton heard of it and commanded his Son, when on the ground, to reserve his fire 'till after Mr E, had shot and then to discharge his pistol in the air." If he had to fight, he told his son, throw away the shot. No one would get hurt, and it would discharge the debt of honor. But Alexander urged his son and his friends, as well, to find another settlement.

Alexander assumed the lads would find a solution. He only heard that the duel was going ahead as planned when Philip was already on his way to Powles Hook, New Jersey. Gripped with anxiety and a terrible sense of foreboding, Alexander rushed to the home of their family physician, Dr. Hosack. He planned to ask the doctor to accompany him out to the dueling grounds, just in case there were an injury.

Alexander arrived too late. His son's friends had already summoned the doctor, who was even now on his way to Greenwich Village. Alexander, filled with horror, fainted in the doctor's parlor from sheer terror. He realized too late that Eliza had been right to worry about Philip. When he came around, Alexander set off at a breakneck speed on horseback.

On a sandy bank just a mile from New York City, the two young men had faced off, after pacing out the distance. Perhaps nineteen-year-old Philip meant to follow his father's instructions and had simply misunderstood the ritual. Perhaps he was acting with his customary bravado and machismo. But form gave George Eacker the first shot, and, instead of giving any hint of his intention to throw away his own shot, at the word "present," Philip had aimed his gun carefully and held steady. For a full minute, nothing happened.

Then George Eacker pulled the trigger.

The shot rang out and an instant later the bullet struck, tearing through the groin, shattering Philip's right hip on its hot path through the body, and lodging in his left arm as he fell.

Friends carried a bloodied and half-conscious Philip as far as they could, to John and Angelica's country home in Greenwich Village, and that was where Alexander found them. Alexander knew the moment he saw his son. The faint pulse in Philip's wrist and the quantities of blood lost told him it was hopeless. Dr. Hosack stood by the bed. Alexander grasped his hand and whispered in agony, "Doctor, I despair." The doctor could only shake his head.

Angelica sent word for Eliza to come the moment the men arrived with her nephew's broken frame. Eliza knew something terrible had happened when she saw her sister's message. Fear made it hard to breathe, but there was no fast way to reach Philip or Alexander. To cross Manhattan in 1801 was already a slow and laborious process, and by the time Eliza arrived from Harlem, darkness had fallen. Angelica's ashen face warned her, and she ran up the stairs to find Alexander. She could only think of what she saw after as a scene of horror.

Alexander stood at the side of a bed. The slump in his shoulders scared her. Standing vigil beside him was one of Alexander's oldest friends, his college roommate Robert Troup, and her son's friend Thomas Rathbone. Eliza looked. Between them was the pale and delirious body of her eldest baby.

The men remembered afterward, too, the terrible moment Eliza entered the room. Alexander, racked with quiet sobs, could barely stand as his eyes met Eliza's. Philip was incoherent and in agony, and there was no question that he was dying. "Never did I see a man so completely overwhelmed with grief as Hamilton has been," Robert Troup wrote after. "The scene I was present at, when Mrs. Hamilton came to see her son on his deathbed (he died about a mile out of the city) and when she met her husband and son in one room, beggars all description!"

Thomas Rathbone's description of how Eliza and Alexander passed that night is even more heartrending: "On a Bed without curtains lay poor Phil, pale and languid, his rolling, distorted eye balls darting forth the flashes of delirium—on one side of him on the same bed lay his agonized father—on the other his distracted mother." Holding their son between them, their hands touching, Eliza and Alexander lay together until just before dawn, when Philip stopped breathing.

Elizabeth De Hart Bleecker reported sadly in her journal, "Philip Hamilton linger'd of his wound till about five o'clock this morning when he expired in the arms of his afflicted Mother—the cause of the unhappy affair was a few words that passed between Mr Eacker, Mr Hamilton, and young Mr Price at the Theatre."

Philip had been all their pet, since his first arrival. It was a tragedy for the entire Schuyler family.

Friends supported Alexander as he followed his son's coffin to the Trinity Church graveyard. Eliza was too distraught to attend the funeral. Then, Eliza and Alexander had no choice but to turn their attention to their daughter Angelica. She was descending into madness.

Angelica's moods had been volatile for years, although no one spoke of this publicly.

Rather, it is the fact that Angelica did not circulate in society like her Church cousins or her young aunt, Catherine Schuyler, that speaks most clearly of Alexander and Eliza's struggles with their eldest daughter. Her cousin Catherine Church danced at balls and lived in high society. Aunt Caty, as Catherine Schuyler was called in the family, went on visits and to house parties. But Angelica Hamilton stayed close to home, near her parents or her grandparents and her pianoforte. She was shy, and some described her as extraordinarily modest and simple. She relied—more perhaps than was healthy—on her eldest brother, Philip.

Eliza's grandson Allan McLane Hamilton wrote decades later that "upon receipt of the news of her brother's death in the Eacker duel, [Angelica Hamilton] suffered so great a shock that her mind became permanently impaired" with something he called "insanity." But the truth was sadder and more complicated. Philip's funeral and the family's despair tipped the scales in what had already been a precarious balance, and the underlying condition was probably schizophrenia. What is certain is that the trauma of her brother's death triggered psychosis and sent the seventeen-year-old young woman into a spiral.

Sometimes Angelica lived in a world in which Philip had not died, and Eliza listened, heart heavy, as she played the same old songs from their childhood obsessively. Sometimes she became withdrawn and catatonic, and Eliza could not reach her daughter. Other times, Alexander and Eliza caught glimpses of the old Angelica and dared to believe things would get better. And sometimes, for a while, they did. Hope was agony for Eliza.

Eliza was not managing well into the winter either, as grief consumed her. She struggled with depression and despair, and her father wrote her loving but stern letters, reminding her that she still had a husband and other children who needed her and that resignation was her Christian duty. "Considerations like those my Child," he urged, "will produce such a degree of calmness in Your mind, as that your health may not be injured and ultimately, with the favor of indulgent heaven, restore you to peace and give happiness to your heart to your beloved Hamilton, to Your children and relations." And religion now did help to console her.

Horseback riding was one of her great pleasures, too, and her father pressed Eliza to rouse herself. "Exert therefore my dearly beloved child that energy, which was so conspicuous in you Ride out frequently," Philip Schuyler advised, "and collect estimable friends about you, that your thoughts may be diverted from painful reflections." By March of 1802, though, Eliza was once again six months pregnant. Now the worry was that her despair would cause her to lose the baby. It certainly would prevent her from fast horseback riding.

Eliza was sick in spirit. Behind the sadness also burned a small, hot flame of anger. Eliza knew as well as anyone that her son had died trying to protect the reputation of his father in the aftermath of scandal. It tore at her that he would never know that his father had not broken faith with her or with any of them. She realized now that she would never be able to tell the unvarnished story to any of the children. They would live in a world where their father was reflected back at them through the eyes of a hostile public. It seemed like a poor inheritance.

When Eliza gave birth to another little boy on June 2, they named him Philip after his lost brother. "May the loss of one be compensated by another Philip," wrote her father. "May his virtues emulate those which graced his brother, and may he be a comfort to parents so tender." But one child could never replace another.

The next blows came in such a rapid succession that Eliza could barely catch her breath. She certainly had no chance to get her bearings. As Alexander said of those next few years, "In the later period of life misfortunes seem to thicken round us."

While a handful of happy family events punctuated the calamities—the wedding of Angelica's oldest daughter, Catherine Church, in the spring to a prominent city lawyer, and the completion of the house at the Grange chief among them—the next few years were a constant train of sorrows. Peggy's widowed husband shocked the family with a hasty remarriage, and, in August, Angelica's eleven-year-old boy, Alexander, came down with the influenza that swept the city that summer. For two weeks, the doctors bled the little boy in a futile attempt to drain the fevers, until he finally perished. Eliza sat for a long time in darkened rooms with Angelica after the men carried away the small body.

Then a letter arrived in early March that shattered any equilibrium Eliza had managed. Her mother had suffered a massive stroke on March 7, 1803. She died within minutes. Eliza again could not stop crying.

Angelica and Eliza set off immediately for Albany by coach, with the young Philip Church driving, intent on returning to the Grange with Philip Schuyler and their sister Catherine.

Alexander had his doubts about Eliza going. "Remember that the main object of the visit is to console him," he urged Eliza, "that his own [burden] is sufficient, and that it would be too much to have it increased by the sorrows of his Children." Alexander wasn't sure Eliza could hold it together well enough to offer anyone else comfort. Alexander stayed behind with their smallest children and tried to buoy Eliza with tender, reassuring news, reporting that their little daughter "pouts and plays, and displays more and more her ample stock of Caprice," and "my two little boys John & William . . . will be my bed fellows." Eliza lived in constant fear of something happening to one of the other children.

If there was one silver lining, for Eliza it was only that her daughter Angelica seemed to be improving. Eliza's father wasn't ready to leave Albany, "after giving and receiving for nearly half a century a series of mutual evidences of an affection and of a friendship which increased as we advanced in life." Eliza and her sister Angelica stayed a few weeks longer, but by April both were eager to get home to their small children. Staying behind, though, to cheer up her father was his favorite daughter, Catherine, and two granddaughters, Betsey Church and a much more stable Angelica Hamilton. Soon, the two older Hamilton boys, James and Alexander, would travel upriver to join them.

On the long journey home, Eliza and Angelica clung to each other. Just like always.

CHAPTER 16

The Duel, 1804

The death of Philip Hamilton had come at a low point in their marriage, but mourning him and rebuilding together had drawn Alexander and Eliza closer. Now, the death of Eliza's mother in 1803 bound them even more tightly. It was their pattern. At a distance, they faltered. In crisis, they turned to each other. Setting off for home, Alexander now wrote Eliza flirtatious letters again from the road. "I shall be glad to find that my dear little Philip is weaned, if circumstances have rendered it prudent," Alexander teased her. "It is of importance to me to rest quietly in your bosom."

The yellow fever hit New York City again that summer, and the children spent the season between Albany and the Grange. By autumn, with the baby weaned and their marriage closer and stronger, Eliza and Alexander spent a quiet Christmas season together. Alexander went shooting on crisp mornings with the older boys and the family dog, Peggy, while Eliza worked on embroidery by the fire with the babies. All was not perfect. Their daughter Angelica had gotten a bit better in her mind and then faltered, and gloomy thoughts possessed Alexander, especially when he looked at his eldest daughter and thought of their lost Philip. But Eliza dared to hope, as 1804 began, that the hardest times were behind them.

So did Alexander. He struggled to shake off the depression that gripped him, and he knew that, compared to what might have been, his troubles in the first months of that year were petty ones. That did not make them, though, the less annoying. Colonel Aaron Burr, ending a term as vice president of the United States under President Thomas Jefferson and planning a run for the New York State governor's office, continued to irritate Alexander, and in legal correspondence between the two men they took little jabs at each other. Alexander wrote in one a snarky postscript: "I observe in your warrant of Attorney a new error. You add the Shillings & pence to the penalty whereas they belong to the condition. The penalty is simply ⟨–⟩." The tone was professional but glacial, and buried beneath the pokes was mutual contempt that had been growing since the duel with John Church in 1799.

Aaron Burr's supporters emerged as a group of Northern politicians agitating for secession and the end of the fragile American union. Alexander was horrified. "For God's sake . . . cease these conversations and threatenings about a separation of the Union," he pleaded with fellow politicians.

In mid-February Burr's run for office was at a fever pitch. Eliza just sighed when Alexander announced that he would be in Albany for most of the month, trying an important legal case the outcome of which would set a precedent for political speech and seditious libel. It was no secret that Alexander was fighting hard to see Aaron Burr defeated in the election, but the two men had been staunch political opponents for years already. There would have been no particular reason for Alexander to write to Eliza in any of his letters that he and her father, General Schuyler, had talked politics with some gentlemen at a private dinner party one evening. By the end of March, Alexander was back in New York City for the rest of the spring anyhow.

During the second week of May, Eliza's sixteen-year-old son, James, brought to the Grange a note from his father. Eliza's heart sank when she read it. Alexander had invited sixteen people to the house for a dinner party on the following Sunday, including the brother of the emperor of France, Napoléon. That would be the end of any other plans at home for Eliza. Alexander acknowledged that it would mean a great deal of work and that their plan for her to come into the city might now be impossible. "If not prevented by the cleaning of your house," Alexander wrote, "I hope the pleasure of seeing you tomorrow."

Alexander then announced additional plans to throw a ball at the Grange a month later for their eldest daughter and her cousins, with another seventy-five guests invited, and Eliza and her sisters were again thrown into a frenzy of preparation. The girls were delighted, and it was good to see their daughter Angelica in good spirits.

One other strange event disturbed their peace that spring, but Eliza only thought more of it later. Just as the early-summer sun was coming up over Harlem, a great pounding on the door startled Eliza from her sleep beside Alexander. Eliza and Alexander exchanged looks that asked what could be the matter, and Eliza's first thoughts were of the older children. Shrugging into a dressing jacket, Alexander went down to investigate. Eliza curled back up among the sheets and waited. The light crept across the floor now as the sun rose higher.

When Alexander stepped back into the room and sat down on the side of the bed, he turned to Eliza, and his expression was puzzled. "Who do you think was at the door?" he asked Eliza.

Eliza shook her head. She could not imagine who would pound on their door at such an hour.

"Colonel Burr."

And before Eliza could ask why, Alexander offered, "He came to ask my assistance."

Broke and in a panic, Burr urgently needed ten thousand dollars to pay loans on his Richmond Hill mansion, and Alexander did help him. He turned to John Church and a few other gentlemen, and they tided Aaron Burr over.

Later, it seemed very odd to Eliza that Aaron Burr should so cruelly return such a favor.

All the planning and work between the dinner party in May and the ball in June meant that Eliza took no notice of a newspaper article,

originally published in late April in the Albany paper and reprinted
in the city in mid-June, about her father and Alexander. A gentleman
named Charles Cooper, writing in response to a letter on political
matters published by her father, alleged that Alexander had dispar-
aged the reputation of Aaron Burr at a dinner party in Albany. "Gen.
Hamilton, the Patroon's brother-in-law, it is said, has come out decidedly against Burr, indeed when he was here he spoke of him as
a dangerous man and ought not to be trusted," the article asserted.
"Judge [James] Kent also expressed the same sentiment," the author
continued, and "the Patroon was quite indifferent about it when he
went to New York—it is thought that when he sees Gen. Hamilton and his [other] brother-in-law Mr. Church (who Burr some
time ago fought a duel with, and who, of course, must bear Burr
much hatred)—I say many feel persuaded that Mr. Rensselaer will be
decidedly opposed to Burr."

When the letter was reprinted in the city papers, the editor of
the *New-York Evening Post* couldn't resist a bit of editorializing
that appeared to question his veracity and infuriated Charles Cooper. He responded by putting Alexander squarely in the middle of a
brewing squabble. He now alleged that Alexander had made other,
even worse claims about Burr, which he would not repeat but which
showed a "still more despicable opinion which General Hamilton has
expressed," and, with spectacularly bad timing, this article appeared
in print the week Burr lost his contested election for governor. Aaron
Burr, stinging from defeat and suspecting dark machinations behind
it, was furious when he saw it a few weeks later.

Historians have long speculated about what Alexander might
have said, but he may have made some remark or another about
one of Burr's "perversions." Aaron Burr was famously louche and
horny. At the height of the election, the admittedly partisan *American Citizen* newspaper alleged that it could name "upward of twenty
women of ill fame" that Aaron Burr had bedded. But prostitutes
were not even the worst of it. The editor followed up those claims
with the shocking assertion that Aaron Burr was seen cavorting with

a well-endowed black woman at a "ball" thrown by his slaves. More recently, there has been some evidence that Burr, like Thomas Jefferson, had mixed-race illegitimate children, including a son and a daughter born in the late 1780s and early 1790s to a woman from India who worked as a family servant. Whether or not there was any truth in these scurrilous assertions hardly mattered in the bruising world of early nineteenth-century American politics. Another theory is that Alexander may have remarked upon Burr's spendthrift ways and reckless way with money, a sensitive topic. Or perhaps it was simply that Alexander believed that Burr—raised in the extended family of Benedict Arnold's wife and already caught up in what Burr's enemies claimed was a nefarious plot to betray the Americans in the West and which would lead to his trial for treason—was more than usually dangerous to the union of the republic.

When Aaron Burr saw the article, fresh on the heels of his defeat, in an election that he had hoped would mark his comeback, visited by spies, pressed by creditors, and—as he must have felt—pursued doggedly by Alexander Hamilton, years of anger hardened into hatred. The tensions in their relationship went back decades, to the earliest days when the young upstart Alexander had been given the run of General Schuyler's law library as a son, and Aaron had had to make a supplicant's application. And the anger was as recent as the governorship election. All the world could read that Alexander behind his back mocked him—Alexander, the self-confessed adulterer—and Burr was desperate to defend his honor. He promptly challenged Alexander to a duel.

Letters flew back and forth. Alexander quibbled over words, and, rather than simply disavow the insult, he dissected the logic of the challenge like a lawyer. When Alexander began spinning out elaborate rhetorical arguments, it was generally a sign that he was guilty of something, and it's more likely than not that whatever Alexander had said was indeed offensive. Burr, backed further into a corner and infuriated at the lawyerly evasions, grew increasingly obstinate and was determined to be offended. The stubbornness of both men and the complex partisan politics that fueled their personal animosity meant that none of their friends was able to resolve the matter. The duel was on. Alexander made sure that Eliza had no knowledge of it.

Alexander delayed until after Angelica's ball at the Grange at the end of June, where lanterns lit the nighttime garden, and their children later remembered Alexander as relaxed and vivacious. There was another small delay so the two men could wind up some business matters, and they agréed to meet with their seconds on the field of honor in New Jersey at dawn on Wednesday, July 11.

Alexander borrowed dueling pistols from John Church, drew up a schedule of his debts and assets, and, as a precaution, wrote a last letter to Eliza.

Aaron Burr began target practice.

The outcome of the duel is famously known.

Eliza would remember always that last, idyllic weekend. On Saturday night, they laughed with old friends around the dinner table at the Grange, and on Sunday morning Alexander asked Eliza to come for a walk with him in the gardens. They strolled for a long while, in companionable silence, with Eliza's arm tucked under Alexander's elbow, and looked out over orchards and toward the distant river. All day, Alexander stayed at home, under Eliza's feet, and she smiled to wonder what had gotten into her normally busy husband. As the evening came on, Alexander called to the children, even the older ones, and urged them out into the garden. There, sprawled among the limbs and tousled hair of his children, Alexander "laid with them upon the grass," one of the smaller boys, eleven-year-old John, later remembered, "until the stars shone down from the heavens." Six-year-old William wriggled, four-year-old Betsey snuggled close to her father, and the older children teased their mother to come join them with the baby. Little Phil was two that summer, and it was hard not to think of his namesake and brother there under the starlight.

On Monday, Alexander went back into the city as usual, taking with him eleven-year-old John and sixteen-year-old James, who went to school during the week in the city. On Tuesday night, Alexander sat up writing some letters, and sometime after ten o'clock he turned off the lantern. The younger of the boys was up late studying his Latin, and Alexander went to stand behind him and put his hand on John's head. The boy's hair was so soft and warm, like when he had been just a baby. Do you want to sleep with Papa? Alexander asked John, and the drowsy boy nodded. When Eliza had been away in Albany in the summers, visiting her parents, this had been Alexander's tradition with his middle sons, and they had listened rapt under the bedcovers or at his feet in the armchair as their father told stories of Roman senators and warriors. "With what emphasis and fervor did he read of battles," the boys remembered; "it would seem as though Caesar were present." Other times, it was stories of the great heroes of the American Revolution and how the patriots he had known beat back the British.

That night, though, Alexander didn't tell any stories. He took his son's hand and intertwined his own hand with the boy's small fingers. They said the Lord's Prayer together. *Thy will be done.* Those words echoed for Alexander, who lay very still until he heard the quiet breath of his child sleeping.

In the morning, Alexander was gone. He set off not long after dawn from New York City with Dr. Hosack and his second, Nathaniel Pendleton. Their destination was the marshland of Weehawken, New Jersey, across the Hudson River from what is today Midtown West and Hell's Kitchen, and the dueling grounds on a grassy, hidden ledge not far above the tidewater. The bargemen pulled against the currents and toward the sea cliffs, startling gulls, as the morning sun climbed over the Atlantic. Alexander surely thought in that moment of his son, shot on the bluff ahead of him. He had already decided to throw away his shot, just as he had advised Philip to do.

By seven o'clock, the barge was grating at the shoreline, and Alexander and Nathaniel climbed the rocky path to the dueling grounds, where Aaron Burr was already waiting. After the ritual exchange and squaring off at ten paces, the men turned toward each other, and moments later in the exchange of fire a hot bullet tore through Alexander's abdomen, shattering his rib cage. Alexander fell to the ground. Burr took a few paces forward and then, urged by his second, fled for the waiting boat. Dueling was illegal, and in the eyes of the law was simply murder. Burr must have realized in a moment what an outcry there would be. Perhaps it dawned on him now, for the first time, that his life, as he had known it, would also end if Alexander perished. And the shot was clearly fatal.

Dr. Hosack was waiting below with the bargemen—he could not be prosecuted for what he did not witness—but raced up the path at the first cries from Burr's second. He arrived to find Nathaniel holding Alexander, who looked for a moment into the doctor's eye, whispered the words "This is a mortal wound," and sank unconscious. The bargemen rushed to carry Alexander to the boat, and fifty yards from shore smelling salts and the sea air brought him around. "He asked me once or twice how I found his pulse," the doctor remembered later, "and he informed me that his lower extremities had lost all feeling, manifesting to me that he entertained no hopes that he should long survive."

By the time they landed on the river docks of Manhattan, the pain was tremendous. Alexander felt it course through him as he was carried toward the city mansion of his weeping friend, William Bayard. All he could think was: *Eliza.* "Let Mrs. Hamilton be immediately sent for," Alexander whispered; "let the event be gradually broken to her; but give her hopes." Alexander knew that it would take hours for Eliza to travel from Harlem to the West Village, where the barge landed. Grief would come soon enough. For the moment, Alexander asked them to spare her. "My beloved wife and children," Alexander kept repeating.

The news spread across the city in a fury. Eliza's cousin Elizabeth De Hart Bleecker heard within hours. A duel had been fought between General Hamilton and Colonel Burr, and General Hamilton had received a mortal wound in the side, she recorded in her journal that evening. In the pubs and on the wharves, it was the talk of all the citizenry, as the shocked city waited.

When a message reached Eliza at the Grange, ahead of her was a ride of a dozen miles, and at first she was told only of an illness. Slowly, as bits of the story were meted out to her, the dawning realization came to her that some unnamed tragedy was unfolding. As she entered Greenwich Village, people stopped on the streets and stood quietly. Tears shone in the eyes even of the men, and Eliza felt panic rising. What was happening? Was it one of her sons? Her husband? Where, she asked, her voice breaking, was Alexander? Why would no one answer? Dr. Hosack standing at the door, with a grave look, told her in that instant everything.

Alexander lay on a large bed upstairs, and Eliza could scarcely breathe for crying. Alexander opened his heavy eyes and squeezed her hand gently. He said, "Remember, my Eliza, you are a Christian." His eyes said, *Be Roman.*

All that afternoon, Eliza sat with him into the darkness. She sat with Alexander through the night as well, and he could still at moments talk to her.

In the quiet of the night, who knows what words passed between them. They are words unlikely to have been very different from the words that Alexander had written already to Eliza in his very last love letter. "If it had been possible for me to have avoided the interview," he wrote to her,

> *my love for you and my precious children would have been alone a decisive motive. But it was not possible, without sacrifices which would have rendered me unworthy of your esteem. I need not tell you of the pangs I feel, from the idea of quitting you and exposing you to the anguish which I know you would feel. Nor could I dwell on the topic lest it should unman me.*

In his last words, he harkened back as well to the orations of Valerius Maximus and wrote of his love and praise for Eliza in what he suspected would be his funeral oration. He urged Eliza to embrace religion and the hope of meeting once more. "Fly to the bosom of your God and be comforted," he wrote. "With my last idea; I shall cherish the sweet hope of meeting you in a better world." Then he thanked her for her stoicism, sacrifice, and always her devotion, when state enemies accosted them, in words with rich, private meaning, words at the heart of their twenty-three-year marriage. "Adieu best of wives and best of Women. Embrace all my darling Children for me."

When dawn broke on Thursday, Alexander was still alive, but a cold paralysis had spread over his limbs. Dr. Hosack felt for a pulse. Alexander's heart was only weakly beating. Eliza ushered in their seven children now to say farewell to their father. Alexander could not speak, but at the sight of them closed his eyes, tears falling. Eliza took his hand and resumed her quiet vigil. At two o'clock in the afternoon, his breath stopped at last, and then the bells across the city of New York began tolling.

Their old friend Gouverneur Morris, so moved by the scene, fled to the garden to try to compose himself. Angelica lay curled on a sofa next door, "weeping her heart out."

As for Eliza, "the poor woman was almost distracted," those who watched her anguished remembered later. When she saw Gouverneur Morrris, Alexander's closest friend, she begged him, between sobs, "to join her in prayers for her own death, and then to be a father for her children." Soon, Gouverneur Morris was also crying.

All day Friday, the church bells in New York City rang from "dawn to dusk" in honor of Alexander. Businesses shut their doors, closed for a city in mourning, and Eliza's friend Elizabeth Seton, the wife of William Seton, recorded privately in her journal that his death was "a melancholy event—the circumstances of which are really too bad to think of."

Eliza dressed that morning for the first time in the black widow's weeds that she would wear until her death more than fifty years later. Although Eliza could not know it, she had more than half her life still ahead of her. When Alexander died, she was not yet forty-seven. There was a ritual of death, and Eliza mustered all her reserves. She set off to do her duty. "Mrs and Miss Hamilton"—Eliza and her daughter Angelica—visited at noontime her kinswoman Elizabeth De Hart Bleecker in one of their first social calls of mourning.

Alexander was buried on Sunday, July 14, with military honors. A slow procession, led by a riderless horse draped in black crape, Alexander's boots turned backward in the stirrups, wound solemnly for miles through a tearful city toward Trinity Church. Soldiers on the streets who remembered Alexander Hamilton's wartime gallantry stepped in to join the march. In New York City harbor, naval officers lit cannons to salute the fallen general. At the side of Alexander's grave, the eloquent Gouverneur Morris gave an emotional eulogy, his voice cracking.

Eliza did not attend the funeral. She sat instead inside a darkened parlor, holding her two-year-old little boy to her. She knew that she would collapse in grief long before she ever reached the churchyard. It took all her emotional reserves to take the older children in the evening to Trinity Church to hear the bishop preach their father's funeral sermon. Sitting in the family pew, she could feel everyone's eyes on her. She wished she could disappear and fly to Alexander. In the decades ahead, she would never stop wishing.

CHAPTER 17

The Widow, 1805–6

The scandal of Alexander's death consumed the city. Aaron Burr fled, as much to avoid a beating at the hands of a mob as to evade arrest. In the weeks to come, a grand jury would indict Burr on charges that, "not having the fear of God before his eyes, but being moved and seduced by the Instigation of the devil," he "feloniously and willfully did Murder" General Hamilton.

Eliza was deaf to all of it. She retreated into her family circle and turned to her sister. Eliza and the younger children traveled up the Hudson to visit her father at the end of July. When she returned to New York City a few weeks later, she felt more steady. She and the older children resumed regular Sunday church services and visited Alexander's grave after the sermon. Eliza and her daughter now made a habit after church of visiting Elizabeth De Hart Bleecker, her brother Andrew Bleecker, and his young wife, Frances. Here, Eliza could talk about Alexander with those who knew and admired him. As a Christmas gift for one of Elizabeth's sons Eliza tenderly wrapped a miniature statuary bust of Alexander.

The frequent references in Elizabeth's journal to "Miss Hamilton," who visited with her mother but also came alone for tea and parties with the other young people, show that, in the immediate aftermath of her father's death, Angelica Hamilton's mental state remained in balance. That was a relief. Eliza had enough troubles.

Her greatest worry was for the future of her oldest boys—especially when she understood the appalling state of her finances.

By the end of August, still caught up in the dreadful business of responding to heartfelt letters of condolences, Eliza was only beginning to grasp the full extent of the financial catastrophe bearing down upon her.

Alexander had drawn up a list of assets and debts, and the plain facts were that the latter significantly outstripped the former. There was a large mortgage on the Grange and precious little in savings. Alexander—like Eliza, only in his late forties—had counted on another decade of working. Or more.

His friends, left to unravel the estate for his widow, were more concerned even than they let on to Eliza. And Eliza already knew enough to panic. Alexander had left his widow in a very difficult position. Letters went back and forth among the friends in July, debating what should be done, and a group of Alexander's friends "immediately set about the execution of the plan suggested . . . to raise a competent sum of money to relieve General Hamilton's family from the possibility of embarrassment and to provide a fund for their support." On August 6, a sultry Monday morning in New York City, Oliver Wolcott called to order a meeting, "on the Subject of Gen. Hamilton affairs . . . at the election room in the Bank of N.Y.," attended by a half-dozen men, including Edward and William Tilghman, to discuss the matter with some urgency. Among other plans to provide for Eliza and the children, more than thirty-five men donated to a trust of income-producing lands in Pennsylvania. John Church took a lead in arranging matters and added his contribution.

But Angelica was left to break the news to Eliza that she still could not afford to return permanently to her home in Harlem. John advised that carrying on alone at the estate, without Alexander's income, would be difficult, even with her father's offer to send down in the fall from Albany any supplies of beef, pork, and butter that Eliza and the children wanted. The Grange had been an extravagance they could barely afford, even when Alexander was furiously working. "Your brother[-in-law] deems it the most prudent," Angelica wrote Eliza, "that you remain where you are, as it is utterly impossible for you to be at the Grange without horses, and their expense will pay for your house rent. He thinks the Grange might be let." But renting the Grange would just delay the inevitable. Eliza's heart broke to think of losing her last ties to a home with Alexander under the gavel at public auction, but there was no other choice. She rented a small home on Warren Street in the city, and toward the end of October Eliza began moving special items from the Grange into the city. Her father encouraged her not to stint, at least, on her rental accommodation. He would make up any shortfall. Philip Schuyler urged her to find a place "sufficiently large that you may not be in the least crowded, for remember, that it is my intention that you should be well accommodated, and make Every want immediately known to me that I may have the pleasure of obviating it."

It was the end of October before Eliza could face the Grange. How painful it would be, her father perceived, to return to "a place where the Sweet Smiles, the Amiable affability, the Chearful and enduring Attentions of the best of men had been wont to meet your Eyes." There was nothing for it but to start packing. "I have removed the Bust [of Alexander]," she wrote her father the next week, "from that habitation that I had expected it would have been for a length of time you will easily imagine my dear papa my feelings."

How to launch her older sons into adulthood was her greatest concern. Eliza was the mother of seven children, ranging from two to twenty, and she needed urgently to find a career position for her now eldest son, Alexander Jr., who had graduated in August from Columbia. He was away in the autumn, traveling through the New York frontier as far as Montreal in the age-old coming-of-age Schuyler tradition, but when he returned, he would need suitable employment. Alexander's second, Nathaniel Pendleton—indicted as an "accessory before the fact" in the murder of Alexander and still dealing with the fallout of his role in the duel in Weehawken—looked for a place for the young man in a merchants' accounting house in New England. Eliza's father and Oliver Wolcott had other ideas for the young man, and Eliza found herself in the unenviable position of having a half-dozen bossy and opinionated men, each with a different idea, all taking charge simultaneously of her future.

She was determined to make her own decisions, especially about the children. This was not easy to do and was met with opposition. She needed help, both with the boys and with money, and women without husbands were not encouraged to be independent. When Eliza resisted one of the men's plans for her children, she softened the blow by playing to the hilt the role of the hapless, helpless widow. In time, it became a habit.

What she wanted more than anything else, in the end, was to have the children near her. She had never wanted to be apart from them or from Alexander. Now, the thought was unbearable. "The Grievous Affliction I am under," Eliza wrote, rejecting the plan for Alexander Jr.'s prospective move to New England, "will be added [to] the trembling mother's anxiety for her child least he should fall in to evil. I have every assurance from him that he will be careful of himself but [even] New York has a thousand snares for an unprotected young man." She was thinking of her eldest son and George Eacker. "Do I not owe it to the memory of my beloved Husband," she pressed Nathaniel Pendleton, "to keep his children together? It was a plan he made in his last arrangement of his family that they should not be with out a parents care at all times. A plan in which I made the greatest sacrifice in my Life, it was that of being one half the week absent from him to take care of the younger while he took care of the Elder."

Eliza got her way, as she always intended. Alexander Jr. entered into a merchants' house in New York City. Then she set about securing a place for her third son, John, at Columbia, where he would join his brother James, already a student.

Philip Schuyler was a constant support now, support that was importantly financial but also emotional. The idea to write a biography of Alexander—a book that would set straight libelous attacks on his reputation and character and tell the story of the man, the father, and the hero of the American Revolution—was one that Eliza and General Schuyler first began to discuss together in November. For Eliza, the dream of someday telling her story of her husband was a lifeline, and she and her father were already deep in discussions about who would be the best author. "My dear papa," Eliza wrote, "I have not said anything to Mr. [John] Mason respecting the subject that you and my self wished he should undertake. It is doubted weather his mode of writing would be equal to it. There is a Mr. [John] Johnston thought of and tis said is desirous of it. Judge [James] Kent is acquainted with him and perhaps could give you an opinion."

Already, Eliza was beginning to imagine the day when she would have the courage to read again Alexander's letters and to gather up anecdotes of her husband. Philip Schuyler had piles of correspondence, too, and decades of memories of a man whom he unreservedly admired. In warm, loving letters, Eliza and her father together laid out their modest plans for a future.

Those plans were interrupted on November 18, 1804.

Philip Schuyler had suffered for years from gout, and the Schuyler siblings considered it the family affliction. That autumn, it had flared badly, but Philip assured his daughter that his most recent bout was no worse than usual and mending.

He had sent her on November 3, 1804, a sympathetic, heartwarming letter, assuring Eliza that her sorrow was not a burden. "That your afflictions, my dear, dearly beloved child, had added to mine," he wrote, "was the natural result of a parent's tenderness for so dutiful and affectionate a child, as he invariably experienced from you."

His gout, he assured her, too, was much better: "Since my last letter to you I have no gout; [and] although the ulcers in my feet and above my knee have been extensive, they bear a most favorable aspect of healing." He was unable to walk about, but he had no pain, and as far as he was concerned, things were looking up.

The trouble was not gout per se. It was the kidney damage caused after decades of the disease's progress and the infected wounds in a seventy-year-old body. Peggy had died when gout went to her stomach. Faster than anyone in Albany thought possible, Philip Schuyler now succumbed, too, to organ failure.

By the time Eliza got the news in New York City, her father had already been buried. The ulcerous sores and cankers urged a hasty service in the Schuyler family parlor followed by a speedy interment.

The letter fell to the floor. Eliza was untethered.

The death of her father was the beginning of a bitter inheritance dispute that would further devastate Eliza. She would not have believed that autumn that further devastation was possible.

The passing of Philip Schuyler also meant that Eliza's financial situation quickly went from precarious to dire. At those rare moments when her grief receded, worries about money and the children rose up instead to consume her.

The crux of the family debate—also the subject of public commentary and more of the gossip Eliza hated—revolved around claims that their father had made generous financial provisions for Eliza after Alexander's death, provisions that her siblings now viewed as an advance on her share of the inheritance.

Alexander's powerful friends had unwittingly fueled the rumor. When they'd met to untangle Alexander's estate and had brought up the issue of raising money for a trust fund to support Eliza and the children, no one wanted to insult a rich man like Philip Schuyler by suggesting that he couldn't or wouldn't take care of his daughter. No matter what kind of a hash Alexander had left his finances in, surely, the men said, her wealthy father would support her.

And, if Philip Schuyler had lived, there is no doubt that he had planned to help Eliza with the children's college fees and promised to fill gaps in her ongoing household expenses. Her other siblings were all on firm financial ground, and, with the marriage of the youngest sister, Catherine, to a rich, if rather unpleasant, man named Samuel Malcolm, Philip Schuyler's other daughters were provided for. Alexander's death had left Eliza alone without a good income.

The truth, however, was that the Schuyler fortune was smaller than the public at large imagined. Angelica, John, Alexander, and Eliza may have been the only ones in the family who knew the truth, and even Angelica assumed that the boom times of the 1790s had repaired some of her father's earlier misfortune. What wealth existed was not only modest but largely illiquid, tied up in the family properties and real-estate investment. In the will recorded in early December at the Albany courthouse, the estate of Philip Schuyler showed a value of only $30,000 or $40,000, split among a half-dozen grown children and some grandchildren. Alexander's debts were above $50,000, and Eliza's share of the inheritance was nowhere near enough to provide her with a steady widow's income, never mind the kind of windfall that might allow her to save the property in Harlem. Eliza accepted the inevitable, but it broke her heart to lose the house that had been Alexander's family vision. The Grange would go on the auction block come springtime.

It was too much. Eliza tumbled into the darkness of depression.

She found herself now in the painful situation of also having to defend herself against accusations that she was double-dipping on her siblings. The family communications were tense and deeply complicated. Doubting Eliza's integrity most openly were her brother Rensselaer, her sister Catherine, and Catherine's husband, Samuel Malcolm. Cornelia and Washington Morton wavered. Angelica and John, who knew Alexander's household affairs and finances intimately, sided with Eliza. The family divide left Eliza and her remaining brother, Philip Jr., as the eldest surviving son and an executor of his father's will, to negotiate a wounding—and wound-ingly public—conversation that felt to Eliza a great deal like airing family laundry.

She wished nothing more than that the earth would swallow her. She wished that she were dead, so she could be with Alexander. "A report has prevailed," Eliza wrote her eldest brother somewhat hysterically,

> that my father gave me six thousand Dollars before I left it, let me assure you it is an untruth, it has given me some pain that I should be held up to the public in so unfavorable a point of view as on the one hand to request you to make provision for me, by some arrangement, and on the other, (as it is said) to be so amply provided for by my father. What but ill intent toward me could have been the motive to have given such an idea to the world and to my sisters and brothers? But this world is a world of evil passions, and I thank my God He strengthens my mind to look on them as steps to an entire resignation to His will, which I pray may fast approach me.

In his last love letter to her, Alexander implored Eliza to turn to religion and the hope that they would meet again in heaven. Eliza clung to faith now like a drowning woman. She carried on in those darkest months only by remembering that she was the mother of Alexander's small children.

John Church acted in the estate matter for Eliza and Angelica, infuriating Samuel Malcolm and pitting the younger generation of Schuyler siblings against their two older sisters. John and Samuel butted heads, and things did not go smoothly. Some of the most hurtful accusations against Eliza were fueled by Samuel's personal animosity toward Alexander and Philip Schuyler. Samuel and Catherine, like so many of the Schuyler girls before her, had eloped, but Philip Schuyler's doubts about Samuel Malcolm had gone deeper than this ceremonial irregularity. The couple would not have needed to elope if the general had endorsed the marriage or this particular son-in-law. He must have wondered, at the end of his life, why so many of his daughters chose such dubious husbands. Alexander had been the exception.

Politics were, as ever, part of the conflict. Samuel Malcolm's staunch allegiance was to John Adams, and John Adams had not taken kindly to Alexander savaging his character and public conduct in an open letter in 1800. Adams was among Alexander's most vituperative enemies, and that he helped to spread and likely believed some of the most scurrilous of the rumors about Alexander did not help family matters. More than a decade after the death of General Schuyler, years yet in the future, Samuel Malcolm could still be found complaining to Thomas Jefferson—another of Alexander's political opponents—of the injustice of Alexander's promotion and of the damage to his career when "my marriage with the youngest daughter of General Schuyler, invited me to Separate myself, from all public Services." He had felt pressured to resign in the wake of the family scandal. But Samuel was also in the newspapers himself in 1805, facing accusations of fraud and financial misdealing, making Catherine's inheritance and money a sensitive issue.

Catherine, naturally, took the side of her husband, although her siblings tried to remember that she had little choice in the matter. Where Samuel led, she followed. When John Church tried to see Catherine to go over the will, she cut him and curtly sent word back with her housemaid that she was not "at home." She also stopped calling on her older sisters and avoided her family.

"Dear Sister," Angelica wrote to Catherine on December 8, hoping to smooth things over, "Mr Church waited on you to deliver the enclosed paper, but you were not at home. I have not sent it before expecting every day to have the pleasure to see you—any other papers respecting my Father's Estate in Mr. Church's possession you may recall whenever it suits your leisure to call." Catherine still kept her distance, although she felt guilty. Eliza was deeply hurt. She and Alexander had opened their home to her youngest sister for years so she could enjoy society and life in the city with her cousins, and Catherine's betrayal felt intimate.

The squabble about the inheritance went on for the better part of a year, but reached its lowest point in January of 1806. The terms of their father's old-fashioned will left the largest portions of the estate to his sons. The lion's share went to the young son of their late first-born brother, John, and much of what remained was left to Eliza's brothers, Philip Jr. and Rensselaer. The will, written before the two youngest girls were settled into marriages, left legacies of $2,000 for Cornelia and $5,000 for Catherine. Otherwise, the surviving sisters, along with Peggy's young son, Stephen, were left to inherit, as tenants in common, one-fifth shares of a partition of farms and land in the Saratoga Patent. Theirs was a modest inheritance.

The question of whether Eliza cheated the estate by hiding a gift of $6,000 poisoned even the simplest financial conversations with Samuel Malcolm and made working together as siblings and tenants in common impossible. Eliza learned in January from the Albany attorney managing the estates that she was due income of $62.35 from her share of the estates, but that the payment couldn't be released because of the conflict with her siblings. Eliza was mortified—not least because she desperately needed the sixty-two dollars.

Her brother Philip Jr., at wits' end, tried to broker the family peace with a compromise and saw clearly that Eliza was not the problem. "My Dear Brother," Eliza wrote him,

> *Thus is our family situated, differences have arisen, and neither can recollect how much it is encumbent on them to be at peace, but ill will must prevail, against all the claims that goodness, and Religion Demand. . . . Mr. Church has read your letter to me and as it is my sincere wish that all differences should be done away, and your requests be complied with, I have called on all around and proposed a meeting at my house to endeavor to affect what you mention in your Letter but have no hopes.*

Eliza had tried to bring all of Philip Schuyler's children together and find a solution. But her siblings and Samuel Malcolm, especially, were determined, it seemed, to quarrel. Eliza was exhausted, and it all seemed hopeless. She considered that the only silver lining in any of this was that it had brought her and her younger brother Philip Jr. closer. Nearly a decade separated them in age, and they hadn't grown up together as children. But the stress of the past year and her brother's calm, steady demeanor drew them into a deep adult friendship.

The stress overwhelmed Eliza. Was it perhaps better to sell up, rather than quarrel? Eliza considered it. "I am told a farm has lately been sold at the rate of six dollars per Acre," she wrote to Philip in March; "my mother expected a handsome Inheritance and certainly their was a considerable tract. . . . With respect to the Saratoga property, the selling of it at present must be at a Considerable." But the estate limped on encumbered.

After it was all said and done, by spring Eliza was left with an inheritance of $15,000—less than $300,000 today. It was nowhere near enough to allow her to dream of buying back the Grange from Alexander's creditors. Their home went on the auction block at last and sold for $30,000. Eliza took the news calmly, but her heart ached when she turned her back for the last time and walked away from the home she and Alexander had built together.

What she did not know was that behind the sale lay a marvelous secret.

Alexander's friends knew how hard she and the children had taken leaving the Grange, and they had searched for a way to show their affection, too, for Alexander and his family—a way that would give the family back some kind of equilibrium. So a group of them, including her brother-in-law Washington Morton, banded together, and, when the Grange went under the hammer, put up the money together to buy it. They wanted to sell it back to Eliza. They would take for a price the $15,000 she had in her savings. Eliza was humbled and deeply grateful.

The summer of 1805 marked the first anniversary of Alexander's death. It was a hard rite of passage, made all the harder by the yellow fever epidemic that once again devastated New York City, with a virulence the locals compared only to the fevers of the 1790s.

Her son James graduated from Columbia, and Eliza and the smallest children spent the summer in Harlem. Home. Eliza smiled at the thought and walked again for a long time in her garden, where she and Alexander had strolled together on their last weekend. Her oldest daughter, Angelica, stronger and better as well, accepted an invitation to spend the summer in the countryside outside Boston with the minister John Mason, who had been with Alexander at his deathbed and whom Eliza and her father had considered engaging to write Alexander's biography. Angelica remained with the Mason family until the start of autumn. "Dear Madam," John Mason wrote to Eliza on September 23,

> *We have this moment parted with your daughter Angelica*
> *with much regret. . . . This good girl of yours has made herself*
> *extremely acceptable to Mrs. Mason & my daughter—& we shall*
> *anticipate with pleasure some future opportunity to enjoy her*
> *society in Boston—If she is spared to you, I most sincerely think,*
> *you have in her a promise of great consolation & Comfort, &*
> *a companion that will alleviate & soothe the sorrows, which*
> *probably never can be removed.*

Angelica Hamilton might never marry. Both Eliza and Reverend Mason saw that. Angelica was childlike and sometimes simple and was perhaps a better companion than wife and mother. But Eliza had prayed for the return of her reason, and for the moment that prayer had been answered.

All summer, the smallest children ran riot at the Grange, and Eliza was glad to hear the house full of life and little people. Her three youngest—Betsey, William, and Philip—ranged from three to eight, but the house was also full of other motherless children.

Eliza was once again collecting around herself waifs and orphans. Sarah, the thirty-five-year-old wife of her brother Philip, died in September, leaving behind two sons under the age of ten, Eliza's nephews Robert and John Schuyler. Would Eliza mother the boys? Philip asked his sister. Eliza did not hesitate. She was a warm and gentle mother, and nothing gave her as much pleasure as children. For the next year, her two young nephews lived with their aunt and cousins at the Grange, while their father courted a suitable stepmother. It was the third time that Eliza had taken motherless children into her home, beginning as far back as the adoption of Fanny Antill, now a young woman of twenty. Alexander, too, had been an orphan.

And that started Eliza thinking. When the next opportunity came along, she embraced it.

Eliza wanted to live up to Alexander's vision of her as the "best of wives and best of women." Too many times, she had been cross or impatient. She had not always borne the burden of sacrifice or public abuse, she knew, with complete equanimity. In his final words, Alexander had asked her to trust in religion and reminded her of the Roman ideal—piety, stoicism, charity, loyalty, motherhood—at the foundation of their marriage. Eliza was determined now not to fail Alexander.

Through church circles, Eliza had been friends with a small group of women, most of them widows, for years already. There was the widow Isabella Graham and her married daughter, Joanna Bethune, whom Eliza knew from the 1780s. There was Elizabeth Seton, the young and pious widow of Alexander's old friend from the Treasury days William Seton, who died of tuberculosis in 1803. There was Sarah Clarke Startin, Elizabeth Seton's godmother, and another Seton family relation, Sarah Hoffman, the widow of Nicholas Hoffman, whose nephews were Alexander's legal partners.

These five women—Isabella Graham, Joanna Bethune, Elizabeth Seton, Sarah Hoffman, and Sarah Startin—had all been involved for a number of years as the leading lights in the Society for the Relief of Poor Widows with Small Children, led by Isabella Graham and Elizabeth Seton and organized as a Christian response to the yellow fever devastation of the 1790s. Eliza was already a casual member and subscriber.

When Alexander's friend William Seton gasped his last in Italy, where doctors had hoped the weather could cure him, his wife embraced Catholicism. It was, all the ladies said, a shocking and "barbaric" thing to do in Protestant America. Her horrified godmother broke off all contact, and the ladies agreed that Elizabeth Seton would not carry on in the Society for the Relief of Poor Widows, based out of Trinity Church in Lower Manhattan. Elizabeth Seton, ironically, would go on to become the first Catholic saint born in America.

Elizabeth Seton's departure—from their society and, to their view, from her senses—would need to be filled by some other strong woman of devout purpose. Ideally someone prominent. Ideally a widow. Eventually, the ladies asked Eliza Hamilton to take Elizabeth Seton's place in their evolving social mission.

Eliza was not a saint and didn't strive to be one. But she did want to be a widow Alexander would admire. And in 1806, after the massive outpouring of grief at Alexander's funeral, she was already New York City's most famous and most cherished widow.

So when Sarah Hoffman discovered in a shabby tenement the heartbreaking scene of five young children weeping over the body of their dead mother and proposed the establishment of a society for orphans, she spoke to Isabella Graham. Isabella, who had been reading about the seventeenth-century church father August Hermann Francke, the founder of an innovative orphanage in Germany, proposed an American "ragged school" on his model. Orphanages did not yet exist in New York. The idea was revolutionary.

Sarah and Isabella went straight to Eliza. Would "Mrs. General Hamilton" join them in the radical project of building a home especially for orphaned children? Eliza only had to think of her two small nephews and how they cried at night for their mother. She thought of Fanny Antill, whom she had loved as a daughter, and how she saw in her the face of Marie-Charlotte and Edward. She thought of a young Alexander and the scars he'd carried with him in private, left alone to survive as an island orphan, and of the note in which he'd asked her to care for the woman who'd saved him. But above all, Eliza thought of her own children still mourning the death of their father, and thought what it would be to leave them without any parents. She knew instantly in her heart the answer. She immediately accepted.

And Eliza needed the society as much as they needed her. In the darkness of grief, she needed a focus. The fate of widows and children spoke to her and let her remember that, even in the loss of Alexander, she was fortunate. Eliza was also a natural organizer.

She threw herself into the society with the same determination and efficiency with which she regulated her household. All these women had been born and bred, in one fashion or another, to manage estates, and running a charitable institution was well within their skill set. At society meetings, Eliza and the other society widows considered and deliberated. They planned their projects. And then, in an act of faith, they signed a lease on a small two-story house on Raisin Street in Greenwich Village, hired a respectable man and his wife to care for the children, and gave a name to their new organization.

On March 15, 1806, the Orphan Asylum Society—the first charitable orphanage in New York—was founded. Eliza and her compatriots put out a public call for other society ladies to join them, and a dozen showed up at their first meeting at the City Hotel. By the time the meeting was over, "Mrs. General Hamilton" had been elected the second directress, essentially the organization's founding vice president. Among the trustees were more society women, almost all of whom had long been part of Eliza and Alexander's inner circle. These friendships were not new to Eliza; rather, they represented a deepening of old ones.

The aim of the asylum, the ladies proclaimed in their public state-

ment, was to educate indigent and orphaned children, teach them
to read the Scripture, and place them in apprenticeships or indentures. The asylum took in twelve orphans in the first few months,
and by the time the ladies met again in January of 1807, with rather
less fanfare and acrimony than the Founding Fathers, to ratify their
constitution, it was already clear that they would need to find space
for more children.

By April, twenty clean and well-fed children appeared before the
board for applause and inspection. The names of those children were
neatly recorded in the asylum record books, today preserved in the
New-York Historical Society archives, and they were boys and girls
with names like Thomas Birch, John Wilkinson, or—the only death
among their children—Sarah Ann Morrison, who died as a four-
year-old from illness. Most of the children were between the ages
of three and ten when they arrived at the orphan asylum, and they
went on to be mantua makers, bakers, and farmers. One girl joined
the household staff of Sarah Startin as a housemaid. A little boy went
on to become the gardener at the estate of Eliza's kinsman Philip
Livingston.

They had taken in twenty children that first year. But they had
turned away nine times as many. The need was immense, and Eliza
felt sure that this was her calling. Growing the orphanage quickly
was a risk and a challenge, and the finances were daunting. But when
the secretary asked Mrs. General Hamilton which way she voted
on the question of pushing ahead, Eliza gave her resounding yes to
the project. The ladies were determined to build a new, bespoke orphanage, large enough to accommodate more children, and, in the
spring of 1807, they started fundraising. Sarah Startin donated a
one-acre parcel of land on Bank Street, in Greenwich Village. Jo-
hanna Bethune's husband said he would guarantee the $25,000 loan
the widows would need to take out to finance the construction of
a three-story orphanage able to accommodate fifty children. The
women turned to the local churches and newspapers, asking min-
isters to encourage donations in their sermons and journalists to

spread the word in their columns, and twisting the arms of their rich friends and neighbors. Eliza's sons, watching her trudge out in even the worst weather when she heard of an orphaned child or saw the chance of rounding up a donation, teased her that she worked not like a lady of leisure but like a peasant.

They were on their way, but the ladies had not yet raised all the money to complete the project. On June 5, the *New-York Evening Post* gave the society a plug, advising that "the attention of the public is most respectfully solicited to the merits, the importance, the wants of a recent but valuable institution, 'The Orphan Asylum of New-York.'" "In the space of fourteen months," the editors gushed, "many of the children who knew not the alphabet when they entered, can now read the Bible fluently, and their progress in writing is also considerable." The public was urged to contribute. By the end of June, church donations had reached $873.38. It was a long way off from $25,000. So Eliza and the ladies turned to their rich network of connections in government and convinced the legislature of the State of New York to donate the last $10,000 toward the building.

When the women triumphantly laid the cornerstone to start the construction of the new orphanage, Eliza, dressed still in the black of mourning, was there. But her heart felt so much lighter.

CHAPTER 18

Legacies, 1807–27

Family quarrels plagued Eliza still, but they touched her less now. The Schuyler family was fracturing, Cornelia's health was failing, and Eliza didn't see her or her sister Catherine much any longer. Catherine's husband, Samuel Malcolm, who still nursed old grievances and guarded jealously his share of the Schuyler fortune, took his family upstate to take personal control of his wife's farmland inheritance. Washington Morton, caught up in a second fatal duel, fled New York one step ahead of an arrest warrant. The thirty-two-year-old Cornelia and their children followed him to Philadelphia, where she died of illness months later.

Angelica remained Eliza's stalwart, but Angelica and John had troubles now, too, with money. After years of easy speculation and fast living, John Church's finances were collapsing as a result of the trade embargo of the winter of 1807–8, as tensions again ratcheted up with Britain, and of being caught out short at last speculating in real-estate investment. Eliza felt badly for her nephew Philip Church, who paid the price of his father's financial disaster. The young man scrambled to try to save his father's worst real-estate gamble by moving to the edge of the wilderness with his society bride. When that didn't work, Philip left his hapless bride to hold down the fort upstate while he headed off to London to try to collect on unpaid gambling debts owed his father. His actions smacked of desperation.

Eliza understood Angelica's panic. The farms in the Hudson Valley continued to cause endless squabbles, and Eliza was sometimes so short of cash that she was forced to cadge a loan to make ends meet. Their spendthrift and high-rolling brother Rensselaer was once again in financial trouble, and Washington Morton put the cat among the pigeons afresh when he asked to be bought out of Cornelia's share of the family land in Saratoga as a widower. The siblings couldn't agree on the value of the land, and the lawsuit that followed ended up in the newspapers. How she would raise her share of the money caused Eliza sleepless nights.

It was also becoming increasingly difficult to deny that her twenty-six-year-old daughter, Angelica, was once again unraveling. Her illness had come and gone before, terrifying the family for a time after the death of her brother and resulting in her, as one of Eliza's friends remembered, again "losing her reason amid the sudden horrors of her father's death." Angelica Hamilton disappeared from society after 1806 and this time did not mend, although Eliza and her sister clung to hope for another decade. The rest of the family shook their heads. Angelica and Eliza's optimism was plainly false. As one sister-in-law confided in a letter to Catherine sometime after 1810, "I have returned home my jaunt to the city was more fatiguing than pleasant I was there only a few days—saw all our friends however & left them well excepting poor Angelica Hamilton who remains far from rational, though they flatter themselves she is recovering."

Years of financial instability had taken their toll on Eliza, and early in 1810 she was determined to take action. She scrimped and saved the money to travel to Philadelphia and then on to Washington, DC, accompanied by her son John, now seventeen, to petition Congress in person and ask them to restore Alexander's veteran's stipend, which he had gallantly—but foolishly—waived at the end of the American Revolution. The annual income of a pension would mean the difference between living on the edge and being economically safe, and Eliza needed an answer. She was tired. Congress, however, was in no hurry. Action on any legacy regarding the family of Alexander Hamilton languished.

Some relief came, as unkind as the thought might be, with the death of Washington Morton that spring in Paris, where he was vacationing. With him died the pressure to buy out his share of Cornelia's farm inheritance; when his will was read, it turned out he was dead broke as well. Wild rumors made their way back from France that he had died there in a duel with the exiled Aaron Burr, intending to avenge the death of Alexander.

Eliza's eldest sons were now young men, and that meant they were of an age for war and dueling. Her oldest, Alexander Jr., in his mid-twenties, headed off for Europe to fight in the Spanish War of Independence. James, soberly practicing law in Saratoga County, where he looked after Eliza's lands and collected rents from her tenants, was married.

The death of Washington Morton and the rumors of a second duel with Aaron Burr, however clearly fanciful, put Alexander's legacy back in the spotlight, and with the renewed attention came a fresh round of political abuse of Alexander. One of the uglier attacks on Alexander's reputation, retreading the same old ground about financial corruption and Maria Reynolds, came from an attorney in Albany, John Cramer, and, when the newspapers picked up the story, some of James's friends most unhelpfully called for a duel to satisfy Alexander Hamilton's honor. James had no option but to issue the challenge. To refuse was either to be branded a coward or, worse, to be seen to be conceding that his father was a scoundrel. Reading reports in the papers was agony for Eliza. She was saved from the horror of another son fighting only by John Cramer refusing the duel. The newspapers gleefully excoriated his cowardice in columns.

But war was the greatest threat to Eliza's sons. All the Hamilton boys except little Philip were old enough to be caught up in the War of 1812 before it ended. James, twenty-four when the war started, moved back to New York City with his young family in the spring of 1814. He remembered later that "at that time an attack on New York city, by the British, was considered imminent," and he would protect his mother. He joined the New York militia and was made deputy quartermaster of an infantry regiment, then promoted to major of another brigade and inspector. James was the bossy oldest brother and Eliza's estate manager, and he saw himself as the patriarch of the family, to the great annoyance of his younger siblings. Eliza's adventurous second son, Alexander Jr., returned from the Spanish peninsula and served as a captain in the United States Army from August 1813 until the summer of 1815. The bookish and dreamy John enlisted as an aide-de-camp for Major William Henry Harrison, and William, fifteen, her rebellious and willful boy, with his father's quick wit and impulsive temper, registered at the United States Military Academy at West Point, New York, although he abandoned the academy (or it abandoned him) short of graduation.

Eliza, however, was fighting a private war of sorrow. She could see that her sister Angelica was dying, probably of tuberculosis.

Angelica wheezed and could not shake a cough that had plagued her since at least as early as 1810. Once a beautiful woman, with her love of art and daring French fashions, she looked thin and haggard and much older than fifty-seven. Around her, the Church family fortune was collapsing, and soon there would be no more mansions or flashy carriages, no more stock-market bubbles and gambling. John Church was already broken in spirit, and by 1814 Angelica was tired of fighting.

Eliza walked through the snowy streets of New York all throughout February and into the first days of March to sit with her sister in the quiet. Outside the bedroom window, snow fell gently, and from the streets the sisters could hear the bells of carriages and the shouts of boys running errands. When bloody coughs racked Angelica's body, Eliza held her and thought back on the years they had been best friends to each other. They had watched each other's children be born and sometimes buried. They had faced the world together in unbreakable solidarity. But above all, they had both loved and been loved by Alexander. Eliza could not imagine a world without the ballast of Angelica. But that world was coming nonetheless.

On Sunday, March 13, 1814, Eliza sat with her sister for the last time. In the distance, the church bells of Trinity rang, and in the days to come Eliza would bury another part of her heart there in the graveyard. Angelica was laid into the vault of their Livingston relations, not far from the grave of Alexander. At the funeral, John Church looked beaten, and when Eliza shook his hand goodbye, she guessed that it would be the last time she would see him also. There was nothing to keep John in New York. He set off on the next packet to London, to see what he could salvage of his ruined finances. Eliza never saw him again. John Church died abroad in 1818, and if any letters of friendship and grief passed between them, Eliza did not save them.

Eliza culled much of her correspondence in that decade.

In the spring of 1816, Congress—after years of struggle and privation—passed at last An Act for the Relief of Elizabeth Hamilton, awarding her "five years' full pay for the services of her deceased husband." With thirty-two years and 165 days of interest, the total sum was $10,609.64, and for Eliza it was life changing. She was not a wealthy woman. But she would be able to live in quiet comfort as a widow and provide for her daughter Angelica's care and for the education of her three youngest children.

Her petition to Congress was based on the financial documents that Alexander had left for safekeeping before his duel with Aaron Burr. "Shortly after the death of General Hamilton," Nathaniel Pendleton, his dueling second, swore to Congress,

I received a packet, Sealed and addressed to me, which inclosed a note from him, in substance among other things importing that that packet would only be delivered to me in the event of his death. It inclosed also his will, and three other papers, in his own

hand writing. In one of them, containing some observations upon his pecuniary affairs, he declared among other circumstances that he had never received the half pay for life, nor the equivalent for it, which other officers, who had served in the Army, in the Revolutionary War had received.

Among those letters had been Alexander's last love letters, which Eliza cherished. Lately, however, she was determined to resume a project that had languished since the death of her father, when they'd talked together of publishing Alexander's biography. John Mason, one of the clergymen at Alexander's deathbed, had been talked of as the writer, but Eliza had been uncertain of the reverend's abilities as a writer. Against her better judgment, she'd given him the project. She'd been right to hesitate. Eliza had gathered together Alexander's papers and passed them—albeit carefully edited—to the clergyman. But John Mason dithered. He had an inability to get started.

Among the papers Eliza did not pass to Reverend Mason were the papers contained in a small leather trunk and marked with the initials of James Reynolds.

A good deal of ink has been spilled over the mystery of the trunk and its letters. It was at the heart of the story about Maria Reynolds and of the allegations that had riveted the nation and said that Alexander, to cover up financial indiscretions, had forged blackmail notes and love letters.

The papers traveled a circuitous route, the details of which even now are murky. What is known for sure is that Alexander, in advance of a threatened duel in 1795, at the height of scandal, asked a friend to look after the contents of the leather trunk and, especially, to take care of something inside that trunk: a "small bundle inscribed thus—J R To be forwarded to Oliver Wolcott Junr. Esq." "I entreat that this may be early done by a careful hand," Alexander emphasized. "This trunk contains all my interesting papers."

Assuming "J.R." stood in 1795 for "James Reynolds," the papers may have been the same documents lodged with a friend in Philadelphia, which Alexander proclaimed in the infamous pamphlet could be reviewed by any "gentleman" who doubted the authenticity of Maria Reynolds's adulterous love letters. Gentlemen, however, by definition, did not doubt the word of other gentlemen, and when the journalist James Callender asked to see them, he was smartly refused. So the papers remained sealed, apparently as late as the summer of 1801, when Alexander and Eliza's Philadelphia neighbor, the land speculator William Bingham, wrote to Alexander, returning at Alexander's request "a Packet of Papers . . . which were deposited."

That Eliza knew of the existence of this mysterious bundle is certain. On Alexander's 1795 letter documenting the importance of the "J.R." packet, Eliza wrote the words "to be retained by myself" and removed the letter about the bundle from the biographer's resources. What precisely happened to those "interesting papers" no one ever recorded. Historians have searched for and never found them.

But there is one person who destroyed large parts of Eliza and Alexander's most private correspondence. Eliza.

Eliza was determined by 1817 to bring the biography of Alexander to press. She was growing increasingly weary of nagging John Mason. "I have been so disappointed by the promises of Mr. Masson in writing the life of your brother[-in-law]," Eliza wrote to her sister Catherine in 1818, "that I have requested his papers to be returned to me and have been very much occupied in endeavouring to obtain all the correspondence that I can." The new author "who will devote himself to it [is] a Mr [Joseph] Hopkinson now in Congress," and Eliza made uncomfortable trips to Long Island and New Jersey, even traveling as far as George Washington's Mount Vernon in Virginia to gather up Alexander's far-flung letters.

She was spurred on now by the increasingly preposterous rumors that were being publicly bandied about in regard to Alexander. There was something petty and ungenerous about insulting someone after his death, it seemed to Eliza, but his political enemies were as insistent as ever. Eliza was furious watching them attack Alexander's reputation. She had defended him in life, and she would defend him no less loyally in his death. Someday, in the afterlife, she was certain she would see him.

Behind the rumors, Eliza noted with disgust, were the same old players. As early as 1816 and with an increasing tenacity by 1818, Alexander's longtime political rival, Thomas Jefferson—the "friend" in Virginia with whom James Monroe had deposited his notes of the Reynolds scandal—was revisiting the debate from a generation earlier about the federal bank and Alexander's time in the Treasury. Jefferson's view, espoused snidely in publications, was that "the more debt Hamilton could rake up, the more plunder for his mercenaries." As Eliza's son James succinctly put it, "The charge against Hamilton is, substantially, that he enabled his myrmidons to amass fortunes by informing them of the measures to be pursued by him." In other words, the allegation was that Alexander was guilty of insider trading. Eliza was dismayed that the old charges of financial corruption—the very charges that had driven Alexander to publish his pamphlet, the charges that had led to the scandal of Maria Reynolds—were being levied again when he was not alive to rebut them.

Thomas Jefferson, however, was not the worst of the gossips, not by a long shot. There were whispers, bandied about by John and Abigail Adams, that Alexander had left behind a string of bastard children in Philadelphia and New York City, and John Adams—whose close relationship with Catherine's now also recently deceased husband, Samuel Malcolm, gave him the air of having direct family knowledge—spoke privately of his disgust at Alexander's "debauchery of all the Sisters of his Wife."

So vile and outrageous was John Adams's scandalmongering in the 1810s that even his cousin William Cunningham felt compelled to warn him,

Should you now refuse to recal the calumny you have spread of
Hamilton in secret; or to supply the evidence of your heinous
charges, will you not oblige his friends to strip from your hands,
before you slip out of life, the poisoned chalice whose contents you
have infused into the minds of many around you[?]

Something of these slanders surely made their way back to Eliza and her children long before the unguarded letters between John Adams and his cousin—detailing all manner of attacks on Alexander's character and churning up again the Reynolds controversy—were published in 1823 in a book that became an instant *succès de scandale*. Alexander's old friend Colonel Timothy Pickering took up the pen a year later, in the midst of the 1824 presidential election, and published a devastating "review" of the correspondence that demolished Adams's reputation and was so hotly contested that, as one nineteenth-century commentator put it, "no publication of the kind ever produced a deeper or wider sensation." The political classes might have found it all titillating. Eliza, of course, found it infuriating and deeply painful.

Colonel Pickering had staunchly defended Alexander's name to the world. Pickering, Eliza decided, was clearly the man who should write the biography. It would take Eliza the better part of a decade to convince him to do it, but in 1827, when the Joseph Hopkinson biography also failed to materialize, the colonel finally agreed to take on the project and spent several months in New York City with "Mrs. Hamilton and her children." In the contract drawn up between them, Eliza promised to pass to the author "all the papers relating to the subject."

And, strictly speaking, Eliza probably kept that promise.

Whether it happened in 1818 or 1827, the result was the same, and the scene is all too easy to imagine. Eliza, whose loyalty to Alexander was as passionate and fierce as ever, filled with righteous indignation at the calumny and taunts of enemies and scandalmongers, lifted each aging sheet gently.

She heard again Alexander's voice in the letters.

Some she would set into a growing pile for his biographer and for her children, documents showing his rectitude and passion, his brilliance and his wisdom, his place among the pantheon of the men and women who had fomented and won the American Revolution and built a new republic on a classical foundation.

Some went into another pile, and it was not a small one. Into that stack went her letters, the ones she'd written to him, speaking of love and fear, longing and desire for her husband, letters written in her faulty spelling and in a style that still, decades later, embarrassed her and showed how unworthy she had been, with her rudimentary education and halting way with words, of such a husband.

Hers were letters, too, that showed clearly what Alexander thought the letters of a woman in love looked like. They were not entirely unlike those Alexander had published in the name of Maria Reynolds. Perhaps the echoes came too near. Perhaps the spelling errors, a turn of phrase here or there, even had something in common. Even if Eliza had wanted to write herself into the history of their life in her own voice, could she risk giving Alexander's opponents any ammunition?

Into that pile, too, went Alexander's 1795 letter, alluding to the existence of a packet with the initials "J.R.," the one with her note on it. And in went, almost certainly, that bundle of letters, wrapped in paper, tied by Alexander's hand with a ribbon—the packet that had once sat in that mysterious leather trunk.

Eliza remembered it all too well, remembered how Alexander had begged for her forgiveness. She could not know how long she would still live. Eliza turned seventy in the 1820s. Those around her were dead or dying. Among her siblings, only Rensselaer, Philip, and Catherine were still living, and all of them were more than a decade younger. The Schuyler children of her generation were gone. Angelica. Peggy. John. Even Cornelia. She could not risk it.

Placing a tremulous hand on a thick pile of papers, taking up the most private and most dangerous among them, Eliza drew a chair close to the fire, alone in the parlor. One by one, she placed each gently into the flames and watched the fire consume them and the floating ash settle. It was like saying goodbye again to Alexander, and she wept as she burned them. She hated to destroy anything that spoke of him.

But she had kept his secret then. She would keep it now and forever. No one would ever be able to examine the papers that exposed Alexander's rash cover story, even if it meant she went down in history as a woman betrayed by a husband she knew had loved her. Even if it meant the world thought he had not cherished her enough to be faithful. Her loyalty was to her family and, above all, to Alexander.

And she did not question that he had kept faith with her either.

CHAPTER 19

Twilight, 1827–46

Although Eliza could not have known it, her death was still a long way in the future.

Among her siblings, only her youngest sister, Catherine, nearly twenty-five years her junior, would outlive her. Quarrels over their parents' estate had come between Eliza and Catherine, and Eliza laid much of the blame at the foot of Catherine's husband, Samuel Malcolm. But when he died in 1817, Eliza reached out to her sister, and Catherine, living in the Hudson Valley, gladly responded. A sisterly correspondence blossomed again between the only two remaining Schuyler sisters. It was with Catherine, now, that Eliza shared her news and her confidences.

She wrote to Catherine with the news that her son Alexander Jr. was engaged, and she fretted over the departure of her son William, tired of life at West Point, for adventure in Illinois, America's westward frontier. She sent word throughout the 1820s of the steady stream of children born to her son John and his wife, Mary, now living in a little two-story house on Varick Street, and shared news of the death of John Church in London.

Eliza also increasingly pressed "big sister" invitations on a cash-strapped and widowed Catherine, urging her sister to bring her small children and spend the winter at the Grange, where "I can make it agreeable to you as we have an excellent clergyman near us let me intreat you to come down." When Catherine delayed, "[Come] with them and live with me," Eliza followed up tenaciously,

and let my wishes be complied with in making you and your
Children comfortable. . . . [Come here] to live as soon as you can.
Adieu my beloved and remember we are to be together as long as
we live Sister and Comply with my Earnest request yours always
Affectionately.

The loss of Angelica had left a hole in Eliza's heart, and she missed the confidences of a sister.

Thoughts of the biography still consumed Eliza too. She pressed members of the family and people who had met Alexander for information to pass to the biographers, for "domestic anecdotes" and recollections of his bearing, his character, "style of conversation—and indeed everything which will illustrate the elasticity of his mind, variety of his knowledge, playfulness of his wit, excellence of his heart, firmness, forbearance, virtues, &c."

The undercurrent of gossip about Alexander, however, grew ever darker, especially in the aftermath of the death of John Church. Now there were tales that John, too, had challenged Aaron Burr to duel in Europe, again determined to avenge the murder of Alexander, and that Burr had shot him. It was almost enough to make one feel sorry for Aaron Burr, who had now been falsely accused of killing both John Church and Washington Morton.

When Aaron Burr returned to New York City from his exile in Paris, those rumors took a dark turn in the mind of some prankster. Eliza's sons were constantly in danger of being pushed into duels on account of their father, and now someone forged a note and sent it to Aaron Burr, hoping to foment a duel between Burr and Alexander's children. The letter was purported to be from James Hamilton, and it read: "Sir: Please to meet me with the weapon you choose, on the 15th May, where you murdered my father, at 10 o'clock, with your second."

An indignant Burr sent a mutual friend, Robert Troup, to speak to James and reply to the challenge, and only Troup perceiving the prank and smoothing the waters prevented fighting. "It was done," James put it later, "in the hope that I might be disgraced or destroyed." Such a vicious joke—if it had been a joke—rattled Eliza.

Throughout it all, Eliza worked tirelessly at the orphan asylum where, after the death of Isabella Graham, she took the leadership role as director. Shopkeepers in Greenwich tipped their hats and then smiled, watching General Hamilton's widow, with her black lace cap and old-fashioned air, disappear around a street corner. More often than not, she was on her way to pick up a new young charge on her way to the orphanage. In the tidy orphanage books, the name of "Mrs. Hamilton" appears on page after page as the sponsor of new children. By 1820 the facility was home to more than a hundred children; Eliza saw that need continued to outpace resources. When the orphanage was full to capacity, Eliza couldn't bear to turn a child away. So she brought them home with her. One little boy named Henry McKavit she took herself from the arms of the fireman who saved him from the burning house where his parents perished when he was five. When the time came in the next decade, despite her modest widow's budget, she personally paid for Henry's education. And that, too, got her thinking.

Eliza had struggled to put her own sons through school on her meager resources as a widow. Alexander had risen in the world as an orphan only because some good-hearted souls had seen in the boy a talent worth caring about and had paid for his schooling. Education became a new charitable passion. So, through tireless fundraising and by herself donating a parcel of land on Broadway in Harlem, Eliza opened the first public school in Washington Heights. "Whole familys have been unbaptised some persons in their neighborhood have [taken] up by subscription a school," she wrote modestly, while pressing for a donation, but "there is still about one hundred dollars wanted to complete the expenditure and to give benches and writing desks." Before long, the Hamilton Free School was open.

By the mid-1820s, Eliza's sons were grown and her youngest daughter, Betsey, married, and the responses of the Hamilton children to their famous family divided them into those who stayed near and joined Eliza in her growing obsession with Alexander's biography and those who cut themselves loose from their father's saga.

James stuck close and remained in the thick of his mother's finances and her hunt for letters. He made a fortune in the mid-1820s as a land speculator and real-estate investor in New York and Brooklyn and later, after meeting the war hero Andrew Jackson, garnered a small role in the Jackson administration. Wealthy and dedicated to the memory of his father, even if he had not inherited his father's brilliance, James had the money and the inclination to pursue his mother's project, which sometimes took a fair bit of arm-twisting. Some of those in possession of Alexander's papers did not relinquish them willingly, sometimes because they wanted to protect the reputation of George Washington. On at least one occasion Eliza, assisted by James, was compelled to bring a lawsuit against one of Alexander's old friends to regain possession of the manuscript drafts of Washington's iconic Farewell Address—which Alexander had written.

Her son John—married and the father of three young children—wandered through a legal career and also dedicated himself to his father's story. At the Grange on the weekends, Eliza filled the house with grandchildren, who made the trip by the stagecoach that left from the corner of Bayard Street and the Bowery on Saturday afternoons and stayed until Monday morning.

Her son Alexander Jr. fled. Perhaps his bearing his father's name had always made that inevitable. A brief stint as New York state representative to Congress gave him a taste of bitter partisanship, and Alexander traveled instead to the new American territory of Florida, ultimately becoming the United States attorney, a land commissioner, and a colonel.

William, having qualified as an attorney like his brothers, also threw off the family legacy and went West. Of all the children, he looked the most like his father, and those who knew him described William as "a man of great intellectual powers" but "unsteady in his habits." Not, perhaps, unlike his father either. William lived a bachelor's life as a frontiersman, speculator, and woodsman, and, despite a brief stint in the state legislature, too, few who met him would have guessed that he was the son of the famous General Hamilton. By mid-decade, he was driving cattle for the federal government from Illinois to Wisconsin, where he fought as a captain in the Winnebago War, staked a mining claim, and struck it rich at a place he named Hamilton's Diggings.

Then there was Philip, Eliza's youngest. She had not been able to give her last child the same private education as the older boys, and, of all the children, he had suffered most from her reduced widow's income. She couldn't afford to send him to college. But young Phil, six feet tall, strikingly handsome, and carrying with him the legacy and the burden of his namesake and brother, was perhaps the most cheerfully resilient and the sweetest of her children, and he was the most like his mother in his passion for good works and in his native modesty. He diligently studied law books at night and quietly passed the bar exam, under his own steam, qualifying as an attorney. Then he moved upstate and enjoyed a quiet life far from the limelight. It was a life Eliza herself might have chosen.

Her youngest daughter, Betsey, and her husband, the wealthy New York merchant Sidney Augustus Holly, joined Eliza in the family project of the biography and helped in caring for the unfortunate Angelica. Angelica Hamilton had been lost to reason already for more than a decade, and she lived in a twilight world of madness, where her father had never died and the Hamilton tragedy had never happened.

By the 1830s, Eliza was approaching eighty.

James, long accustomed to being in charge and having his mother's ear as a confidant, made her feel like an old lady. The property in

Harlem, he insisted, was too much for her. He pressed Eliza to sell. He had long managed her rents and finances, and he was sure he knew what was best. His younger brother John, never a forceful personality, was not one to mount any objections. Eliza must live with him and his wife, James insisted now, and, though she knew his motives were good-hearted, he started to annoy Eliza.

When her son Alexander Jr. swept back into New York City in the early 1830s, everything shifted. Alexander, who soon established a position as a wealthy Wall Street real-estate investor that rivaled his brother's, took stock of the situation and asked his mother what she wanted. Eliza didn't want to live with James, and she didn't want to be bossed around either. She was ready to give up the Grange—it was too far out of town and too expensive to manage—but she wanted a place in Greenwich Village near the orphan asylum. And she needed to figure out what to do about Angelica.

New luxury town houses were planned on a pretty street nearby called St. Marks Place, and Alexander Jr. asked if she possibly wanted a home there. That Eliza could imagine. So she sold the Grange for $25,000 and put the money toward the purchase of a five-story brick home. All that James would not have minded. But sibling relations were not improved when he learned that Eliza planned to live there with Betsey and Sidney, Alexander Jr. and his wife, and the latter couple's young Spanish-born nephew. James could be forgiven for feeling cut out of the family.

Eliza placed Angelica under the medical supervision of Dr. James MacDonald, who specialized in mental illness, and, in a sign of how far advanced her illness was now, Angelica does not seem to have lived with the family at St. Marks Place. She likely resided instead at the progressive lunatic asylum that Dr. MacDonald directed in Bloomingdale, in Upper Manhattan, and that might explain why, in the 1830s, Eliza selected a large parcel in Bloomingdale as the future home of a new and growing orphanage campus.

For Eliza, the townhome on St. Marks came as a relief and a joy. They had merry times now at number four, and when the next spring their distant cousin James Fenimore Cooper and his family took up residence at number six, Eliza was the center of attention. Cooper's novel *The Last of the Mohicans* was not yet a decade old, but, set in 1757, in the Hudson River Valley during the French and Indian War, it had made famous the world of Eliza's girlhood.

Eliza regaled her younger kinsman with stories of the past, and perhaps they talked as well of the news from her son William, who had fought in the bloody Indian wars in the Midwest, leading native allies from the Winnebago and Menominee bands in battles against the Sauk chieftain Black Hawk and his "British Band," whose massacres and scalping raids horrified the nation.

One of the most famous of the Sauk attacks took place just five miles from William's land, when a scalping party raided a nearby farm, setting off a national incident. William's mining operation at Hamilton's Diggings—quickly renamed Fort Hamilton—had played a central role in the skirmish, and it was here that families and the militia retreated.

When Black Hawk and his handsome son were captured, Andrew Jackson ordered the chieftain brought east to impress upon the natives the futility of fighting against the American nation. Crowds turned out to gawk at the vanquished chief and the young brave. The *New York Courier* reported, "Wherever they go, great numbers are sure to follow them, wherever they stop, hundreds and sometimes thousands, besiege them." Fashionable ladies swooned at the romance and thrilled to the encounter. Eliza was sanguine. Somewhere, she still kept the beads placed around her neck as a girl by the sachem during her initiation at the grand council.

The socialites flocked to catch a glimpse of the chieftain, but Black Hawk was less impressed with the New York ladies of fashion. He was recorded to have muttered, "What in the devil's name do these squaws want of me!" When the chieftain told his story to a government translator, who in 1833 published the account under the title *Autobiography of Ma-Ka-Tai-Me-She-Kia-Kiak, or Black Hawk*, the book was an instant bestseller. And the scruffy, gruff woodsman, black sheep of his family, "Billy" Hamilton, was now lauded as the son of Alexander.

That year, another piece of history resurrected itself.

If there were two men whom Eliza blamed for the death of Alexander, they were James Monroe and Aaron Burr. If Eliza hated one man more than the other, it was actually the former, but she had already had her final showdown with James Monroe one weekend in Harlem.

She had always blamed James Monroe for the Reynolds scandal and for the rumors that Alexander was engaged in insider trading and speculation. That political agenda had brought about Alexander's "confession."

She had been in her garden, talking with a teenage nephew, when a maid brought her the card of a visitor. "What has that man come for?" she asked, rising, and her nephew remembered later how her voice got very quiet when she was angry. Eliza strode determinedly to the front parlor and glared at James Monroe, already a former president. She notably did not ask him to make himself comfortable.

"It has been many years since we have met, the lapse of time has brought its softening influences. We are both nearing the grave when past differences might be forgiven and forgotten . . ." James Monroe faltered.

"Mr. Monroe," Eliza promptly interrupted, "if you have come to tell me that you repent, that you are sorry, very sorry for . . . the slanders . . . you circulated against my dear husband . . . no lapse of time, no nearness to the grave, makes any difference."

Then Eliza turned on her heel and marched back out to her garden.

And now Aaron Burr was getting his comeuppance. Not only did Eliza have the satisfaction in 1834 of seeing the first volume of Alexander's biography published at last—written finally not by any of the clergymen or by the old colonel but by her bookish son John

Hamilton—but Burr's rich new wife, Eliza Jumel, wanted a divorce and she wasn't being quiet about the reasons. Mrs. Burr had discovered her randy husband *in flagrante* and asked Eliza's son Alexander Jr. to act as her divorce attorney. Alexander Jr. not only accepted, he filed the motion on the anniversary of his father's murder, setting tongues in New York City wagging.

Alexander Jr. and his wife were still living with Eliza and the Holly family in the townhome on St. Marks Place, and, sitting in the front parlor with her needlework, Eliza chuckled at news of how the case proceeded. Eliza Jumel, the daughter of a prostitute, was a survivor if ever there were one, and she had traded on her beauty and intelligence to marry first a rich merchant and then, in 1833, the seventy-seven-year-old former vice president. After just four months of living with the notoriously unfaithful Aaron Burr and suspecting he was squandering her hard-earned fortune on trysts in New Jersey, where, according to one newspaper report, "many a night he wandered around the hillside, breathing in [his young mistress's] ear love and devotion," his stout fifty-eight-year-old bride followed him on one nocturnal adventure and caught him red-faced and red-handed. After giving Burr and his young lady companion a tongue-lashing that harkened back to her bawdy house origins, Eliza Jumel decided she'd had enough.

Aaron Burr, for his part, resented that his bride was, in the words of one of his biographers, "overbearing and domineering beyond human endurance and . . . a devil incarnate."

The couple retained dueling lawyers. The aggrieved wife, showing a laudable, if perverse, sense of humor, wanted a showdown with Alexander Hamilton Jr. in her corner. When Burr shortly thereafter had a stroke that left him half paralyzed and broken, Eliza Jumel cared not one whit. She insisted they carry on with the proceedings.

Home at St. Marks Place, Eliza tried to feel pity. But it was hard not to see the hand of God and divine retribution.

Eliza Jumel was awarded her divorce in 1836, and Aaron Burr died the day the judgment was awarded. And that year, Eliza's children, all middle-aged now, were beginning to scatter again in different directions.

Her son James gave up his family home on Varick Street and purchased a large rural property in Irvington, New York, called, in honor of his father's childhood home, Nevis. While raising the grand estate was left in the hands of contractors, the family spent the winter at the City Hotel, below Liberty Street, in preparation for a voyage in the spring to Europe. Not far away, in the New York Merchants' Exchange, stood a statue of Alexander Hamilton, which Congress in 1826 had approved to reside there as a testament to his legacy as the first secretary of Treasury.

Just after 11 p.m. on the night of December 16, when gale-force winds were whipping across the city in the grip of a cold snap, a loud knock and frantic voice calling out fire woke James. The whole area was ablaze.

James set off to try to save the statue. By midnight, the entire financial district was a conflagration and boats on the wharfs were in flames. Witnesses remembered heat so intense that the copper fittings from the roofs melted down the sides of the buildings. The frigid weather froze the water supplies, and James joined a group of men determined to battle the inferno.

At St. Marks Place, Eliza and her daughter paced the floors as the sentries wailed out the news on the street corners.

One of James's group of men set off in an open boat in the midst of the storm to fetch gunpowder from the Brooklyn Navy Yard, so they could explode buildings in the path of the fire to create a containment barrier. They would have to deprive the fire of fuel by sacrificing buildings. By dawn the fire had spread to more than five hundred buildings and nearly twenty blocks and could be seen on the horizon as far away as Philadelphia. When the gunpowder arrived, James lit one of the fuses and watched as buildings exploded. The strategy was a success and ultimately confined the losses to seven hundred buildings. "My cloak was stiff with frozen water," James remembered later, and "I was so worn down by the excitement that when I got to my parlor I fainted. The scene of desolation and demoralization was most distressing."

When James and his family sailed for Europe following the great fire, Eliza asked him to call on her old friend Charles Maurice de Talleyrand in Paris and to see Jérôme Bonaparte, whom she and Alexander had entertained at the Grange in the last weeks before the death of Alexander. James dutifully "took a letter from my dear mother to Prince Tallyrand, which was left at his hotel in Paris," and when the men met, the prince told a story of how, years earlier, he had encountered by chance at an inn a homesick American man, whom he learned at parting was Benedict Arnold and who took him to his rooms and showed him a portrait miniature, given to him during the Revolutionary War and carried by him ever since, of his former friend Alexander Hamilton. The prince promised to send James the portrait.

In Paris, he also met another of his mother's old acquaintances, Louis Philippe d'Orléans, now the king of France, and his sister Adélaïde, who had spent part of their exile during the French Revolution in the 1790s in New York and Philadelphia, where they became friends with Alexander, Eliza, and the Churches.

In Florence, Italy, Eliza's name was again a passport to the royal houses. "King Jerôme [Bonaparte], who was living there, hearing my name, [talked] about my father and the courtesies he had received at his country-house" and "of the dinner at my father's house" in those last days of Eliza's marriage, James later noted.

James then traveled to Scotland, to see his father's ancestral home, also called the Grange.

James sent back glittering reports of his father's fame from Europe; meanwhile, Alexander Jr. passed long evenings with his mother by their shared fire telling Eliza stories about the haunting swamps of Florida and how the moss from the branches touched the river. He told her about his travels to the American West and of seeing once again his younger brother.

Eliza never heard from William. And she had some unfinished business.

Eliza had made up her mind. The boys advised against it. Eliza straightened her frail old-lady shoulders. She was a Schuyler and the wife of a general. Wives of soldiers showed no fear. That was what her mother, on her way to burn the fields in advance of the British, told fleeing refugees and, throughout their childhood, General Schuyler's daughters. There was no deterring her. Eliza was going to set off herself on a last adventure.

CHAPTER 20

Last Adventures, 1847–54

Eliza wasted no time in setting off. Who knew at eighty how much time was left to her?

Eliza had never been to Europe. The Old World did not tempt her. She had seen it all, decades before, through the eyes of her sister Angelica. What could a scuffed and tattered reality offer her that could rival the magic of a sister's youthful letters? To break the magic would feel like losing Angelica all over.

No, it was the American West, with its mighty rivers and broad, rolling prairies, that Eliza hankered after. She was part of this vast, striving continent, and rivers and mountains had been in her blood since her girlhood on the Hudson, when she had wondered what lay on the far side of the Catskills and the answer had come: the future. Eliza felt sure there were adventures ahead of her. When the train rattled along now toward Harlem and the fields rushed past her, Eliza sometimes asked the bewildered conductor to let her off at an empty junction, just for the pleasure of knowing she could still climb hills—and fences—at eighty.

But she wanted to touch the past again, too, on this last great adventure. She would touch the past and pass the torch of her love and Alexander's to the most wayward and independent of her children. How like his father. She wanted to see William, the boy who looked most like Alexander, too, and who carried with him most clearly the raw spirit of the Schuyler frontiersmen. She had not laid eyes on her son for more than fifteen years, and Eliza longed to embrace him as his mother once more before she died. She knew that he would not come home, and that she would need to set off to find him. His brother Alexander had already made a journey west to see William and had come back with wondrous tales that piqued even the steady Eliza's curiosity. In Illinois, he met the up-and-coming state senator Abraham Lincoln, he exclaimed, "lying upon the counter in midday telling stories." Her Alexander would never have believed that one day this odd thin man would be president.

Eliza wanted to give to William a gift that he alone, perhaps, of her children could appreciate as his inheritance, and she wanted to give it to him in person. It was foolish and unnecessary, her sensible sons assured her. But was it foolish to want to hold a clod of earth in your palm and to tell your son to grow strong and rich and happy on it? As part of the tangle of his father's unpaid pension, only recently settled with Congress, came a claim to a large parcel of public lands in Illinois and Wisconsin. William had wanted his freedom. She would bless him with it.

Let her other boys fuss. James and John and Alexander: one of them was always fussing or quarreling with the other, to the annoyance of their sister. Drawing near to the fire, watching the heat rise with satisfaction, Eliza, alone in the afternoons, sometimes set aside her embroidery and thumbed the pages of well-worn river guidebooks, thinking and planning. In January, she set into a sturdy leather trunk her provisions and organized some pressing domestic matters. What to do with her daughter Angelica was a question she had lived with now for almost half a century. Dr. James MacDonald's resignation from the Bloomingdale Insane Asylum had thrown the care of Angelica into question.

When she set off, she had a solution. She did not depart for the West that winter, when the cold had settled. Eliza turned, instead, north over frozen ground by sleigh to her childhood home in the

Hudson River Valley to the small-town bachelor residence of her mild-mannered and sweet-tempered youngest son, Philip. Her ghost boy. The one who could never take the place of his dead brother and who kept aloof to save his mother's feelings. Philip had agreed to take charge of his sister during Eliza's absence.

Steeling herself against the biting cold and pulling her woolen petticoats and buffalo wraps tightly around her and her eldest daughter, Eliza wondered. She had wanted to be a good mother—a republican mother—but she knew herself at eighty. There had been wounds. She, like Alexander, had favorites among the children. And somehow her favorites were the distant ones, the ones with wild streaks of independence. Eliza settled back and smiled to herself. Alexander would have liked that.

When Angelica was settled with her bachelor brother, Eliza turned her sights westward, waving goodbye to Philip at the wharf in the first days of March. Her father used to have just that same habit. The ground was still cold, but the river ice had broken, and Eliza felt her spirit carried along with the rush of waters. She didn't know precisely where the current would take her, but she was ready to welcome it.

Eliza rattled along for nearly three weeks, over rickety plank turnpikes and swaying in barges dragged along by horses across the shallows, wondering for the first time what she had been thinking. It was hard going. As hard as anything she remembered from those bygone days of the revolution. In her narrow cot, she cursed the cold until dreams came to her, and in the morning the corn mush gruel was lumpy and unpalatable, just as she remembered. At mid-month, as reward for her privations, Eliza reached the ugly town of Pittsburgh, which she found "gloomy from the use of coal" and generally hideous.

She planned to set off immediately for Cincinnati, though, and her tone was jubilant. Never mind what had passed. The continent

and William were before her. Besides, steamboat packets were floating grand hotels, and the captain warmly welcomed the small, elderly
lady he soon discovered was Mrs. General Hamilton. She must dine
at the captain's table and drink his Madeira. He would not brook opposition. "Adieu!" she wrote to Philip in high spirits before the steamboat pulled away. "Write to me and let me know how Angelica is."

Traveling with only a maidservant, Eliza was on an adventure
that few women half her age would have braved in the 1830s. Some
of the dangers were real. Steamships snagged and sank with alarming
regularity. Eliza wrote letters home describing the muddy waters of
the turbulent springtime river and a difficult navigation. But it was
the fear of the wilderness that kept most women and most men, too,
confined to the salon and the parlor, and Eliza was having none of
that. She was still the same fearless tomboy.

And so, mostly, her letters home at each riverside village were
filled with descriptions of the great beauty of the frontier and the
awesome power of the river that carried her. On warm evenings, as
winter turned to spring, Eliza settled comfortably into a deck chair
and let time and the shore slip past her. How she wished Alexander
were here beside her. Who could blame an old lady if she sometimes
closed her eyes and spoke aloud her greetings? April saw her as far
as Louisville, Kentucky. In May, they were gliding past the wilderness of forest into what Eliza thought was the very beautiful city of
St. Louis.

There, for the first time, the disastrous news from the East reached
her. Urgent voices asked, "Have you heard? Have you heard?" Eliza
did not know what the men were talking about, but she had seen
enough of stock markets and the Treasury to guess that it was bad
business. Eliza called over to the boys along the docks to ask for
word from New York, and when the eager reply came back, "Crash,
madam, crash in the city," as word trickled west of the great financial
collapse that would destroy the fortunes of both her sons James and
Alexander and lead to the bank foreclosing on the St. Marks Place
property, Eliza calmly sent her maid off to find newspapers.

Eliza took it all in stride. She had been poor before, and her only true home had been the Grange and Alexander. Cutting her trip short was not going to restore the family fortunes. Eliza wrote back home to the children, warning them that her business with the land claims would not allow her to return immediately, news from the city or no, and she carried on toward the far horizon. By June 5, 1837, she had passed the great junction where the Ohio River met the Mississippi and was on her way to the Wisconsin Territory, the river coming to life all around her.

The truth was, Eliza didn't wish to return any time soon. The trip was exciting. She was done with men and their financial crises. She felt like that same girl who had once scampered over rocks and up waterfalls and left the fussy, helpless Miss Lynch and the other ladies crying out in terror at her courage. God knew that courage had in the years since sustained her. But when Eliza saw William at last—a "cultured gentleman, speaking French and having his cabin shelves filled with books . . . his furniture a rude bedstead with some blankets and buffalo robes for bedding, and oak table, wood stools"—smiling out at her with his father's eyes, it was still hard not to cry a little.

It was the better part of a year before Eliza set foot back in New York City, a spectacle of financial ruin, and she had not forgotten her projects or the orphans on her travels. While Eliza was away, carpenters had been busy breaking ground for new buildings for the orphan asylum in Bloomingdale, on a gentle slope that looked down over the Hudson River, with fundraising thankfully behind them.

Construction was completed at last three years later, in 1840, near what is now Seventy-Fourth Street and Riverside Drive. On July 4, at a grand celebration covered in the New York press, Eliza Hamilton, the orphanage's sprightly directress, was the lady of the hour. That year, her John would publish, too, the long-awaited second volume of the life of Alexander, the second of a four-volume planned series. It was the perfect homecoming.

Her journey to the West and the news of the financial crash had given Eliza time to consider. Her boys were men and had careers and lives ahead of them. Women had no prospects. When that wicked man had murdered Alexander, what options had been left before her except dependence and charity? She had two daughters. One, Betsey, was by now twice a widow. One would spend her life, Eliza accepted, in an asylum. Eliza was determined that neither of her daughters should have to rely on the prudence and wisdom of their brothers for their survival. Eliza could remember all too easily how, after the death of their parents, her siblings had turned on her in inheritance battles.

On her return from the West, with her land business settled and worried about Angelica's future, Eliza set about changing her will and quarreled with her son James, who continued to exercise a heavy hand over his mother's finances and his father's legacy. She was determined now to leave Betsey the sole executrix not only of her estate but also of her father's papers, which they hoped to sell to the United States government to fund the care of Angelica. James, who possessed power of attorney, intervened and set about attempting to rewrite his mother's will, provoking a confrontation. On February 15, 1841, Eliza wrote to him an angry letter. "I am much dissatisfied," Eliza reprimanded her son. "My first intention in requesting you to take charge of the papers was to make a codicil to my will. You objected. . . ." Now she wanted the legal papers surrendered. "I have looked for you day after day and with the expectation of your bringing that paper with you, and cannot rest until I have received it and seen it destroyed," her letter instructed.

James had long been her most challenging child, but now she feared his motive was "an illegal one." She was certain that his goal was to prevent his sister from having financial independence. That rankled mightily. James had suffered devastating losses in the crash, and Eliza knew enough of financial speculation and panic to have a clear idea of the lengths to which a man and a father might be driven. Eliza was sensitive to the ways in which the men around her managed finances, for reasons that should have needed no explanation to any of Alexander Hamilton's children. They had read the papers and knew what was said about their father. Eliza didn't mean the change to her will as a criticism of Alexander and the position in which he had placed her as a widow. Never that. But Alexander Hamilton's untimely death had left her and the children in dire straits, and she did not forget. She preferred to trust her steady, sensible, widowed daughter. She left to her sons—James, John, Alexander Jr., Philip, and William—a mother's love. Everything else she left to her widowed daughter, in trust for the care of the orphaned Angelica, who would live "lost to her herself," as those who knew her put it, for decades.

James, hurt and angry, set off for Europe in a fit of pique and stayed away for the better part of the next half decade. With the house at St. Marks Place lost to the bank following the crash, Alexander Jr. and his wife left as well again for Spain, and in 1842 Eliza's youngest son, Philip, married at last, to a young woman of abolitionist sympathies named Rebecca McLane. Philip and Rebecca, alongside Eliza's "orphan" daughter Fanny Antill and her husband, Arthur Tappan, joined the secret resistance movement known by the 1830s as the Underground Railroad. Years later, Philip's young boys remembered discovering a "very black and ragged man in the cellar who was being fed by my father himself."

By the 1840s, Eliza and her daughter Betsey— now living together in a rented house on Prince Street in New York City and considering what to do next—had also embraced the cause of the abolitionists and spoke out against slavery.

What to do next? They were, mother and daughter, two widows, not rich but not poor now either, and the world was before them. Eliza was unsteady sometimes when she walked, though, and her gout ached in the biting weather. Like her father, she had inherited the family malady. Winters in New York City were cold and painful.

The ladies decided to live a little. They would spend the cold months farther south, in the new capital city of Washington, near the heartbeat of the republic. Eliza missed those days when everything was still beginning, and Alexander was shaping the future. She missed Alexander.

In the capital—the capital Alexander had helped to found, she could not help but remember—Eliza quickly became friends with a spunky and already famous young woman named Jessie Benton Frémont, the daughter of a United States senator and the wife of one of her generation's foremost military explorers, a man whose guide, a certain Kit Carson, was already a legend. Jessie Frémont had turned her husband's army notes into a book, *Report of the Exploring Expedition to the Rocky Mountains* (1843), and it enthralled the country. Eliza recognized something in this slight and vibrant young woman and delighted in her company. The older woman could see a new era breaking, and she knew she wouldn't be there to see it. She was already in her nineties and, though her mind was sharp as ever, her body was failing. But Eliza knew that whatever was coming, Jessie would be part of it.

For her part, Jessie Frémont reached out to take the torch from a woman who seemed to many Americans already mythical, part of the pantheon of men and women who had stood beside George Washington and sparked the revolution. Jessie's books had opened the West to the American imagination. But she would tell the world, too, of the day in 1845 when Eliza Hamilton went to church in the morning, on the occasion of the fiftieth anniversary of the founding of the orphan asylum, where Eliza remained directress.

Eliza attended the newly founded Church of the Epiphany in the capital, but her bones ached with pains that came and went, and she was too frail to sit through an entire sermon. Come for whatever part you can, the preacher assured the devout old lady. Eliza and her daughter arrived this day at the close of the service. What Eliza did not know was that the sermon that day had been on the vast decency of the small group of women who decades ago had founded and built the orphan asylum. The "work and its greatly extended good were told over" to the congregation, Jessie recalled, and "our minds and hearts were filled with the good work of this gentle lady when she entered—a very small, upright little figure in deep black."

"As she moved slowly forward supported by her daughter, Mrs. Holley, one common feeling made the congregation rise, and remain standing until she was seated in her pew at the front." Eliza held her daughter's hand tightly.

Eliza's mind remained as clear as ever, even as her body failed her, and increasingly visits to the parlor of Mrs. Hamilton became a living history lesson for a new generation of Americans in the capital. President James Polk recorded in his diary a dinner party in her company in the winter of 1845, noting that "Mrs. General Hamilton, upon whom I waited at table, is a very remarkable person."

When gold-rush fever swept the nation, Eliza's heart traveled with her son William when, following in the footsteps of Jessie Frémont's husband, he set off for California, driving a "spanking black team hitched to a bright new red wagon." William landed up in Sacramento, which he described as a "miserable hole," and, finding no gold, opened a store selling supplies to other hopeful miners. His younger brother, Philip, still an ardent abolitionist now like his mother, followed after William to the gold rush not long after.

William would not return or again see his mother. He died of "mountain fever"—cholera—in a place he hated. Eliza cried for her darling boy with his father's eyes the way she had not wept in fifty years. She wept for him and for his lost father and brother.

Eliza had turned ninety-one in 1848, and she supposed that it was time, at last, to pass stewardship of the orphan asylum to another generation of women that year. The orphanage she cofounded exists still today in New York, under the name of Graham Windham, carrying on the work of Eliza's living legacy.

Upon retiring at ninety-one, Eliza moved with her daughter permanently to Washington, DC, taking a house on H Street near the intersection with Fourteenth Street, not far from the White House. When the historian Benson Lossing met Eliza that year, he noted, "The sunny cheerfulness of her temper and quiet humor . . . still made her deportment genial and attractive." But Eliza was a restless soul. Retirement did not mean retreat or inaction. Eliza instead threw herself full-time into the work of helping her old friend Dolley Madison raise donations to build a fitting monument to General Washington, and on July 4, 1848, in a grand ceremony, the cornerstone of the Washington Monument was laid.

Eliza sat beside George Washington Parke Custis, the grandson of Martha and the general, and she could hardly believe that this was the little boy who, decades earlier, had gone to dancing lessons in Martha Washington's coach with her own young children.

As fireworks burst over the city that night, a crowd of twenty thousand roared, and Eliza touched gently the burnished locket she wore around her neck and had worn since the week of Alexander's funeral. It contained the scraps of a love poem and Alexander's last letter to her. Did she think back, perhaps, to the fireworks on that summer night in 1780, when she and Alexander, in love and newly engaged, had celebrated the arrival of the French fleet? She did not regret the battles or the sacrifices she had made for Alexander to shape so profoundly the destiny of this republic.

Eliza and Dolley Madison, the last widows of the men who had fought beside George Washington for that liberty, could only smile at each other sadly as they remembered. They were the last of a passing generation. Once, they had danced at the same wartime balls as young belles and brides, when independence seemed like a dream. Now they were bent, and Eliza's hands sometimes trembled.

Eliza went out very little as old age slowed her body. But the world came to Eliza. And Eliza remained keenly interested in young people. Two of Sidney Holly's nieces, nineteen-year-old Elizabeth and her sister, Marianna, came to spend the winter social season of 1852–53 with their aunt and her famous mother, Mrs. General Hamilton. The girls' chatty, vibrant letters home to family and friends describe a glittering social scene in the capital, with Eliza in the thick of it. One of the girls reported to an aunt, with some astonishment, that on New Year's Day, Eliza had more than two hundred visitors. "Gentlemen brought their children to see Mrs. Hamilton, many called who went to no other place, and as you are fond of hearing all, I wish I had room to tell you the names of the most distinguished senators, members," she wrote, but she noted that among the callers was the president of the United States, who "sat with Mrs. Hamilton some time and asked her to appoint some time to dine with him."

And Eliza did. For dinner with the president of the United States, she made an exception to her life as a homebody. Millard Fillmore was not, after all, the first president she had dined with. She had spent quiet evenings with George Washington in her parlor, and laughed when he ducked behind a screen with a wink to escape the tedium of diplomats and society ladies to play with his grandchildren and her children. She had been at dinner parties where a young Thomas Jefferson sported an absurd electric-blue waistcoat, direct from Paris, and made eyes at her sister Angelica. Eliza understood too well how Alexander and her father and all their old friends had fought to make such a thing as the White House or the presidency possible. A few weeks later, in the year she turned ninety-six, Eliza and her daughter put on their finest evening wear and sat down, in the twilight days of the Fillmore administration, to an intimate dinner in the White House, where the first lady, Abigail Fillmore, insisted on Eliza taking the place of honor.

The year of 1853 had been a dazzling last season. When the spring came in 1854, Eliza felt time ebbing. She wanted to go home to New York City. She wanted to sit again in her old pew at Trinity Church, where she once sat with Alexander. She wanted to walk the old churchyard, where Alexander and Angelica and so many of her friends were buried. She wanted to see, too, her former home in Lower Manhattan, where they had lived in the heady days of the first inauguration when they were young and so much seemed possible.

Her son John agreed to take her for a last visit. On a glorious and clear May morning, her son, his wife, and Eliza's grandson, yet another Alexander, rode in silence to the corner of Broad and Wall Streets and were ushered into her old front parlor. Eliza's heart pounded. The memories flooded back. It was so hard. So exquisite. She could feel Alexander's presence. Turning to her grandson, Eliza mused, "I, with Mrs. Knox and other ladies, looked from this window over to Federal Hall and saw George Washington inaugurated the first President of the United States. Then we all walked up Broadway to St. Paul's Chapel, Fulton Street. Washington, Chancellor Livingston, General Knox and your grandfather . . . went into the chapel and occupied the pew on the north side. We ladies sat just in back of them."

Eliza stood for a long while looking out the window. She let her hand touch the mantel of the fireplace, where Alexander, coming in from the cold, stood and gaily recounted to her the day's gossip and political machinations. She did not linger in their old bedroom. She couldn't. When Eliza closed the door, she knew it was forever.

She guessed, as well, that it would be her last summer. Back in Washington, she stood as godmother to the infant daughter of the Reverend John French, named Eliza in her honor, and it was a final passing of the torch for the elderly woman. Something was unwinding inside her. On November 8, 1854, Eliza felt weak and called for the doctor. She knew that her heart was failing. A worn-out heart, tired of grieving, she thought to herself. To die of a broken heart seemed fitting.

Her daughter Betsey sent word immediately to her brothers. Only James, back in Manhattan, was close enough to travel to the capital. He set off that night and arrived bleary-eyed on the morning of November 9. The doctor told him bluntly: she is dying. Eliza had no illness and no pain, but she was tired. *It is so long. I'm so tired. I want to see Hamilton.* Those were the thoughts of her reveries. Those thoughts had been her companions now for decades.

"James, I sat up with mother last night," his sister said. "I wish you do so to-night; I will sleep on the sofa in the next room; there is no medicine to be given her." James and his mother needed to make their peace, after years of misunderstanding. There was little time left. In the dim bedroom, with the heavy curtains falling gently around them, James sat beside his mother, holding Eliza's hand, and for two long hours, in silence, he felt it growing colder.

What thoughts went through Eliza's mind in those quiet hours? Did she think back to her childhood at the edge of the wilderness? Did she think of her youthful passions and crushes, her bond with her sisters as they grew up together?

Or perhaps she thought, as she had for more than fifty years, only of Alexander.

Of the times she and her cousin Kitty Livingston rode, giggling and blushing, in Alexander's sleigh to a ball at Morristown, of how she and her colonel danced together under the watchful eyes of George and Martha Washington, of their marriage and their happiness. Of her beloved sister Angelica. Of Alexander's pranks and ghost stories. What a fuss those stories caused. Of their children. And of that moment, in a parlor in Philadelphia, when Alexander wept at the foolishness of men and their gambling. Wept at his missteps and asked for her loyalty and forgiveness, which she knew she had given him, at great cost, to its fullest measure. She had done her duty. She hoped that she had been both a Roman wife and an American one. This was what the Livingston and Van Rensselaer and Schuyler women were born for, and she had not shirked.

She was certain that when the veil parted, waiting for her would be her beloved sister Angelica and her beautiful lost son Philip. Her handsome boy William. And waiting for her would always be Alexander.

At just after eleven o'clock, Eliza spoke into the darkness. James leaned close. *The bedsheets at my feet. They feel so heavy.* She saw in James's eyes his pain and disappointment as he bent to untangle them. He wanted more before she departed. James had been a complicated son. Sometimes he had made her angry, but she loved him with all her heart, as she loved all her children—those she had borne, those she had adopted. Eliza took a deep breath and said in a clear, firm voice, as he leaned in to see if she was still breathing, "God bless you, you have been a good son." She listened to his sharp breath. They were the words the boy needed.

And then she let go. She let her arm go limp, let her spirit flutter. A thin stream of blood spilled gently from the sides of her mouth. James leaned in again to hear if she would whisper something else, but Eliza had fled to Alexander.

The Hamilton children's mother was dead, and all that was left for James was to wake his sister. In the days to come, the siblings would gather together, one last time, to bury Eliza in the grave in Trinity Church cemetery next to their father. She had lived fifty-five years waiting to see Alexander.

Author's Note

Her Story

The final lines of the musical *Hamilton* belong to Eliza: "Will they tell my story?"

A chorus of voices responds only with more questions: "Who lives, who dies, who tells your story?" The life of Eliza Hamilton does sometimes seem to be more about questions than about answers.

In contrast, the life of Alexander Hamilton is familiar cultural ground as I put the final touches on this book in 2018. Since the turn of the new millennium alone, there have been, by my count, no fewer than a dozen full-length biographies of the most flamboyant of our Founding Fathers. The best known of those, of course, is the sweeping biography by Ron Chernow, adapted for the stage in the Broadway musical phenomenon known simply as *Hamilton*.

The musical was the first introduction for many people to the story of Hamilton's wife, Eliza, who emerges on the stage along with Angelica and Peggy, as part of the spunky trio of Schuyler sisters. They captivate us just as surely as they captivated Alexander Hamilton. When Alexander's infidelity with Maria Reynolds becomes public and the scandal prompts Eliza to burn her love letters in rage and defiance, she becomes the story's heartbroken heroine.

The answer to the musical's final questions, though, is that Eliza's story has largely not been told in print. You hold in your hands the first full-length biography of Eliza Hamilton. And while there are rich sources, many of them untapped because they come before or after her life with Alexander, few of those sources are in Eliza's own voice. As the world knows from *Hamilton*, she wrote herself out of history, and it seems clear that she did burn scores of letters, including her love letters to Alexander. Eliza being Eliza, though, she didn't talk about that either.

Why did Eliza burn correspondence, all of her own and apparently some of Alexander's? As her biography shows, the reasons are a bit more complicated than heartbreak.

Part of it was cultural: women's lives were rarely documented in the eighteenth and nineteenth centuries, unless those women were queens or the mistress of someone famous. Men had lives in the public square. Alexander's letters were destined, Eliza hoped, for the national archives of Congress. She not only hoped for that, she expected it. But she could see no reason why history would be interested in her letters. Respectable women lived resolutely domestic existences and shuddered at the thought of exposing themselves in public.

Part of it is that Eliza also hated writing letters, something that boggled the fast-talking Alexander. She could not spell well and was embarrassed. In this, Eliza was not alone either. Only rarely did even an upper-class girl of the time get a formal, bookish education like her brothers. If there was one argument that Eliza and Alexander had throughout their long and overwhelmingly happy marriage, it was about Eliza and her discomfort with writing letters.

And part of it is the question of this affair with Maria Reynolds. That is the part that most needs unraveling.

I began this book with an epigraph written by Germaine de Staël, a celebrated French writer in Eliza's time, published in the year before the scandal surrounding Alexander and Maria Reynolds broke. Madame de Staël, as she was known, observed that "love is the whole history of a woman's life; it is an episode in a man's." This was not a recommendation but a statement of fact: whom a woman married in the eighteenth century shaped her life completely. Men had lives outside their marriages.

In the story of the life of Alexander Hamilton, the telling of his liaison with Maria Reynolds is a small blot on a larger, epic story. For

Eliza Hamilton, it is the defining moment in a career as a wife and mother. And as I began drafting this biography of Eliza Hamilton, poring over what testimony she left behind, trying to make sense of what Alexander wrote and her reaction, this became part of what I puzzled over for months.

In the context of the life of Alexander Hamilton—the one who committed the infidelity and paid the price with a confession—nothing about the story of Maria Reynolds is jarringly out of character. Alexander was impulsive, flirtatious, intemperate, contradictory, and brilliant. He was a scrapper, who worked his way up from a start as an orphan on a remote island, marked by his illegitimate birth, to the highest reaches of American political life. He married into a family that was, for all intents and purposes, aristocratic. Like the husbands of Eliza's sisters, he was one of life's gamblers. The Schuyler sisters—not only Angelica and Peggy but also their next-youngest sister, Cornelia—all had a thing for men who, like their father, Philip Schuyler, were risk takers and fortune hunters.

Eliza's story, however, is less straightforward.

When we look at the letters and documents that survive, when we track the story of Eliza Hamilton from her girlhood through her death nearly a century later, it is hard to make sense of her reaction. In the musical *Hamilton*, she burns with anger and indignation and sends Alexander off to sleep in his office. In private Schuyler family correspondence and in Alexander Hamilton's surviving letters to her, she steadfastly refuses to accept that Alexander has betrayed her and places the blame squarely and exclusively on the shoulders of his political enemies. Behind closed doors, she and Alexander did not pull apart either. They drew ever closer, into a universe of two, precisely at the moment of a spectacularly public breach of trust between them. For this, Alexander's letters breathe his gratitude. "A thousand blessings upon you," he wrote to her in the months after. "While all other passions decline in me, those of love and friendship gain new strength. . . . In this I know your good and kind heart responses to mine. . . . Heaven bless you My Dear Wife & reward you with all the happiness you deserve," he offered her.

In Eliza's case, it is harder to square the circle. Here is a young woman—passionately in love, fiercely loyal, relentlessly pragmatic, and deceptively strong-minded and independent, for all her self-effacing modesty—who, confronted with the affair of her husband, in fact does not get angry and kick him to the couch. Instead, if the story of the affair is true, she apparently clings to him, makes excuses, and insists to her dying day that he was an admirable husband. She does this despite Alexander having published an entire pamphlet as "evidence" of his infidelity, offering up sordid details of sex in their marital bed and publishing transcripts of another woman's love letters.

What makes it hard to reconcile the life of Eliza Hamilton with her response to Alexander's infidelity is that we have to posit a personality change occurring suddenly in the summer of 1797. We have to believe that the affair crushed her spirit and turned her from a feisty child of the frontier to a victim of her own self-deception. We have to posit that Eliza simply could not handle the reality of Alexander's affair and would do anything to keep him. When he dies, in a duel fueled at least in part by the scandal, she carries on for decades insisting that Alexander has been maligned, idolizing him and insisting on his virtue.

In short, when it comes to Alexander, Eliza begins to look a bit foolish.

But Eliza Hamilton was nobody's fool. After Alexander's death, in all the other aspects of her long life, she carries on being just as strong-minded, pragmatic, and independent as always. She raises children as a single mother who is strapped for cash. She takes in the children of others. She builds a formidable charitable institution that still exists today as her living legacy, and, in her eighties, with energy and resources that astonished those around her, she set out for the new frontier, the American West, just because she still relished an adventure and didn't trust her boys with her business interests.

What if the piece of history that doesn't fit the puzzle of this life story is not Eliza but the publicly accepted story of Alexander's affair with Maria Reynolds?

As her biographer, I struggled to write the chapters that came after the publication of the pamphlet, because I couldn't make sense of how the person I had come to know as Eliza up to that point—as a biographer I was spending more time each day "with" Eliza than with anyone in my family—suddenly changed in her essential character.

So I went back to the scholarship and the archives, and I found something astonishing and eye-opening. There exists a completely different version of this story. It is not a story that is a belated, modern invention either. It's the story that in the 1790s was splashed all over the newspapers, and it's the version of the story that was believed by James Monroe and any number of men in Congress. It's the story Maria Reynolds told.

It is also a story that makes perfect sense of Eliza's reaction.

Eliza and Alexander, though, wanted to bury it.

What if Alexander Hamilton never had an affair with Maria Reynolds? That is the crux of what I found in the scholarship and in the newspapers from the 1790s. What if something else—something to which infidelity was preferable—happened?

The idea that Alexander Hamilton's relationship with Maria Reynolds and her husband, James Reynolds, is more complex than it appears is an idea with a long history, and there is no evidence that an affair with Maria Reynolds ever happened, apart from Alexander Hamilton's sole say-so. Everyone else connected with the scandal— from Maria Reynolds and James Monroe, who investigated the matter in Congress, to muckraking newspaper journalists—said it was a convenient cover story for a bigger, financial scandal that went to the heart of the government.

In American presidential history, the intense political and personal rivalry between Alexander Hamilton and Thomas Jefferson has played out in the field of biography. When Hamilton has been in, Jefferson has been out, and vice versa. As the musical phenomenon testifies, this is a Hamilton moment. In the 1960s and 1970s, however, the groundbreaking research was on Jefferson, led by the

world's foremost expert, Professor Julian Boyd at Princeton University, who happened to be the editor of the papers of the third president of the United States.

In Alexander Hamilton's own time, the authenticity of Maria
Reynolds's letters and the truth behind Alexander's pamphlet were
hotly debated and questioned. Julian Boyd asked the simple question: What if we took seriously the claims of Alexander's doubters?
What is the evidence in the archives? He argued, in long, scholarly
notes, that taking Alexander Hamilton's word against the word of
everyone else posed some thorny problems.

If manuscript letters from Maria Reynolds existed—because the
only evidence that they did were the transcriptions published by Alexander in his printed pamphlet—why would Alexander not produce
them? Maria Reynolds was alive and well when the scandal broke,
and it would have been an easy thing to obtain a writing sample. The
newspapers suggested it. An indignant Maria Reynolds was willing.
But Alexander refused to release the documents and claimed to have
lodged them with a gentleman friend in Philadelphia, who later professed bewilderment at the idea of having ever seen them, making far
more plausible the charges of forgery brought against Alexander by
his political enemies.

And why, Alexander's contemporary critics asked in the newspapers, were the transcriptions that were published such strange, chi-
merical compositions? Why does Maria Reynolds consistently use
and spell complex words and phrases correctly but change the spelling of the simplest words, sometimes correctly, sometimes not, from
paragraph to paragraph, in ways that don't make any sense in respect
to the phonetics? It looks, Boyd grimly concluded after reconsider-
ing the evidence, a lot like what a well-educated man might imagine
to be the misspellings of a woman's love letter. As one of Alexander
Hamilton's biographers in the late 1970s observed, more than this,
the published letters bear more than a passing resemblance to the letters between Alexander and Eliza. Is it possible that Alexander used
some of the things Eliza wrote, too, as the basis for those published

transcriptions of Maria Reynolds's putative love letters? If so, there might be another reason Eliza burned them.

There were only two people who ever knew for certain whether Alexander Hamilton and Maria Reynolds shared a passion, and the truth can only rest with one of their stories. One of the two of them was lying. Alexander said that they were lovers. Maria Reynolds was prepared to testify to Congress that they weren't. The further evidence that might have proven the case conclusively, one way or another— Alexander asserted as proof of his claims that there were blackmail notes and love letters—was burned by someone. That someone was most plausibly Eliza.

While there is no smoking gun to prove that Alexander fabricated his affair with Maria Reynolds to distract congressmen from an investigation into the Treasury, neither has evidence emerged to prove that Alexander's contemporaries were wrong or that Maria Reynolds was lying. Julian Boyd, in effect, makes the case for the veracity of Maria. Others argue that we should take the word of Alexander.

As the editors of the Hamilton Papers at the National Archives of the United States judiciously note, it remains very much an open question. "Many historians like to view themselves as experts," the archivists observe,

> and as such they are reluctant to admit that at times they encounter questions for which they can find no satisfactory answers. But such questions exist, and the "Reynolds Affair" poses not one such question but a host of them. Despite the most rigorous scholarship and the best intentions, historians have been forced to leave the "Reynolds Affair" in essentially the same enigmatic state in which they have found it. . . . In this respect historians, both past and present, are little better than Hamilton's contemporaries, for what they have been wont to call conclusions are in reality little more than acts of faith.

And where the book in question is a biography of Alexander Hamilton, few of us would not place our faith in the word of our subject. The stakes, anyhow, are not vast ones. Whether Alexander Hamilton took a tumble between the sheets with a woman about whom history remembers nothing else, after all, is hardly the most important part of his story. In the life of Alexander, Maria Reynolds happens in square brackets, as an unfortunate lapse in a brilliant career, something that damaged his chances of higher political office, to be sure, but not definitive of the man or his life story. And, so, few contemporary biographies of Alexander Hamilton raise the questions of whether Alexander might have been fibbing. The best biographies—Ron Chernow's notably among them—mention them only in the footnotes and then proceed to tell the story of the Maria Reynolds affair as if we are certain that it did happen, because that is the only way to write a life story.

But the story here is of the life of Eliza Hamilton, and their shared history looks differently from the perspective of her character and reactions. If Alexander Hamilton fibbed about an affair with Maria Reynolds and flirted, instead, with insider trading, the story of the life of Alexander gets a bit murkier for certain.

And if he fibbed and asked for loyalty and devotion, the story of the life of Eliza Hamilton suddenly becomes coherent.

Biographers, this one included, are inclined to take the word of their subjects. "Taking the word" of Eliza Hamilton, however, means reading not what she wrote—and burned—but reading the outlines of her convictions and character in her actions and how others described them. It also means acknowledging that Eliza, more than any other person, was responsible for making knowing impossible and that more than anything she cared about protecting Alexander. That was the principle at the heart of their marriage.

The story I tell here is the story in which there was no breach of faith between them.

Some readers will be understandably curious to learn more about the tangled and fascinating history of the Reynolds crisis, which also riveted newspaper readers in the 1790s. For any reader who wishes to track the historians and to draw his or her own conclusions, two comprehensive sources are the extensive introductory note provided by Harold C. Syrett, editor of the twenty-seven-volume *Papers of Alexander Hamilton*, to a letter of Oliver Wolcott Jr. dated July 3, 1797, published in volume 21 and available online, along with all the relevant primary source material related to the Reynolds investigation and pamphlet at the United States National Archive's website Founders Online; and the detailed appendix, titled "The First Conflict in the Cabinet," provided by Julian P. Boyd in volume 18 of *The Papers of Thomas Jefferson*.

This book is not a scholarly dissertation. The life of Eliza Hamilton is too lively and exciting for that, and, apart from the author's note here and my extensive citations at the end of the book, I proceed to tell her story without equivocation or hedging. The only liberties that I have taken with her story are instances in which, where her voice is absent, I have used other historical sources—mainly Alexander's replies to her lost letters, in which he alludes to specific content—or have extrapolated from her character or from the letters of others to offer a glimpse into what I believe was Eliza's lived experience of her story. Those are instances of historical triangulation and inference, however, and not invention.

In telling Eliza's story, I am persuaded from what I know of Eliza Hamilton and her character, as reflected in the testimony of her life and the lives of those who loved her, that the affair with Maria Reynolds was fabricated by Alexander in an attempt to end a political inquisition that would damage him and several of their extended family members. I am persuaded that Eliza knew and that she swore to keep the secret.

Whether Alexander was guilty of financial indiscretion or whether it was only that the appearances were so strongly against him that he felt cornered is impossible to know for certain. The fact that money passed between Alexander and James Reynolds tends to suggest that Alexander was speculating, at least in a small way, probably on army pensions. What is certain is that Alexander was surrounded by men who were making huge financial bets at the peak of a bubble and playing fast and loose with inside information, and that some of that information led back to the Treasury. It is not impossible that he was trying to protect some of those other men, including John Church and Philip Schuyler, from being taken down in a financial investigation.

And when the story of the affair with Maria Reynolds broke, Eliza vowed to protect Alexander and her family, even if it meant the world believing Alexander had betrayed her. Her loyalty was ferocious. Alexander was profoundly grateful and was determined to make this up to her.

What was Eliza's motivation?

Believe in me, Alexander had asked implicitly of Eliza in their letters. *I am flawed, and I am not worthy. Love me. Forgive me.* That was what he meant when he called her his "nut brown maid" and when he called her "the best of wives, the best of women." He had poured out his heart in the earliest days of their courtship, with a raw need that made Eliza love him. He had asked her to let it be them against the world, come what might. She had promised, and she would go on promising.

Eliza would keep her promise all through the decades of her widowhood. Among Alexander's surviving papers is a letter composed in advance of a duel he nearly fought as the scandal was crashing over them in 1795. All his most interesting papers, Alexander wrote, were in a small leather trunk. Inside the trunk was a sachet of letters, bound in a ribbon, and marked with the initials of James Reynolds.

Eliza set this letter aside when it came time for biographers to write the story of Alexander's life, with a note in firm handwriting, "to be retained by myself." As far as anyone knows, the little leather trunk and the bundle of letters sealed "J.R." also made their way, in the end, to Eliza.

Then the letters disappear from history. Historians have scoured the archives and have never found a trace of them. Their fate is also speculative and circumstantial. But it is not hard to imagine an elderly widow, with a trembling hand, tracing one last time the ink from his pen with her finger, and consigning them to a winter fire.

This, and all that came before and after, is Eliza's story.

Acknowledgments

I owe debts, large and small, to those who helped in the process of bringing this book to completion.

I would like to extend a particular thanks to Selby Kiffer and his associates at Sotheby's in New York City and especially to the owner(s) of the major collection of Hamilton and Schuyler family materials sold at auction in January 2017, just as I was completing the research for this book, for permission to conduct research in and to quote from this important historical collection of materials on the life of Elizabeth Hamilton prior to sale. It was a rare and final chance for a scholar to work with those materials as a single collection and added immeasurably to my sense of Eliza Hamilton as a person.

I am grateful as well to the librarians at Hobart and William Smith Colleges, the New-York Historical Society, Columbia University, the University of Michigan, and the New York Public Library, all of which hold archival materials that are not published and, unlike many of the Hamilton papers, are not available online. I wish to thank particularly Dr. Mary Tibbetts Freeman at Columbia for her efforts in tracking down family correspondence, and a particular thanks as well to the senior staff at the New York Public Library who assisted in arranging access to the Schuyler-Malcom family papers in the midst of digitalization; their efforts were heroic and hugely appreciated. Thanks as well at the New York Public Library to Melanie Locay, who helped to arrange space in the Allen Room, and to the retired librarian David Smith, who was an invaluable research assistant. I am likewise indebted for research assistance to Rachel Betts and Derek Frasure, in New York and Michigan, respectively, and would like to acknowledge their work in helping to hunt down unpublished sources and the help of Catherine Delannoy in fact-checking the manuscript.

Finally, a thanks to all the staff at the National Arts Club in New York City for all those small kindnesses toward the perennially distracted and occasionally disheveled writer up in the garret. Without all their assistance, this book could not have been completed in a timely manner, especially in the midst of my teaching responsibilities at Colby College.

Harry Berberian and his colleagues at Graham Windham in Brooklyn—Eliza's orphanage—generously shared not only their archives and knowledge but also their enthusiasm for this project. It is a small, private wish that readers might consider sharing their enthusiasm for Eliza's story by supporting her legacy; Eliza would have loved that, I am certain. Fellow Eliza enthusiast Chelsea Geiger shared leads and a passion, and my thanks to her and, once again as well, to Mark Lee, slayer of obstacles, for that most important of gifts between writers.

I was fortunate enough to have two fabulous editors on this book. My thanks to Karen Kosztolnyik for making Eliza's story happen and for continuing to support this project after her move to Grand Central. And very warmest thanks to my second editor at Gallery, Natasha Simons, for wise counsel on all things Eliza. I am grateful at Gallery Books, as well, to Jennifer Bergstrom and Meagan Harris; to Polly Watson for her keen eye as copyeditor; to Hadley Black at the Simon & Schuster speakers bureau; and, as always, to my literary agent, Stacey Glick, and my film agent, Lou Pitt, for clearing the space for a good story.

Above all, my abiding love to Robert Miles, who is not a man of many words (Eliza would approve) but who, among his other acts of kindness, without fail brought coffee at dawn to a cranky and irascible writer and quietly closed the door behind him. I steal from Alexander the only fitting words for my gratitude and devotion: best of men and best of husbands.

Notes

Notes here are generally limited to occasions of direct quotation and paraphrase only, so that interested readers may conveniently locate passages of particular interest. However, the author wishes to note that she has drawn from the works cited in the following notes as primary sources of material of the life and times of Elizabeth Hamilton. The early biographies of Alexander Hamilton and the memoirs of his friends and children; the early biographies of Catherine Schuyler, Philip Schuyler, and the Schuyler family; the memoirs of Tench Tilghman; and the letters of Elizabeth Hamilton, Alexander Hamilton, their family members, and their friends and colleagues are among the most important of those sources, and the author wishes to acknowledge her debt to these materials, as well as to the important scholarship of the authors whose works are referenced here.

Throughout this biography, the term "cousin" is used, for the sake of simplicity, to refer not only to first cousins but to a larger and more extensive range of family relations of cousinhood and kinship, including second cousins, third cousins, and cousins at generational removes.

PROLOGUE

1   *"I have told you and I told you truly that I love you"*: Alexander Hamilton
    to Elizabeth Schuyler, 5 October 1780, Hamilton Papers, Founders Online,
    National Archives of the United States. All further references to Founders
    Online, National Archives, direct readers to the relevant collections and ex-
    tensive notes at www.founders.archive.gov. The Hamilton Papers are sourced
    from *The Papers of Alexander Hamilton*, ed. Harold C. Syrett, 27 vols. (New
    York: Columbia University Press, 1961–87).

2   *popular folk song of that same title—"The Nut-Brown Maid"*: Thomas Percy,
    *Reliques of Ancient English Poetry, Consisting of Old Heroic Ballads, Songs, and
    Other Pieces of Our Earlier Poets* (London, J. Dodsley, 1765; New York: E. P.
    Dutton, 1906), 2:303–14; the text has been updated from the original by the author
    to conform more nearly to Standard American English to ease comprehension.

3   *"I ought at least to hear from you by every post"*: Alexander Hamilton to Eliz-
    abeth Schuyler, 5 October 1780, Hamilton Papers, Founders Online.

3   *"If that ye were with enemies day and night"*: Percy, *Reliques*, 303–14.

CHAPTER I

5   *outpost at German Flatts along the Mohawk River*: Nelson Greene, ed., *His-
    tory of the Mohawk Valley: Gateway to the West 1614–1925* (Chicago: The
    S. J. Clarke Publishing Company, 1925), 1:581–87.

8   *the most prominent Dutch entrepreneurial families in the New World*: Patri-
    cia U. Bonomi, *A Factious People: Politics and Society in Colonial New York*
    (Ithaca, NY: Cornell University Press, 2014), 179.

8   *the Rensselaerwyck boundaries*: Details here and throughout from Warren
    Roberts, *A Place in History: Albany in the Age of Revolution, 1775–1825* (Al-
    bany, NY: SUNY Press, 2010), 26, etc.

8   *Kitty was a striking woman*: Details here and throughout on the Schuyler fam-
    ily from Mary Gay Humphreys, *Catherine Schuyler* (Albany, NY: C. Scrib-
    ner's Sons, 1897), 28, etc.

10 *"on your escape and arrival and extreme good fortune"*: Humphreys, *Cather-
    ine Schuyler*, 63.

10 *Kitty's construction budget was 1,400 pounds sterling*: Historical dollar values
    from MeasuringWorth, www.measuringworth.com; figure here represents
    historical economic-status-value comparison.

11 *Anne MacVicar, later left an account of growing up with the Schuyler girls*:
    Jane Williams, *The Literary Women of England* (London: Saunders, Otley,
    and Company, 1861), 519ff. See also Anne McVicar Grant, *Memoirs and Cor-
    respondence of Mrs. Grant of Laggan*, ed. J. P. Laggan (London: Longman,
    Brown, Green, and Longman, 1844); and Anne McVicar Grant, *Memoirs of an
    American Lady, with Sketches of the Manners and Scenery as They Existed in
    America, Previous to the Revolution* (New York: George Dearborn, 1836).

12   *Forty percent of children born in the 1760s died*: Max Roser, "Child Mortal-
      ity," 2018, Our World in Data, https://ourworldindata.org/child-mortality.

12   *the winter that year was particularly hard, with the first snows coming in early
      November*: Noah Webster, *A Brief History of Epidemic and Pestilential Dis-
      eases; With the Principal Phenomena of the Physical World, Which Precede
      and Accompany Them, and Observations Deduced from the Facts Stated*
      (Hartford, CT: Hudson & Goodwin, 1799), 1:216ff.

12   *Smallpox continued to plague the Mohawk and Hudson Valleys*: Kirrily
      Apthorp, "As Good as an Army: Mapping Smallpox During the Seven Years'
      War in North America" (thesis, University of Sydney, Australia, 2011), 73;
      S. L. Kotar and J. E. Gessler, *Yellow Fever: A Worldwide History* (Jefferson,
      NC: McFarland Publishing, 2017), 284.

CHAPTER 2

16   *Albany County sheriff, Harmanus Schuyler, laid siege to a farmhouse*: Col-
      lin Jay Williams, "New York Transformed: Committees, Militia, and the
      Social Effects of Political Mobilization in Revolutionary New York" (PhD
      diss., University of Alabama, 2013), 53, http://acumen.lib.ua.edu/content
      /u0015/0000001/0001205/u0015_0000001_0001205.pdf.

17   *Prendergast was ordered "hanged by the neck, and then shall be cut down
      alive"*: William A. Evans, "The Prendergast Family: Loyalists" (lecture, Chau-
      tauqua County Historical Society, Jamestown, NY, April 10, 1976), http://
      mcclurgmuseum.org/collection/library/lecture_list/prendergast_loyalists_by
      _evans.pdf.

18   *unleashed fresh complaints about years of British mismanagement*: Hum-
      phreys, *Catherine Schuyler*, 93.

19   *"Angelica's early air of Elegance & dignity"*: Anne Grant to Elizabeth Hamil-
      ton, 18 November 1834, private collection, Sotheby's, New York.

19   *"two of the children for 50 a year, two pounds of tea, one of loaf sugar"*: Hum-
      phreys, *Catherine Schuyler*, 123.

19   *"the young ladies are in perfect health and improve in their education"*: Hum-
      phreys, 123.

19   *all three of the Schuyler girls learned to play the English "guittar"*: Art
      Schrader, "Guittars and Guitars: A Note on Musical Fashion," *American
      Music Research Center Journal* (University of Colorado, Boulder) 11 (2001),
      http://www.colorado.edu/amrc/sites/default/files/attached-files/0506-2001-011
      -00-000001.pdf.

20   *"With respect to the distribution of your time"*: Thomas E. Cone Jr., "Thomas
      Jefferson Writes to His 11-Year Old Daughter," *Pediatrics* 51, no. 4 (April
      1973), http://pediatrics.aappublications.org/content/51/4/715.

22   *the grand Indian council of the Six Nations*: "Grand Council," Haudenosaunee
      Confederacy, accessed April 1, 2018, http://www.haudenosauneeconfederacy
      .com/grandcouncil.html.

22 *they almost certainly stopped overnight at Johnson Hall, the estate of Sir William Johnson:* For details on the life of Sir William Johnson, see, for example, James Thomas Flexner, *Mohawk Baronet: A Biography of Sir William Johnson* (Syracuse, NY: Syracuse University Press, 1990).

23 *He and Sir William joined more than two thousand representatives of the Iroquois and Cherokee nations:* For the history of the complex relations between colonial settlers and the Iroquois, see, for example, Daniel K. Richter and James H. Merrell, *Beyond the Covenant Chain: The Iroquois and Their Neighbors in Indian North America, 1600–1800* (University Park, PA: Penn State Press, 2010), 148; John Romeyn Brodhead, *Documents Relative to the Colonial History: Procured in Holland, England and France* (Albany, NY: Weed, Parsons, and Company, 1857), 234.

23 *To accept the gift of wampum meant to accept an agreement as binding:* Francis Jennings, *The History and Culture of Iroquois Diplomacy: An Interdisciplinary Guide to the Treaties of the Six Nations and Their League* (Syracuse, NY: Syracuse University Press, 1995), 88.

24 *she was proud of her Indian name, which her father said meant "One of Us":* For details on naming rituals, see "Constitution of the Iroquois Nations," National Public Telecomputing Network and the Constitution Society, Harvard University, http://cscie12.dce.harvard.edu/ssi/iroquois/simple/7.shtml; for details on Eliza Hamilton's name, see Ron Chernow, *Alexander Hamilton* (New York: Penguin, 2005), 126ff.

24 *satin and brocade dresses cut low enough to raise modern eyebrows:* Edwin G. Burrows and Mike Wallace, *Gotham: A History of New York City to 1898* (New York: Oxford University Press, 1998), 174.

25 *Slaves made up roughly a quarter of the population of New York City:* Marc Egnal, *A Mighty Empire: The Origins of the American Revolution* (Ithaca, NY: Cornell University Press, 2010), 138.

25 *"A very Pretty Young Lady," as one visitor noted emphatically:* Humphreys, *Catherine Schuyler*, 134.

25 *"a Brunette with the most good-natured, lively dark eyes":* Humphreys, 134.

26 *Now "Lovely Polly," as she was known:* Humphreys, 345.

26 *"Rich and nervously irritable":* W. Stewart Wallace, ed., *The Encyclopedia of Canada* (Toronto: University Associates of Canada, 1948), 3:304. Reprinted at Claude Bélanger, "Sir John Johnson," The Quebec History Encyclopedia, Marianopolis College, 2005, http://faculty.marianopolis.edu/c.belanger/quebechistory/encyclopedia/SirJohnJohnson-QuebecHistory.htm.

26 *The wedding took place at the end of June in New York City:* W. Max Reid, *The Story of Old Fort Johnson* (New York, G. P. Putnam's Sons, 1906), chap. 5, http://montgomery.nygenweb.net/johnson/Chap05.html.

27 *their common aunt, Judith Van Rensselaer:* Judith Bayard married first Jeremiah Van Rensselaer, Catherine Schuyler's brother, who died in 1764; Judith after married William Bruce and was widowed again in 1779. Eliza knew her

as Aunt Bruce. According to Thomas Jones, *History of New York During the Revolutionary War: And of the Leading Events in the Other Colonies at That Period* (New York: New-York Historical Society, 1879), 1:588, Judith Bruce and Judith's niece Mrs. Stephen De Lancey were the aunts with whom Lady Mary Johnson was sent to stay during her captivity. Aunt Bruce died in 1817 and left $100 to Eliza's orphanage.

27 *Mary Watts would get drawn into espionage*: Ian Mumpton and Danielle Funiciello, "I Desire You Would Remember the Ladies," Schuyler Mansion State Historic Site, December 9, 2016, http://schuylermansion.blogspot.com/2016/12/i-desire-you-would-remember-ladies.html.

CHAPTER 3

29 *"Much as I love peace," Philip Schuyler wrote to a friend*: Benson John Lossing, *The Life and Times of Philip Schuyler* (New York: Sheldon and Company, 1860), 2:307.

30 *"brunette with dark eyes, and a countenance as animated and sparkling"*: Tench Tilghman, *Memoir of Lieut. Col. Tench Tilghman, Secretary and Aid to Washington: Together with an Appendix, Containing Revolutionary Journals and Letters, Hitherto Unpublished*, eds. S. A. Harrison and Oswald Tilghman (Albany, NY: J. Munsell, 1876), 89.

30 *"Mr. [Walter] Livingston informed me that I was not mistaken"*: Tilghman, *Memoir*, 89; Walter Livingston was the husband of Eliza's cousin Cornelia Schuyler, a daughter of Aunt Gertrude Schuyler.

30 *the very elegant Miss Lynch*: Miss Lynch was either the twenty-eight-year-old Sabina or, more likely, the twenty-one-year-old Elizabeth; further identification has not been possible.

32 *"made herself merry at the distress of the other Ladies"*: Tilghman, *Memoir*, 91.

32 *"beating their drum, sticking sticks together in Exact time and yelling"*: Tilghman, 92.

32 *"I accepted the proposal with thanks"*: Tilghman, 95.

33 *"pretty and extremely cleanly they speak tolerable English too"*: Tilghman, 96–7.

33 *"the Belle of the Town and therefore a little of the Coquette"*: Tilghman, 96–7.

33 *"I sat among them like an old Acquaintance"*: Tilghman, 96.

34 *"Who should bless my eye sight this evening"*: Tilghman, 98.

35 *"Miss Ransolaer," he recorded in his journal, "is pretty, quite young"*: Tilghman, 98.

35 *"I lamented that my short stay in Albany would so soon deprive me"*: Tilghman, 99–100.

35 *captured British officer John André stayed briefly in the Schuyler family*: For John André's pencil portrait of Abraham and Jannetje Cuyler of Albany, see

sale 2420, lot 31, Swann Auction Galleries, sales catalogue, June 2016, http://catalogue.swanngalleries.com/asp/fullCatalogue.asp?salelot=2420++++++31+&refno=++719250&saletype=.

36 *"The lively behavior of the young ladies"*: Humphreys, *Catherine Schuyler*, 148.

37 *by November 1776, John Carter was a regular visitor*: Weymer Jay Mills, *Historic Houses of New Jersey* (Philadelphia: J. B. Lippincott, 1902); Melissa Carrie Naulin, "All That a Genteel Family Need Require: The Church Family's Frontier Experience at Belvidere, Allegany County, New York" (thesis, University of Delaware, 2000), 9; see "Church Family Papers, 1784–1957, 2000: A Finding Aid S.C.08," Hobart and William Smith Colleges, March 15, 2018, http://library.hws.edu/ld.php?content_id=28360194.

37 *The Schuyler sisters were already part of that network*: Mumpton and Funiciello, "I Would Desire You Remember the Ladies."

40 *"father was so alarmed by the killing of Miss McCrea"*: Jessie Benton Frémont, *Souvenirs of My Time* (Boston: D. Lothrop, 1887), 119.

CHAPTER 4

45 *"nothing remarkable to distinguish her save her gilding"*: Naulin, "A Genteel Family," 9.

46 *"entered into a partnership with another man, but then took 5000 guineas of the pair's money"*: Naulin, 9; see also R. G. Thorne, ed., *The History of Parliament: The House of Commons, 1790–1820* (London: Secker & Warburg, 1986), 5:441, reprinted at The History of Parliament: British Political, Local, and Social History, www.historyofparliamentonline.org/volume/1790-1820/member/church-john-barker-1748-1818. MeasuringWorth, purchasing-power calculation.

46 *"Dear Alice, Gr. Grandfather Trumbull writes his wife as follows"*: [Unidentified correspondents], 30 June 1777, Church Family Papers, Special Collections, Hobart and William Smith Colleges.

47 *"unacquainted with his Family, his Connections, and Situation in Life"*: Lossing, *Philip Schuyler*, 2:207.

48 *"Mrs. Carter requests you to buy her 5 or 6 Pounds of Hyson Tea"*: Lossing, 2:207.

48 *the American currency entered what some feared was a death spiral*: James E. Newell, "How Much Is That Worth?," The Continental Line, www.continentalline.org.

48 *"The General will pay you for them when you come here"*: Lossing, *Philip Schuyler*, 2:207.

48 *"Whether or not Schuyler had agreed to assume Carter's debts in addition to his married daughter's"*: Naulin, "A Genteel Family," 13.

49 *prevented Philip Schuyler from being murdered in his bed by the intruder*: Eliza Susan Morton Quincy, *Memoir of the Life of Eliza S. M. Quincy* (Boston: J. Wilson and Son, 1861), 316.

50   *"she possessed courage and prudence in a great degree"*: Quincy, *Memoir*, 312.

51   *"The wife of the General must not be afraid"*: Quoted in Samuel Sidney, *The Book of the Horse* (London: Cassell & Company, 1893), 370.

51   *Kitty ordered the post rider to take back to the general at Fort Edwards*: Quincy, *Memoir*, 318.

51   *"Very well." Kitty sighed. "If you will not do it, I must do it myself"*: Humphreys, *Catherine Schuyler*, 142.

53   *"wearied out with the Disputes and Bickerings"*: Naulin, "A Genteel Family," 13.

53   *"No part of your buildings escaped their malice"*: Quincy, *Memoir*, 322.

53   *"I must candidly confess that I did not present myself . . . with much courage to the enemy"*: Edward St. Germain, "Frederica de Riedesel," AmericanRevolution, accessed April 1, 2018, http://www.americanrevolution.org/women /women9.php.

53   *"Do not be alarmed," he assured her, and he lifted her three little girls*: Una Siknickson, "Frederika Baroness Riedesel," *Pennsylvania Magazine of History and Biography* 30, no. 4 (1906): 392.

54   *"You are too kind to me—who have done you so much injury"*: Humphreys, *Catherine Schuyler*, 159.

54   *"Our reception from General Schuyler, and his wife and daughters"*: Una Siknickson, "Frederika Baroness Riedesel," 392.

CHAPTER 5

57   *"I entreat you to purchase for Mrs. Carter"*: Lousie Hall Tharp, *The Baroness and the General* (Boston: Little, Brown, and Company, 1962), 262.

57   *John and Angelica owned at least one slave*: Alexander Hamilton to John Chaloner, 11 November 1784, Founders Online, National Archives; Bradford Verter, "Interracial Festivity and Power in Antebellum New York: The Case of Pinkster," *Journal of Urban History* 28, no. 4 (May 2002): 398–428.

57   *Angelica, "who, with her sister Betsy, was living in Boston"*: Tharp, *The Baroness and the General*, 242.

57   *"Curiosity and desire urged me to pay a visit to Madame Carter, the daughter of General Schuyler"*: Friederike Charlotte Luise Freifrau von Riedesel, *Letters and Journals Relating to the War of the American Revolution, and the Capture of the German Troops at Saratoga* (London: J. Munsell, 1867), 140.

57   *"Madame Carter," the baroness decided, "was as gentle and good as her parents"*: Riedesel, *Letters*, 140.

58   *"I did not understand you . . . in what you mention'd in your note about Carter"*: Tharp, *The Baroness and the General*, 264.

58   *"salt them down in small barrels, and send over to the English one of these barrels"*: Tharp, 264.

59   *"the little Fellow of two Days old 'grows finely' "*: John Carter to Philip Schuyler, 8 May 1788, Church Family Papers.

61   *"where all is under the secure lock and key of Friendship"*: Bernard Christian Steiner, *The Life and Correspondence of James McHenry, Secretary of War Under Washington and Adams* (Cleveland: Burrows Brothers Company, 1907); see also Humphreys, *Catherine Schuyler*, 169; and "Beverwyck Site," National Register of Historic Places, United States Department of the Interior, National Parks Service, application, May 2004, https://npgallery.nps.gov/GetAsset?assetID=78cac489-7e8c-4e04-920c-51ba81d9f87c.

62   *Cornelia Lott, daughter of the wealthy but rather shady merchant*: Cornelia Lott was the sister-in-law of General Greene's aide-de-camp Lieutenant Colonel William Smith Livingston, another of the Schuyler-Livingston cousins; for more on the Lott family, see Lott Family Papers, ARC.186, Brooklyn Historical Society; and Alexander Van Cleve Phillips, *The Lott Family in America: Including the Allied Families: Cassell, Davis, Graybeal, Haring, Hegeman, Hogg, Kerley, Phillips, Thompson, Walter and Other* (Ann Arbor, MI: Edwards Brothers, 1942).

63   *"Such a wife as I want will, I know, be difficult to be found"*: Alexander Hamilton to Lieutenant Colonel John Laurens, [April 1779], Founders Online, National Archives.

64   *"After knowing exactly your taste, and whether you are of a romantic"*: Alexander Hamilton to Catharine Livingston, 11 April 1777, Founders Online, National Archives.

65   *"What bend the Stubborn knee at last"*: Quoted in Chernow, *Hamilton*, 94.

65   *Abraham Lott was hopelessly indebted*: "Abraham Lott, the Colony Treasurer," American Archives: Documents of the American Revolutionary Period, 1774–1776, Southern Illinois University Libraries, accessed April 1, 2018, http://amarch.lib.niu.edu/islandora/object/niu-amarch%3A106007.

66   *Mary, known as "Polly," the daughter of Colonel Edward Tilghman*: Mary "Polly" Tilghman (1762–1793), the daughter of Tench's uncle, Colonel Edward Tilghman of Philadelphia, and his first cousin. This identification is conjectural, but the evidence for the identification is very strong. Tench Tilghman's reference to Polly by her Christian name, in a letter to a relation, among other facts, indicates that she was a member of his family, and Colonel Edward Tilghman was in and out of Morristown in 1780 and remained in contact with Alexander Hamilton afterward. Edward Tilghman assisted Elizabeth Hamilton financially after her widowhood.

66   *Anna Tilghman was a young lady who knew precisely*: Tilghman, *Memoir*, 112.

67   *applauding Anna for not "surrendering at the first Summons"*: Daniel Blake Smith, *Inside the Great House: Planter Family Life in Eighteenth-Century Chesapeake* (Ithaca, NY: Cornell University Press, 1986), 133.

67   *"evidently very attractive and must have possessed a great charm"*: C. V. Hamilton, "The Erotic Charisma of Alexander Hamilton," *Journal of American Studies* 45, no. 1 (February 2011): 1–19, http://d-scholarship.pitt.edu/5848/.

67   *"his complexion was exceedingly fair and varying from this"*: Hamilton, "Charisma of Alexander Hamilton."

67   *"Alas poor Polly! Hamilton is a gone man"*: Tilghman, *Memoir*, 173.

CHAPTER 6

69   *"cavalry-like advances on the latest feminine arrival"*: Phillip Thomas Tucker, *Alexander Hamilton's Revolution: His Vital Role as Washington's Chief of Staff* (New York, Skyhorse Publishing, 2017), n.p.

69   *more trunks of extravagant French fashion than was strictly decent*: Pamela Murrow, "The Role of Dancing," *Journal of the American Revolution*, March 14, 2013, https://allthingsliberty.com/2013/03/the-role-of-dancing/.

70   *Wrapped in thick cloaks, their hands protected in beaver muffs*: Details here and throughout from Harry M. Ward, *The War for Independence and the Transformation of American Society: War and Society in the United States, 1775–83* (New York: Routledge, 2014), 90; and Benson John Lossing, *The Pictorial Field-Book of the Revolution or, Illustrations, by Pen and Pencil, of the History, Biography, Scenery, Relics, and Traditions of the War for Independence* (New York, Harper and Brothers, 1851), 307.

71   *"Her hair in front is craped at least a foot high"*: Lyman Henry Butterfield and Margaret A. Hogan, *Adams Family Correspondence: March 1787–December 1789* (Cambridge: Harvard University Press, 1963), 268.

71   *"Coiffures dressed* à la Americaine": Ward, *The War for Independence*, 223.

71   *Peggy, had sat for a wedding portrait*: Victoria Cooney, "Love and the Revolution," *Humanities: The Magazine of the National Endowment for the Humanities* 34, no. 5 (September/October 2013), www.neh.gov/humanities/2013/septemberoctober/statement/love-and-the-revolution.

72   *Eliza called it later her "Marie Antoinette coiffure"*: John Sedgwick, *War of Two: Alexander Hamilton, Aaron Burr, and the Duel That Stunned the Nation* (New York: New American Library, 2015), 107.

73   *"good natured affability and vivacity unembellished"*: Alexander Hamilton to Margarita Schuyler, [February 1780], Founders Online, National Archives.

74   *"I am a stranger in this country"*: Alexander Hamilton to Lieutenant Colonel John Laurens, 8 January [1780], Founders Online, National Archives.

74   *when General Schuyler passed through camp briefly in early March*: Philip Schuyler to Alexander Hamilton, 8 April 1780, Founders Online, National Archives; Philip John Schuyler to George Washington, 12 March 1780, Founders Early Access, Charlottesville: University of Virginia Press, http://rotunda.upress.virginia.edu/founders/default.xqy?keys=FOEA-print-01-01-02-1113.

74   *"You cannot, my dear sir,"* Philip Schuyler wrote to Alexander: Quoted in Roberts, *A Place in History*, 124.

75   *"she consents to Comply with your and her daughters wishes"*. Philip Schuyler to Alexander Hamilton, 8 April 1780, Founders Online, National Archives.

75   *"You will see the Impropriety of taking the dernier pas"*: Philip Schuyler to Alexander Hamilton, 8 April 1780.

76   *"If I were not afraid of making you vain"*: Alexander Hamilton to Elizabeth Schuyler, 17 March 1780, Founders Online, National Archives.

76   *"I cannot tell you what extacy I felt in casting my eye over the sweet effusions"*: Alexander Hamilton to Elizabeth Schuyler, 17 March 1780.

76   *"Have you not heard that I am on the point"*: Alexander Hamilton to John Laurens, 30 June 1780, Founders Online, National Archives.

77   *Kitty was determined to see to it that no early infant arrival*: *Notable American Women, 1607–1950: A Biographical Dictionary*, eds. Edward T. James, Janet Wilson James, and Paul S. Boyer (Cambridge: Harvard University Press, 1971), 1:244.

77   *"kicked up a hell of a dust" until June*: Kate Van Winkle Keller, *Dance and Its Music in America, 1528–1789* (Hillsdale, NY: Pendragon Press, 2007), 549.

78   *"A love like mine so tender, true"*: Alexander Hamilton to Elizabeth Schuyler, [2–4 July 1780], Founders Online, National Archives.

78   *"I intend to restore the empire of Hymen"*: Alexander Hamilton to John Laurens, 16 September, 1780, Founders Online, National Archives.

79   *"The sweet softness and delicacy of your mind and manners"*: Alexander Hamilton to Elizabeth Schuyler, [2–4 July 1780], Founders Online, National Archives.

80   *"It is an age my dearest,"* he wrote: Alexander Hamilton to Elizabeth Schuyler, 20 July 1780, Founders Online, National Archives.

81   *"Do you soberly relish the pleasure of being a poor mans wife"*: Alexander Hamilton to Elizabeth Schuyler, August 1780, Founders Online, National Archives.

81   *"I know too you have so much of the Portia in you"*: Alexander Hamilton to Elizabeth Schuyler, [August 1780], Founders Online, National Archives.

83   *"When I come to Albany, I shall find means to take satisfaction"*: Alexander Hamilton to Elizabeth Schuyler, [8 August 1780], Founders Online, National Archives.

83   *Eliza responded teasingly by sending Alexander a cockade*: Alexander Hamilton to Elizabeth Schuyler, [3 September 1780], Founders Online, National Archives.

83   *"If America were lost"*: Alexander Hamilton to Elizabeth Schuyler, 6 September 1780, Founders Online, National Archives.

83 *"I was once determined to let my existence"*: Alexander Hamilton to Elizabeth Schuyler, 6 September 1780.

84 *"I have no body between me and the Enemy except two poor famalies"*: Philip Schuyler to Alexander Hamilton, 19 October 1780, in *The Works of Alexander Hamilton, Comprising His Correspondence*, ed. John C. Hamilton (New York: John F. Trow, 1850), 5:191; also available at Founders Online, National Archives.

CHAPTER 7

86 *in accordance with an ancient Schuyler family recipe*: "Schuyler Wedding Cake 1690," What America Ate, Michigan State University, http://whatamericaate .org/full.record.php?kid=79-2C8-30A&page=1.

86 *As evening fell, the house rang with laughter and the clink of glassware*: Details here and throughout from "1779 Rev War General Philip Schuyler Slave Sale," Live Auctioneers, lot 0114, April 2015, https://new.liveauctioneers.com /item/36094021_1779-rev-war-general-philip-schuyler-slave-sale.

88 *a small gold ring, engraved simply*: "Gold double-band wedding ring of Elizabeth Schuyler Hamilton, and wedding handkerchiefs of Alexander and Elizabeth Hamilton, 1780," Special Collections, Columbia University Libraries, www.columbia.edu/cu/lweb/eresources/exhibitions/treasures/html/39b.html.

88 *Mac read a poem he'd composed*: Poem by Major James McHenry, [14–15 December 1780], Founders Online, National Archives; Roberts, *A Place in History*, 154.

88 *"Hers," he said, "was a strong character with its depth and warmth"*: Quoted in Chernow, *Hamilton*, 131.

90 *"a handsome house, halfway up the bank opposite the ferry"*: Humphreys, *Catherine Schuyler*, 65.

90 *"found ourselves in an instant in a handsome drawing room near a good fire"*: *The Schuyler Mansion at Albany: Residence of Major-General Philip Schuyler* (New York: DeVinne Press, 1911), 10.

90 *Alexander set off for camp immediately after the New Year*: Michael E. Newton, *Hamilton: The Formative Years* (Phoenix: Eleftheria Publishing, 2015), 691.

91 *Benjamin Franklin asked a mutual acquaintance in 1778*: J[ohn] C[arroll] to Benjamin Franklin, 18 January 1778, Founders Online, National Archives.

91 *"persuade all her friends to embark with her in the matrimonial voyage"*: Alexander Hamilton to Margarita Schuyler, 21 January 1781, Founders Online, National Archives.

92 *"Mrs. Carter told me you was soon to be married to her sister, Miss Betsy Schuyler"*: Marquis de Fleury to Alexander Hamilton, 20 October 1780, Founders Online, National Archives; Mary Duane, b. 1762, later married General William North; James Duane's wife was Mary Livingston.

92   *"I am composing a piece"*: Alexander Hamilton to Elizabeth Schuyler, [5 October 1780], Founders Online, National Archives.

92   *in love "with an old man of fifty"*: Alexander Hamilton to Elizabeth Schuyler, [2 October 1780], Founders Online, National Archives.

93   *"Mrs. Carter is a fine woman. She charms in all companies"*: James McHenry to Alexander Hamilton, 11 August 1782, Founders Online, National Archives. The allusion to Swift's Vanessa in the letter is a reference to Jonathan Swift, "Cadenus and Vanessa" (1713), Luminarium Editions, December 2006, www.luminarium.org/editions/cadenusvanessa.htm.

93   *"Pray do you talk of a Jaunt to New York"*: Kitty Livingston to Elizabeth Hamilton, 11 February 1781, in Allan McLane Hamilton, *The Intimate Life of Alexander Hamilton* (New York: Scribner's Sons, 1910), 101.

94   *"If I did not know any apology made a bad thing worse"*: Kitty Livingston to Elizabeth Hamilton, 7 February 1781, in McLane Hamilton, *Intimate Life of Alexander Hamilton*, 101.

95   *Edward's increasingly desperate letters*: Mary Van Deusen, "The Antill Branch," Memories of People I Never Knew, www.iment.com/maida/family tree/antill/antill.htm; Gavin K. Watt, *Poisoned by Lies and Hypocrisy: America's First Attempt to Bring Liberty to Canada,1775–1776* (Toronto: Dundurn, 2014), 124.

95   *prisoner exchange to free Edward took place*: George Dawson, "Washington's Valley," *The Link* (Raritan Millstone Heritage Alliance) 7, no. 1 (February 2005), www.raritanmillstone.org/linknewsletters/TheLink_vol7_issue1.pdf.

96   *"Lieutenant Colonel Antill appears to have been captured"*: Mary Van Deusen, "Lt. Colonel Edward Antill," Memories of People I Never Knew, www .iment.com/maida/familytree/antill/coledwardletters1781.htm.

97   *Orders flew to John Carter's business partner, Jeremiah Wadsworth*: See, for example, Alexander Hamilton to Jeremiah Wadsworth, [16 April 1781], Founders Online, National Archives.

97   *a slave woman from the wife of General George Clinton*: Alexander Hamilton to George Clinton, [22 May 1781], Founders Online, National Archives. The text of the letter reads: "I expect by Col Hay's return to receive a sufficient sum to pay the value of the woman Mrs. H had of Mrs. Clinton," and as the archivists at the National Archives note, "This sentence provides one of the few pieces of extant evidence that either H[amilton] or his wife owned slaves."

97   *Alexander also bought a small boat*: Alexander Hamilton to Major Richard Platt, [28 April 1781], Founders Online, National Archives.

97   *"riches enough, with common management, to make the longest life very comfortable"*: Quoted in R. G. Thorne, *The House of Commons* (London: Boydell and Brewer, 1986), 5:441.

98   *"proceed immediately with Colonel [Moses] Hazen's Regiment to Albany"*: *Proceedings of the New Jersey Historical Society* (Edison, NJ: New Jersey Historical Society, 1899), 42–48. Some historians have suggested that Marie-

Charlotte Antill resided with her mother-in-law rather than removing to Albany to join her husband. However, her mother-in-law was a Loyalist in occupied New York, making this extremely unlikely given Edward's active military engagement in support of the Americans; see also Van Deusen, "Lt. Col. Edward Antill."

98   *"Though I know my Betsy would be happy to hear I had rejected this proposal"*: Alexander Hamilton to Elizabeth Hamilton, [10 July 1781], Founders Online, National Archives.

98   *"I impatiently long to hear from you the state of your mind since our painful separation"*: Alexander Hamilton to Elizabeth Hamilton, [10 July 1781].

98   *"I am inexpressably happy . . . to find that you seem at present to be confirmed"*: Alexander Hamilton to Elizabeth Hamilton, 16 August 1781, Founders Online, National Archives.

99   *By nine o'clock in the evening, the family gathered in the front hall for dinner*: Details here and throughout from Jeptha R. Simms, *The Frontiersmen of New York* (Albany, NY: 1883), 2:487, http://threerivershms.com/simms1781.htm.

99   *"carry[ing] off some of the most inveterate and active Leaders in the Rebellion"*: *Dictionary of Canadian Biography* online, s.v. "Meyers, John Walden," by Robert J. M. Shipley, accessed April 1, 2018, www.biographi.ca/en/bio /meyers_john_walden_6E.html.

100   *"The attack and defense of the house was bloody and obstinate, on both sides"*: Mary Beacock Fryer, *Loyalist Spy, The Experiences of Captain John Walden Meyers During the American Revolution* (Brockville, ON: Besancourt Publishers, 1974), 124ff.

101   *came instead face-to-face with Captain John Meyers*: *Dictionary of Canadian Biography* online, s.v. "Meyers, John Walden."

101   *"Wench, wench, where is your master?" demanded John Meyers*: Humphreys, *Catherine Schuyler*, 34.

101   *The attackers fled, taking the family silver and the three sentinels*: Humphreys, 34.

101   *"Upon the whole I am glad this unsuccessful attempt has been made"*: Alexander Hamilton to Elizabeth Hamilton, 16 August 1781, Founders Online, National Archives.

102   *"I am unhappy my Betsey," he wrote. "I am unhappy beyond expression"*: Alexander Hamilton to Elizabeth Hamilton, 22 August 1781, Founders Online, National Archives.

103   *"the caprices of her father and then she will enslave"*: Alexander Hamilton to Elizabeth Hamilton, 12 October 1781, Founders Online, National Archives.

CHAPTER 8

104   *"Two nights ago, my Eliza, my duty and my honor obliged me to take a step"*: Alexander Hamilton to Elizabeth Hamilton, 16 October 1781, Founders Online, National Archives.

105   *"the assurance of never more being separated"*: Alexander Hamilton to Eliza-
      beth Hamilton, 6 September 1781, Founders Online, National Archives.

105   *Aaron Burr, living by now with the Van Rensselaer family*: James Parton, *The
      Life and Times of Aaron Burr* (New York: Mason Brothers, 1861), 138.

105   *"I am told Miss is in great distress"*: Alexander Hamilton to Major Nicholas
      Fish, [29 December 1781], Founders Online, National Archives.

106   *The young teenage patroon Stephen Van Rensselaer*: Richard A. Harrison,
      Princetonians, 1776–1783: A Biographical Dictionary (Princeton, NJ: Prince-
      ton University Press, 2014), xxviii; George Rogers Howell, *Bi-centennial
      History of Albany: History of the County of Albany, NY from 1609 to 1886*
      (Albany: W. W. Munsell & Company, 1886), 1:261.

106   *"You cannot imagine how entirely domestic I am growing"*: Alexander Hamilton
      to Richard Kidder Meade, March 1782, Founders Online, National Archives.

106   *Could an acquaintance help him find four pint-size wine decanters?*: Alex-
      ander Hamilton to Richard Kidder Meade, March 1782, Founders Online,
      National Archives.

107   *Aaron Burr, who had been introduced to the Schuyler family by the good offices
      of General Alexander McDougall*: *The Schuyler Mansion at Albany*, 9.

107   *But when Aaron Burr soon became fast friends with Stephen Van Rensselaer,
      Aaron confided in his amorous letters*: Aaron Burr, *The Private Journal of
      Aaron Burr, During His Residence of Four Years in Europe, with Selections
      from His Correspondence* (New York: Harper Brothers, 1836), 1:234.

107   *"I have been employed for the last ten months in rocking the cradle"*: Alexan-
      der Hamilton to Marquis de Lafayette, [3 November 1782], Founders Online,
      National Archives.

108   *"Remember your promise"*: Alexander Hamilton to Elizabeth Hamilton, [18
      December 1782], Founders Online, National Archives.

108   *When a letter arrived at the Pastures warning that Peggy and Angelica were
      both gravely ill*: James Duane to Alexander Hamilton, 17 February 1783,
      Founders Online, National Archives.

108   *"When you are in the Jerseys write me of your arrival and I will come for you"*:
      Alexander Hamilton to Elizabeth Hamilton, 27 October 1780, Founders On-
      line, National Archives.

109   *Eliza's favorite cousin, Kitty Livingston, was both older and richer*: Susan E. Klepp,
      *Revolutionary Conceptions: Women, Fertility, and Family Limitation in America,
      1760–1820* (Chapel Hill, NC: University of North Carolina Press, 2012), 28.

111   *"Stephen's precipitate marriage has been to me a source of surprise and indeed
      of regret"*: Humphreys, *Catherine Schuyler*, 195.

112   *George Washington, who dreamed of a horseback tour through the Hudson
      River and Mohawk country*: John C. Fitzpatrick, ed., *The Writings of George
      Washington from the Original Manuscript Sources 1745–1799*, vol. 27, *1783–
      1784* (Washington, U.S. Government Printing Office, 1938), 106.

112 *Philip Schuyler, Abraham Ten Broeck, and Peggy's new husband, Stephen Van Rensselaer, joined the touring party*: "Washington's Mohawk Valley Tour," Three Rivers, http://threerivershms.com/washington.htm.

113 *increasingly exasperated with his mother-in-law*: Alexander Hamilton to Robert R. Livingston, [13 August 1783], Founders Online, National Archives.

113 *On July 27, John, Angelica, and their children set sail*: Philip Schuyler to Alexander Hamilton, 5 February 1781, Founders Online, National Archives.

113 *upwards of a modern equivalent of $46 million*: MeasuringWorth, labor-value calculation.

113 *Banks of fog and a persistent haze blanketed harbors*: Greg Neale, "How an Icelandic Volcano Helped Spark the French Revolution," *Guardian*, April 15, 2010, https://www.theguardian.com/world/2010/apr/15/iceland-volcano -weather-french-revolution.

113 *"Mr Carter has found all his friends and relatives well"*: Naulin, "A Genteel Family," 14.

114 *"I intended to have called my little girl Eliza after Mr. Church's mother"*: Angelica Church to Elizabeth Hamilton, 27 January 1784, quoted in McLane Hamilton, *Intimate Life*, 107.

114 *controversial fraternity, the Society of the Cincinnati*: "The Society and Its Critics, 1784–1800," The Society of the Cincinnati, accessed April 1, 2018, www.societyofthecincinnati.org/about/history/critics; "History," The Society of the Cincinnati in the State of Connecticut, accessed April 1, 2018, http://theconnecticutsociety.org/history/.

114 *the inveterate gambler and wheeler-dealer William Duer*: On the Cincinnati in general and William Duer's association, see, for example, Embry Clark, "The Society of Cincinnati," Bauman Rare Books, accessed January 15, 2018, www .baumanrarebooks.com/blog/society-cincinnati/; Martha Joanna Lamb and Burton Harrison, *History of the City of New York: Its Origin, Rise, and Progress* (New York: A. S. Barnes, 1880), 2:445; "Fraunces Tavern, New York City, Jan. 11, 1785–Apr. 30, 1788," Office of the Historian, United States Department of State, https://history.state.gov/departmenthistory/buildings/section11; "Honorary Members," New York State Society of the Cincinnati, accessed April 1, 2018, www.nycincinnati.org/HonoraryMembers.htm; James Grant Wilson, ed., *The Memorial History of the City of New York, from Its First Settlement to the Year 1892*, vol. 3 (New York: New York History Company, 1893).

CHAPTER 9

117 *"You have I fear taken a final leave of America and of those that love you here"*: Alexander Hamilton to Angelica Church, [3 August 1785], Founders Online, National Archives.

118 *Eliza said a less tragic goodbye, too, to her favorite, little Harriet Antill*: On the Antill family, see *Proceedings of the New Jersey Historical Society*, 42–48. See also "Descendants of Antill Progenitor-422090: Eighth Generation," Merchants Network, accessed April 1, 2018, www.merchantnetworks.com

.au/genealogy/web/antill/pafg08.htm; Harriet Antill married first Charles Blake, a British army surgeon and businessman, in 1804; after his death she married Bernard Panet, of Quebec, in 1814.

118 *"fade before the generous and benevolent action of My Sister in taking the orphan Antle"*: Angelica Church to Alexander Hamilton, 2 October 1780, Founders Online, National Archives.

119 *Abraham Lott was locked away as debtor*: Abraham Lott to George Washington, 7 August 1789, Founders Online, National Archives.

119 *Criminal inmates were fed and clothed by their jailers, however abjectly*: Peter J. Coleman, *Debtors and Creditors in America: Insolvency, Imprisonment for Debt, and Bankruptcy, 1607–1900* (Washington, DC: Beard Books, 1999), 116.

120 *Of the 1,162 debtors in New York City prisons that year*: Steve Fraser, "The Politics of Debt in America: From Debtor's Prison to Debtor Nation," *Common Dreams*, January 29, 2013, www.commondreams.org/views/2013/01/29/politics-debt-america-debtors-prison-debtor-nation; MeasuringWorth, real price-commodity value.

120 *The incarcerated artist, Ralph Earl*: Bruce Mann, *Republic of Debtors: Bankruptcy in the Age of American Independence* (Cambridge: Harvard University Press, 2002); "Ralph Earl," National Gallery of Art, accessed April 1, 2018, www.nga.gov/content/ngaweb/Collection/artist-info.1261.html; "Ralph Earl," Worcester Art Museum, accessed April 1, 2018, www.worcesterart.org/collection/Early_American/Artists/earl_r/biography/index.html?PHPSESSID=b7b9aa9e2ce5c0b4f48b0cbeacb41ead.

121 *Methodism, with its holy-roller enthusiasm, and Catholicism*: *Our Excellent Women of the United Methodist Church in England and America* (New York: J. C. Buttre, 1878), 149.

122 *"Unfortunately neither of the children had the pleasure of receiving an honorable wound"*: Elizabeth De Hart Bleecker, diary, Mss. 318, Archives & Manuscripts, New York Public Library, http://archives.nypl.org/mss/318.

122 *"rather a stupid visit"*: Bleecker, diary.

122 *On weekends, the entire family went to church services*: Kyle Bulthuis, *Four Steeples over the City Streets: Religion and Society in New York's Early Republic Congregations* (New York: NYU Press, 2014), 215.

123 *"But whither, my pen, are you hurrying me?"*: John Jay and Sarah Livingston Jay, *Selected Letters of John Jay and Sarah Livingston Jay: Correspondence by or to the First Chief Justice of the United States and His Wife*, ed. Landa Freeman (Jefferson, NC: McFarland Publishing, 2005), 74.

124 *"head is full of politics, he is so desirous of making one in the British House"*: Angelica Church to Alexander Hamilton, 2 October 1787, quoted in "John Church," R. G. Thorne, *The History of Parliament*, 5:441.

125 *"indulge me in returning to my family and my country"*: Angelica Church to Elizabeth Hamilton, 1 February 1787, private collection, Sotheby's.

125 *"a superabundance of secretions which he could not find whores enough to*

draw off ": John Adams to Benjamin Rush, 11 November 1806, Founders Online, National Archives.

126 *"He is just what I should like for a military parson except that he does not
whore or drink "*: Alexander Hamilton to Brigadier General Anthony Wayne,
[6 July 1780], Founders Online, National Archives.

CHAPTER 10

127 *Thomas Jefferson, whose dalliance in Paris with Sally Hemings*: On the critical
consensus surrounding Thomas Jefferson's long-term sexual relationship and
children with Sally Hemings, see, for example, Annette Gordon-Reed, *The
Hemingses of Monticello: An American Family* (New York: W. W. Norton,
2008); Andrew Bernstein, *Jefferson's Secrets: Death and Desire and Monticello* (New York: Basic Books, 2006); and the report of the Thomas Jefferson Foundation, "Report of the Research Committee on Thomas Jefferson
and Sally Hemings," www.monticello.org/site/plantation-and-slavery/report
-research-committee-thomas-jefferson-and-sally-hemings; for Angelica Church's
presumed role in communicating this information to Alexander Hamilton and
Alexander Hamilton's anonymous political pamphlets on this rumor, see Chernow, *Hamilton*, 316–18, 406, passim.

128 *"Mrs Carter, a handsome woman"*: Humphreys, *Catherine Schuyler*, 191.

128 *"because she [was] engaged at cards with her children"*: Howard Swiggett, *The
Extraordinary Mr. Morris* (New York: Doubleday, 1952), 145.

128 *"young enough and handsome enough "*: Swiggett, *Mr. Morris*, 178.

129 *Peggy—still thought of as "a young wild flirt from Albany, full of glee & ap-
parently desirous of matrimony"*: Harrison Gray Otis, *The Life and Letters of
Harrison Gray Otis, Federalist, 1765–1848*, ed. Samuel Eliot Morrison (New
York: Houghton Mifflin, 1913), 142.

130 *At the inaugural ball in early May, all eyes were on Eliza*: Keller, *Dance and Its
Music in America*, 515.

130 *"I had little of private life"*: Chernow, *Hamilton*, 335.

130 *"I mingled . . . in the gaieties of the day"*: Chernow, 335.

131 *"I am glad to hear that my Brother is likely to be so well established"*: Angelica
Church to Catherine Schuyler, 8 March 1787, private collection, Sotheby's.

132 *"I love him very much and if you were as generous as the Old Romans"*: Cassandra
A. Good, "The Flirtatious Friendship of Alexander Hamilton and Angelica Church
Hits Broadway," Oxford University Press (blog), November 17, 2015, https://
blog.oup.com/2015/11/friendship-alexander-hamilton-angelica-church-broad
way/. See also Linda K. Kerber, "The Republican Mother: Women and the En-
lightenment: An American Perspective," in *Toward an Intellectual History of
Women* (Chapel Hill, NC: University of North Carolina Press, 1997), 43.

132 *By early June, their runaway younger brother and his bride had made peace
with Eliza's parents*: On the complex movements of the Schuyler–Hamilton–
Church families in New York this summer and on the Schuyler family fi-

nances, see Alexander Hamilton to Elizabeth Hamilton, [28 May 1789], Founders Online, National Archives; Philip Schuyler to Catherine Schuyler, 13 May 1789, Mss. 23867, Schuyler-Malcom Family Papers, Archives & Manuscripts, New York Public Library, http://archives.nypl.org/mss/23867; Angelica Church to Alexander Hamilton, 11 June 1789, private collection, Sotheby's.

133   *"If papa requires money I hope that he will draw on Col. Hamilton who will supply him"*: Angelica Church to Catherine Schuyler, 23 July 1789, private collection, Sotheby's.

133   *"an eligible situation, and if my Brother [Hamilton] should be appointed to the finance"*: Angelica Church to Catherine Schuyler, 23 July 1789.

133   *"On the first floor there are two rooms"*: On the rental house in New York City, see Philip Schuyler to Catherine Schuyler, 29 July 1789, Schuyler-Malcom Family Papers; Philip Schuyler to Catherine Schuyler, 9 August 1789, Schuyler-Malcom Family Papers.

135   *"I am completely at sea"*: Angelica Church to Alexander Hamilton, [5–7 November 1789], Founders Online, National Archives.

135   *"After taking leave of you on board of the Packet"*: Alexander Hamilton to Angelica Church, 8 November 1789, Founders Online, National Archives.

137   *"went to church from the bed of the wife of his friend"*: Roger Kennedy, *Burr, Hamilton, and Jefferson: A Study in Character* (Oxford, UK: Oxford University Press, 2000), 79.

137   *"If you ever get to the East Indies . . . you will see little Hamilton"*: Kennedy, *Burr, Hamilton, and Jefferson*, 79.

137   *"size, make, quality of mind and body . . . do justice to the length of my nose"*: Alexander Hamilton to John Laurens, April 1779, Founders Online, National Archives.

137   *"intercourse . . . with my friend"*: Alexander Hamilton to John Laurens, April 1779.

CHAPTER II

139   *"So many people concerned in the business may really make the fools fight"*: William Maclay, *Journal of William Maclay: United States Senator from Pennsylvania, 1789–1791* (New York: D. A. Appleton, 1890), 418.

140   *"He made your government. . . . He made your bank"*: Chernow, *Hamilton*, 353.

140   *"one of the largest dealers in public papers"*: Charles Austin Beard, *An Economic Interpretation of the Constitution of the United States* (Clark, NJ: Law Book Exchange, 2011), 109.

141   *"the most abandoned system of speculation ever broached in our country"*: Maclay, *Journal*, 418.

143   *Alexander—whose concerns for their personal finances were acute*: Alexander
      Hamilton, cash book, March 1, 1782–1791, Founders Online, National Archives.

143   *"I believe it would be best to part with them"*: Susan Winchell-Sweeney et. al.,
      "Mapping the Archaeology of Slavery in the Hudson River Valley," New York
      State Museum, www.academia.edu/24741582/Mapping_the_Archaeology_of
      _Slavery_in_the_Hudson_River_Valley; Don R. Gerlach, "Schuyler the Man,"
      chap. 9 in *Philip Schuyler and the Growth of New York, 1733–1804* (Albany,
      NY: Office of State History, 1968), http://threerivershms.com/schuylerman
      .htm. On other details see also Philip Gilje and Howard Rock, *Keepers of the
      Revolution: New Yorkers at Work in the Early Republic* (Ithaca, NY: Cornell
      University Press, 1992), 21; and Cuyler Reynolds, *Hudson-Mohawk Genea-
      logical and Family Memoirs: A Record of Achievements of the People of the
      Hudson and Mohawk Valleys in New York State, Included Within the Present
      Counties of Albany, Rensselaer, Washington, Saratoga, Montgomery, Fulton,
      Schenectady, Columbia and Greene* (New York: Lewis Historical Publishing
      Company, 1911), 1:14–16.

144   *"Little as the prospect is that I should find My Dear Child Alive:"* Philip Schuy-
      ler to Catherine Schuyler, 18 August 1795, Schuyler-Malcom Family Papers.

145   *"The accounts we have of the prevalence of the Yellow fever at N York"*: Philip
      Schuyler to Elizabeth Hamilton, 31 August 1790, private collection, Sotheby's.

146   *"I leave the matter to yourself"*: Alexander Hamilton to Elizabeth Hamilton,
      [11 September 1790], Founders Online, National Archives; Alexander Ham-
      ilton to Elizabeth Hamilton, 15 September 1790, Founders Online, National
      Archives.

147   *Home now was a three-story redbrick row house*: Alexander Hamilton to Wal-
      ter Stewart, [5 August 1790], Founders Online, National Archives.

147   *William Seton, went searching at Eliza's request for yards of imported French
      upholstery*: Alexander Hamilton to William Seton, [3 December 1790], Found-
      ers Online, National Archives.

147   *Anne Bingham, whose husband, William, was, like Alexander, involved in gov-
      ernment*: Abigail Adams to Abigail Adams Smith, 26 December 1790, Adams
      Family Correspondence, vol. 9, Adams Papers, Massachusetts Historical Soci-
      ety, www.masshist.org/publications/apde2/view?id=ADMS-04-09-02-0088.

147   *pressed his flattery on one of the Chew daughters*: William Cunningham to
      John Adams, 18 April 1811, Founders Online, National Archives.

148   *"Do you live as pleasantly at Philadelphia as you did at New York?"*: Angelica
      Church to Elizabeth Hamilton, after October 1790, McLane Hamilton, *Inti-
      mate Life of Alexander Hamilton*, 106.

148   *Philadelphia was the second-largest city in the nation*: For information on late
      eighteenth-century Philadelphia, see Edward M. Riley, "Philadelphia, the Na-
      tion's Capital, 1790–1800," *Pennsylvania History: A Journal of Mid-Atlantic
      Studies* 20, no. 4 (October 1953): 357–79; Billy Smith, ed., *Life in Early Phil-
      adelphia: Documents from the Revolutionary and Early National Periods*

(University Park, PA: Penn State University Press, 2010), 79; Thomas H. Keels, *Wicked Philadelphia: Sin in the City of Brotherly Love* (Mt. Pleasant, SC: Arcadia Publishing, 2010).

149   *The chancellor, passed over for lucrative appointments*: Alfred F. Young, *The Democratic Republicans of New York: The Origins, 1763–1797* (Chapel Hill, NC: University of North Carolina Press, 2012), 164.

150   *"There is so much Rottenness"*: William Duer to Alexander Hamilton, [19 January 1791], Founders Online, National Archives.

150   *"The Chancellor [Robert Livingston] hates, & would destroy you"*: James Tillary to Alexander Hamilton, [January 1791], Founders Online, National Archives.

150   *In January, a heat wave unexpectedly hit the city*: Anthony Watts, "In 1790, Philly 'Had a Fever,' Today Not So Much," WUWT, February 3, 2010, https://wattsupwiththat.com/2010/02/03/in-1790-philly-had-a-fever-today-not-so-much/.

150   *"I fear," Philip Schuyler wrote of Eliza to Alexander, "that if she remains where she is"*: Philip Schuyler to Alexander Hamilton, 15 May 1791, Founders Online, National Archives.

151   *planning to see their friends Rufus and Mary King*: Alexander Hamilton to Rufus King, 8 July 1791, Founders Online, National Archives.

151   *"the hot City of Philadelphia; but in good health"*: Alexander Hamilton to Elizabeth Hamilton, 2 August 1791, Founders Online, National Archives.

151   *"I have been to see your new house"*: Alexander Hamilton to Elizabeth Hamilton, 2 August 1791.

151   *"barley water with a dash of brandy"*: Alexander Hamilton to Elizabeth Hamilton, 2 August 1791.

151   *"I am myself in good health but I cannot be happy without you"*: Alexander Hamilton to Elizabeth Hamilton, 9 August 1791, Founders Online, National Archives.

152   *"Dear Betsey—beloved Betsey—Take care of yourself"*: Alexander Hamilton to Elizabeth Hamilton, [4 September 1791], Founders Online, National Archives.

152   *"my extreme anxiety for the restoration of your health will reconcile me to your staying longer"*: Alexander Hamilton to Elizabeth Hamilton, [21 August 1791], Founders Online, National Archives.

CHAPTER 12

154   *"once, on a reception evening, when the drawing-room in [the president's] house"*: Lewis Tappan, *The Life of Arthur Tappan* (New York: Hurd & Houghton, 1871), 262.

154   *"We have just taken house in Markett Street nearly opposet the President"*: Alexander and Elizabeth Hamilton to Angelica Church, 2 October 1791, Founders Online, National Archives.

157   *Eliza's father liquidated $67,000 worth of securities*: Beard, *Economic Interpretation of the Constitution*, 108.

158   *But the nail in the coffin was William Duer*: On William Duer and his role in this affair, see Robert Francis Jones, *The King of the Alley: William Duer, Politician, Entrepreneur, and Speculator, 1768–1799* (Philadelphia: American Philosophical Society, 1992), 133; and Bob Schoone-Jongen, "William Duer: America's First Wall Street Villain," Historical Horizons, Department of History, Calvin College, May 15, 2015, https://historicalhorizons.org/2015/05/15/william-duer-americas-first-wall-street-villain/.

159   *"Betsey has lately given me stronger proof than she ever did before of her attachment"*: Alexander Hamilton to Angelica Church, November 1791, Founders Online, National Archives.

159   *Eliza busied herself with hunting down Latin textbooks*: Alexander Hamilton to Philip A. Hamilton, 5 December 1791, Founders Online, National Archives.

160   *"suspicion is ever eagle-eyed. And the most innocent things may be misinterpreted"*: *Works of Alexander Hamilton*, 5:447.

160   *William Duer "will speculate on you"*: Quoted in David Dill Jr., "Portrait of an Opportunist: The Life of Alexander Macomb," *Watertown Daily Times*, September 9, 1990, http://mlloyd.org/gen/macomb/text/amsr/wt.htm. See also Bryan Taylor, "The Panic of 1792," Global Financial Data, accessed April 1, 2018, https://www.globalfinancialdata.com/gfdblog/?p=3462.

161   *Mobs of furious investors stormed the jail*: Thomas Fleming, "Wall Street's First Collapse," *American Heritage* 58, no. 6 (Winter 2009), http://www.americanheritage.com/content/wall-street's-first-collapse.

161   *"I have learned from a friend of yours that [Eliza] has as far as the comparison will hold as much merit as your treasurer"*: James McHenry to Alexander Hamilton, 3 January 1791, Founders Online, National Archives.

161   *"a man whose history, from the moment at which history can stoop to notice him"*: Thomas Jefferson to George Washington, 9 September 1792, Founders Online, National Archives.

161   *"dealing out of Treasury-secrets among his friends"*: Thomas Jefferson to George Washington, 9 September 1792.

162   *Alexander looked the other direction*: Julian P. Boyd, "The First Conflict in the Cabinet," *The Papers of Thomas Jefferson*, vol. 18 (Princeton, NJ: Princeton University Press, 1971), http://rotunda.upress.virginia.edu/founders/TSJN.html.

163   *until it reached the Speaker of the House of Representatives, Frederick Muhlenberg*: Jacob Clingman, Appendix No. IV (a), 13 December 1792, Founders Online, National Archives.

163   *"in confidence, that if [William] Duer had held up three days longer"*: Clingman, Appendix No. IV (a).

164   *"Mr. Reynolds has once or twice mentioned . . . that he had it in his power to*

hang Col. Hamilton": Clingman, Appendix No. IV (a). See also James Reynolds to George Washington, 26 June 1789, Founders Online, National Archives.

164 *"burned a considerable number of letters from him to her husband"*: Boyd, "First Conflict."

166 *"Last night we waited on Colo. H."*: Boyd, "First Conflict."

166 *"Mrs. Reynolds . . . appeared much shocked"*: Boyd, "First Conflict."

167 *"Beauty in Distress"*: Alexander Hamilton, draft of the "Reynolds Pamphlet," 25 August 1797, Founders Online, National Archives.

167 *"The Chancellor hates, & would destroy you"*: John Church Hamilton, *Life of Alexander Hamilton* (New York: D. Appleton, 1840), 7:505.

168 *"Never was poor Creature so unhappy, and so barbarously used, as poor Pamela!"*: Samuel Richardson, *Pamela; or, Virtue Rewarded* (New York: Dover, 2015), 59.

168 *"Alas my friend . . . want want what [I] can ask for but peace"*: Maria Reynolds to Alexander Hamilton, [23 January–18 March 1792], Founders Online, National Archives.

168 *"was innocent and . . . the defense was an imposition"*: Boyd, "First Conflict."

169 *"Tis the malicious intrigues to stab me in the dark"*: Alexander Hamilton to John Jay, 18 December 1792, Founders Online, National Archives.

169 *"designs . . . on the chastity of Mrs. [Tobias] Lear"*: John Adams to Benjamin Rush, 11 November 1806, Founders Online, National Archives.

170 *"contrived to get into Mrs. Jay's bedchamber"*: John Adams to Benjamin Rush, 11 November 1806.

170 *"unpretending good sense"*: Alexander Hamilton to Elizabeth Schuyler, [2–4 July 1780], Founders Online, National Archives.

171 *"It remains with you to show whether you are a Roman or an American wife"*: Alexander Hamilton to Elizabeth Schuyler, [August 1780], Founders Online, National Archives.

CHAPTER 13

173 *"Clingman [reports] that Mrs. Reynolds has obtained a divorce"*: Oliver Wolcott Jr., introductory note [3 July 1797], Founders Online, National Archives.

174 *"Mrs Washington sends her Love to Mrs Hamilton"*: Joseph E. Fields, ed., *Worthy Partner: The Papers of Martha Washington* (Westport, CT: Greenwood Publishing Group, 1994), 253.

174 *"I am truly glad my Dear Madam to hear Colo. Hamilton is better"*: Martha Washington to Elizabeth Hamilton, 9 September 1793, Martha Washington Collection, Washington Library, http://catalog.mountvernon.org/cdm /singleitem/collection/p16829coll7/id/86.

174   *"I pray she may be handsome, for the sake of my nephews and niece"*: Angelica Church to Elizabeth Hamilton, 1 January 1793, Alexander Hamilton Papers Publication Project, Columbia University, finding aid at http://www.columbia.edu/cu/lweb/archival/collections/ldpd_4078858/index.html.

174   *"declare war in favor of the French Revolution"*: Sandy Hingston, "Eleven Things You Might Not Know About Philly's 1793 Yellow Fever Epidemic," *Philadelphia*, February 5, 2016, www.phillymag.com/news/2016/02/05/11-things-you-might-not-know-about-philly-yellow-fever-epidemic/#0BFzdWQC70gv4TLb.99/.

174   *"I hear the Jacobins have made a attack at home"*: Angelica Church to Elizabeth Hamilton, 1 January 1793, Alexander Hamilton Papers Publication Project.

175   *"Considerations, relative both to the public Interest and to my own delicacy"*: Alexander Hamilton to George Washington, 21 June 1793, Founders Online, National Archives.

175   *"It has been whispered to me that my friend Alexander means to quit his employment of Secretary"*: Angelica Church to Elizabeth Hamilton, 25 January 1794, Alexander Hamilton Papers Publication Project, Columbia University AH Papers Box 268.

176   *"I have not seen a fever of so much malignity, so general"*: Robert John Thornton, *The Philosophy of Medicine: Or, Medical Extracts on the Nature of Health and Disease, Including the Laws of the Animal Oeconomy, and the Doctrines of Pneumatic Medicine* (London: C. Whittingham, 1799), 310.

177   *"Your enemies are at work upon Mr. Francis"*: William Willcocks to Alexander Hamilton, 25 August 1793, Founders Online, National Archive; see also Larry Tise, *The American Counterrevolution: A Retreat from Liberty, 1783–1800* (Mechanicsburg, PA: Stackpole Books, 1998), 191.

177   *"As it is an affair of delicacy . . . I will thank you to request some gentleman"*: Alexander Hamilton to Catharine Greene, 3 September, 1793, Founders Online, National Archives.

178   *"With extreme concern I receive the expression of your apprehensions"*: George Washington to Alexander Hamilton, 6 September 1793, Founders Online, National Archives.

179   *"I must give you some information concerning the dreadful distress which prevails in Philadelphia"*: Philip Ten Eyck to Philip Schuyler, 10 September 1790, private collection, Sotheby's.

179   *"We have visited Col. Hamilton and his lady at Greenbush"*: Joel Munsell, *The Annals of Albany* (Albany: J. Munsell, 1850) 1:257.

180   *"Exercise & Northern air have restored us beyond expectation"*: Alexander Hamilton to George Washington, 24 October 1793, Founders Online, National Archives.

180   *"It is very natural . . . that you and my Dear Eliza Should be anxious to have your children"*: Philip Schuyler to Alexander Hamilton, 17 November 1793, Founders Online, National Archives.

180   *"others we all agree must remain until Spring"*: Philip Schuyler to Alexander Hamilton, 17 November 1793.

180   *Albany in mid-November, during the slave uprising*: David Levine, "History of the 1793 Fire in Albany," *Hudson Valley Magazine*, January 22, 2014, www.hvmag.com/Hudson-Valley-Magazine/February-2014/History-of-the -1793-Fire-in-Albany/.

181   *Their oldest daughter, nine-year-old Angelica, who was studying French in Albany*: Philip Schuyler to Alexander Hamilton, 15 December 1794, Founders Online, National Archives.

181   *"alarmed at the state of my Dear Elizas health"*: Philip Schuyler to Alexander Hamilton, 5 January 1794, Founders Online, National Archives.

181   *"When am I to hear that you are in perfect health"*: Angelica Church to Elizabeth Hamilton, 25 January 1794, Alexander Hamilton Papers Publication Project, AH Papers Box 268.

182   *Alexander noted too little the beauty of his wife*: Marquis de Tallyrand to Angelica Church, 11 May 1794, University of Virginia Library, https://explore .lib.virginia.edu/exhibits/show/church/angelica.

182   *Dr. Stevens again ordered Eliza and baby James to the country*: George Washington to Alexander Hamilton, 11 July 1794, Founders Online, National Archives; George Washington to Alexander Hamilton, 23 July 1794, Founders Online, National Archives; Elizabeth Hamilton to Alexander Hamilton, 31 July 1794, Founders Online, National Archives.

182   *"You press to return to me"*: Elizabeth Hamilton to Alexander Hamilton, 17 August 1794, Founders Online, National Archives.

183   *"My dear Hamilton . . . [Mrs. Hamilton] has had, or has been in danger of a miscarriage"*: Henry Knox to Alexander Hamilton, 24 November 1794, Founders Online, National Archives.

184   *"I confess I should not like to settle at Philadelphia"*: Angelica Church to Elizabeth Hamilton, 11 December 1794, Philip Church Papers, New-York Historical Society.

185   *"I have built houses . . . I have cultivated fields"*: James McHenry to Alexander Hamilton, 17 February 1795, Founders Online, National Archives.

185   *"Negro boy & woman"*: Philip Schuyler to Alexander Hamilton, 31 August 1795, Founders Online, National Archives.

186   *"that Hamilton had vested £100,000 sterling in the British funds"*: James Nicholson to Alexander Hamilton, 20 July 1795, Founders Online, National Archives.

187   *"if Hamilton's name is at any time brought up as a candidate for any public office"*: James Nicholson to Alexander Hamilton, 20 July 1795.

188   *"simplicity and humility afford but a flimsy veil to the internal evidences of aristocratic splendor"*: Quoted in Chernow, *Hamilton*, 531.

188 *a certain muckraking anti-Federalist journalist named James Callender ended up with copies*: Angela Serratore, "Alexander Hamilton's Adultery and Apology," *Smithsonian*, July 25, 2013, www.smithsonianmag.com/history/alexander-hamiltons-adultery-and-apology-18021947/#RR0tfMPy95ywTMH1.99.

CHAPTER 14

189 *"a gloom upon the family"*: Alexander Hamilton to James McHenry, 29 April 1797, Founders Online, National Archives.

189 *"I shall be so free to tell you I hate you for not acquainting me"*: Schuyler Mansion State Historical Site, "This Day in History: Birth of Cornelia Schuyler," Facebook, December 22, 2016, www.facebook.com/schuylermansion/posts/1500369353311270:0.

190 *Cornelia, a "charming girl"*: Humphreys, *Catherine Schuyler*, 164.

191 *James Callender's* History of the United States for 1796: James Thomson Callender, *The History of the United States for 1796: Including a Variety of Interesting Particulars Relative to the Federal Government Previous to That Period* (Philadelphia: Snowden and McCorkle, 1797).

191 *"We now come to a part of the work, more delicate, perhaps, than any other"*: Callender, *History of the United States for 1796*, 2:204.

191 *"in consequence of his intrigue with Hamilton to her prejudice"*: Oliver Wolcott Jr. to Alexander Hamilton [3 July 1797], Founders Online, National Archives.

192 *Alexander immediately published a letter of denial*: Alexander Hamilton, letter to the editor, *Thomas's Massachusetts Spy; or, Worcester Gazette*, July 26, 1797.

192 *"I have perused your observations"*: James T. Callender to Alexander Hamilton, [29 October 1797], Founders Online, National Archives.

192 *"According to my information"*: Quoted in Alexander Hamilton to James Thomson Callender, 10 July 1797, Founders Online, National Archives.

192 *"place the matter more precisely before the public"*: Quoted in Alexander Hamilton to James Thomson Callender, 10 July 1797.

192 *"You are in the right . . . for they have at present some unlucky doubts"*: Quoted in Alexander Hamilton to James Thomson Callender, 10 July 1797.

193 *"the very derogatory suspicion"*: Quoted in Alexander Hamilton to James Thomson Callender, 10 July 1797.

193 *"Alexander Hamilton has favoured this city with a visit"*: Quoted in John Church to Alexander Hamilton, 13 July 1797, Founders Online, National Archives, n. 1.

194 *"How is my Dear Eliza? We are anxious to know"*: Philip Schuyler to Alexander Hamilton, 8 July 1797, Founders Online, National Archives.

194 *"Eliza is well . . . It makes not the least Impression on her"*: John Church to Alexander Hamilton, 13 July 1797, Founders Online, National Archives.

195 *"The affair, My Dearest Eliza, upon which I came here has come to a close"*: Alexander Hamilton to Elizabeth Hamilton, 19 July 1797, Founders Online, National Archives.

195 *"I apprehended the vile calumny of my Dear Hamilton's villainous enemies"*: Philip Schuyler to Elizabeth Hamilton, 30 July 1797, Library of the Late Benson J. Lossing.

195 *"poor Mrs. H. Account whose feelings on the Occasion"*: John Barnes to Thomas Jefferson, 3 October 1797, Founders Online, National Archives.

196 *"When my Brother returned from the sloop"*: Angelica Church to Elizabeth Hamilton [after 4 August 1797], New York State Library, http://www.nysl.nysed.gov/msscfa/sc19811.htm, 3:31.

196 *"I have been [charged] . . . with being a speculator, whereas I am only an adulterer"*: Alexander Hamilton, draft of the "Reynolds Pamphlet," 25 August 1797, Founders Online, National Archives.

197 *"Art thou a wife?" the newspapers mocked Eliza*: Quoted in Serratorre, "Alexander Hamilton's Adultery and Apology."

197 *"in the event of certain political movements"*: "Seen and Heard in Many Places," *Philadelphia Times*, March 29, 1800, 7.

198 *"Great distress then existing in [the] family"*: Letter from Dr. David Hoscack to John Hamilton, quoted in Alexander Hamilton to Elizabeth Hamilton, 12 September 1797, Founders Online, National Archives, n. 2.

198 *"Mother, overwhelmed with distress"*: Letter from Dr. David Hosack to John Hamilton, quoted in Alexander Hamilton to Elizabeth Hamilton, 12 September 1797, Founders Online, National Archives, n. 2.

198 *"speculate in the public securities lest it should be inferred that their speculations"*: Quoted in "The United States Treasury Department," *Harper's New Monthly Magazine* 44, no. 262 (March 1872): 481–98, 487.

198 *The debts "are too numerous," Philip Schuyler wrote grimly. "No alternative is now left"*: Philip Schuyler to Elizabeth Hamilton, 4 November 1797, private collection, Sotheby's.

199 *"Her mother and myself had a difference which extended to the father"*: Allynne Lange, "Women of the Schuyler Mansion," Hudson River Maritime Museum, April 14, 2017, www.hrmm.org/history-blog/category/albany.

199 *"slackened his pace to the sober rate befitting a steady-going married man"*: Lange, "Women of the Schuyler Mansion."

199 *"Come into the library"*: Lange, "Women of the Schuyler Mansion."

200 *"I got my wife in opposition to them both"*: Lange, "Women of the Schuyler Mansion."

200   *"if she can possibly enjoy it, with a man of such an untoward disposition as her husband"*: Philip Schuyler to Elizabeth Hamilton, 26 November 1797, private collection, Sotheby's.

200   *"His conduct, whilst here has been as usual, most preposterous"*: Philip Schuyler to Elizabeth Hamilton, 26 November 1797.

201   *"If the letters published by Mr. Hamilton in the name of Maria are genuine"*: Oliver Wolcott Jr., introductory note [3 July 1797], Founders Online, National Archives.

201   *"These letters from Mrs. Reynolds"*: Oliver Wolcott Jr., introductory note [3 July 1797].

202   *"Copy Right not secured according to the Act of Congress"*: Oliver Wolcott Jr., introductory note [3 July 1797].

202   *"No Body can prove these things, but every body knows them"*: Maclay, *Journal*, 394.

202   *"Why has the subject been so long and carefully smothered up?"*: Oliver Wolcott Jr., introductory note [3 July 1797], Founders Online, National Archives.

202   *Eliza knew whom she blamed for all the heartache*: The real culprit was likely Thomas Jefferson's campaign manager, John Beckley; see Serratorre, "Alexander Hamilton's Adultery and Apology."

CHAPTER 15

204   *found Angelica "the mirror of affectation"*: Otis, *Life and Letters*, 142.

204   *"makes it a habit of receiving while lying down in her bedroom"*: Naulin, "A Genteel Family," 25.

204   *"I rely on your promise to compose your dear heart"*: Alexander Hamilton to Elizabeth Hamilton, 14 January 1798, Founders Online, National Archives.

205   *"I have been extremely uneasy, My beloved Eliza"*: Alexander Hamilton to Elizabeth Hamilton, 3 June 1798, Founders Online, National Archives.

205   *"dear boys & myself continue in good health & that they thus far behave well"*: Alexander Hamilton to Elizabeth Hamilton, 5 June 1798, Founders Online, National Archives.

206   *the Harlem Heights area was a popular summer retreat*: "Neighborhood," Hamilton Heights–West Harlem Community Preservation Organization, accessed April 1, 2018, http://westharlemcpo.org/neighborhood-history/.

206   *"You are my good genius; of that kind which the ancient Philosophers called a familiar"*: Alexander Hamilton to Elizabeth Hamilton, [19] November 1798, Founders Online, National Archives.

208   *it was the virtues of the Roman wife recounted by Valerius Maximus*: Mary Letkowitz, Maureen Fant, eds., *Women's Life in Greece and Rome* (Baltimore: John Hopkins, 2005), 134ff.

208 *"Why... should I now hold up to view our intimate and secret plans"*: Women's *Life in Greece and Rome*, 137.

209 *"Aided by our natural credulity and the respect paid"*: Letter from Peter Augustus Jay to Ann Jay, 14 February 1799, quoted in "Alexander Hamilton Talks to a Ghost," *FoundingFatherFest* (blog), September 27, 2011, http://foundingfatherfest.tumblr.com/post/10718081295/alexander-hamilton-talks-to-a-ghost.

209 *"to frighten the family for amusement"*: Letter from Peter Augustus Jay to Ann Jay, 14 February 1799, quoted in "Alexander Hamilton Talks to a Ghost."

209 *"It seems it was a plot laid by General Hamilton, Mrs. Church, young Church"*: Bleecker, diary.

210 *"dug in the filthiest corners of the town"*: Andy Newman, "Intact Pipes from 1800s Once Carried Water, Though Not Very Well," *New York Times*, April 18, 2013, https://cityroom.blogs.nytimes.com/2013/04/18/early-water-delivery-system-in-the-city-cut-corners-and-trees/?smid=pl-share.

210 *"in some company intimated that Burr had been bribed"*: Chernow, *Hamilton*, 589.

212 *"a gentleman called this instant to tell me a duel was to take place between General Hamilton and myself"*: John Skey Eustace to Alexander Hamilton, January 1799, private collection, Sotheby's.

212 *"You are perfectly right, Sir, in calling the story you mention a more than ridiculous one"*: Alexander Hamilton to John Skey Eustace, 10 January 1799, private collection, Sotheby's.

212 *"measured the distances [for the building] as though marking the frontage of a [military] camp"*: Quoted in Thomas Fleming, "Duel: Alexander Hamilton, Aaron Burr and the Future of America," New York: Perseus Books, 1999, republished online at *Washington Post*, March 31, 2000, www.washingtonpost.com/wp-srv/style/longterm/books/chap1/duel.htm.

213 *"Tell the Renowned Philip... I have been told that he has out stript all his Competitors"*: Gertrude Lewis to Elizabeth Hamilton, 17 October 1800, quoted in McLane Hamilton, *Intimate Life of Alexander Hamilton*, 103.

213 *"Don't be alarmed that Kitty is sent for"*: Alexander Hamilton to Elizabeth Hamilton, 23 September 1801, Founders Online, National Archives.

214 *"On Saturday, My Dear Eliza, your sister took leave of her sufferings"*: Alexander Hamilton to Elizabeth Hamilton, 2 October 1801, Founders Online, National Archives.

215 *"I was extremely disappointed, My Dear Eliza"*: Alexander Hamilton to Elizabeth Hamilton, 2 October 1801.

215 *"Naughty young man," Alexander sympathized*: Alexander Hamilton to Elizabeth Hamilton, 25 October 1801, Founders Online, National Archives.

216 *in the words of one of his father's friends, a "sad rake"*: Remark by Robert Troup, quoted in Fleming, *Duel*.

216 *A Friday night at the Park in the early 1800s was not a staid affair*: Timothy J. Gilfoyle, *City of Eros* (New York: Norton & Co., 1992), 67.

217 *"replete with the most sarcastic remarks"*: "The Duels Between Price and Philip Hamilton and George I. Eacker," *New York Gazette and General Advertiser*, November 24, 1801; [Philip Hamilton], obituary, *New-York Evening Post*, November 28, 1801.

217 *"It is too abominable to be publicly insulted by a set of rascals"*: "The Duels Between Price and Philip Hamilton and George I. Eacker," *New York Gazette and General Advertiser*.

217 *Circa 1801, "rascal" retained its original sense*: Francis Grose, *Dictionary of the Vulgar Tongue* (London: S. Hooper, 1785; rpt. 1811), s.v. "rascal."

217 *"Who do you call damn'd rascals?"*: *American Citizen and General Advertiser*, November 26, 1801; *New-York Evening Post*, November 28, 1801; for Thomas W. Rathbone, November 21–December 9, 1801, see Benjamin Rush to Alexander Hamilton, 26 November 1801, n1, Founders Online, National Archives.

218 *His challenge followed, just before midnight*: Lamb, *History of the City of New York*, 2:478.

218 *"On Monday before the time appointed for the meeting"*: Thomas Rathbone, November 21–December 9, 1801; see Benjamin Rush to Alexander Hamilton, November 26, 1801, n1, Founders Online, National Archives.

219 *But form gave George Eacker the first shot*: Fleming, *Duel*.

219 *"Doctor, I despair"*: See Alexander Hamilton to Benjamin Rush, November 26, 1801, n. 1, Founders Online, National Archives.

220 *"Never did I see a man so completely overwhelmed with grief as Hamilton"*: Charles R. King, ed., *The Life and Correspondence of Rufus King, Comprising his Letters, Private and Official, his Public Documents and His Speeches* (New York: G. P. Putman's Sons, 1900), 4:28.

220 *"On a Bed without curtains lay poor Phil"*: "The Duels Between—Price and Philip Hamilton, and George I. Eacker," *Historical Magazine* 2, no. 2 (October 1867): 203–4.

220 *"Philip Hamilton linger'd of his wound till about five o'clock"*: Bleecker, diary.

221 *"upon receipt of the news of her brother's death in the Eacker duel"*: McLane Hamilton, *Intimate Life of Alexander Hamilton*, 219.

221 *the trauma of her brother's death triggered psychosis*: On the connections between trauma and schizophrenia, see Mick P. Fleming and Colin R. Martin, "Post-Traumatic Stress Disorder and Schizophrenia: Case Study," in Colin Martin, Victor Preedy, Vinood Patel, eds., *Comprehensive Guide to Post-Traumatic Stress Disorders* (New York: Springer, 2016), 2275–84.

221 *"Considerations like those my Child"*: Philip Schuyler to Elizabeth Hamilton, 19 February 1802, Alexander Hamilton Papers Publication Project, AH Papers Box 278.

222 *"Exert therefore my dearly beloved child that energy"*: Philip Schuyler to Elizabeth Hamilton, 19 February 1802.

222 *"May the loss of one be compensated by another Philip"*: Philip Schuyler to Elizabeth Hamilton, 23 August 1802, Schuyler Mansion Archives, https://parks.ny.gov/historic-sites/33/details.aspx.

222 *"In the later period of life misfortunes seem to thicken round us"*: Alexander Hamilton to Elizabeth Hamilton, March 1803, Founders Online, National Archives.

223 *"Remember that the main object of the visit is to console him"*: Alexander Hamilton to Elizabeth Hamilton, 16–17 March 1803, Founders Online, National Archives.

223 *"pouts and plays, and displays more and more her ample stock of Caprice"*: Alexander Hamilton to Elizabeth Hamilton, 20 March 1803, Founders Online, National Archives.

223 *"after giving and receiving for nearly half a century a series of mutual evidences of an affection"*: Philip Schuyler to Alexander Hamilton, 16 April 1803, Founders Online, National Archives.

CHAPTER 16

225 *"I shall be glad to find that my dear little Philip is weaned"*: Alexander Hamilton to Elizabeth Hamilton, October 1803, Founders Online, National Archives.

226 *"I observe in your warrant of Attorney a new error"*: Alexander Hamilton to Aaron Burr, 10 October 1803, Founders Online, National Archives.

226 *"For God's sake . . . cease these conversations and threatenings"*: Quoted in John Torrey Mores, *The Life of Alexander Hamilton* (New York: Little, Brown, and Company, 1876), 354.

227 *"If not prevented by the cleaning of your house"*: Alexander Hamilton to Elizabeth Hamilton, 7–11 May 1804, Founders Online, National Archives.

227 *"Who do you think was at the door?"*: Church Hamilton, *Life of Alexander Hamilton*, 7:802.

228 *"Gen. Hamilton, the Patroon's brother-in-law, it is said, has come out decidedly"*: Peter Hess, "The Albany Connections of Burr, Hamilton, and Schuyler," *New York History Blog*, May 14, 2015, http://newyorkhistoryblog.org/2015/05/14/the-albany-connections-of-burr-hamilton-and-schuyler/.

228 *"still more despicable opinion which General Hamilton has expressed"*: Alexander Hamilton to Aaron Burr, 20 June 1804, Founders Online, National Archives.

228 *"upward of twenty women of ill fame"*: Sedgwick, *War of Two*, 326.

229 *Burr, like Thomas Jefferson, had mixed-race illegitimate children*: Greg Ip, "Aaron Burr Fans Find Unlikely Ally in Black Descendent," *Pitts-*

burgh Post-Gazette, October 4, 2005, www.post-gazette.com/news/nation/2005/10/05/Aaron-Burr-fans-find-unlikely-ally-in-black-descendant/stories/200510050184.

229 *nefarious plot to betray the Americans in the West*: R. Kent Newmyer, "Burr Versus Jefferson Versus Marshall," *Humanities: The Magazine of the National Endowment for the Humanities* 34, no. 3 (May/June 2013), www.neh.gov/humanities/2013/mayjune/feature/burr-versus-jefferson-versus-marshall.

230 *"laid with them upon the grass"*: Church Hamilton, *Life of Alexander Hamilton*, 7:823.

231 *"With what emphasis and fervor did he read of battles"*: Church Hamilton, *Life of Alexander Hamilton*, 7:827.

231 *Their destination was the marshland of Weehawken*: Jason George, "A Duel Evokes Emotions over a Unique Place in History," *New York Times*, July 5, 2004, www.nytimes.com/2004/07/05/nyregion/a-duel-evokes-dueling-emotions-over-a-unique-place-in-history.html?mcubz=3.

231 *He had already decided to throw away his shot*: William Coleman, *Collection of the Facts and Documents Relative to the Death of Alexander Hamilton, with Comments Together with the Various Orations on His Life and Character* (New York: I. Riley and Company, 1804), 20.

232 *"This is a mortal wound"*: David Hosack to William Coleman, 17 August 1804, Founders Online, National Archives; Church Hamilton, *Life of Alexander Hamilton*, 7:829.

232 *"He asked me once or twice how I found his pulse"*: David Hosack to William Coleman, 17 August 1804; Church Hamilton, 7:829.

232 *"Let Mrs. Hamilton be immediately sent for"*: David Hosack to William Coleman, 17 August 1804; Church Hamilton, 7:829.

232 *"My beloved wife and children"*: Church Hamilton, 7:829.

233 *"Remember, my Eliza, you are a Christian"*: Church Hamilton, 7:836.

233 *"If it had been possible for me to have avoided the interview"*: Robert Brammer, "My Beloved Eliza: The Final Letters from Alexander Hamilton to his Wife," *In Custodia Legis* (blog), Library of Congress, September 19, 2016, https://blogs.loc.gov/law/2016/09/my-beloved-eliza-the-final-letters-from-alexander-hamilton-to-his-wife/.

234 *"Fly to the bosom of your God and be comforted"*: Brammer, "My Beloved Eliza."

234 *"Adieu best of wives and best of Women"*: Brammer, "My Beloved Eliza."

234 *Angelica lay curled on a sofa next door, "weeping her heart out"*: Richard Brookhiser, "July 11, 1804: How Alexander Hamilton's Friends Grieved," *New York Post*, July 10, 2015, http://nypost.com/2015/07/10/july-11-1804-how-alexander-hamiltons-friends-grieved/.

234 *"to join her in prayers for her own death"*: Brookhiser, "How Hamilton's Friends Grieved."

234 "*a melancholy event—the circumstances of which are really too bad to think of*": Joan Barthel, *American Saint: The Life of Elizabeth Seton* (New York: Macmillan, 2014), 98.

CHAPTER 17

236 "*not having the fear of God before his eyes*": The State of New Jersey v. Aaron Burr: indictment for murder, October 23, 1804, Founders Online, National Archives.

236 *a habit after church of visiting Elizabeth De Hart Bleecker*: Bleecker, diary.

237 "*immediately set about the execution of the plan suggested*": "Oliver Wolcott Jr. Papers: Letters and Documents Concerning Alexander Hamilton, July 1804," Connecticut Historical Society, http://collections.ctdigitalarchive.org /islandora/object/40002:27304#page/38/mode/2up.

237 "*on the Subject of Gen. Hamilton affairs*": "Oliver Wolcott Jr. Papers."

238 "*Your brother[-in-law] deems it the most prudent*": Angelica Church to Elizabeth Hamilton, n.d., quoted in McLane Hamilton, *Intimate Life of Alexander Hamilton*, 355–56.

238 "*sufficiently large that you may not be in the least crowded*": Philip Schuyler to Elizabeth Hamilton, 22 July 1804, Schuyler-Malcom Family Papers.

238 "*a place where the Sweet Smiles, the Amiable affability*": Philip Schuyler to Elizabeth Hamilton, 25 October 1804, private collection, Sotheby's.

238 "*I have removed the Bust*": Elizabeth Hamilton to Philip Schuyler, 6 November 1804, Schuyler-Malcom Family Papers.

238 "*accessory before the fact*": "Guide to the Papers of Nathaniel Pendleton 1767– 1867," New York Historical Society Museum and Library, MS 483, accessed April 1, 2018, http://dlib.nyu.edu/findingaids/html/nyhs/pendleton/; the trial was ultimately abandoned.

239 "*The Grievous Affliction I am under*": Elizabeth Hamilton to Nathaniel Pendleton, 17 September 1804, Alexander Hamilton Papers Publication Project.

239 "*Do I not owe it to the memory of my beloved Husband*": Elizabeth Hamilton to Nathaniel Pendleton, 29 September 1804, Alexander Hamilton Papers Publication Project.

240 "*My dear papa . . . I have not said anything to Mr. [John] Mason*": Lossing, *Life and Times of Philip Schuyler*, 2:476.

240 "*That your afflictions, my dear, dearly beloved child, had added to mine*": Lossing, 2:476.

240 "*Since my last letter to you I have no gout*": Lossing, 2:476.

242 *Her other siblings were all on firm financial ground*: Lange, "Women of the Schuyler Mansion."

243 *"A report has prevailed . . . that my father gave me"*: McLane Hamilton, *Intimate Life of Alexander Hamilton*, 140.

244 *Adams was among Alexander's most vituperative enemies*: "Introductory Note: Letter from Alexander Hamilton, Concerning the Public Conduct and Character of John Adams, Esq. President of the United States, [24 October 1800]," Founders Online, National Archives, https://founders.archives.gov /documents/Hamilton/01-25-02-0110-0001.

244 *"marriage with the youngest daughter of General Schuyler"*: Samuel B. Malcom to Thomas Jefferson, 15 May 1812, Founders Online, National Archives.

244 *But Samuel was also in the newspapers*: Edwin Burritt Smith, *Reports of Cases Adjudged and Determined in the Supreme Court of Judicature and Court for the Trial of Impeachments and Correction of Errors of the State of New York* (New York: Lawyer's Cooperative Publishing Company, 1883), 3:563.

244 *"Dear Sister . . . Mr Church waited on you"*: Angelica Church to Catherine Malcolm, 8 December 1804, Schuyler-Malcom Family Papers.

245 *The will, written before the two youngest girls were settled*: Philip Schuyler, "Last Will and Testament," 1803, New York State Museum, accessed April 1, 2018, https://exhibitions.nysm.nysed.gov/albany/wills/willphschuyler1750.html.

245 *she was due income of $62.35*: John Henry to Elizabeth Hamilton, 3 January 1805, Alexander Hamilton Papers Publication Project, AH Papers Box 280.

245 *"My Dear Brother . . . Thus is our family situated"*: Elizabeth Hamilton to Philip J. Schuyler, 1805, Alexander Hamilton Papers Publication Project, AH Papers Box 280.

246 *"I am told a farm has lately been sold"*: Elizabeth Hamilton to Philip J. Schuyler, 13 May 1805, Elizabeth Schuyler Hamilton Papers, New-York Historical Society.

246 *What she did not know was that behind the sale lay a marvelous secret*: John L. Brooke, *Columbia Rising: Civil Life on the Upper Hudson from the Revolution to the Age of Jackson* (Chapel Hill, NC: University of North Carolina Press, 2013), 542.

247 *"Dear Madam . . . We have this moment parted"*: John Mason to Angelica Church, 23 September 1805, private collection, Sotheby's.

249 *So when Sarah Hoffman discovered in a shabby tenement*: *Notable American Women, 1607–1950*, 1:139.

249 *Would "Mrs. General Hamilton" join them*: Anne M. Boylan, *The Origins of Women's Activism: New York and Boston, 1797–1840* (Raleigh, NC: University of North Carolina Press, 2003), 104.

250 *Among the trustees were more society women, almost all of whom had long been part of Eliza and Alexander's inner circle*: Ellin Kelly, "Elizabeth Seton: Key Relationships in Her Life, 1774–1809," *Vincentian Heritage Journal* 14, no. 2 (Fall 1993): 305–27.

251   *But they had turned away nine times as many*: "History," Graham Windham, accessed April 1, 2018, http://www.graham-windham.org/about-us/history/.

251   *The women turned to the local churches and newspapers*: Boylan, *Origins of Women's Activism*, 104.

252   *"In the space of fourteen months," the editors gushed*: Boylan, 104.

CHAPTER 18

253   *Catherine's husband, Samuel Malcolm, who still nursed old grievances*: Samuel B. Malcom to John Adams, 26 September 1797, Founders Online, National Archives.

253   *Washington Morton, caught up in a second fatal duel*: J. Jefferson Looney and Ruth L. Woodward, *Princetonians, 1791–1794: A Biographical Dictionary* (Princeton, NJ: University of Princeton Press, 1991), 201–2.

254   *"losing her reason amid the sudden horrors of her father's death"*: George Washington Bethune, *Memoirs of Mrs. Joanna Bethune* (New York: Harper and Brothers, 1863), 116.

254   *"I have returned home my jaunt to the city was more fatiguing than pleasant"*: Mary Anna Hamilton to Catherine Malcolm, n.d., Schuyler-Malcom Family Papers, New York Public Library.

255   *"at that time an attack on New York city, by the British, was considered imminent"*: James Hamilton, *Reminiscences of James A. Hamilton; Or, Men and Events, at Home and Abroad, During Three Quarters of a Century* (New York: Charles Scribner and Co., 1869), 41.

257   *An Act for the Relief of Elizabeth Hamilton*: Alexander Hamilton, explanation of his financial situation, [1 July 1804], Founders Online, National Archives; citing Nathaniel Pendleton, ADS, RG 233, Records of the Committee on Pensions and Claims, National Archives.

257   *"Shortly after the death of General Hamilton"*: Oliver Wolcott Jr., introductory note [3 July 1797], Founders Online, National Archives.

258   *"small bundle inscribed thus—J R To be forwarded to Oliver Wolcott Junr. Esq."*: Oliver Wolcott Jr., introductory note [3 July 1797].

259   *"a Packet of Papers . . . which were deposited"*: Oliver Wolcott Jr., introductory note [3 July 1797].

259   *"to be retained by myself"*: Oliver Wolcott Jr., introductory note [3 July 1797].

259   *"I have been so disappointed by the promises of Mr. Masson in writing the life of your brother[-in-law]"*: Hamilton, *Reminiscences*, 17.

259   *"who will devote himself to it [is] a Mr [Joseph] Hopkinson now in Congress"*: Hamilton, *Reminiscences*, 18.

260   *"the more debt Hamilton could rake up, the more plunder for his mercenaries"*: Hamilton, *Reminiscences*, 17.

260 *"The charge against Hamilton is, substantially, that he enabled his myrmidons to amass fortunes"*: Hamilton, *Reminiscences*, 18.

260 *"debauchery of all the Sisters of his Wife"*: William Cunningham to John Adams, 18 April 1811, Founders Online, National Archives.

261 *"Should you now refuse to recal the calumny you have spread of Hamilton"*: William Cunningham to John Adams, 18 April 1811.

261 *"no publication of the kind ever produced a deeper or wider sensation"*: Arthur Schlesinger Jr., "The War Between Adams and Hamilton," *New Republic*, December 31, 1961, https://newrepublic.com/article/63493/the-war-between -adams-and-hamilton; Octavius Pickering and Charles Wentworth Upham, *The Life of Timothy Pickering* (Boston: Little, Brown, 1873), 4:338.

261 *"Mrs. Hamilton and her children"*: Pickering and Upham, *Timothy Pickering*, 339–40.

261 *"all the papers relating to the subject"*: Pickering and Upham, 343.

CHAPTER 19

264 *"I can make it agreeable to you as we have an excellent clergyman near us"*: Elizabeth Hamilton to Catherine Malcolm, 8 November 1818, Schuyler-Malcom Family Papers.

264 *"[Come] with them and live with me"*: Elizabeth Hamilton to Catherine [Malcolm] Cochrane, 1819, Alexander Hamilton Papers Publication Project, AH Papers Box 280.

265 *"domestic anecdotes . . . style of conversation—and indeed everything"*: Elizabeth Hamilton to Catherine [Malcolm] Cochrane, 25 October 1819, Alexander Hamilton Papers Publication Project, AH Papers Box 280.

265 *"Sir: Please to meet me with the weapon you choose, on the 15th May"*: Hamilton, *Reminiscences*, 55.

266 *"It was done . . . in the hope that I might be disgraced or destroyed"*: Hamilton, *Reminiscences*, 56.

266 *"Whole familys have been unbaptised some persons in their neighborhood"*: Elizabeth Hamilton to unknown correspondent, 4 March 1819, Elizabeth Schuyler Hamilton Papers, New-York Historical Society.

268 *"a man of great intellectual powers"*: *History of Sangamon County, Illinois: Together with Sketches of Its Cities, Villages and Townships, With Portraits of Prominent Persons, and Biographies of Representative Citizens* (Chicago: Inter-State Publishing Company, 1881), 78.

270 *their distant cousin James Fenimore Cooper*: Wayne Franklin, *James Fenimore Cooper, The Later Years* (New Haven, CT: Yale University Press, 2017), 610.

270 *One of the most famous of the Sauk attacks took place just five miles from William's land*: Patrick Jung, *The Black Hawk War of 1832* (Norman, OK: University of Oklahoma Press, 2008), 109.

270 *William's mining operation at Hamilton's Diggings—quickly renamed Fort Hamilton*: Tom Fey, "Lead Cannons at Fort Hamilton," *Territorial Tales* (blog), accessed April 1, 2018, http://www.territorialtales.com/lead-cannons -at-fort-hamilton.html.

270 *"Wherever they go, great numbers are sure to follow them"*: "Black Hawk," *Georgia Telegraph* (Macon, GA), May 8, 1833, 2, quoted in Tena Helton, "What the White 'Squaws' Want from Black Hawk: Gendering the Fan-Celebrity Relationship, *American Indian Quarterly* 34, no. 4 (Fall 2010): 498–520, 500.

270 *"What in the devil's name do these squaws want of me!"*: Helton, "What the White 'Squaws' Want from Black Hawk," 499.

271 *"What has that man come for?"*: Quoted in Lanny Davis, *Scandal: How "Gotcha" Politics Is Destroying America* (New York: Palgrave Macmillan, 2007), 258.

272 *"many a night he wandered around the hillside"*: Geoffrey Owen Cobb, "Great American Rogue, Aaron Burr's Visits to Greenpoint," *Historic Greenpoint* (blog), January 7, 2015, https://historicgreenpoint.wordpress.com/2015/01/07 /great-american-rogue-aaron-burrs-visits-to-greenpoint/.

272 *"overbearing and domineering beyond human endurance"*: John E. Stillwell, *The History of the Burr Portraits* (privately printed pamphlet, 1928), 63.

272 *The aggrieved wife, showing a laudable, if perverse, sense of humor*: Kim Dramer, "Eliza Jumel: American Success Story, Maybe," *Huffington Post*, December 6, 2017, www.huffingtonpost.com/kim-dramer-/eliza-jumel-american -success-story-maybe_b_9069018.html.

273 *a statue of Alexander Hamilton, which Congress in 1826 had approved*: Richard Peters, ed., *The Public Statutes at Large of the United States of America, from 1789 to March 3, 1845* (Boston: Little, Brown, 1856), 175.

273 *Witnesses remembered heat so intense that the copper fittings from the roofs melted*: Jasmin K. Williams, "The Great Fire of 1835," *New York Post*, November 16, 2007, http://nypost.com/2007/11/16/the-great-fire-of-1835-3/.

274 *"My cloak was stiff with frozen water"*: Hamilton, *Reminiscences*, 288.

274 *"took a letter from my dear mother to Prince Tallyrand"*: Hamilton, *Reminiscences*, 290.

274 *"King Jerôme [Bonaparte], who was living there, hearing my name"*: Hamilton, *Reminiscences*, 290.

CHAPTER 20

277 *"lying upon the counter in midday telling stories"*: William MacBean, *Biographical Register of Saint Andrew's Society of the State of New York* (New York: St. Andrew's Society, 1925), 2:18–19.

277 *As part of the tangle of his father's unpaid pension*: Chris Naylor, "Those Elusive Early Americans: Public Lands and Claims in the American State Papers,

1789–1837," *Prologue Magazine* (National Archives of the United States) 37, no. 2 (Summer 2005), https://www.archives.gov/publications/prologue/2005/summer/state-papers.html.

278 *"gloomy from the use of coal"*: Elizabeth Hamilton to Philip Hamilton, 19 March 1837, in McLane Hamilton, *Intimate Life*, 220.

279 *"Adieu! . . . Write to me and let me know how Angelica is"*: Elizabeth Hamilton to Philip Hamilton, 19 March 1837.

280 *"cultured gentleman, speaking French and having his cabin shelves filled with books"*: Quoted in Tom Emery, "Wisconsin's Hamilton," *Milwaukee Journal Sentinel*, August 29, 2015.

281 *"I am much dissatisfied"*: Elizabeth Hamilton to James A. Hamilton, 15 February 1841, Alexander Hamilton Papers Publication Project.

281 *"I have looked for you day after day"*: Elizabeth Hamilton to James A. Hamilton, 15 February 1841.

281 his motive was *"an illegal one"*: Elizabeth Hamilton to James A. Hamilton, 15 February 1841.

282 *"very black and ragged man in the cellar who was being fed by my father"*: Allan McLane Hamilton, *Recollections of an Alienist, Personal and Professional* (New York: George H. Doran, 1916), 16.

284 *"work and its greatly extended good were told over"*: Jessie Benton Frémont, *Souvenirs of My Time* (Boston: D. Lothrop and Company, 1887), 116–18.

284 *"As she moved slowly forward supported by her daughter"*: Frémont, *Souvenirs of My Time*, 116–18.

284 *"Mrs. General Hamilton, upon whom I waited at table, is a very remarkable person"*: James K. Polk, *The Diary of James K. Polk During His Presidency, 1845–1849*, ed. Milo Milton Quaife (Chicago: A. C. McClurg, and Company, 1910), 226.

284 *"spanking black team hitched to a bright new red wagon"*: Emery, "Wisconsin's Hamilton."

284 Sacramento, which he described as a *"miserable hole"*: Emery, "Wisconsin's Hamilton."

285 *"The sunny cheerfulness of her temper and quiet humor"*: Quoted in Chernow, *Hamilton*, 730.

286 *"Gentlemen brought their children to see Mrs. Hamilton"*: De Groot Family Papers, 1837–1965, New-York Historical Society.

287 *"I, with Mrs. Knox and other ladies, looked from this window"*: "Mrs. Alexander Hamilton Witness That George Washington Was a Communicant of the Church," *Soldier and Servant Series*, no. 166 (Hartford, CT: Church Missions Publishing Company, 1932), n.p.

287 *"James, I sat up with mother last night"*: Hamilton, *Reminiscences*, 65.

289 *"God bless you, you have been a good son"*: Hamilton, *Reminiscences*, 65.

AUTHOR'S NOTE

293 *"A thousand blessings upon you," he wrote to her in the months after*: Alexander Hamilton to Elizabeth Hamilton, 17 October 1799, Founders Online, National Archives.

293 *"While all other passions decline in me, those of love and friendship gain"*: Alexander Hamilton to Elizabeth Hamilton, 26 January [1800], Founders Online, National Archives.

296 *As one of Alexander Hamilton's biographers in the late 1970s observed*: James Thomas Flexner, "'The American World Was Not Made For Me': The Unknown Alexander Hamilton," *American Heritage* 29, no. 1 (December 1977), http://www.americanheritage.com/content/american-world-was-not-made-me.

297 *"Many historians like to view themselves as experts"*: Oliver Wolcott Jr., introductory note [July 3, 1797], Founders Online, National Archives.

Eliza Hamilton

Tilar J. Mazzeo

This reading group guide for Eliza Hamilton includes an introduction, discussion questions, and ideas for enhancing your book club. The suggested questions are intended to help your reading group find new and interesting angles and topics for your discussion. We hope that these ideas will enrich your conversation and increase your enjoyment of the book.

Introduction

Eliza Hamilton was much more than Founding Father Alexander Hamilton's devoted wife. In Alexander's last letter to Eliza, he called her the "best of wives, best of women." She was a strong pioneer woman, a loving sister, a caring mother, and in her later years, a savvy businesswoman. In this fascinating biography, award-winning author Tilar J. Mazzeo reveals the many sides of one of America's founding mothers.

Eliza Hamilton: The Extraordinary Life and Times of the Wife of Alexander Hamilton follows Eliza through her early years, to the ups and downs of her married life and the aftermath of Alexander's tragic murder, to her involvement in many projects that cemented her legacy as one of the unsung heroes of our nation's early days. This is *her* story.

Topics and Questions
for Discussion

1. Reflect on the Germaine de Staël quotation that opens this biography: "Love is the whole history of a woman's life; it is an episode in a man's." Madame de Staël was a celebrated French writer and intellectual whose work often touched on the status of women in Revolution-era France. Discuss this quotation as it relates not only to Eliza Hamilton's life but also to the status of women during her lifetime.

2. Thomas Jefferson outlines how his eleven-year-old daughter, Polly, should "distribute" her time (page 20). The list closely resembles the expectations that fell on young Eliza as well. Knowing Eliza's entrepreneurial strengths (and affinities), discuss how these restrictive expectations of "elite" colonial girls shaped Eliza's early life and sense of self. What expectations were especially formative for you as a child and teenager, and what did you rail against?

3. Did it surprise you to learn that Eliza owned slaves despite being pro-abolition? How do you suppose she was able to reconcile those conflicting ideas?

4. In the early days of their courtship, Alexander wrote to Eliza in a letter: "Nature has been very kind to you; do not neglect

to cultivate her gifts and to enable yourself to make the distinguished figure in all respects to which you are intitled to aspire" (page 79). This tactless piece of advice tapped into what author Tilar Mazzeo calls Eliza's "greatest insecurity . . . [t]hat she was dull and stupid" (pages 79–80). How did you react to Alexander's tone-deaf suggestion that Eliza undertake intellectual self-improvements? More broadly, how did you react to Alexander's often "swaggering way" (page 137) in general?

5. The level of public scrutiny that Eliza endures during Alexander's meteoric political rise rivals that of modern-day celebrities. Did that surprise you? Why or why not?

6. Describe—and react to—Mazzeo's characterization of George and Martha Washington. How does their relationship with Eliza and Alexander align with or diverge from your preexisting ideas of these historical figures?

7. Mazzeo offers a new perspective on Alexander Hamilton's infamous affair with Maria Reynolds than previous biographers. Her extensive research suggests that it was actually a cover-up for bad financial dealings, and that Eliza was in on it. Was this revelation a shock to you? Does this new take on the affair change your impression of Eliza?

8. Were you surprised by the muckraking that defined the political landscape of Revolution-era America? How does it compare to the role of political journalism in America today?

9. Eliza's sister Angelica has a tumultuous relationship with the Schuyler family, largely due to her choice of husband. Discuss the sisters' close relationship, as well as the way in which Angelica's marriage shapes the trajectory of her life.

10. Consider the portrait of American society in its infancy. As Mazzeo describes: "Philadelphia was the second-largest city in the nation, although its population was under thirty thousand. By modern standards, everything in America in the 1790s had a small-town feeling. Visitors to America cities remarked with astonishment on the feral pigs that ran wild in the streets" (page 148).

11. Discuss the pattern that comes to define Alexander and Eliza's marriage: "At a distance, they faltered. In crisis, they turned to each other" (page 225). Moments of hardship seemed to strengthen their bond over the course of their relationship. What are the moments of adversity and resilience that stood out to you most, and why?

12. Alexander asks Eliza to embody the ideal of a "Roman wife"—a partner fully prepared for the "self-sacrifice and loyalty that building a republic would require" (page 171). Do you believe that this gave Eliza a sense of purpose, or conversely, imposed on her an unfair burden?

13. Eliza's life is defined by the roles assigned to her by others—Alexander needs her to be his "Roman wife"; her peers expect a gracious socialite; her family demands political engagement as the American republic takes form; her children require a doting mother. Based on her own letters and the choices she makes for herself following Alexander's death, what do you sense Eliza wanted most for herself?

14. After Alexander's life is cut short by the infamous duel with Aaron Burr, Eliza is left to tell his story. How did you react to her decision to burn so many of her own letters (pages 262–263)? Discuss Eliza's role as Alexander's biographer.

15. Eliza dedicates her life to a series of significant undertakings in the (nearly fifty!) years following Alexander's death, from her work to preserve Alexander's legacy to serving as director of the first public orphanage in New York. What surprised—or impressed—you most about her life's work after her husband's death?

Enhance Your
Book Club

1. Play the soundtrack to Lin-Manuel Miranda's smash-hit musical *Hamilton* and engage in lyrical analysis. Dissect Eliza's and Angelica's songs, especially; how does Mazzeo's depiction of these women depart from Miranda's portrayal?

2. Engage in some speculation: If Eliza Hamilton were born in the twenty-first century, what do you think she would take on as a career? If Alexander Hamilton were a modern-day politician, with which party do you think he would align himself? Reimagine the central characters of this biography as twenty-first-century figures.

3. Watch the film *The Last of the Mohicans* with your book club. Knowing that it is a romanticized version of the world in which Eliza grew up and came of age, talk about your impressions of the film as you discuss this biography. Can you envision a young Eliza in the context of this film?

4. Select the subject of Tilar Mazzeo's next biography! Identify another female figure from our nation's early history who you're curious to learn more about, and discuss why.

5. Revisit Mazzeo's author's note in the back of this book. She mounts significant historical evidence to support her new take on the infamous Reynolds affair. Dissect the pieces of evidence that you find most compelling, and identify any gaps that you think still leave room for speculation. Does your book club have any alternate readings to propose?